THE CREATOR OF GENESIS 1:1 WHO IS HE?

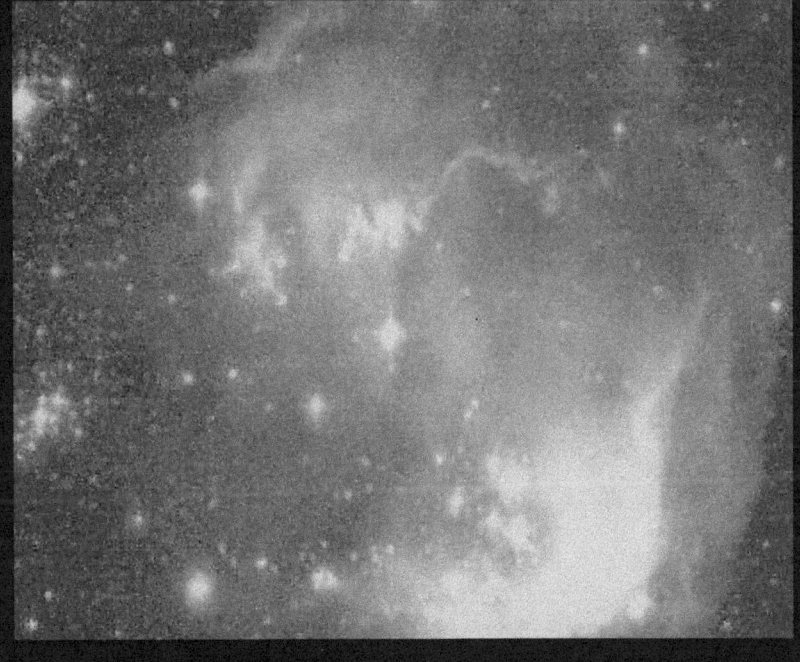

By: Philip Mitanidis

In Memory of: *Donna Gail*

Copyright © 2003, 2014 by Philip Mitanidis
All Rights Reserved

All rights reserved. No part of this publication may be reproduced or transmitted in any form or by any means, electronically or mechanically, including photocopy, recording, or by any information storage and retrieving system now known or hereafter invented without the prior written permission of the publisher.

For further information, or request for permission to make copies of any part of the work should be mailed to the following address:

BEEHIVE PUBLISHING HOUSE INC.
www.beehivepublishinghouse.com
e-mail: info@beehivepublishinghouse.com

First edition of "The Creator of Genesis 1:1 Who is He?" was originally published by BEEHIVE PUBLISHING HOUSE INC. in Canada in 2003. ISBN 0-9733258-0-1

This revised edition of "The Creator of Genesis 1:1 Who is He?" was published by BEEHIVE PUBLISHING HOUSE INC. in 2014, and contains the ISBN 978-0-9866246-6-7

The revised edition of "The Creator of Genesis 1:1 Who is He?" was printed in the USA in 2014.

Author's published work:
 The Creator of Genesis 1:1—Who is He?
 The Covenant—A Contract Rejected
 No God and Saviour Beside Me
 According to a Promise
 Christians Headed Into the Time of Trouble
 Ghosts Demons UFO'S and Dead Men
 Moses Wrote About Me
 Blaspheming the Holy Ghost
 The Apostasy
 What is the Sign of Christ's Second Coming and
  the End of the World
 The Sign in Matthew 24

ACKNOWLEDGEMENTS & ABBREVIATIONS _____ IV

In my references of the (OKJV) Bible, I have changed the first letter of the pronouns into capital letters, which refer to God the Creator; and I have translated the Hebrew word "יהוה" and the Greek word "Κυριος" to read "LORD," whenever the Scriptures refer to God the Creator of Genesis 1:1.

Please refer to the Hebrew and to the Greek inspired Scriptures in order to verify my opinions.

All Bible references are given from the Old King James Version (OKJV) unless otherwise indicated.

Greek Scripture references are quoted from Η Αγια Γραφη, Βιβλικη Εταιρεια, Αθηναι 1961.

"Scripture quotations taken from THE AMPLIFIED BIBLE (Amp.), Copyright © 1954, 1958, 1962, 1964, 1965, 1987 by The Lockman Foundation. All rights reserved. Used by permission. (www.Lockman.org)"

"Scriptures quoted marked (CEV) are from t*he Contemporary English Version* Copyright © 1991, 1992, 1995 by American Bible Society. Used by permission.

The New Testament in The Moffatt Translation by DR. James Moffatt. 1959 Edition. Printed in Great Britain for Hodder & Stoughton, Ltd.

"Scripture taken from the *NEW AMERICAN STANDARD BIBLE* (NAS), © Copyright 1960, 1962, 1963, 1968, 1971, 1972, 1973, 1975, 1977 by The Lockman Foundation. Used by permission." (www.lockman.org)

"Scriptures quoted from *The Holy Bible, New Century Version* (NCV), copyright © 1987, 1988, 1991 by World Publishing, a division of Thomas Nelson, Inc. Used by permission."

Scripture taken from the HOLY BIBLE, NEW INTERNATIONAL VERSION (NIV). Copyright 1973, 1978, 1984 by International Bible Society. Used by permission of Zondervan. All rights reserved.

New World Translation of the Christian Greek Scriptures (NWTCGS), copyright, 1950 by Watch Tower Bible & Tract Society.

Today's English Version (TEV). Copyright © 1992. American Bible Society, 1865 Broadway, New York, NY 10023. Used by permission

The New English Bible (TNEB), © copyright the Delegates of the Oxford University Press and the Syndics of the Cambridge University Press 1961.

Front cover created and designed by Philip Mitanidis (picture provided by NASA) Artwork in this book is created by the Author Philip Mitanidis.

FOREWORD v

The Creator of the universe—who is He?

If you ever wondered who is the Creator of the universe, and everything that is in it and outside of it, this book is for you. But you might find this book controversial because it places the subject matter of God the Creator out of the popular mainstream beliefs of religious institutions and theologians.

Therefore, you will find the message of this book timely and of astounding value; especially, if you are seeking the truth about the subject matter of God the Creator of the universe. This book takes you step by step through the Old and New Testaments of the Bible, in order to show you how the Creator of Genesis 1:1 created the heavens, the earth, ecosystem, and man. This book also reveals the Creator's two Associates, misquoted creation verses, altered creation verse, and in the interim, it leads you to the identity of the Creator. And this book reveals NASA'S findings of the age of the earth, sun, moon, and of the universe. And surprisingly, many of the scientists agree with the Genesis creation account and are at awe!

Now with the new findings, it can be realized that the whole universe and the outer parts of the universe are the handy-work of God the Creator of Genesis 1:1. Nehemiah writes,

"6 Thou [You], even Thou, art LORD alone; Thou hast made heaven, the heaven of heavens, with all their host, the earth, and all things that are therein, the seas, and all that is therein, and Thou preservest them all; and the host of heaven worshippeth Thee [You] (Nehemiah 9:6).

As you have read in the above verse, God the Creator of Genesis 1:1 has placed intelligent beings who live within His governing guidelines within and outside of His universe. And as per the above verse, these intelligent beings worship God the Creator.

And these intelligent beings who worship the Creator and live in the universe are in constant motion. They are in constant motion due to the fact that their worlds and galaxies are in motion.

Having said that, did you know you are flying in the Creator's universe at a very high speed? Yes, while you are reading this book, you are spinning like a top and traveling at the rate of 66,000 miles per hour through space—and you do not have your seatbelt on! At that speed, one would think that a person would be flung off the face of the earth, and into space somewhere; but you are still here! The reason you are not trailing the earth, at this point, is due to the spin of the earth, which produces a gravitational pull upon you and keeps you on the face of the earth, while you are traveling in excessive speeds through the dark cold space. And while you are traveling in the dark cold space, around the sun, you are kept warm by the sun's rays.

And did you know while you are spinning and traveling at the rate of 66,000 miles per hour through space, the sun is also traveling through space with you? But while the sun and the earth are in motion, the other planets in our galaxy are also in motion. And while the planets and the suns in our galaxy are in motion, our own galaxy is also in motion.

And did you know that the earth is older than our sun and the moon? And did you know that the sun is 93,000,000 miles away from the earth, and it takes about eight minutes for the sun's light to reach the earth?

Did you also know that the nearest star to planet earth is about 25 trillion miles away? And did you know how long it takes for man to go to our nearest star? Well, if sinful man was allowed to go there, he would not make it there alive with the technology man possesses. But, do you know how long it takes the saints (holy angels) of God to go from earth to our nearest star? Go ahead; take a guess. It takes few seconds for an angel to travel 25 trillion miles to the nearest star.

That's it!

Are you surprised?

Don't be, angels can travel long distances, without any mechanical devices, in a matter of seconds. They are immensely powerful and knowledgeable of the universe.

Moreover, if you were to look with a modern electronic telescope, in any given area of the night sky, you will see thousands upon thousands of galaxies in that area alone. And while you are looking at the other galaxies in space, you are looking at the other galaxies from the edge of the fifth spoke of your own galaxy, which spirals through space around other galaxies? And, did you know

That there are planets out there, like ours, which can and do sustain intelligent life forms like ours?

Isn't it awesome?

Now don't get the idea that beings from other planets are visiting us. No, they are not allowed to interfere. These sinless beings have not visited us neither will they visit us now; but after the plan of salvation is accomplished, then, they will visit the redeemed. But as for now, the only visitors we have and had are the sinless angels of God the Creator. These angels of God travel throughout the universe and come here, to planet earth, to protect us from the evil satanic angels, who live here (Revelation 12:9), and to help with the plan of salvation for man.

Anyway, if you are familiar with the above information, you probably have an idea of the distances amongst the galaxies and planets; and because of these great distances, the astronomers measure distances in light years (the distance light will travel in one year). Maybe you are even more knowledgeable than that? You probably know or are familiar with quarks, black dust, quasars, pulsars, black holes, novas, the speed of light, light years, blinding light, explosive light balls, etc., etc.

If you are familiar with the above, you are also familiar with the phrase, "The Big Bang Theory." But, if you are not familiar with the "Big Bang Theory," this theory states simplistically that there was a big mass of matter somewhere in space, and at one point, it decided to blow itself up into innumerable pieces of matter. Oh! Correction. Matter turned into gas, light, energy, etc.? In addition, we are told by the theorists that these pieces of matter formed into worlds, suns, galaxies, pulsars, men, women, birds, etc.

But, this kind of theory creates a lot of questions? For example, we can ask, "Where did space come from?" "Where did this mass of matter come from?" "Why was matter in space?" "Why was it not residing in the third heaven?" "Did somebody choose to put it in space, and not in the third heaven?" "What made it blow up?" Something must have made it blow up because scientists tell us that a mass at rest remains at rest until something or someone makes it move. So! Who made the mass of matter move and explode? How did this mass manage to form itself into such a diversified forms throughout the universe? And how did all of these planets, suns, and galaxies manage to be so orderly and in such a precise distance from each other, in order to sustain the life forms in them?

But, since these planets and galaxies are so orderly, why are scientists saying that these galaxies are all flying further and further apart when many of them are traveling inwards from where they originated? Why are some of these galaxies colliding with each other, if they are going further and further away, or apart from each other? And since that is the presentation of the universe and of the "Big Bang Theory," a person has to wonder, where are they going?

On the other hand, some theorists also say that eventually these masses of matter will lose steam one day, and then, they will start coming back into the same spot from where they started. But, I have to ask, "Who or what will bring them back since there is not enough gravitational pull in the entire universe?" If that theory is true, what will happen to the galaxies that are traveling in the opposite direction? Better still, will all of the galaxies that are traveling in the opposite direction create a sling shot effect when they pass by the incoming galaxies? And will these galaxies make the incoming galaxies stop from going back to their original point to become a great mass again? And, if this slingshot effect does take place, will the galaxies change direction again? Or, will these galaxies collide with each other and create new magnetic fields in their respective areas, which will eventually reconstruct into new planets, suns, nebulas, and so on?

But then again, we have a greater problem with all of these theories. The problem with these theories, if we base them on the "Big Bang Theory," is the fact that we know, as per the "Big Bang theory," there is not enough matter at the so called center of the universe to draw or cause all of the matter that exploded to return to its original place? The other question the "Big Bang Theory" does not explain, if the universe is flat, two dimensional, three dimensional, cubical, or is it like a balloon filled completely or partially with something?

Therefore we can ask, is the "Big Bang Theory" credible?

Well, you decide; all I can say is that the theorists can go on with their theories, but this one fact will still remain, they are only unresolved theories.

On the other hand, do you know why the "Big Bang Theory,"

as we know it, never took place? It never took place because the universe, as the scientists know it, was spoken into existence! Matter just did not come into existence by its free will. Remember, the scientists will tell you and agree that nothing creates nothing. Since nothing creates nothing, obviously something or someone created a mature universe, as we know it now. And that something or someone, according to the Bible is God the Creator of Genesis 1:1.

If God the Creator of the universe did not create matter by His command, matter, as we know it now, never existed. And the scientists would not be able to manipulate matter or the elements of matter because matter would not be here and there for them to manipulate. It is as simple as that. But now scientists boast of their findings! Well, that's just what they are! They are findings.

Just remember dear reader; somebody had to create this universe. Somebody brought it into existence. Just think for a moment, space did not decide one day to come into existence; and then, a piece of lump of matter decided to park itself into space; and when this lump of matter got tired of sitting around in the cold dark space, one day, it decided to blow itself up and form itself into the precision planetary systems we see now. And on top of all that, this lump also decided to form intelligence called man?

Woo! That is a smart piece of lump of matter, isn't it?

So, how is it when I pick up a piece of matter, it does not talk to me? Why does it not show any intelligence? Oh! Excuse me, some scientist believe that matter, which is made up of molecular structure, does have intelligence. And their proof is that the electrons of the molecular structure maintain their orbits in order to sustain its structure. That is a good theory, but I cannot see any intelligence in that theory because all the electrons do is to spin in their orbit all the time. In fact, I can disrupt their orbits, as and example by turning the lights on and off, at will because I have intelligence, and they cannot disrupt their orbits because they do not have intelligence. So, how can anyone say that rocks, wood, water, or matter, per say, have intelligence?

Anyway, we can further speculate and say, "Is space dumber than the lump of matter?" Is that why space allowed matter to park itself in the midst of it? Or was it the other way around? Can we say that a lump of matter was sitting in nowhere, and then, space

Came along and gave it a place to blow itself up? Or, was the high density of luminance, which surrounds space, placed space and matter in its center to contain them both?

What do you think?

Need I go on?

You know, it is harder to believe in chance than to believe the Bible because at least the Bible talks to you and tells you how things came into existence. And on top of that, it even tells you to prove what it says. God says, "Come let us reason together."

So, let us reason with the Biblical claims.

The Bible claims that there is an Individual who calls Himself "LORD God," and this Individual, who calls Himself "LORD God," claims that He created the universe and everything that is in it. But first, He gives us a challenge; He says, "Look up and tell us who created all these things so that we may know." Then He further questions, "Can you tell us for sure, who created all these things?"

In addition to the above questions, God the Creator of Genesis 1:1 says, "I created all things by the breath of My mouth." "I hung the earth on nothing." "I spread the heavens." "I call them all by their names," and so on go the claims of God the Creator of Genesis 1:1.

Having said that, do you know who He is?

Do you know who the Creator of the universe is? If you do not know, don't feel bad because I can safely say that over ninety percent of the people on planet earth don't know who is the sole Creator of "all things."

If you want to prove my statement, do a little experiment.

For example, if you were to go and talk to a number of theologians and ask them the question, "Who is the Creator of the universe?" most probably they will each tell you that the Creator of the universe is God.

Does that sound about right to you?

But, what if you were to walk down the street tomorrow, and you stopped a handful of passers-by, and asked them the same question you asked the theologians, do you think they will give you the same answer? I would say, more than likely.

If that was the case, I have to ask you, would you be satisfied with their answers?

If you said, "Yes," I would probably agree with you, to a point, but how would you sift through the theologian's answers, if they were answering you from a different school of thought without revealing that thought to you?

You see, although a Jew, a Muslim, and a Christian will identify the Creator of Genesis 1:1 by the name of God, it does not necessarily mean that these individuals or religious institutions are referring to the same God. In fact, they will tell you that they are not. That being the case, how will you know to whom they are referring to?

Having said that, would you still be satisfied with their answers?

Personally, I would not be satisfied. And the reason I would not be satisfied with their answers is due to the fact that they have not identified the Creator of the universe as per the revelation of the prophets of old. All they would have done with their answers is to give you someone's name. That's all!

Let me explain: Their answers will be similar to the question, "Who is that racecar driver?" Somebody answers, "It is Joe." That answer will be acceptable if there was only one racecar driver by the name of "Joe." But, what if there were more than one racecar drivers with the name of "Joe"? How would you know to which "Joe" that person is referring? Obviously, you would need more information in order to identify the correct "Joe."

Do you agree?

Logically, your answer will be "Yes."

We have the same scenario in the Bible when it refers to God the Creator of the universe and everything that is in it.

As you can observe, the first verse of the Bible opens by saying: "1 IN the beginning God created the heaven and the earth." Genesis 1:1

Although Moses is referring to the Creator by the name "God," and then reveals how He went about to create the heavens and the earth, in Genesis chapter one, he does not identify the Creator in that chapter. All Moses has done is to reveal God's name!

Therefore, if we were to identify the Creator of Genesis chapter one, a person has to bring other verses and compile them in order to identify Him. Without the compilation of other verses, the Creator of Genesis 1:1 will remain known as "God," unless, we conjure up an identity out of thin air for Him. To avoid our own personal injections of His identity, we should allow Scripture to interpret Scripture in order to identify Him. And that is the intent of this book. It will take you step by step in order to reveal to you God the Creator of Genesis 1:1 by separating Him from His two Associates who have the same name as He has.

Yes that is what I said; "His two Associates."

By accomplishing that task, you will not only know who is the Creator, but, you will also know who are the Creator's Associates whose names are "LORD God," as well.

Having said that, I want you to know, the prophets of old have stated that every person on planet earth will know who is the Creator of the universe before the Second coming of Jesus Christ the LORD takes place.

Here are the prophet's words: "6 And I saw another angel fly in the midst of heaven, having the everlasting gospel to preach unto them that dwell on the earth, and to every nation, and kindred, and tongue, and people, "7 Saying with a loud voice, Fear God, and give glory to Him; for the hour of His judgment is come: and worship Him that made heaven, and earth, and the sea, and the fountains of waters." Revelation 14:6, 7

Did you hear that?

We are told that the "gospel" will be preached "unto...every nation, and kindred, and tongue, and people." And the Gospel will also reveal, to all of the people on planet earth, who is the Creator that "made heaven, and earth."

In addition, according to the above verses, the people of the earth are all admonished to "worship Him," the Creator "that made heaven, and earth, and the seas, and the fountains of waters" (Revelation 14:7).

Please note, the prophet states that worship is to be given to "Him," to the Individual who created the heavens and the earth. The Creator is placed in the singular pronoun (Him) in the above presentation in order to reveal to you and to me that there is only one Creator and not two, three, or more, as some religious institutions want you and me to believe. Unfortunately, contrary to Christ's will, some of these beliefs will be enforced by law upon the people of planet earth, during the coming events of the "great tribulation." (See Revelation 13:11-18.) (If you want more information on "the great tribulation" read my book called "The Sign in Matthew 24.)

In the last days of the earth's history, God's people, who ever they are, will be preaching the above message of John and drawing people to the Creator of Genesis 1:1. In doing so, they will be persecuted like the beloved Apostle John, who preached and believed in Jesus Christ the LORD. Because John preached the Gospel message of Jesus Christ the LORD of hosts, he was asked to appear before the Roman Senate. When he was brought before Caesar for his beliefs, he was told to stop preaching Christ to the citizens of Rome. John replied that he could not do that. He was sentenced to die a cruel death, as an example to those who would not conform to Rome's dictates. The Roman soldiers took John, bound him, and led him to the square to be boiled in oil, publicly.

As the on lookers beheld the eerie scene, the fire became more intense underneath the huge pot; and the oil began to bubble and spill over the caldron. And, as the oil spilled over into the fire, the fire would burst into huge flames and lick the hot oil as it slid downwards into the blazing fire. And when the oil stopped spilling over the mouth of the caldron, the fire subsided, but, the caldron was still bellowing smoke from its opening above. When the Roman soldiers thought it was safe to lower Apostle John into the boiling oil of the caldron, the commander gave the order to lower John into it. In the first few tries, a number of the Roman soldiers caught on fire from the extreme heat; but, the command was given again, and the soldiers finally managed to lower Apostle John in the boiling pot of oil.

As John was lowered through the billowing smoke of the boiling oil, the crowd cheered on; and as the excessive oil spilled over into the fire, the intense heat upon the caldron caused the oil to boil even hotter. In doing so, it burst like a volcano over-spilling into the fire. By now the crowd thought that John's flesh had melted into the scorching oil. But the Creator had compassion on the deceived crowd. He wanted John to witness for Him. So He sent one of His angels to make sure that there was no harm done to John. The ropes, which bound John, burnt off him, and he surfaced on top of the oil in the caldron. When the crowd saw John surface from his torture chamber, they were sore afraid. In fact they thought that they were seeing a ghost! But, it was not a ghost. John was raised out of the boiling oil, and he immediately preached unto them Jesus Christ the LORD. Many believed his words.

Fear set in the Roman Senate when the soldiers brought John back to them. And because they feared him, John was sent in exile to the Greek Isle of Patmos. Patmos is mostly made up of rock. There John was placed under the Roman guard for the rest of his life.

When Caesar died and a new Caesar came to power, he released many Christians from their shackles. One of those individuals who was released from prison was Apostle John. When John was released, he continued to preach the Gospel of Jesus Christ (Mark 1:1) to the people, and explained how Jesus Christ was crucified and raised from His grave.

But, before John was released from the Isle of Patmos, Jesus Christ the LORD gave him a number of prophetic visions. These visions encompassed many time periods, and even the time period, which John was living in. In fact, the visions span beyond a thousand years after the second coming of Jesus Christ the LORD of hosts takes place.

According to one of the visions, John saw Jesus Christ the LORD between the candlesticks walking towards him. Then Jesus told John that He was "the first and the last." And that He was the One who was dead, but now He is alive. After Jesus revealed Himself to Apostle John, on the Greek Isle of Patmos, one Saturday (LORD'S day Mark 2:28) two thousand years ago, Jesus gave him a number of specific messages to preach. Later on, while John was still in exile on the Isle of Patmos, in a vision, he saw an angel preaching three messages. One of these messages was to direct the people of earth to the Creator and tell them to:

> "7 worship Him that made heaven, and earth, and the sea, and the fountains of waters." Revelation 14:7

According to the above verse, one of the final messages to the residents of planet earth will be to one, identify and reveal the

Creator who "made heaven, and earth, and the sea, and the fountains of waters." And two, to invite the people of planet earth to "worship Him that made heaven, and earth, and the sea, and the fountains of waters." And that is the Gospel message of this book.

Having said that; let me present to you, in the following chapters of this book, the unknown Creator of the universe, which Paul spoke about on Mars hill, in Athens Greece, nearly two thousand years ago.

> Paul said to the Athenians, "22 Ye men of Athens, I perceive that in all things ye [all of you] are too superstitious. 23 For as I passed by, and beheld your devotions, I found an altar with this inscription, TO THE UNKNOWN GOD, Whom therefore ye ignorantly worship, Him declare I unto you. 24 God that made the world and all things therein, seeing that He is LORD of heaven and earth, dwelleth not in temples made with hands; 25 Neither is worshipped with men's hands, as though He needed anything, seeing He giveth to all life, and breath, and all things; 26 And hath made of one blood all nations of men for to dwell on all the face of the earth, and hath determined the times before appointed, and the bounds of their habitation;" Acts 17:22-26

> "8 **Our help is in the name of the LORD, who made heaven and earth."** Psalms 124:8
>
> The author

CONTENTS

- iv   Acknowledgement
- v   Foreword
- 16   Contents
- 17   <u>Creation of the Earth</u>
  - The Scientific Community..........................17
  - The Genesis Account................................19
- 28   The Antediluvians
- 47   The Journeys of God the Creator
- 140   The Translator's Inconsistencies
- 157   Misapplying Bible verses
- 169   The Creator's Name
- 173   One Creator or More
- 177   The Identity of God the Creator
- 192   The Creator's Associates
- 206   The Creator's Transformation
- 217   <u>God the Creator in the New Testament</u>
  - Christ (Messiah)......................................219
  - Christ "with God"....................................222
  - God the Christ..222
  - Christ the Creator 223
  - Creating "through" Christ?.......................226
  - Romans 11:33-36; Colossians 1:16, 17.........245
  - Summation of the word "through"............266
  - Ephesians 3:9..267
  - Revelation 3:14.......................................272
- 280   <u>Three Religious Doctrines</u>
  - The Trinitarian Theory.............................280
  - The One God Theory...............................285
  - The Arian Theory....................................288
- 309   A Question
- 320   The Rejection of God the Creator
- <u>Supplements</u>   A Prophet and a Man....................344
  - Re Bible Translations................................345
  - Commentators...351
  - Does a day equal 24 hours?.......................354
  - The Experiment.......................................358
  - Declaration...365
- 366   Questions
- 371   Bibliography

"8 Our help is in the name of the LORD, who made heaven and earth."
Psalms 124:8

Creation of the Earth

I have broken down the presentation of the "Creation of the Earth" in the following manner:

1). The Scientific Community   2). The Genesis Account

The Scientific Community _____ There is a lot of debate and energy inserted by the scientific community in the search for answers as to when the heavens and the earth were created or came into existence by some unknown force? This effort, it appears, is on going because every time the scientific community thinks it has found the answer, the scientists run into another stumbling block, which thwarts their new findings regarding the formation of the heavens and of the earth. And because of these inconsistencies, the search for an answer as to how the universe and planet earth came into existence has become an intriguing question for the scientific community, ever since its inception.

Therefore, if your were to look into the growth and the findings of the scientific community, you would notice that the scientific community has moved on from its former stance of telling people that the earth is flat, it is held by a big pivot underneath it, and the water from the ocean drops into an unknown abyss. In fact, with those types of claims, the scientists use to be at odds with the claims of the Bible; now, due to recent findings, reluctantly many acknowledge the creation week of Genesis one.

Formally, when the believers in the Bible, starting with Moses' writings, which were written about 3,400 years ago, continued to claim that the earth was round and the LORD "7 hangeth the earth upon nothing" (Job 26:7), and "stretcheth out the heavens as a curtain, and spreadeth them out as a tent to dwell in" (Isaiah 40:22), many in the scientific community continued to ridicule their claim. But today, the scientific community acknowledges that we are living in a tent because recently the scientists discovered that the earth contains two protective layers of magnetic fields, which envelope the earth, in order to protect us from outside debris and from overwhelming inferno plasma from the sun. And when the believers

The Scientific Community

stated that the continents broke away from one landmass (Genesis 1:9, 10), during the flood, they snickered at their claims. And when the believers claimed that the sun runs in an orbit (Psalms 19:6), they said that the sun was the center of the universe and it did not move. And when the believers stated that the sun and the moon were younger than the earth and older by two days than Adam and Eve (Genesis 1:16, 27), they were laughed at, but not any more!

In fact, up until recently, it was believed by the majority of the scientists that the earth came into existence twelve and a half billion years ago, during the formation of the universe. And the ecosystem of the earth began to flourish about 165 million years ago. And, as for the universe, some of the new models of the Big Bang theory dispute the claim that the universe exploded into existence. Now, some scientists claim that the universe has imploded. But, then again, if you want to believe that the universe imploded or exploded it does not matter because the scientists substantiate both models. The problem they have with those models is the fact that they see, with their new electronic gadgetry that both theories have some validity; and wonder, how can that be?

In the foreword, if you recall, it was stated that there are collisions of galaxies and new formations of planets and suns throughout the universe. Some of the suns are 1,000 times greater than our own sun; and these new formations have a tendency to travel inward to the center of the universe and outward in the universe. Although these events can be seen taking place by an array of telescopes, the scientists cannot put their finger as to how the universe came into existence. And since today the scientists think that they have reached the edge of the universe, they wonder what is the "wall of black matter" they have observed there? Although the scientists wonder what is behind the "wall of black matter," some of them, in order to substantiate their claims about their findings, already have formed an opinion; and others are forming theoretical models about our universe and what is beyond it.

Nonetheless, irrespective as to how the universe came into existence, the scientists, through their theoretical models, today claim that the universe is about twelve to thirteen billion years old.

The Genesis Account

And regarding planet earth, they claim that the earth is about four and a half billion years old. But, in reference to the ecosystem of the earth, a resent scientific model, which has been accepted by some scientists, claims that the ecosystem began about three billion years ago!

So, if we were to consider the "Big Bang" theory against the Bible, we can ask, how can the earth be younger than the universe?

If the scientific community says that the earth is younger than the universe because it formed later, then we can ask, why is the earth's moon and sun younger than the earth?

If planet earth, in our galaxy, for some reason or another, formed after the planetary system in our galaxy formed, don't you think that the moon and the sun should be the same age? So, why are the scientists claiming now that the moon and the sun are younger than the earth?

Did they just pop in out of nowhere and parked themselves here?

How?

Although the scientists cannot explain it, they still wonder how is it possible for the sun and the moon to be younger than the earth?

These are some of the questions the scientific community cannot answer. But, at least, we can say that they are still trying to give us an answer; and that is good. Moreover, I am sure you can assume that they will continue to give us answers as they obtain new findings. But, the question is, will they ever come to the conclusion that the universe and everything that is in it was spoken into existence by the word of the LORD of hosts and accept the answers that are given in the Bible?

For that answer, we can conclude; only time will tell.

The Genesis Account Although NASA and the rest of the scientific community are still divided on the creation of the universe, the majority, of late, appear to agree on the latest proposed model that the earth is about four and a half billion years old; and the ecosystem of the earth is less than three billion years old. By accepting that model, notably, many of these scientists, if

The Genesis Account

not all, unknowingly agree and support the Genesis creation account!

Here is why?

We are told; "1 IN the beginning God [אלהים] created the heaven and the earth" (Genesis 1:1).

So! When did God create the heaven, earth, ecosystem, and man?

According to the scientific community, as it was stated before, the existence of the earth is about four and a half billion years old. But, as far as the ecosystem of the earth is concerned, recently some of the scientists say that it has been in existence for less than three billion years.

Therefore, according to the above information, we can conclude from the inspired Scriptures (Bible), when God came with the angels and other created beings to planet earth, about three billion years ago, they saw the earth completely covered with frozen water (Genesis 1:2), void, and hanging here in the cold dark space.

The prophet of the LORD says,

"7 He [God] stretched out the north over the empty space, and hanged the earth upon nothing." Job 26:7

As per the above verse, when the angels came here, to planet earth, with the Creator of Genesis 1:1, about three billion years ago, they saw the earth hanging "upon nothing," and "2 the earth was without form, and void; and darkness was upon the face of the deep. And the Spirit of God [the Creator] moved upon the face of the waters" (Genesis 1:2).

And, during that time, when God the Creator of Genesis 1:1 began to create the earth into a habitable place in six days, the angels "shouted for joy" (Job 38:7).

This is what happened, on the *first day*, about three billion years ago. God created a temporary light so that the angels and the rest of the beings, who were with Him, were able to see clearly the formation of the ecosystem of the earth as it was spoken into

The Genesis Account

existence. And in reference to that light, "5 God called the light Day, and the darkness He called Night. And the evening and the morning were the first day" (Genesis 1:5).

On the *second day*: God made the "firmament," which is the expansion between heaven and earth. Above the expansion, He placed water. What this means is that there was water that enveloped the earth above the atmosphere, which was not yet created, and below the atmosphere was the water (ocean, already in existence), which covered the entire earth.

And on the *third day*: God called the water, which covered the entire earth (ocean) to be gathered into one place, and allow dry land to appear. And when land appeared, God called for the vegetation to appear (grass, fruit trees, herbs, flowers, etc., etc.).

The *fourth day*: As I have stated before, during the first day, the temporary light was brought forth first for the benefit of the angels and other beings, who were with God the Creator of "all things," in order to be able to see the creation of the earth's ecosystem taking place before their eyes. Later on during the fourth day, the Creator replaced the temporary light with the moon and sun in our Galaxy. The LORD created the moon and the sun to give light upon the earth; the moon, to give light at night and to keep the earth steady in its rotation; and the sun, to keep the earth in a relative constant temperature, in order to sustain the ecosystem and all life forms.

By replacing the temporary light with a sun, it gave the Creator's audience the beauty of the creation stages of the earth while the sun shined upon the earth and on the other planets in our system. And it also gave the on-lookers the delight in the beauty and the spectacular changes that were taking place in the nearby planets because of the sun's heat, and because of the property of light and its magnetic field that is in it.

For example, the heat from the sun's rays caused gases to evaporate and ice to melt in the surrounding planets of the earth, as in Mars, which eventually the water from the ocean almost completely evaporated because there was no system in place to hold the water vapor from escaping into outer space. Now, pockets of water can be found within the planet and some water can be seen

The Genesis Account

falling in the form of snow and ice in the north and south poles of the planet.

Gases, ice, water, magnetic fields, air, and gas currents, to mention a few, were the phenomenon's that sprung up all around to the beholder's delight. The sun's rays, also gave the observers the enchantment of color all around them as far as the eye could see. And planet earth was becoming more and more like a blue jewel sparkling in space during the progression of the creation week.

On the *fifth day* God created creatures to live in the water, on land, and birds to fly in the air, to fill the empty space, and so on.

And on the *sixth day* God created man and gave him dominion over the earth and everything that was in it and on it.

In confirmation to the above comments, here are the references that are found in the Torah (the five books of Moses).

Moses wrote:

"1 IN the beginning God created the heaven and the earth. 2 And the earth was without form, and void; and darkness was upon the face of the deep. And the Spirit of God moved upon the face of the waters.

"3 And God said, Let there be light: and there was light. 4 And God saw the light, that it was good: and God divided the light from the darkness. 5 And God called the light Day, and the darkness He called Night. And the evening and the morning were the first day.

"6 And God said, Let there be a firmament in the midst of the waters, and let it divide the waters from the waters. 7 And God made the firmament, and divided the waters which were under the firmament from the waters which were above the firmament: and it was so. 8 And God called the firmament Heaven. And the evening and the morning were the second day.

"9 And God said, Let the waters under the heaven be gathered together unto one place, and let the dry land appear: and it was so. 10 And God called the dry land Earth; and the gathering together of the waters called He Seas: and God saw that it was good. 11 And God said, Let the earth bring forth grass, the herb yielding seed, and the fruit tree yielding fruit after his kind, whose seed is in itself, upon the earth: and it was so. 12 And the earth brought forth grass,

The Genesis Account

and herb yielding seed after his kind, and the tree yielding fruit, whose seed was in itself, after his kind: and God saw that it was good. 13 And the evening and the morning were the third day.

"14 And God said, Let there be lights in the firmament of the heaven to divide the day from the night; and let them be for signs, and for seasons, and for days, and years: 15 And let them be for lights in the firmament of the heaven to give light upon the earth and it was so 16 And God made two great lights; the greater light to rule the day, and the lesser light to rule the night. He made the stars also. 17 And God set them in the firmament of the heaven to give light upon the earth, 18 And to rule over the day and over the night, and to divide the light from the darkness: and God saw that it was good. 19 And the evening and the morning were the fourth day.

"20 And God said, Let the waters bring forth abundantly the moving creature that hath life, and fowl that may fly above the earth in the open firmament of heaven. 21 And God created great whales, and every living creature that moveth, which the waters brought forth abundantly, after their kind, and every winged fowl after his kind: and God saw that it was good. 22 And God blessed them, saying, Be fruitful, and multiply, and fill the waters in the seas, and let fowl multiply in the earth. 23 And the evening and the morning were the fifth day.

"24 And God said, Let the earth bring forth living creature after his kind, cattle, and creeping thing, and beast of the earth after his kind: and it was so. 25 And God made the beast of the earth after his kind, and cattle after their kind, and every thing that creepeth upon the earth after his kind: and God saw that it was good.

"26 And God said, Let us make man in our image, after our likeness: and let them have dominion over the fish of the sea, and over the fowl of the air, and over the cattle, and over all the earth, and over every creeping thing that creepeth upon the earth. 27 So God created man in His own image, in the image of God created He him; male and female created He them. 28 And God blessed them, and God said unto them, Be fruitful, and multiply, and replenish the earth, and subdue it: and have dominion over the fish of the sea, and over the fowl of the air, and over every living thing that moveth

The Genesis Account

upon the earth. 29 And God said, Behold, I have given you every herb bearing seed, which is upon the face of all the earth, and every tree, in the which is the fruit of a tree yielding seed; to you it shall be for meat. 30 And to every beast of the earth, and to every fowl of the air, and to every thing that creepeth upon the earth, wherein there is life, I have given every green herb for meat: and it was so.

"31 And God saw every thing that He had made, and, behold, it was very good. And the evening and the morning were the sixth day" (Genesis 1:1-31).

So! How was the earth and its ecosystem created?

According to the above verses, Moses clearly stated three thousand and four hundred years ago, before all of the High-Tec electronic gadgetry was invented that at the beginning of each new day, God, of Genesis 1:1, created something by speaking it into existence. Likewise King David agrees with Moses and states that God created the ecosystem of the "earth," "the heavens," and "the hosts of them" into existence "by the breath of His mouth."

He says, "6 By the word of the LORD were the heavens made; and all the host of them by the breath of His mouth." "9 For He spake, and it was done; He commanded, and it stood fast" (Psalms 33:6, 9). They were all created by His "power," by His "outstretched arm," and by His "discretion." Jeremiah 10:12

When were the earth, ecosystem, sun, heaven, and man created in our galaxy?

As it was stated before, according to the scientific community, the earth has been here for four and a half billion years; and the ecosystem of the earth has been here for less than three billion years. Therefore, in acknowledgement to the scientific findings, if their findings are correct, according to the Bible, man, the earth's ecosystem, the earth's moon, and sun were created about three billion years ago. And that acknowledgement by the scientific community places Adam, Eve, and their children in a sinless life for

The Genesis Account

about three billion years before Eve and Adam sinned six thousand years ago, in which time, Cain, their son, followed in their rebellion, and plunged their offspring into relentless evil living.

Nonetheless, in spite of the rejection of the Biblical facts by many scientists, let me say again that recent theoretical scientific models confirm the creation week, the flood, and the statements that are made in Genesis chapters one to nine and elsewhere.

Here is a summation of the scientific and Biblical facts.

Recent scientific findings	The 3,400 year old Biblical facts
	Pre-creation of the earth
Antimatter	Third heaven. (1st heaven is between earth and space. 2nd heaven is between stratosphere and to the edge of deep space, and the 3rd heaven is outside of the universe.)
Universe 13 billion years old	Created beings existed before the universe was created (Nehemiah 9:6).
Earth 4.5 billion years old	Hung on nothing (Job 27:6).
Earth is round	Isaiah 40:22
Earth turns	Job 38:14
Earth had an ocean	Covered with frozen water (Gen. 1:2).
Earth	In darkness (Gen. 1:2).
	Lifeless and void (Genesis 1:2).
	No landmass (Genesis 1:7, 9).
	No sun or moon (Genesis 1:16).
	No stars in our solar system (Gen. 1:16-18).
	Creation of the earth
As per the scientists, the earth's ecosystem is less than 3 billion years old.	1st day. The temporary light more than likely caused the vast ocean's frozen water to melt (Genesis 1:3, 4) because the following day the frozen ocean had already melted.
	2nd day. Water placed above the firmament to envelope the earth in order to keep the whole earth in a constant tropical temperature (Genesis 1:6, 7).

The Genesis Account

3rd day. One mass of dry land was created in the midst of the ocean and was caused to yield grass, herbs, fruit trees, etc., and multiply (Gen. 1:9-12). And the ocean was told not to go beyond the shore (Job 38:11).

Sun and moon less than 3 billion years. (Earth is 4.5 billion years old.) Stars in our solar system?

4th day. The sun and the moon were created on the fourth day (Gen. 1:16). Stars and clusters (bands) were created in our solar system (Gen. 1:14, 15; Job 38:31).

Massive suns that are 1,000 times greater than our own sun called "Arcturus" travels at unheard of speeds (Job 38:32).

5th day. God created all the life forms in the sea, land, and air and told them to multiply (Genesis 1:20-22).

6th day. God created man after His own image and in the image of His Associate and told them to multiply (Genesis 1:26, 27).

7th day (Saturday) the Creator rested from His work (Genesis 2:4).

Earth's ecosystem less than 3 billion years old.

Therefore man lived in a sinless state for less than 3 billion years before he sinned 6,000 years ago.

During the flood

Earth has more than one continent. The scientists acknowledge that the present continents broke from one massive continent.

During the flood, the earth's one continent was broken by the sheer weight and by the huge water currents, which coiled around the earth's under water highways. The massive force of the water not only broke the single continent into multiple continents that we see today, but at the same time, it created an upheaval of the ocean floor and pushed upwards the Tec-Plates and the landmass to create gigantic mountains in the broken continents

The Genesis Account

And the massive deluge also killed the huge antediluvians, animals such as dinosaurs, birds, whales, and fish. And only eight persons were saved and a myriad of life forms. (Gen. chap's 6-9).

<u>After the flood</u>

The scientists thus far acknowledge that the earth's ecosystem is degenerating, and the life forms are dying and gradually becoming extinct

Up until the flood, man lived on an average of 1,000 years; but after the flood, like the other life forms, man started to degenerate; and today he would be lucky if he lives for 100 years. (Gen. chap. 5.)

Fossils also reveal to us that many species, which lived for many millions of years, on land and water, are extinct, and even current species that live among us are at risk of extinction

As per the above information, although some scientific models place the formation of the sun and the moon and the ecosystem taking place three billion years ago, Moses disagrees with that theory, just as some of the other scientific models disagree with that theory. Some scientific models claim that the ecosystem began three billion years ago by a huge mass of matter colliding with the earth. According to theoretical models, it took almost three billion years for the ecosystem to develop. But that cannot be true because the sun and the moon were created in one day; and so it was with the ecosystem, it was created in six days. Therefore it did not take tree billion evolutionary years for the sun, moon, and ecosystem to crawl into existence. According to the Bible, the sun, the moon, the ecosystem, and its residents of the earth were created in six literal Days in a mature state. They did not take three billion years to develop. Therefore as per the scientific data, if it is correct, we can conclude that the sun, moon, the ecosystem, Adam, and Eve were placed on earth within one week from the beginning of the three billion years. And, as per the Bible, Adam and Eve chose to sin (broke the Ten Commandments) six thousand years ago.

A lot more can be said of how, today, the scientific community continues to acknowledge, by their scientific findings, the Biblical facts of the 3,400 year old statements in the book of Genesis and elsewhere; but, will the scientists accept the Creator's invitation to "come and let us reason together" and acknowledge that He is the Creator of "all things"? Unfortunately, it appears, in spite of their own scientific facts, which confirm the Genesis Biblical statements, today, many scientists reject the Creator of Genesis 1:1 and think that God the Creator of Genesis 1:1 is some kind of a particle called the "God particle"?

Go figure?

THE ANTEDILUVIANS

Oh! Those antediluvians. They have become a thorn to the scientist's theoretical side because the antediluvians are commonly associated with the worldwide flood. And because the antediluvians are connected with the global flood, some of the scientists on one hand ignore the flood as if it never happened; and yet on the other hand, they acknowledge that the present handful of continents of planet earth did sever themselves from one landmass (Genesis 1:9, 10) during the global flood (Genesis chapters 6-8), as the Genesis account so aptly reveals.

Although the scientific community may willfully close their eyes to the three thousand and four hundred year old statements of the Genesis account, they cannot make the Biblical facts go away because the more they try to avoid the statements in the Genesis account, the more their theoretical models confirm the Genesis account; and that does not sit too well with many of them—for whatever reason. The fact that the archeologists are finding fossils in different layers of soil, with all manner of life forms that are millions of years old, should suffice as concrete evidence that the Genesis statements are accurate.

The Antediluvians

Therefore, if you read the Genesis account, you would have noticed how the heavens, the earth, and man came to exist. But, if you have not read the Genesis account, here is a brief overview of what happened before the antediluvians, during the antediluvians, and during the global flood.

Moses tells us when the Creator of Genesis 1:1 came to the lifeless planet earth with the holy angels (saints), and with other beings to watch the creation of the ecosystem of the earth take place; he said;

"2 the earth was without form, and void; and darkness was upon the face of the deep [water]" (Genesis 1:2).

Moses, in the above verse, is stating a simple fact. He says that the earth was in total darkness; there was no moon or sun to give light and warmth to planet earth. Therefore, when the Creator started to create, He caused a temporary light to appear (Genesis 1:3, 4), which revealed the earth in its void condition, and hanging frozen in the cold dark space, which it occupied. The earth did not have land mass. And the earth's single ocean was largely frozen, rugged, irregular, broken, rough, and in a jagged form. In that state, the earth did not sustain life, as we know it.

Moreover, it is very apparent by reading chapter's one and two of Genesis and Job chapter thirty-eight that the living beings, who came with God the Creator of Genesis 1:1 to watch the earth being created into a habitable place, lived billions of years before the earth, Adam, and Eve were created and placed upon planet earth to live. What the above and the following verses also reveal is the fact that those beings who came with God the Creator, and the other beings who watched from afar, had places of their own to live in. It also means that God the Creator created the habitats for those beings way before the ecosystem was created on planet earth for Adam and Eve to live in.

And to confirm the fact that holy angels and other beings were with the Creator during the creation week, the Creator said to Job, "4 Where wast [were] thou [you] when I laid the foundations of the

The Antediluvians

earth? declare, if thou [you] hast understanding. 5 Who hath laid the measures thereof, if thou knowest? or who hath stretched the line upon it? 6 Whereupon are the foundation thereof fastened? or who laid the corner stone thereof; 7 When the morning stars [angels] sang together, and all the sons [other created beings who live in other worlds] of God shouted for joy?" Job 38:4 -7.

There with the morning stars (angels), Lucifer in his sinless state was singing and shouting for joy while they all saw the earth being transformed and appear as a blue joule ready to receive Adam and Eve. Lucifer was there with the other sinless angels watching, on the 6th day, Adam and Eve being created while they all shouted for joy.

So! When did the angels and the other sons of God shout for joy?

The answer is given; they shouted for joy when God the Creator was creating the ecosystem of the earth, Adam, and Eve.

By considering the above presentation, a person can obviously conclude that the earth pre-existed in its void form, before the ecosystem was created for man. That being the case, a person has to also conclude, as per the scientific research, the earth has been here for approximately one and a half billion years in its void form. And according to some new scientific research, the ecosystem has been here on planet earth for less than three billion years. Therefore, if today's scientific research is correct, we can conclude, Adam and Eve, and their children, occupied the earth in their sinless state for less than three billion years. And, we can also conclude, Adam and Eve lived a sinless and satisfying life for at least two billion years before they learned the bad news about Lucifer's (Satan's) sin. And for another one billion years, they watched diligently for Lucifer's wily deceptions, until, at one point, Eve arrogantly entangled herself into his deceptive web, which led to her deception and plunged Adam and Eve into the horrors of sin. But, even if we were to exclude the scientific research, which tells us that the ecosystem has been here for less than three billion years, we can conclude that Adam and Eve lived here on planet earth way beyond the time they sinned; and that places Adam and Eve in their sinless state many,

The Antediluvians

many millions of years before they sinned six thousand years ago.

To expand on the above comments, let me say that it is commonly known that Eve sinned first, but in all fairness to Eve, we should note that she was not the one who sinned first; it was the archangel Lucifer who sinned first in heaven after Adam and Eve were created. We are told about thirty percent of the heavenly angels chose to support Lucifer in his underhanded cause to overthrow their Creator from His lofty throne. They wanted to dethrone God the Creator of Genesis 1:1, and make Him subservient to them, and usher in a kingdom of anarchy.

Can you imagine that?

Again, it was Lucifer (Satan) who sinned in heaven first. After his fall from grace, he implemented his wily tactics upon his fellow angels, which caused many of them to eventually sin against their Creator. After he accomplished that task, he went about throughout the galaxies to deceive other beings for his cause and failed miserably. Well, he almost failed. Even though Adam and Eve were warned about their wily foe and could communicate face to face with God their Creator, when Satan came to planet earth, he still managed to deceive Eve. After he caused Eve to sin, his name became synonymous with the media he used to deceive Eve. Now, he is most commonly known by the names of Satan, dragon, serpent, and devil. (See Revelation 12:9.) After she sinned, Satan was able to work through her, and eventually she became Adam's demise. Adam could have averted his death by choosing not to sin and allow Eve to die. Instead, he chose to die with her?

You know, God could have created another woman for Adam; so, why did he choose to perish?

Do you have an answer?

Eve and Adam sinned (broke the 10 Commandments: Romans 5:13) against their Creator. In doing so, they threw their allegiance with Satan and became his subjects. And by becoming his subjects, the dominion that was given to Adam and Eve, by the Creator, over the earth and every thing that was in it, Adam and Eve forfeited their dominion to Satan. Now, Satan had dominion over the earth and everything that was in it. Well, almost everything, today, he does

The Antediluvians

not have dominion over the repentant sinners. He is not their God; Christ the LORD of hosts is their God.

At this point, Satan and his evil angels were very happy for the victory over Adam and Eve; and since he and his angels were not allowed to return to their heavenly abode, Satan was in his glory because now, he and his evil angels had a place to live—here on earth. Satan had claimed the earth for himself, and claimed to be the god of this world.

Now, all Satan had to do is to get rid of the humans, or perhaps, use them in the future to expand into other worlds, which exist in other galaxies and cause other sinless beings to join him in his revolt against God their Creator? Or use them as his toys?

Needless to say, Lucifer's victory was going to be short lived because God the Creator did not want Lucifer to expand sin into other worlds, and neither did God the Creator wanted Lucifer and his evil angels to live forever on planet earth or anywhere else for that matter. The Creator was going to implement the plan of salvation for the human race. And that meant that Satan's evil plans sooner or later were going to end.

Irrespective to the Creator's plans to save man, Lucifer's aim was, and still is today, to continue with his plans to have full control over every human being on earth. As you probably know, the record reveals that Satan and his evil angels eventually succeeded once, to a large degree, to saturate the minds of the antediluvians with sin. Planet earth was drenched in sin because Satan, his evil angels, Eve, and Adam chose to live in unrestrained acts of sin. And since they all chose to live in sin, they all imposed upon themselves the death penalty (Romans 6:23), and the destruction of the ecosystem of planet earth.

After Eve sinned, the effects of sin did not appear right away in their lives and in the ecosystem. It was not until after Adam sinned, he and his wife finally realized that the ecosystem began to degenerate. They also understood that the animals, birds, fish, and all the life forms, which Adam recognized by their names, which he had given them, became fearful of them. They not only realized what was happening to their surroundings, but they also realized

The Antediluvians

that they lost their robe of righteousness (the light that emanated and covered their naked bodies). Realizing that the robe of righteousness disappeared from them, they quickly became conscious of the fact that they were naked and degenerating. And when they saw that their robe of righteousness was gone from their bodies, they were ashamed because their sinless children saw them naked. To their horror, it finally sunk in their heads what their sinful acts had done! They remembered the Creator's words when He said to them:

> "16 Of every tree of the garden thou [you] mayest freely eat: 17 But of the tree of the knowledge of good and evil, thou shalt not eat of it: for in the day that thou eatest thereof thou shalt surely die" (Genesis 2:16, 17).

The Creator allowed enough time to pass before He confronted Adam and Eve with their sinful acts. He wanted to allow enough time, so that Adam and Eve could experience their sinful environment, and give them time to repent for their sins. And sure enough, Adam and Eve did realize, and were experiencing the horrors of sin. And when the time was right, the Creator spoke to them, without appearing before them. The guilt-ridden pair recognized the Creator's voice and quickly hid from the Creator while He was speaking to them. They hid because they thought it was retribution time. At that time, the Creator began to ask them questions regarding their sinful acts, in order to give them the opportunity to confess their sins and repent; but they would not take the blame for their sinful acts. They each replied that they were deceived because of the other person, and because of the dragon. In other words, Adam blamed the woman by saying, "If you did not give me the woman, I would not have sinned." And Eve, said, "the serpent beguiled me."

Although Adam and Eve were very afraid of God the Creator at this point, they were surprised when they received from God the Creator "coats of skins" to cover their naked bodies, instead of the "wages" for their sins, which is "death" (Gen. 3:21; Romans 6:23).

The Antediluvians

The record shows that they did not acknowledge their sins right away. But, when they saw that God the Creator did not come in vengeance, Adam and Eve finally chose to repent. When they repented from their sins, God their Creator spoke to them in the Garden of Eden and gave them the opportunity to save themselves and their offspring. And when they accepted the plan of salvation, God the Creator promised that He would come in the "flesh" from the "seed" of a woman and pay the penalty of death for them, in order to save them and their children from eternal destruction.

Adam and Eve were overwhelmed with the Creator's love for them, with the plan of salvation, and with the promise of the supreme sacrifice of the Creator on their behalf. Knowing that the Creator was willing to die for their sins, in order to save them, caused them to love their Creator even more than before they sinned. They were in awe to learn that God the Creator was willing to die for their sins in order to save them. After that, Adam and Eve became zealously obedient to the Covenant (the Ten Commandments of Exodus 20) and to the plan of salvation.

And unto the dragon that was perched on top of the forbidden tree, in the Garden of Eden, God the Creator said:

> "15 I will put enmity between thee [you] and the woman, and between thy [your] seed [litter] and her seed [offspring]; it shall bruise thy head, and thou shalt bruise his heel" (Genesis 3:15).

And so it was after Adam's fall, and so it is today. Man lost planet earth, eternal life, happiness, contentment, and the Garden of Eden. Then, man's needs were all supplied. Now, he has to toil and struggle in order to survive. The dragon has lost its legs and wings, and its litter is slithering on its belly breathing the dust of the ground. And, whenever the dragon (snake) was or is confronted by man, it strikes at man's heel; and man strikes upon its head.

Nonetheless, after Adam and Eve sinned, the Creator sent angels of mighty stature and strength to guard the tree of life, in the Garden of Eden, which gave Adam and Eve their perpetual youth and vigor. Adam, Eve, their offspring, Satan, and his evil angels

The Antediluvians

were not allowed to take the fruit of the "tree of life" and eat it. If they did eat of the tree of life, they would have received nutrients to replenish their youthful bodies, which would have caused their longevity to be prolonged. Therefore because of their sins and of the benefits of the tree of life, they were banished from the Garden of Eden to eliminate their perpetual youth and the encouragement of confrontation with the holy angels who were guarding the tree of life, and for few other reasons, which I will not go into.

Consequently, after Adam sinned, they knew, as we know today that sooner or later they would die. And so it was, Adam lived, after he sinned, for nine hundred and thirty years, and then he died (Genesis 5:5).

It should also be noted that Adam and Eve had more children after they sinned 6,000 years ago. Scripture tells us that Adam had "sons and daughters" (Genesis 5:4). And, it should be eminent that many of their children did not sin prior to or after Adam and Eve sinned. To confirm that fact, the record tells us that

"14 Death reigned from Adam to Moses, even over them that had not sinned after the similitude of Adam's transgression," Romans 5:14.

But, after Adam sinned, about 6,000 years ago, and forfeited the dominion of planet earth to Satan, as I have stated before, the condemnation of the law (the Ten Commandments) upon the dominion of planet earth and everything that was in it began to erode, age, and disappear, as many of the species and plants continue to become extinct today

In addition to the planetary effects that were caused by Adam's sins—the aging of Adam and Eve, and of the life forms in the water and above the water—they instilled the condemnation of the Ten Commandments (Romans 6:23) indirectly upon the emotions of Adam's sinless children. By observing the deadly events taking place around them, they became emotionally stressed out and fearful that Adam's sins might affect them. But, after a time, they noticed that they were not influenced.

The Antediluvians

As time went on, beyond their sinless three billion years (according to the scientific community), many of Adam's children rejoiced in their steadfastness and abstinence from sin; but unfortunately for many of the children of Adam, eventually sin began to attract them when their brother Cain sinned a number of years after Adam sinned. (See Genesis chapter four.)

By dwelling upon the sins that were progressively committed by Cain and by his brothers and sisters, the rest of the children of Adam were influenced to a degree to join their rebellious sinful life style. Although a number of the children of Adam abhorred sin and the sinful acts of their brothers and sisters, many of them did not remain loyal to God the Creator; eventually they abandoned God and chose to live in sin.

Sin eventually divided the children of Adam into two camps. One camp was identified as the "sons of God" (those who did not sin), and the other camp was identified as the "sons of Satan" (sons and daughters of men). And, as the "sons of God" watched the enticing evil acts of the sinners (sons and daughters of men), the "sons of God" became attracted to them and many of them committed fornication and many of them intermarried. These acts further enticed many of the "sons of God" to fall from their sinless state; and eventually, deserted God the Creator.

The record states;

> "1 AND it came to pass, when men began to multiply on the face of the earth, and daughters were born unto them. 2 That the sons of God saw the daughters of men that they were fair; and they took them wives of all which they chose." Gen. 6:1, 2

Although the "sons of God" were enticed by the beauty and by the flirting of the sexual dress and luring sensual acts of their fallen brothers and sisters, it appears that there was no restraint by many of them.

As you have read in the above verses, many of them gave their allegiance to Satan.

But those individuals who hated sin, and the results of sin,

The Antediluvians

chose to follow God the Creator, remained steadfast, and loyal to God. They communicated with Him and He with them. God the Creator would hear their petition, grant them His blessing, advise them what to do, and how to further implement the plan of salvation, so that people would not lose sight of eternal life and of their Creator.

Although the record does not fully reveal what happened to the sinless children of Adam (sons of God), it is reasonable to conclude that those individuals who had not sinned were taken to another world to live, until the second coming of Christ the LORD takes place (See Genesis 5:24 as an example). And, at the second coming of Jesus Christ the LORD, the holy angels will gather the redeemed from earth and the redeemed from that planet and they will all go together to heaven.

We are also told that there were sinners who repented after Adam sinned and were taken away from the earth. One such person was Enoch. Enoch loved God the Creator very much. Enoch, at the age of sixty-five, had a son called Methuselah. After Enoch had his son, he began to contemplate what would it be like to lose his son? The more he thought about it the more compassionate he became towards his son and towards God the Creator. One day Enoch fully realized the impact of the barbaric death, which God the Creator was going to suffer for the human race, and the extreme sacrificial cost to Him, in order to save the human race. The more he pondered upon the Creator's sacrifice for the sins of the world, the more he began to abhor sin and the fruit of sin.

Finally, Enoch got so disgusted with sin and the results of sin that he focused upon the sinless Creator, and lived within the precepts of the Decalogue. Daily, Enoch found himself drawn closer and closer to the sinless Creator; and more and more he pulled himself away from sin. In doing so, we are told that Enoch walked with the Creator for three hundred years after his son Methuselah was born, and the Creator took Enoch to live on another planet, with other sinless beings, until the second coming of Jesus Christ takes place.

If you are wondering why I said "Enoch was taken to another

The Antediluvians

planet to live," it is simple; Christ said that "no man hath ascended up to heaven" neither has any man come down from heaven (John 3:13); therefore, Enoch had to be taken to another world to live.

Here is the account: "21 And Enoch lived sixty and five years, and begat Methuselah: 22 And Enoch walked with God after he begat Methuselah three hundred years, and begat sons and daughters: 23 And all the days of Enoch were three hundred sixty and five years: 24 And Enoch walked with God: and he was not; for God took him" (Genesis 5:21-24).

On the other hand, unfortunately, many of Adam's children lost sight of the Creator during the time period of Enoch and right up to the time when Noah entered in the ark (ship). In those days, they had plenty of food, and lacked for nothing. Life was good, so what did they need God the Creator for? Satan and his evil angels provided all the vile and sinful enticements they wanted. Their lives were full of debase and sinful acts. And those sinful acts, like today's crowd, they called enjoyment. They were losing their reasoning and wisdom to a point where they preferred to live in sin. In fact, to them, living in sin was natural. They abandoned God the Creator and chose to worship the gods of their imaginations, which they produced by their hands, as statutes, icons, and other paraphernalia.

There is nothing new in that department—is there?

After the flood, the children of Israel, hundreds of years later, did the very same thing before God the Creator, over and over again. They worshipped, astrologers, sorcerers, witchcraft, idols, molten images, seers, psychics, fortune-tellers, and so on.

Does that sound like today's crowd?

Anyway, Isaiah writes regarding the molten images, which the people worshipped: "6 Worshipers of idols comfort each other, saying, "Don't worry!" 7 Woodcarvers, goldsmiths, and other workers encourage one another and say, "We've done a great job!" Then they nail the idol down, so it won't fall over" (Isaiah 41:6, 7). (CEV).

And God the Creator adds the following regarding those man-made idols, which are called gods: "21 I am the LORD, the King

The Antediluvians

of Israel! Come argue your case with me. Present your evidence. 22 Come near me, you idols. Tell us about the past, and we will think about it. Tell us about the future, so we will know what is going to happen. 23 Prove that you are gods by making your predictions come true. Do something good or evil, so we can be amazed and terrified. 24 You idols are nothing, and you are powerless. To worship you would be disgusting" (Isaiah 41:21-24). (CEV)

God the Creator reveals that these gods, which are made by human hands, are all vanity and abomination; they are full of confusion because it is the work of man. Referring to these man-made idols, icons, etc., the Creator says: "28 None of these idols are able to give advice or answer questions. 29 They are nothing, and they can do nothing—they are less than a passing breeze" (Isaiah 41:28, 29). (CEV)

Then, like today, people still worship men, women, idols, icons, sorcerers, fortune-tellers, seers, soothsayers, psychics, evil spirits (angels) who more often masquerade dead people, and false prophets who claim and promise all sorts of things; but God the Creator says that they are workers of iniquity, confusion, and an abomination. The workers of "iniquity" are individuals who are prompted by the evil angels to work miracles and prophecy through them. But, let it be known, even satanic influence cannot prophecy accurately of things to come. They can only create phenomenon to deceive the ungodly and bring them false hope in order to hold them in their iron clutches of sin and cause them to reject the Creator as their God.

There upon the altars of those man-made gods, and false prophets, the antediluvians not only offered their gifts, but they also offered their children as a sacrifice of gratitude and of appeasement.

Those antediluvian men, woman, and children were so smart, and of such enormous height and strength that one would think that they would be more attentive to their Creator instead of Satan and his evil angels? They were not! They enjoyed their evil acts and preferred to live in them. (See Job 21:14.) In fact, their characters were so evil that their thoughts were continually evil. Instead of going to sleep at night, they would spend the time to think of what

The Antediluvians

evil things they could do when they got up from their beds.

> Here is the record: "5 God saw that the wickedness of man was great in the earth, and that every imagination of the thoughts of his heart was only evil continually." "12 And God looked upon the earth, and, behold, it was corrupt; for all flesh had corrupted his way upon the earth"(Genesis 6:5, 12).

Their depraved acts reached the Creator's patience to a point where He wanted to eradicate the human race from the face of the earth. Moses wrote, "6 And it repented the LORD that He had made man on the earth, and it grieved Him at His heart. 7 And the LORD said, I will destroy man whom I have created from the face of the earth;" (Genesis 6:6, 7).

Because evil was so rampant throughout the earth, God the Creator chose not to allow those evil acts to spread and overtake the whole human race; neither would He allow evil man and evil angels to occupy planet earth for ever. If He did, they would destroy the ecosystem, and eventually destroy the earth; and that was not acceptable, and it is still not acceptable to God the Creator today.

In fact, today, God the Creator has said to His holy angels not to allow man to harm the earth, to a point, where it will not be able to sustain His repentant people. These mighty angels of God are commissioned to restrain man and prevent the complete destruction of the ecosystem of planet earth until God's people are sealed shortly after the sign of Christ's second coming appears in heaven and before the plagues begin to fall upon the ungodly and upon the ecosystem of the earth. And just before Christ comes the second time, to take His people to heaven, the angels are commissioned to remove their restraint from sinful man, allow them to destroy each other, and the ecosystem of planet earth.

Here is the account: "1 AND after these things I saw four angels standing on the four corners of the earth, holding the four winds of the earth, that the wind should not blow on the earth, nor on the sea, nor on any tree. 2 And I saw another angel ascending from the east, having the seal of the living God: and he cried with a

The Antediluvians

loud voice to the four angels, to whom it was given to hurt the earth and the sea, 3 Saying, Hurt not the earth, neither the sea, nor the trees, till we have sealed the servants of our God in their foreheads" (Revelation 7:1-3).

The above verses are self-explanatory. You know as well as I do what happens if the vegetation of the earth is destroyed. No food! No air! Right? And you also know what happens if there is drought or the water becomes undrinkable. That is why the LORD sent the angel to the four angels who are on the earth. He told them to stop man, Satan, and his evil angels from destroying the ecosystem of the earth completely. They are to prevent the destruction of the earth's ecosystem until such time God's people are "sealed" for heaven, after that the protection upon man, beast, and upon the ecosystem is to be removed.

God the Creator could have avoided all of the above by allowed the human race to destroy itself, during Adam's time, but His love and mercy for man endured. He chose to fulfill the "promise" He made to Adam and Eve. Therefore, He picked Noah to preach the plan of salvation, by the power of the Holy Spirit (1 Peter 3:18-20), and to give the warning of the deluge that was to come upon the earth. Noah preached to the antediluvians for one hundred and twenty years. And during that period of time, Noah's three sons were born. "Japheth," the oldest was born when Noah was 500 years old. Two years later "Shem" was born. "Ham" was the youngest. He was the one who was cursed by his father after the flood.

Although Noah spent considerable time giving the warning of the coming crises, he also spent many hours building a ship (ark) as per the specifications that were revealed to him by God the Creator of Genesis 1:1.

For one hundred and twenty years the message of grace and mercy went forward to the giant descendents of Adam and Eve. In spite of their high intellect and stature, many of these individuals were incapable of making a moral judgment and save themselves from the flood that was to come upon them. With the help of the evil angels, they were steeped in sin so deep that it clouded their

The Antediluvians

judgment. They had become like the evil angels who emulate Satan their leader. The antediluvians had put on the evil character of Satan. In doing so, they hated God the Creator for not letting them live in sin and therefore they loved death.

Thus, God the Creator was left with no choice. If God was going to save the repentant sinners; He had to stop sin and the unrepentant sinners from overtaking the whole earth. "13 And God said unto Noah, The end of all flesh is come before Me; for the earth is filled with violence through them; and, behold, I will destroy them with the earth." "18 But with thee [you] will I establish My covenant; and thou [you] shalt come into the ark, thou, and thy [your] sons, and thy wife, and thy sons' wives with thee" (Genesis 6:13, 18).

The Creator's patience was running out. The sinners on earth went beyond the Creator's forbearance. They were gone to the point of no return. God the Holy Spirit could not reason with them any more. They abandoned him and the Creator. (See 1 Peter 3:18-20.)

God the Creator gave the antediluvians plenty of time to repent, but they chose not to. He also gave them plenty of evidence of the things Noah was preaching about. That evidence was true because the Creator foretold what was going to take place before the flood came. But, the antediluvians laughed at Noah when he said to them that the rain would precede the catastrophic events of the world. In response, they said, "It does not rain Noah! We do not have rain—remember? Why are you making this up?" And when Noah said that he was going to build a ship, they said, "There is no water here Noah; can't you see? You are standing on dry ground?" When Noah said to them that the animals were going to come into the ark (ship) two by two, and the clean animals will come in the ark by sevens, they said, "It is impossible to accomplish that task Noah." "The animals and the dragons will tear you apart Noah, if you try to capture them!" "Besides Noah, how are you going to collect all of these animals and birds in your lifetime? Are you going to sprout wings?" "Noah, you are going to be too old to walk by the time you gather all of the species in the ark!"

The Antediluvians

The antediluvians ridiculed Noah and his sons, but seven days before the flood came, the animals and the birds started to come into the ark as Noah had said. People began to wonder how this was done? How were all of the animals and birds coming into the ark so orderly by themselves without killing each other—they wondered?

Instead of wondering how Noah managed to get the animals into the ship, so orderly, they should have thought of the signs, which Noah gave them, and of the events that were going to take place before the flood came upon them. And they should have taken heed to these signs, which Noah revealed to them. They should have repented and entered into the ship and be saved. Instead they continued to mock and ridicule Noah and his family.

While the antediluvians were wondering about the animal procession, Lucifer (Satan) and his evil angels were not wondering at the scene. Although man could not see God's angels bringing the animals into the ark, Lucifer and his angels saw the holy angels directing the animals and the birds into the ark. And that brought chills upon Lucifer's spine. He began to worry because he did not take the Creator's words seriously enough, when Noah said that a flood was coming. A flood could not harm Lucifer and his angels. But now, he realizes that this is more than a flood, and he wondered how catastrophic it was going to be? But, he was not worried because he thought he could always hitch a ride in the ark (ship).

Meanwhile, Noah, after one hundred and twenty years of warning the people, his sons, and their wives went into the ark as God the Creator advised them. When everybody had settled in, and no one else wanted to go in, an unseen hand lifted the huge door of the ark, and closed it. The Creator, personally, closed the door and no one could open it. Not even the mighty evil angels. Noah's ark was protected by the Creator's hand, and no one could enter in it; and that included the millions of evil spirit beings, who dwell on earth, called evil angels (Revelation 12:9).

At this point Lucifer began to really worry because he saw with his own eyes how the Creator closed the huge door of the ark (ship). Satan remembered the words of the Creator that were spoken by

The Antediluvians

Noah. He also knew that God the Creator does not lie. In his anxiety, Lucifer began to plan for his safety because now, he knew that he could not hitch a ride in the ark. He started to think how the water, which enveloped the earth, was going to come down upon the earth, and what role and effect the water that was upon the earth and beneath the crust of the earth would have upon him; and what would he do to escape a crushing death? At this point, Lucifer was not worried about anybody else; he was worried mainly about his own safety.

When his evil commanding angels saw Lucifer acting strange, they inquired of their outcome during the deluge. He told them that the water would not be detrimental upon them; but they were not that stupid, they were concerned because, if the deluge was going to be prolonged, they would not be able to stay in the water too long. Nonetheless, Satan managed to assure them that if they could hover and stay sandwiched between the water that was above the ark and below the ark, they would be OK. Although they were still skeptical, they thought that the plan was logical enough to follow.

But what Satan and his evil angels did not anticipate was the awesome lightning that were going to take place during and before the release of the water, which enveloped planet earth? You see, the millions of kilowatt lightning and thunder that was going to drape the sky, at will, worried Satan. He wondered if that wattage was large enough to kill him or any of his evil angels. He knew that any one of his angels who fell in the path of these awesome deadly lightning bolts would have a severe time to survive its destructive strike.

Although the evil angels spent a lot of time planning their escape, there was nothing they could do at that point but to wait for the deluge to come. They were left on their own. It was a solemn time for the evil angels because they were not allowed to leave planet earth and take refuge somewhere else. As far as the human race was concerned, it was going to have a rude awakening. All of those individuals who chose not to enter in the safety of the ark were headed on the road of dismay, pain, anxiety, terror, and destruction.

The Antediluvians

As I stated before, after the birds, reptiles, animals, Noah, and his family went into the ark, the Creator closed the ark's door. For seven days, the antediluvians laughed and scorned Noah and his zoo; but then, raindrops were felt! Could it be that Noah was right—some reasoned. The rain came lightly at first, and then, it became progressively stronger. When the people saw what was happening, they rushed towards the ark; but the ark's door was closed! They could not get in. As the rain got stronger, and streams of water began to flow violently towards the low lands, those mighty giants began to rush to the ark screaming for the door to be lowered. But, the call of mercy that fell upon their deaf ears for one hundred and twenty years was over. The antediluvians made their choice to stay out of the ark, and when the door of the ark was closed, probation was over. The door was sealed, and no un-repented sinner could go in.

The crowd that was pushing, shoving, and trampling each other on the way to the ark was in frenzy because they could not get to the ark fast enough. Children, wives, husbands, and old people were abandoned. It was survival time for every one. Many that were able to reach the ark clung to the wooden hull to only find themselves overtaken by someone stronger than themselves—to no avail. The torrential rains came; and the powerful streams, which turned into huge rivers, came crashing upon the crowds, sweeping them away like refuse. The water currents were so violent and swift, men, women, and children could not hold on to the slippery ark and to the trees, which they thought they had refuge in. Noah's ark, which was as big as a football field, was lifted securely with its cargo to ride the mauling and battering rising water.

The hand of the Creator sustained the ark during the devastating turbulent deluge.

Meanwhile, the deluge, which covered the earth with its mauling and brutal currents of water, churned, and coiled across the globe; and by their shear brute force turned the world upside down, tore the single continent into pieces, and created new landscapes.

We are told, "17 the flood was forty days upon the earth; and the waters increased, and bare up the ark, and it was lift up above

The Antediluvians

the earth. 18 And the waters prevailed, and were increased greatly upon the earth; and the ark went upon the face of the waters. 19 And the waters prevailed exceedingly upon the earth; and all the high hills, that were under the whole heaven, were covered. 20 Fifteen cubits upward did the waters prevail; and the mountains were covered. 21 And all flesh died that moved upon the earth, both of fowl, and of cattle, and of beasts, and of every creeping thing that creepeth upon the earth, and every man: 22 All in whose nostrils was the breath of life, of all that was in the dry land, died. 23 And every living substance was destroyed which was upon the face of the ground, both man, and cattle, and the creeping things, and the fowl of the heaven; and they were destroyed from the earth: and Noah only remained alive, and they that were with him in the ark. 24 And the waters prevailed upon the earth an hundred and fifty days" (Genesis 7:17-24).

And the rest of the story you probably already know.

God the Creator saved only eight people from the destruction of the flood. And through these eight people, the Creator had the earth repopulated, and the plan of salvation continued to be preached by Noah to the residents of the earth. Again, in those days, some chose to follow God the Creator, and others did not. But on the overall, the plan of salvation was in full force, as it is today.

Concerning today, the plan of salvation is being preached to everyone. Stop and think for a moment, Jesus said that His Gospel message was going to be preached to every human being on planet earth before He comes the second time to take His people home (Matthew 24:14). Therefore, all of the skeptics who said it cannot be done because there are regimes in the world that do not want Christianity preached to them, today it is done. The Gospel of Jesus Christ is preached. Many individuals had said that the task of preaching the Gospel to every person on earth was impossible. But, look at the world today, the Gospel message is propagated upon uncharted ground. It is possible! Christ's words will not fail. Every human being on earth will know who is Christ and of His saving power, and then, the end will come. It is as simple as that, just as it was during Noah's time.

Anyway, the hand of God the Creator placed Noah's ark in the region called Mesopotamia. When the water receded, the ark landed in the range of Mount Ararat. The area where the ark landed is better known today as northern Iraq. There in Mesopotamia, the three sons of Noah, Japheth, Shem, and Ham gradually replenished the land of Mesopotamia with their sons and daughters. When their offspring filled the land in Mesopotamia, they branched outward in other areas. Japheth's descendents kept moving northward from the Middle East. Ham's descendents expanded southward from the land of Palestine and into Egypt. Shem's descendents in the beginning remained mostly in the Middle East; later many of them occupied the land of Canaan.

Through the seed of Noah, the earth was repopulated; and without the Antediluvian's evil influence, the plan of salvation was perpetuated and God the Creator blessed those who preached the Gospel message and are preaching its message today. (See Matt. 28:16-20; Mark 1:1, 15; 2 John 9.)

The Journeys of God the Creator

After sin entered into the world of ours, God the Creator spent time protecting and guiding His representatives, which were, Adam, Noah, Abraham, Isaac, Jacob, the children of Israel (Jacob), Daniel, and so on. From one generation to the next, God the Creator traveled with His people while they preached the Gospel message to the residents of planet earth.

One such individual, after the flood, who was blessed because he loved righteousness and God the Creator and preached the Creator's Gospel, was called Abram (Abraham). Abram was a descendent of the line of Shem, and lived with his parents in

The Journeys of God the Creator

Mesopotamia, in an area called "Ur." Ur is located in Iraq, about 1/3rd north of the Persian Gulf, and a small distance southwest from the Euphrates River; and about 130 miles south of Babylon. Although Abram's relatives worshipped pagan gods, he remained loyal to God the Creator. There, one day the Creator said to Abram, take your belongings and go to a land, which I will show you and give it to you, and to your offspring.

Abram responded to the command of the Creator and went first to lived in Haran (North-west part of Iraq) until his father Terah died there. At that point in time, Abram was seventy-five years old. After his father's death, the Creator told Abram to go into the land of Canaan and live there. The land of Canaan encompassed the area from the city of Dan, which is north of Damascus to the Negeb, which is south of the Salt Sea; and eastward from the Mediterranean Sea coast, beyond the River Jordan.

Here is the account: "1 NOW the LORD had said unto Abram, Get thee [you] out of thy [your] country, and from thy kindred, and from thy father's house, unto a land that I will shew thee: 2 And I will make of thee a great nation, and I will bless thee [you], and make thy name great; and thou shalt be a blessing: 3 And I will bless them that bless thee, and curse him that curseth thee: and in thee shall all families of the earth be blessed. 4 So Abram departed, as the LORD had spoken unto him: and Lot went with him: and Abram was seventy and five years old when he departed out of Haran. 5 And Abram took Sarai his wife, and Lot his brother's son, and all their substance that they had gathered, and the souls that they had gotten in Haran; and they went forth to go into the land of Canaan; and into the land of Canaan they came" (Genesis 12:1-5).

And when Abram settled in Canaan, Abram was given the promise that through his seed the Gospel message will be preached. In fact, Abram, whose name was changed to Abraham, after he and God the Creator made a covenant, was also promised that through his seed God the Creator was going to come in the "flesh" to save repentant sinners. No! It is not a misprint. I did say, "God the Creator was going to come in the 'flesh' to save repentant

The Creator of Genesis 1:1-Who is He?   By: *Philip Mitanidis*

The Journeys of God the Creator

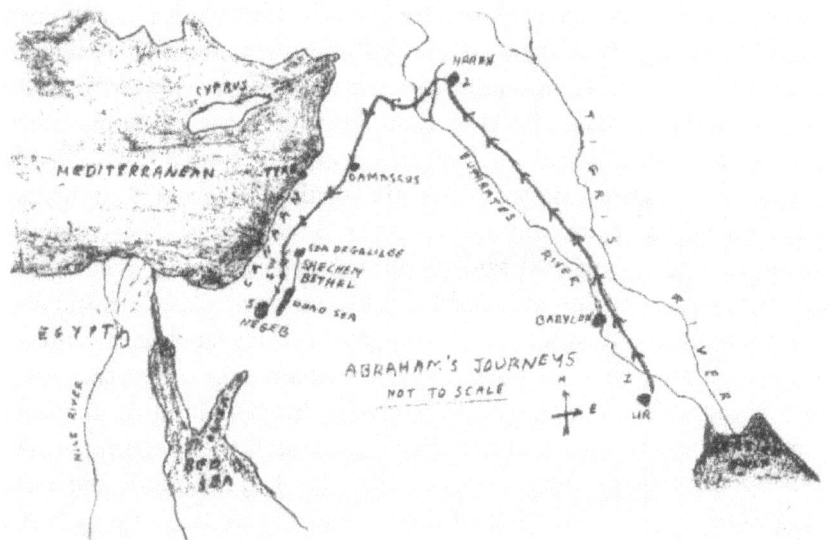

sinners." Do you remember Genesis 3:15, and the "promise" that was made to Adam and Eve? The "promise" that was made to Adam and Eve, by God the Creator, was passed on to Noah, and later, it was passed on to Abram. The Creator swore that the "promise" would be fulfilled through Abraham's seed. And when the Creator swore, He swore by His own name (יהוה אלהים) because there was no greater than Him.

> *Please remember; God the Creator of Genesis 1:1 swore by His own name because there is no one greater than Himself to swear by, as we continue to study the subject matter of who is God the Creator of Genesis 1:1?*

But Abraham did not have any children. He was getting old, and his wife was not able to conceive. So, how was the "promise" of the Creator going to be fulfilled through Abraham's seed? Abraham said to God the Creator, "2 what wilt Thou [You] give me, seeing I go childless, and the steward of my house is this Eliezer of Damascus? 3 And Abram said, Behold, to me Thou hast given no seed [offspring]: and, lo, one born in my house is mine heir [Eliezer]. 4 And, behold, the word of the LORD came unto him, saying, This shall not be thine heir; but he that shall come forth out of thine own bowels shall be thine heir. 5 And he brought him forth abroad, and said, Look now toward heaven, and tell the stars, if thou be able to number them: and He said unto him, So shall thy seed be. 6 And he believed in the LORD; and He counted it to him for righteousness" (Genesis 15:2-6).

Abraham waited patiently for the birth of a son. But when Sarah, his wife became old, hope of a son was diminishing. Sarah approached Abraham and said to him; if you want to have a son, you take Hagar, our servant, and have sex with her. Abraham finally consented and did what Sarah suggested. Hagar the Egyptian woman did give birth to a son when Abraham was eighty-six years old. Abraham's son was named Ishmael. In the taking of another woman to bear them a son, Abraham and Sarah thought they were fulfilling the will of their Creator. But God the Creator did not recognize Ishmael as the heir of the Covenant. He had other plans. And those plans were not the plans of Sarah and Abraham.

When Abraham was ninety-nine years old, God the Creator appeared to Abraham and told him again that He was to have a son from his wife Sarah. He was to be blessed, and his seed [offspring] after him.

God the Creator said to Abraham,

"19 Sarah thy wife shall bear thee a son indeed; and thou shalt call his name Isaac: and I will establish My covenant with him for an everlasting covenant, and with his seed after him" (Genesis 17:19).

But, Abraham reminded the Creator that he already had a thirteen year-old son. His name was Ishmael. And after all, now, Sarah was too old to have children.

In His next appearance, again, God would not recognize Ishmael as the successor. He said, "15 As for Sarai thy [your] wife, thou [you] shalt not call her name Sarai, but Sarah shall her name be." "17 Then Abraham fell upon his face, and laughed, and said in his heart, Shall a child be born unto him, that is an hundred years old? and shall Sarah, that is ninety years old, bear? 18 And Abraham

The Journeys of God the Creator

said unto God, O that Ishmael might live before Thee! 19 And God said, Sarah thy wife shall bear thee a son indeed; and thou shalt call his name Isaac: and I will establish My covenant with him for an everlasting covenant, and with his seed after him. 20 And as for Ishmael, I have heard thee: Behold, I have blessed him, and will make him fruitful, and will multiply him exceedingly; twelve princes shall he beget, and I will make him a great nation. 21 But My covenant will I establish with Isaac, which Sarah shall bear unto thee at this set time in the next year" (Genesis 17:15, 17-21).

Shortly after the above experience, God the Creator reappeared to Abraham and Sarah, in the "plains of Mamre," disguised in the form of a man, and reminded them that Sarah was going to have a son. She laughed within herself at the idea of having a child because she was too old. So, how was she going to have a son? Sarah was stunned when the Creator revealed to them of how she laughed within herself at His statement!

Here is the account: "9 And they said unto him [Abraham], Where is Sarah thy wife? And he said, Behold, in the tent. 10 And He said, I [the LORD] will certainly return unto thee according to the time of life; and, lo, Sarah thy wife shall have a son. And Sarah heard it in the tent door, which was behind him. 11 Now Abraham and Sarah were old and well stricken in age; and it ceased to be with Sarah after the manner of women. 12 Therefore Sarah laughed within herself, saying, After I am waxed old shall I have pleasure, my lord being old also? 13 And the LORD said unto Abraham, Wherefore did Sarah laugh, saying, Shall I of a surety bear a child, which am old? 14 Is any thing too hard for the LORD? At the time appointed I will return unto thee, according to the time of life, and Sarah shall have a son. 15 Then Sarah denied, saying, I laughed not; for she was afraid. And He said, Nay; but thou didts laugh" (Genesis 18:9-15).

How did this man know that Sarah laughed; they wondered?

Then, Abraham remembered what the Creator had said to him earlier in the previous visit. Now, he was hearing almost the same thing. Sarah was going to have a son. Abraham began to wonder who these men were? And to whom was he speaking?

The Journeys of God the Creator

Realizing that they were visited not by mere men, Abraham began to address one of the men by the name "יהוה" (LORD) and "אלהים" (God). In fact, if you were to read the account from Genesis eighteen and onwards, you will notice that one of the men acknowledged that He was the LORD (יהוה).

Nonetheless, as God the Creator promised, "2 Sarah conceived, and bare Abraham a son in his old age, at the set time of which God had spoken to him. 3 And Abraham called the name of his son that was born unto him, whom Sarah bare to him, Isaac. 4 And Abraham circumcised his son Isaac being eight days old, as God had commanded him" (Genesis 21:2-4).

As Isaac grew, Hagar the bondwoman observed that Isaac was going to be the heir of Abraham's house. This was a total contradiction to the original plan. Abraham and Sarah told Hagar that Ishmael was going to be the heir. But now, they changed their plan and told her that Isaac was going to be the heir. This hurt Hagar very much to a point where she began to resent both Abraham and Sarah. As time went on, she also began to resent Isaac. Her resentment of Isaac was also revealed in her son, and in turn Ishmael began not to like Isaac. Hagar's attitude and her son's attitude began to create problems for Sarah and Abraham. There was dissension in Abraham's house.

Hagar turned maliciously upon Sarah and upon Abraham because they rejected her son Ishmael as the heir. According to the custom, the firstborn was to be the heir, and in this case Ishmael should be the heir; she argued. Although she was correct in her argument, she was not correct in the choice God the Creator made. The Creator chose Isaac and that was final. Ishmael was not going to be the heir of his father's estate and the promise of the Covenant. And to make matters worse, she also allowed her son Ishmael to look upon Isaac indifferently. Friction between Sarah and Hagar was getting out of hand. So, Sarah told Abraham to let Hagar and her son Ishmael go and live somewhere else; but Abraham could not bring himself to expel them from his home. He loved Ishmael very much.

Finally, God the Creator stepped into the picture and told

The Journeys of God the Creator

Abraham to send Ishmael and his mother away, and let them go to live somewhere else. "12 And God said unto Abraham, Let it not be grievous in thy sight because of the lad, and because of thy bondwoman; in all that Sarah hath said unto thee, hearken unto her voice; for in Isaac shall thy seed be called" (Genesis 21:12). The Creator reminded Abraham that Isaac was the heir; it was with him, and with his seed (the coming of the Messiah) that the Covenant was going to be established.

The Creator said,

"12 for in Isaac shall thy [your] seed be called." Genesis 21:12

Abraham acted according to the Creator's advice and sent Ishmael and his mother away. Hagar grieved, but the angels of the Creator comforted Hagar by telling her that the lad will prosper. She should not worry about him. Hagar and her son left Gerar and went to live in Shur near the Egyptian border of the wilderness of Sin. Finally, Hagar brought a woman out of Egypt and gave her to Ishmael for a wife. Later on, Ishmael grew in wealth and into a great nation.

Although Abraham's grief was colossal because he was asked to let his son Ishmael go away and live somewhere else, it was nothing compared to what was to follow. At one point, when Isaac was about twenty years old, Abraham was asked by God the Creator to take Isaac and sacrifice him on the altar. This request was devastating and exceedingly sorrowful to Abraham. He questioned within himself as to why God would ask him to sacrifice Isaac? He was not serving a pagan god? If Isaac was sacrificed, how was the Covenant going to be established in Isaac? Why would He ask me to sacrifice my only son, Abraham wondered? On and on, went the questions in his mind.

Nonetheless, Abraham complied with the Creator's request. He took the lad without telling Sarah, few of his servants, fire, put rations on a donkey, and went early in the morning on his way to Mount Moriah. It took three agonizing days to reach Mount Moriah from Beersheba where Abraham lived at that time. Mount Moriah

The Journeys of God the Creator

is the mountain range where Jerusalem sits on. It is the sight where Abraham offered Isaac, where King David made an offering to stop the plague, and where Solomon built the Sanctuary for the LORD God of Israel.

Regarding the event of Abraham and Isaac, we are told that Abraham did not speak very much during his three days journey to Mount Moriah. But when he arrived at the designated place, he revealed everything to Isaac and the reason they had come this far. Isaac agreed to be sacrificed. Abraham laid the wood in order on the altar, they said their goodbyes, bound Isaac—his son—and laid him on the altar upon the wood. Then Abraham stretched forth his hand and took the knife to slay his son. But, "11 the angel of the LORD called unto him out of heaven, and said, Abraham, Abraham: and he said, Here am I. 12 And he said, Lay not thine hand upon the lad, neither do thou any thing unto him: for now I know that thou [you] fearest God, seeing thou hast not withheld thy son, thine only son from Me. 13 And Abraham lifted up his eyes, and looked, and behold behind him a ram caught in a thicket by his horns: and Abraham went and took the ram, and offered him up for a burnt offering in the stead of his son. 14 And Abraham called the name of that place Jehovahjireth: as it is said to this day, In the mount of the LORD it shall be seen [Christ on the cross]. 15 And the angel of the LORD called unto Abraham out of heaven the second time, 16 And said, By Myself have I sworn, saith the LORD, for because thou hast done this thing, and hast not withheld thy son, thy only son: 17 That in blessing I will bless thee, and in multiplying I will multiply thy seed as the stars of the heaven, and as the sand which is upon the sea shore; and thy seed shall possess the gate of his enemies; 18 And in thy seed shall all the nations of the earth be blessed; because thou hast obeyed My voice" (Genesis 22:11-18).

About seventeen years later, when Sarah was one hundred and twenty-seven years old, she died in a place called "Kiriath-arba" (Hebron).

After Isaac's mother died, Isaac was very sad. Noticing Isaac's ordeal, three years later, Abraham sent his faithful servant Eliezer, who was from Damascus, to his brother's house in Haran, which is

The Journeys of God the Creator

north west of Iraq, to bring back Isaac a wife. (Eliezer's round-trip from Beersheba to Haran and back was approximately eleven hundred miles.)

Before Eliezer approached Nahor's house, he stopped the caravan and asked God the Creator for a sign, in order to know, which girl he should take for Isaac to be his wife. Eliezer's petition to the Creator, the LORD God of heaven, was the first girl to come to the well to fetch water, and voluntarily give the camels and him water to drink, was the sign that she should be the wife for Isaac.

Eliezer said, "42 O LORD God of my master Abraham, if now Thou [You] do prosper my way which I go: 43 Behold, I stand by the well of water; and it shall come to pass, that when the virgin cometh forth to draw water, and I say to her, Give me, I pray thee, a little water of thy pitcher to drink; 44 And she say to me, Both drink thou, and I will also draw for thy camels: let the same be the woman whom the LORD hath appointed out for my master's son" (Genesis 24:42-44).

After Eliezer finished praying, Rebekah came to fetch the water out of the well. And there, Eliezer confronted Rebekah and asked her to give him a little bit of water to drink. And she responded by saying to him, I will also draw water for your camels. And that was enough for Eliezer's ears. He asked her, "Whose daughter are you?" and she said, "the daughter of Bethuel, Nahor's son." Then, Eliezer asked if she would take him to her parents.

She did.

Eliezer explained to Rebekah's parents what had happened, and why he had come all the way to their place. They listened intently; and then, "50 Laban and Bethuel answered and said, The thing proceedeth from the LORD: we cannot speak unto thee bad or good. 51 Behold, Rebekah is before thee, take her, and go, and let her be thy master's son's wife, as the LORD hath spoken" (Genesis 24:50, 51).

Eliezer took Rebekah and her maids and left their home. He brought Rebekah to Lahairoi, the daughter of Bethuel Nahor's son, to be a wife for Isaac. Isaac was forty years old when he took Rebekah for a wife. Isaac and Rebekah lived in Lahairoi, which is

The Journeys of God the Creator

south of Beersheba in the Negeb. Isaac's father, continued to live in Beersheba during his twilight years.

Here is the account: "61 And Rebekah arose, and her damsels, and they rode upon the camels, and followed the man [Eliezer]: and the servant took Rebekah, and went his way. 62 And Isaac came from the way of the well Lahairoi; for he dwelt in the south country. 63 And Isaac went out to meditate in the field at the eventide: and he lifted up his eyes, and saw, and, behold, the camels were coming. 64 And Rebekah lifted up her eyes, and when she saw Isaac, she lighted off the camel. 65 For she had said unto the servant, What man is this that walketh in the field to meet us?" She was overwhelmed with what she saw! "And the servant had said, It is my master: therefore she took a vail, and covered herself. 66 And the servant told Isaac all things that he had done. 67 And Isaac brought her into his mother Sarah's tent, and took Rebekah, and she became his wife; and he loved her: and Isaac was comforted after his mother's death" (Genesis 24:61-67).

After this event, Abraham remarried and had many children. He died at the age of one hundred and seventy-five; "9 And his sons Isaac and Ishmael buried him in the cave of Machpelah, in the field of Ephron" (Genesis 25:9).

"11 And it came to pass after the death of Abraham, that God blessed his son Isaac; and Isaac dwelt by the well Lahairoi" (Genesis 25:11). The Covenant was re-established with Abraham's son Isaac.

In passing, I want to say that the well at Lahairoi was named after Hagar, Abraham's bondwoman.

Moreover, Isaac and Rebekah could not have any children. Twenty years later, Rebekah asked Isaac to pray to the "LORD God" of his fathers, and ask Him to bless her, so that she could have children. Isaac prayed to God the Creator, and asked Him to bless Rebekah, so that she could have children. Eventually, Rebekah had twins. The first-born was named Esau and the second-born was named Jacob.

As the boys grew, Esau's passion was to hunt and roam around the countryside. He preferred to be carefree from the responsibilities of his father's household, while Jacob became more like a

The Journeys of God the Creator

homebody. He preferred to stay around his mother.

One day Esau went hunting. He came home empty handed and very hungry. He said to Jacob, "30 Feed me, I pray thee, with that same red pottage; for I am faint: therefore was his name called Edom. 31 And Jacob said, Sell me this day thy birthright. 32 And Esau said, Behold, I am at the point to die: and what profit shall this birthright do to me? 33 And Jacob said, Swear to me this day; and he swear unto him: and he sold his birthright unto Jacob, 34 Then Jacob gave Esau bread and pottage of lentils; and he did eat and drink, and rose up, and went his way: thus Esau despised his birthright" (Genesis 25:30-34).

Esau not only despised his birthright but he also despised his brother Jacob for what he did to him then, and what he did to him later on.

But, before Isaac died, he wanted to pass on the inheritance to Esau. Isaac said to Esau, "Go fetch me some meat and prepare a meal that we may eat and celebrate your inheritance." Esau took his bow and went out to hunt. And when Rebekah heard what Isaac said to Esau, she went to Jacob and said to him, prepare a meal for your father, and impersonate Esau, so that you can receive the inheritance instead of your brother. But Jacob questioned his mother's plan because Esau was a hairy person, and Jacob had hardly any hair. So they went and got few goatskins, and Rebekah tied the skins of the goats upon Jacob's arms and neck, so that when his father Isaac felt Jacob, he would think he was Esau. Jacob and Rebekah prepared themselves for the deception, and when they approached Isaac with the food, which Rebekah prepared, they were able to deceive him because his eyesight was very poor. Isaac's eyesight was so poor that he could not see clearly who was in front of him. Jacob and his mother took advantage of his poor eyesight and tricked him, even though Isaac questioned Jacob's voice. They made him think that it was Esau he was blessing. After they ate, thinking that he was blessing Esau, Isaac blessed Jacob instead. Then, Jacob left the presence of his father's tent.

Later on, Esau came with the food to serve his father, with the hope of receiving his inheritance. To Esau's surprise, Isaac said

The Journeys of God the Creator

to him, I already blessed you? Esau explained to his father that he did not bless him. But, his father insisted!

In his fury, Esau went about asking the servants if they knew who impersonated him and received his inheritance? Finally, he found out that his father blessed Jacob and gave him the inheritance.

Esau was furious to a point where he wanted to kill Jacob.

Jacob was about seventy-seven years old when he fled from home and decided to go to Laban's house, which was in Haran. Laban was the son of Bethuel. Laban was Rebekah's brother.

On the way to Mesopotamia, Jacob stopped to rest one night at a place called "Bethel." There during the night, God the Creator appeared unto him in a dream and said to Jacob, "13 I am the LORD God of Abraham thy father, and the God of Isaac: the land whereon thou liest, to thee will I give it, and to thy seed; 14 And thy seed shall be as the dust of the earth, and thou shalt spread abroad to the west, and to the east, and to the north, and to the south: and in thee and in thy seed shall all the families of the earth be blessed. 15 And, behold, I am with thee, and will keep thee in all places whither thou goest, and will bring thee again into this land; for I will not leave thee, until I have done that which I have spoken to thee of" (Genesis 28:13-15).

Jacob was astonished at the vision because he was running away from his brother for the wrong he did to him. He wondered, how was it that God the Creator was speaking to him in this manner after the wrong he had done? Nonetheless, when he got up in the morning from his sleep, Jacob took the stone, which he used for a pillow, and poured oil over it, and he called the place "Bethel."

When Jacob reached the land of his relatives, in Haran, he noticed a number of sheepherders near a well. Jacob said to them, "5 Know ye Laban the son of Nahor? And they said, We know him. 6 And he said unto them, Is he well? And they said, He is well: and, behold Rachel his daughter cometh with the sheep." "9 And while he yet spake with them, Rachel came with her father's sheep: for she kept them" (Genesis 29:5, 6, 9).

Jacob introduced himself to Rachel, rolled the stone away from the well, and gave the herd water to drink. Then Jacob kissed

The Journeys of God the Creator

Rachel and told her who he was and wept before her. When Rachel heard who he was, she immediately ran home and told her father the news. And when her father heard the news that his sister's son was there, he ran to meet him, embraced him, and took him to his home.

Jacob stayed with Laban for a month; and while he stayed there, he helped Laban with the chores around the house. Finally, Laban said to Jacob, you have been helping me all this time and I have not paid you any wages; so go ahead; tell me what you want in return?

Jacob thought of Rachel. Since he was in love with her, he thought it was appropriate to ask for her to be his wife. But, he did not have a dowry to give to Laban. So Jacob said to Laban, "18 I will serve thee seven years for Rachel thy younger daughter. 19 And Laban said, It is better that I give her to thee, than that I should give her to another man: abide with me. 20 And Jacob served seven years for Rachel; and they seemed unto him but a few days, for the love he had to her." "22 And Laban gathered together all the men of the place, and made a feast" (Genesis 29:18-20, 22).

While Jacob served Laban for seven years, Laban observed that his wealth increased! Laban thought that he had a good thing going in Jacob. Therefore Laban did not want Jacob to leave him; consequently, he tricked Jacob by giving him Leah the older daughter for his wife. Jacob said to Laban, what have you done to me? Did we not agree that Rachel was going to be my wife? Laban said to him that we do not do things like that in this country; we give our oldest to marriage first, then, the youngest.

So, Jacob and Laban struck another deal. Because Jacob's love for Rachel was so great he was willing to serve Laban for another seven years. And he did. Finally Rachel became his wife upon the agreement.

While Jacob and his wives were staying with Laban, there Jacob's wives and maidservants conceived eleven boys whose names are as follows: Reuben, Simeon, Levi, Judah, Issachar, Zebulon, Gad, Asher, Joseph, Dan, Naphtali, and one girl named Dinah. And God the Creator continued to bless Jacob not only with children, but he also blessed him with livestock and other wealth.

Laban observed how God was blessing Jacob. And in turn, he

The Journeys of God the Creator

also observed because of Jacob, he to was also blessed. Therefore, Laban did not want Jacob to leave him or separate himself from him.

One day, Jacob called Leah and Rachel, and told them that their father was using him for his own means. They all agreed that the situation was not good. Jacob said to them: "6 ye know that with all my power I have served your father. 7 And your father hath deceived me, and changed my wages ten times; but God suffered him not to hurt me." Furthermore, God had said to me, "13 I am the God of Bethel, where thou anointedst the pillar, and where thou vowedst a vow unto Me: now rise, get thee out from this land, and return unto the land of thy kindred."

And then, the women responded to Jacob's remarks by saying: "15 Are we not counted of him [their father] strangers? for he hath sold us, and hath quite devoured also our money...16 now then, whatsoever God hath said unto thee, do. 17 Then Jacob rose up, and set his sons and his wives upon camels; 18 And he carried away all his cattle, and all his goods which he had gotten...in Padanaram, for to go to Isaac his father in the land of Canaan" (Genesis 31:6, 7, 13, 15-18).

Three days later, Laban found out, which way Jacob fled from him. Laban was furious. Jacob had left Laban's livestock unattended and wandering in the fields. Laban went back home to Haran, and made provisions for his livestock, which Jacob had abandoned. He delegated the work to others, looked around his house to see if anything was missing; and after he made sure that his household was going to be looked after, he prepared his servants for battle. After that, Laban and his band of warriors took off to find Jacob to punish him.

After seven days of tracking, Laban found Jacob. But God the Creator intervened in a night vision and said to Laban that he was not to do him harm. And when Laban overtook Jacob's band, he confronted Jacob, and said to him, "26 What hast [have] thou [you] done, that thou hast stolen away unawares to me, and carried away my daughters, as captives taken with the sword?" And then, Jacob answered Laban and said to him, "31 Because I was afraid: for I said,

The Journeys of God the Creator

Peradventure thou wouldest take by force thy daughters from me" (Genesis 31:26, 31).

But now, remembering what God had said to Laban in the night vision, he gives the excuse that he really came to take his gods back, which Rachel had stolen and say good-by to them. So, Laban searched for his molten gods everywhere he could think of, but he did not find them because Rachel had hidden the images in the "camels furniture and sat upon them." Out of courtesy, her father would not have her dismount, and therefore they did not search under her to see where she had hid her father's idols.

After few harsh words of exchange, between Laban and Jacob, Laban said, "44 let us make an covenant" that there be no more bickering between us. Jacob agreed, and they built a heap of stones as a witness of their covenant." "55 And early in the morning Laban rose up, and kissed his sons and his daughters, and blessed them: and Laban departed, and returned unto his place" (Gen. 31:44, 55).

After twenty years of service to Laban, at the age of ninety-seven, Jacob was finally going back home to his father. But there was one more massive obstacle for Jacob to overcome; he was wondering how was he going to overcome Esau's death threat?

Although God the Creator did tell Jacob that he will keep, protect, and bless him, Jacob was still terrified of his brother. In order to calm Jacob's fears, the Creator sent two bands of angels to join Jacob's caravan. As Jacob and his group were traveling, all of the sudden, Jacob noticed that his group had enlarged. He saw one band of holy angels at the front of his caravan, and the other band of holy angels he saw at the back of his caravan. And when Jacob saw them, he was astonished. He had seen angels before in a vision, but now, he is seeing them literally. He named the place "Mahanaim," meaning double the number or double the host.

As the band of livestock, men, women, and children moved westward to the land of Canaan, Jacob began to be more fully preoccupied with his sinful past acts that he had committed to his father and to his brother Esau. Indifferent to the fact that the two heavenly bands of angels were traveling with Jacob, for his protection, Jacob began to sink into desperation. He was wondering,

The Journeys of God the Creator

if Esau, after all of these years, was going to forgive him?

Finally, night fell and Esau had not arrived. During that night, Jacob woke his two wives, their maids, his eleven sons, daughter, and made them go over the Jabbok River. This river today is coined as the "Blue River." It connects to the River Jordan, and it is located between Jericho and Shechem, approximately 27 miles north of the Dead Sea. Jacob told them to go on the other side of the river, so that he would be alone with God in prayer.

There at Jabbok that night, Jacob in desperation began to pray. His life and the life of his family were at risk. The weight of his sins, which he had committed against his father and against his twin brother Esau were tormenting and pressing heavily upon his heart. In deep conviction, Jacob reached out to God the Creator and asked Him to cleanse him from all of his sins and deliver him from his brother's hands. He "wept" with deep remorse for his sins and looked for the Creator to forgive him. Jacob repeatedly beseeched the LORD God of his fathers through out the night, but the LORD would not answer. Jacob felt that God abandoned him, and the horrifying thoughts began to surface very predominantly in Jacob's mind that there was no escape from the hand of Esau.

As Jacob was pleading in desperation to God, he heard a noise, and suddenly, he felt a mighty hand upon his shoulder. Fearful for his life he grabbed the intruder and began to struggle with Him. The more Jacob tried to overcome Him, the greater the resistance of the Antagonist. Jacob continued trying to overcome Him, but he was unable to overpower Him. The struggle persisted through the night; and just before the break of day, his opponent touched Jacob on his thigh and crippled him. Jacob suddenly realized that the Individual he was struggling with was not a mere man. "With that kind of power," Jacob thought, "this individual can easily paralyze me or dispose me. So, why has He not destroyed me?" Now, Jacob began to cling unto the Stranger, and kept asking Him to reveal who He was. The powerful and immovable Adversary would not answer him. But finally, the Stranger broke His silence and said to Jacob: "[26] Let Me go, for the day breaketh." But Jacob replied in the following profound words,

The Journeys of God the Creator

"I will not let Thee [You] go, except Thou [You] bless me."

Jacob wanted forgiveness for and a cleansing from all of his sins. And then, Jacob was asked, "27 What is thy [your] name?" Jacob answered Him and said, "Jacob." And then, Jacob's opponent said to him,

"Thy [your] name shall be called no more Jacob, but Israel:"

Jacob's name was changed to "Israel" because "28 for as prince hast thou power with God and with men, and hast prevailed." "30 And Jacob called the name of the place Peniel: for I have seen God face to face, and my life is preserved. 31 And as he passed over Peniel the sun rose upon him, and he halted upon his thigh" (Genesis 32:26-28, 30, 31).

God the Creator left Jacob before the break of daylight and left His blessing upon him. As the break of the morning sun came, Jacob stood up in pain, firmly, on his deformed leg, and as he stood up in agony and pain, the rising sun struck his leg, and he observed the hollow of his thigh. It reminded him that God had not forsaken him. He thanked the LORD for sparing his life and for giving him strength to go and face his brother. He carefully crossed over the river Jabbok and joined his caravan. He organized his group and started his journey.

Jacob began to reminisce over the visitation of God the Creator, His blessings upon him, the change of his name to "Israel," and the overall ordeal he went throughout the night. As he was contemplating on the events of the night, at one point he lifted up his eyes, and behold, he saw Esau with four hundred warriors. Quickly, Israel (Jacob) rearranged his caravan by placing his servants at the front of the caravan with their children, as one group, and then, he placed Leah and her children after as another group, and he placed Rachel and Joseph at the very back of the caravan. And then, he went in front of everybody to lead the way and waited in expectation to meet, what he thought, his angry brother Esau in a final confrontation.

The Journeys of God the Creator

Isn't it strange? In the night, Jacob (Israel) personally encountered God the Creator and lived. His name was changed to Israel to show that he is an over-comer. He received his blessings personally from God the Creator, and the assurance that He was with him; and yet, Israel was still concerned about his safety and the safety of his family and servants. The personal visit by God the Creator should have been enough to disperse Israel's fears, but it did not.

Faith is truly tested when one's life is at stake. Isn't it?

You know, ever since the destruction of the Twin Towers, in NY, which took place on September 11, 2001, we have entered into the final prophetic events. The seven last prophecies are upon us. They will be fulfilled quickly for the "elects sake," before Jesus Christ's second coming takes place. One of these prophecies reveals the events of how the "One World Order" was going to tell the world, "Do as I say or else?" Or as President George Bush has said, to the nations of the world, "Are you with us or against us?" This policy of the One World Order will try to unite the countries of the world, and the churches of the world under one umbrella; and, if you will not conform to the political and to the religious policies, you will not be able to buy or sell your goods in their markets. In fact, they will pass a law saying that if a person will not conform to their laws that person will even be put to death. In those coming events, which already have started, I wonder how many professed Christians will throw in their towel and worship the dictates of man instead of God the Creator?

As Jacob's faith was tested, soon, our faith in God the Creator will truly be tested, dear reader. You see, the days are fast approaching upon us when you will have to make a choice; will you stand firm for God the Creator and His doctrine, and be persecuted, or will you join the One World Order and their political and pagan religious agenda, and become the persecutor? During those events, I wonder in whose camp you are going to be—in Christ's or Satan's?

I hope and pray, you will abstain from your affiliation with the One World secular church and their political oppressive agenda and be found in the LORD'S camp where you will be sheltered from the fearful and destructive last plagues. I those days, dear reader, when the fires of war will rage in the middle east, between the kings of the east and the kings of the west, at one point, the religious and political leaders will proclaim peace, peace, but do you know what, we are told, then, "sudden destruction" will come upon the ungodly. Those last plagues will be poured upon the ungodly without any mercy. My prayer for you is that you will choose life and be saved in the Creator's Kingdom where you will find eternal happiness and contentment.

But, in the interim, how will you respond to the authorities when they come knocking on your door?

Only time will tell, won't it?

If you want more detailed information on the above prophetic events, read my book called: "The Sign in Matthew 24" By: *Philip Mitanidis,* BEEHIVE PUBLISHING HOUSE INC.

However, going back to our story, as Esau approached Israel's caravan, Esau dismounted and ran to meet Israel. Israel's heart started to race. His emotions heightened as he painfully and slowly dismounted and started walking towards Esau in his crippled form. When Esau saw him, he had pity upon him, and "4 embraced him, and fell upon his neck, and kissed him: and they wept." And when Esau raised his eyes and looked at all of the men, women, and children, he said to Israel, "5 Who are those with thee?" Israel said, they are "The children which God hath graciously given thy servant" (Genesis 33:4, 5).

Then they all came, one group after the other and bowed down before Esau. And when they had finished with the introductions, Esau said to Israel, "8 What meanest thou by all this drove which I met?" And Israel said to him, "These are to find grace in the sight of my lord. 9 And Esau said, I have enough, my brother; keep that thou hast unto thyself" (Gen. 33:8, 9).

Nonetheless, Israel wanted Esau to have the gifts. Israel looked up to his brother as his superior; he did not undermine him. In fact, Israel humbled himself before Esau and addressed him with respect by referring to himself as Esau's "servant" and his "lord." Israel did not give cause for any dissention. He did not come to Esau posing as the head of the household. Neither did he seek anything from Esau. In acknowledgement to Israel's humble attitude and servitude, Esau accepted the gifts from his brother.

God had intervened on behalf of Israel. Esau's heart was softened, and Esau did him no harm.

After a cordial stay, Esau recommended that Israel ride with him to Canaan, but Israel humbly refused because of the children and the flock. Esau looked at Israel's caravan again and noticed that he needed help to veer off the many bandits that could easily overthrow Israel's helpless band. So Esau offered some of his warriors to stay with him until they reach Esau's home in Seir. Israel thanked his brother and said to him, "Since we are unable to keep up with you, it will be best if you went back home to Seir with your band, and we will come as soon as possible and visit." Esau agreed and went onward before Israel.

Israel settled for a while near the city of Shechem, before he went onward to meet with his brother in Seir. (Please note: At that time, there was a Mount Seir northwest of Jerusalem, and one in Edom.)

It should be noted that when Israel fled from Esau to Mesopotamia, against his father's aspirations, Esau married his father's niece, and few other women. Esau married women from the family of Ishmael and of the Hittites, or Horites if you like, and lived temporarily in Canaan. Later Esau moved to Mount Seir to live. Eventually, his descendents overthrew the Horites and occupied their land. It should also be noted that Esau was known by the name of Edom. His household and those who were affiliated with him were known as Edomites, or the tribe of Edom.

After a cordial stay, Esau returned to his home in Seir.

It was about two hundred and eighty-eight years later when Moses was confronted with Esau's descendents. The Edomites would not let Moses and the children of Israel pass through their land.

Meanwhile, while Israel's household stayed in Shechem, there one day, Shechem the son of Hamor raped Dinah; in revenge, the brother's of Dinah plotted and killed all of the males of the city of

The Journeys of God the Creator

Shechem. In fear of retaliation, from the surrounding tribes, Israel moved from the vicinity, as God the Creator advised him, to a place, which he called "Bethel." "AND God said unto Jacob, Arise, go up to Bethel" (Genesis 35:1).

And God the Creator appeared to Israel in "Bethel" (Luz) and said unto him, "12 the land which I gave Abraham and Isaac, to thee I will give it, and to thy seed after thee will I give the land. 13 And God went up from him in the place where He talked with him. 14 And Jacob set up a pillar in the place where He talked with him, even a pillar of stone: and he poured a drink offering thereon, and he poured oil thereon. 15 And Jacob called the name of the place where God spake with him, Bethel" (Genesis 35:12-15). Bethel is about ten miles north of Jerusalem, and about thirteen miles west of Jericho. Bethel can be found in the beginning of the mountain range of Ephraim, seated between the city of Ramah and Shiloh.

Before Israel went south to Bethel, he told his wives, his children, and his servants to bring to him all of their pagan gods, which they worshiped. They did so, and Israel took them and buried them under an oak tree, which was not far from Shechem.

The Journeys of God the Creator

After that, he told them to wash and put on clean clothes before they went to Bethel. When they arrived at Bethel, Israel built an altar and offered thank offerings to the Creator for sparing his life and for the blessing He had bestowed upon him.

Israel did not stay in Bethel very long; he decided to move again. He continued his journey southward; and when he reached Ephrath (Bethlehem), there Rachel went into complicated labor and gave birth to a son. She named him "Benoni," but Israel named him "Benjamin." Rachel died while she was giving birth to Benjamin. She was buried there.

Israel continued southward and stayed near Edar for a time. Then he went to Mamre where his father Isaac lived. "27 And Jacob came unto Isaac his father unto Mamre, unto the city of Arbah, which is Hebron, where Abraham and Isaac sojourned" (Genesis 35:27).

While Jacob lived at Mamre, Joseph, the second youngest son of Israel, had a dream regarding himself and his brothers. After conveying the dream to his brothers, his brothers hated him more than before. Before, they hated him for his righteous living; now, they hated him for the idea that they had to serve him. They said, "We cannot have him reign over us." So, they thought of ways to dispose of him and even kill him in order to avoid his sovereignty from taking place.

Needless to say, the opportunity did present itself on one occasion when Israel sent Joseph to find his brothers because he was worried about his sons. Israel was wondering why his sons had not returned with the flock from Shechem, and even failed to send a message explaining their delay. To find out what happened, Israel sent Joseph, who was seventeen years old at that point, to Shechem. He was to go there, find out what was going on, and then, return back home and give the report to his father.

When Joseph arrived, his brothers noticed from a distance that he was coming. They knew it was Joseph from the coat of many colors, which his father had made for him. As he was arriving, they began to think of the opportunity that was presented to them to get rid of him.

The Creator of Genesis 1:1-Who is He?   By: *Philip Mitanidis*
The Journeys of God the Creator

They bound him and threw him in a deep pit. But, Judah said unto them, let us sell him and make some money. They sat down to eat, and as they were eating an Ishmaelite band was going by. They stopped the caravan and sold Joseph to them for "twenty pieces of silver."

When the Ishmaelite caravan arrived in Egypt, the Ishmaelites sold their commodities at the market place, and they also sold Joseph, for profit, to "1 Potiphar, an officer of Pharaoh, captain of the guard" (Genesis 39:1).

Potiphar, the Egyptian, took Joseph and put him to work in his household; and when Potiphar observed that Joseph prospered in everything that he did, he made Joseph an overseer of his house.

When Potiphar's wife saw Joseph, she became very friendly towards him. One day when Joseph came in to her house she became overbearing to a point where she wanted him to have sex with her. Joseph would not act in accordance with her wishes. She became furious with him. How dare he, a slave, have the nerve to turn her down? Joseph said to Potiphar's wife, "The only thing that your husband kept from me is you because you are his wife." But Potiphar's wife did not want to hear Joseph's reasoning. She wanted him to be her lover. Joseph turned around and said to her,

> "how then can I do this great wickedness, and sin against God?" (Genesis 39:9)

In spite of what Joseph said to her, she insisted that he act in accordance with her demand and grant her the pleasure she was seeking; after all, he was her servant.

Joseph stood upon his moral principles. He did not grant her the desire she wanted. She became furious with him. Seeing that he could not reason with her, Joseph started to leave her presence, but in her fury, she grabbed Joseph's mantle and tore it. Unfortunately, Joseph did not try to take the torn garment from her. He quickly departed from her presence.

When her husband, Potiphar, came home, she conjured up a story and said to her husband that the Hebrew slave, who he had bought from the Ishmaelites, was trying to seduce her. She said, I fought him off me, and he ran away.

Potiphar confronted Joseph about his wife's allegations. Joseph told him exactly what happened. Although Potiphar push the issue, Joseph told Potiphar that he was innocent. "The fact that I did not bother to collect my raiment, which she tore off me, should be sufficient proof to you that I did not try to seduce your wife, and neither did I seduce your wife," Joseph said to him.

Although Potiphar wanted to believe Joseph, he sided with his wife and in order to pacify her, he had him confined. Finally, Potiphar took Joseph and put him in prison where Pharaoh's prisoners were kept.

Meanwhile, there, in Pharaoh's prison, the prison keeper found trust in Joseph, so he gradually gave him chores in the prison house. Eventually, Joseph became his right hand man. Joseph more or less looked after lot of the affairs in the prison house.

When Joseph was twenty-nine years old, in the second year of his imprisonment, Joseph's grandfather Isaac died. The record says, "28 And the days of Isaac were an hundred and fourscore [180] years. 29 And Isaac gave up the ghost, and died, and was gathered unto his people, being old and full of days: and his sons Esau and Jacob buried him" (Genesis 35:28, 29). Esau and Israel were one hundred and twenty years old when their father died.

After Isaac's death, Esau and Israel went back to their homes. They did not unite to live together because the LORD had blessed both of them with great wealth. They felt that it would be better to live separately in order to avoid friction amongst their servants, wives, and livestock. So they went their separate ways in peace. Esau went back home to Mount Seir, and Israel went to Mamre.

While Joseph was still in prison, Pharaoh had a disturbing dream. He summoned his advisors, his astrologers, his seers, magicians, wise men, and others who were recommended to interpret Pharaoh's dream, but none could interpret his dream. Pharaoh was wroth with all of them. Pressure was building very intensely upon Pharaoh's servants to come up with a solution, but they continued to fail.

The Journeys of God the Creator

Then, the LORD intervened and brought the chief butler, through various circumstances, before Pharaoh. Standing before Pharaoh, the butler tried to rejuvenate Pharaoh's memory, to the time when he got mad at him, two years ago and put him in prison. The butler explained to Pharaoh that in the ward, which he was put in, there was a Hebrew slave who interpreted his dream and the chief baker's dream. And according to the interpretation, it was fulfilled. I was reinstated in three days to my position, and then, the butler added, "the chief baker was hung in three days as the Hebrew slave had stated."

Pharaoh was impressed with the butler's report and sent for Joseph right away. Joseph cleaned up, shaved, put on new clothes, and then, he came before Pharaoh. Finally, Joseph, after thirteen years of servitude, stood before Pharaoh. And Pharaoh immediately said to Joseph, "I had heard that you could interpret dreams?" Joseph said to Pharaoh that it was not in himself that he could interpret dreams, but God will give an answer to Pharaoh. Encouraged by Joseph's remarks, Pharaoh immediately began to tell the dream to Joseph.

Pharaoh said, "2 behold, there came up out of the river seven well favoured kine and fatfleshed; and they fed in a meadow. 3 And, behold, seven other kine came up after them out of the river, ill favoured and leanfleshed; and stood by the other kine upon the brink of the river. 4 And the ill favoured and leanfleshed kine did eat up the seven well favoured and fat kine. So Pharaoh awoke. 5 And he slept and dreamed the second time: and, behold, seven ears of corn came up upon one stalk, rank and good. 6 And, behold, seven thin ears and blasted with the east wind sprung up after them. 7 And the seven thin ears devoured the seven rank and full ears. And Pharaoh awoke, and, behold, it was a dream. 8 And it came to pass in the morning that his spirit was troubled; and he sent and called for all the magicians of Egypt, and all the wise men thereof: and Pharaoh told them his dream; but there was none that could interpret them unto Pharaoh" (Genesis 41:2-8)

After hearing Pharaoh's dreams, and how the wise men and magicians of Egypt could not tell the interpretation of his dreams,

The Journeys of God the Creator

Joseph made Pharaoh to understand that it was God the Creator who wanted Pharaoh to know what he was going to do in the future. Joseph said that the interpretation comes from God and not of himself.

Joseph said, "29 Behold, there come seven years of great plenty throughout all the land of Egypt: 30 And there shall arise after them seven years of famine; and all the plenty shall be forgotten in the land of Egypt; and the famine shall consume the land; 31 And the plenty shall not be known in the land by reason of that famine following; for it shall be very grievous. 32 And for that the dream was doubled unto Pharaoh twice; it is because the thing is established by God, and God will shortly bring it to pass. 33 Now therefore let Pharaoh look out a man discreet and wise, and set him over the land of Egypt" (Genesis 41:29-33).

When Pharaoh heard the interpretation, he was devastated; but very quickly he asked Joseph what he recommended for the coming crises. Joseph told Pharaoh that he had to appoint officials, now, who were able to go throughout the land of Egypt and store the grain, the corn, and other food that was able to keep, so that they will have enough food for the people when the famine comes for seven years.

Pharaoh's heart was impressed with Joseph's reply. In fact, even Pharaoh's servants were impressed. Pharaoh opened his mouth and said to his servants: "38 Can we find such a one as this is, a man in whom the Spirit of God is? 39 And Pharaoh said unto Joseph, Forasmuch as God hath shewed thee all this, there is none so discreet and wise as thou art: 40 Thou shalt be over my house, and according unto thy word shall all my people be ruled: only in the throne will I be greater than thou" (Genesis 41:38-40).

Pharaoh had set Joseph over all the land of Egypt. At the age of thirty, Joseph was made second in command next to Pharaoh. He gave him his ring and showered him with gifts. And when Pharaoh went somewhere with Joseph, Pharaoh had him ride in the second chariot. In addition to Joseph's position, Pharaoh changed Joseph's name to "Zaphnathpaaneah," and gave him a wife, whose name was "Asenath." She was from an influential family. She was the daughter of Potipherah, a priest of "On."

Shortly before the end of the seven years of plenty, Joseph's wife, "Asenath," bare him two sons. Joseph named the first son "Manasseh" (to forget), and the second son he called "Ephraim" (fruitful).

Nonetheless, when the famine came, it not only arrived upon Egypt, but it covered Libya, Arabia, Canaan, Syria, etc. People, animals, and birds were dying all over the land. There was pain, agony, murders, theft, and strife for a morsel of bread. Even the people in Egypt ran out of food and cried out to Pharaoh to provide them with food or else they to would perish, as many had in other countries. Pharaoh said to his people, "Provisions have been made for you, go to Zaphnathpaaneah (Joseph), and do what he says to you."

And the people of Egypt went before Joseph for their rations.

Israel's family in Mamre was also feeling the need for more food.

While Israel's sons were thinking about food, and what to do, Israel said to them, "I have heard that there was food in Egypt. Why not go down there and get some food before we end up dead?" They agreed that they should go, and ten of Israel's sons went to Egypt. Benjamin, the youngest, stayed home upon his father's request. Israel was afraid something might happen to him. He did not want to lose another son.

When the ten brothers arrived in Egypt, they inquired from the people where they could go and buy some rations? The people gave them direction. They followed the directions, which were given to them, and they arrived to one of the storehouses. There they saw all kinds of people waiting in line to get served. Finally, their turn came to be served. They bowed down before Zaphnathpaaneah (Joseph) and requested to buy food. Zaphnathpaaneah looked at them, and quickly recognized that they were his stepbrothers. Recognizing who they were and observed that they did not recognize him, he spoke to them through an interpreter. And when he spoke to them, he spoke to them rough for a while, then, he asked them through his interpreter, where did they come from? They said that they came

The Journeys of God the Creator

from the land of Canaan. As they were speaking to him, Joseph remembered the dream, how they were going to bow down to him.

Since Joseph's stepbrothers did not recognize him, he began to speak to them with threats. He was accusing them of being spies who came to Egypt to see how they could overtake the stored food. They denied that they were spies and said to Joseph, "11 we are all one man's sons; we are true men, thy servants are no spies" (Genesis 42:11). Then, Joseph's stepbrothers divulged some more information to Joseph, which he welcomed wholeheartedly. They told him that they are ten out of twelve brothers, of whom the youngest is with his father, and one is dead.

When Joseph heard that his father and his brother were still alive, he was overwhelmed with emotion. But, he quickly suppressed his emotions, and listened what they had to say.

While Joseph's stepbrothers were speaking, Joseph devised a plan, which he hoped it would work. He said to his stepbrothers, now I know for sure that you are spies. If you are not spies, one of you will have to go home, get the youngest brother, and bring him here to me, so that you will prove to me that you are not spies. They tried to reason with Joseph, but Joseph would not hear them; instead he locked them up in prison for three days.

Although Joseph could understand his stepbrother's language, after three days Joseph took his interpreter and came to the prison house. He spoke to them again through his interpreter. The interpreter said to them, "19 If ye be true men, let one of your brethren be bound in the house of your prison: go ye, carry corn for the famine of your houses: 20 But bring your youngest brother unto me; so shall your words be verified, and ye shall not die. And they did so" (Genesis 42:19, 20).

His stepbrothers started immediately to decide who should remain in custody until they return with Benjamin, Joseph's brother. While they were talking amongst themselves, Joseph became emotional, so he left them. He wept and when he returned, he took from them Simeon and tied him up before their eyes. "25 Then Joseph commanded to fill their sacks with corn, and to restore every man's money into his sack, And to give them provision for the way:

The Journeys of God the Creator

and thus did he unto them. 26 And they laded their asses with the corn, and departed thence" (Genesis 42:25, 26).

When they arrived home in Canaan, as they were emptying the sacks of corn in the storage place, they told their father what had happened in Egypt and on the way home. They also told their father that everyone's money was found in the sacks of corn. Not knowing why their money was in their sacks, they all feared for their lives. But that was not the end of it, the governor of Egypt, Zaphnathpaaneah, wanted to see Benjamin. And what about Simeon? The governor kept him in his custody in Egypt. If Benjamin was not brought before Zaphnathpaaneah, he was going to kill Simeon. Israel was devastated even further because he feared for the life of his household. He did not like the way he and his sons were manipulated.

On the other hand, if he wanted to save Simeon, he had to let Benjamin go to Egypt at the risk of losing him. Israel decided not to send Benjamin to Egypt at the risk of not seeing Simeon again.

Then, one day, a hard and cold reality set in. The famine was in its second year, and the food that they had secured from Egypt was almost gone. Israel told his sons that they had to go to Egypt and buy more food. But, there was a snag in that request. Judah reminded his father of what Pharaoh's administrator had said to them. The administrator told us that we could not buy food without seeing Benjamin first, and we cannot see him if we do not bring Benjamin to him to prove that we are not spies.

Israel did not want to send Benjamin to Egypt.

Then Judah said to his father, "Send the lad with me," and if anything goes wrong let the blame be upon me "for ever." Israel in his sorrow said, "14 If I be bereaved of my children, I am bereaved" (Genesis 43:14).

Israel's sons got ready and went down to Egypt.

When Joseph saw Benjamin his brother, he was moved with gratitude to see that he was still alive. He thought, perhaps, his stepbrothers disposed of him also. He left their presence and said to the soldiers, take these men away to my house. Fear fell upon the ten brothers because the authorities took them away. Joseph also said to his head housekeeper to prepare enough food because the Hebrews were going to dine with him.

Simeon was released from jail and was told to join his brothers.

When Joseph saw them, he could not help yearning for his brother Benjamin. He talked with them for a while through an interpreter; but he could not contain his emotions for his brother Benjamin, so he left the room and cried. After a while, he washed his face and came back into the room and mingled with them and with the rest of his guests. Then, they were all seated. The eleven brothers sat on one side of the room, in the order according to their birth, and away from the Egyptian guests because the Egyptians did not sit with Hebrew people, and the servants sat in another place. Joseph sat alone before all of them. They ate, they drank, and they were merry.

In the morning, Joseph told his servants to prepare the sacks of corn and place the money, which they bought the corn with, back in the sacks. And on top of that, Joseph also told the steward of his house to take his silver drinking cup and place it in the sack of their younger brother whose name was Benjamin and send them away.

After they had gone for a while from Joseph's presence, Joseph ordered his soldiers to go and intercept the Hebrews and say to them, "4 Wherefore have ye rewarded evil for good?" (Genesis 44:4). Seize them, and bring them back here again with all of their possessions.

And when they appeared before Joseph again, they bowed down before him and said, "Heaven forbid that we should do such a thing. We have brought the money, which we found in our sacks the first time we came here, why would we steal again?" Joseph said to them, "Somebody smuggled my silver-drinking cup from my house, and I aim to find it." In spite of their plea and fairness, Joseph ordered their sacks searched. And when they opened the sacks, behold, the money was found in the sacks, and the silver cup was found in one of Benjamin's sacks. How were they going to explain that?

Joseph said to them, "Don't you know what I can do to you for the crime you committed?"

The Journeys of God the Creator

Judah said to Joseph, "What can we say unto my lord? and how can we clear ourselves. We did not do this thing!" In fear for their lives Judah said, "But, if it pleases my lord we can all be your servants even the youngest."

Finally, Joseph said, "17 God forbid that I should do so: but the man in whose hand the cup is found, he shall be my servant; and as for you, get you up in peace unto your father" (Genesis 44:17). (Read the rest of the chapter and observe the repentant voice of his stepbrother.)

But Judah would not leave the presence of Joseph. He made a final appeal by saying, "34 how shall I go up to my father, and the lad [Benjamin] be not with me? lest peradventure I see the evil that shall come on my father" (Genesis 44:34).

Joseph listened to Judah's repentant voice; and noticed that their father was still alive. He listened to the plea to let Benjamin go back home, and if he did not Benjamin's father will surly die. In exchange for Benjamin, Judah was willing to stay and be his servant, if only he let Benjamin go. Listening to Judah's plea, Joseph became emotional to a point where he could not hold back his tears. He ordered all of his servants out of the room, and he was left alone with his brothers. The first thing he said to his brothers in Hebrew was, "I am Joseph your brother." They did not answer him. They were stunned by that remark! The second thing he wanted to confirm from them was the truth about his father; he wanted to know if he was really alive. So, he asked "Is my father alive?" Again, they did not answer him; they were deeply troubled by what he was saying. Sensing their dilemma, Joseph said unto them, "4 Come near to me, I pray you. And they came near. And he said, I am Joseph your brother, whom ye sold into Egypt. 5 Now therefore be not grieved, nor angry with yourselves, that ye sold me hither: for God did send me before you to preserve life."

"7 And God sent me before you to preserve you a posterity in the earth, and to save your lives by a great deliverance."

"9 Haste ye, and go up to my father, and say unto him, Thus saith thy son Joseph, God hath made me lord of all Egypt: come down unto me, tarry not: 10 And thou shalt dwell in the land of

The Journeys of God the Creator

Goshen, and thou shalt be near unto me, thou, and thy children, and thy children's children, and thy flocks, and thy herds, and all that thou hast: 11 And there will I nourish thee; for yet there are five years of famine; lest thou, and thy household, and all that thou hast, come to poverty" (Genesis 45:4, 5, 7, 9-11).

"Only Joseph knew that we sold him to the Ishmaelites. It must be Joseph our brother!" They agreed. They were pleased to hear that there was no retribution for what they had done to him, and that he wanted them and their father to come down to Egypt to live. They embraced Joseph with heightened and mixed emotions. And after they had a good cry, they talked to him.

The news of Joseph's brothers spread very quickly, and when Pharaoh heard that Joseph's brothers were with him, he called him and said unto him, "Tell your brothers to go to Canaan and bring your father here and all that they can carry. And whatever they lack, they are not to worry, I will provide for them when they come here. Give them wagons and provisions to take with them to Canaan." And Joseph did as Pharaoh commanded.

When Joseph's stepbrothers arrived before their father, in Mamre, they tried to explain how they got the wagons, their new clothes, the food, and animals. And when they said to him that his son Joseph was alive, and that he was the governor of Egypt, Israel's heart fainted because he did not believe them. Israel did not believe his sons just as Joseph's stepbrothers did not believe Joseph when he said to them "I am Joseph your brother."

Israel's sons sat him down, talked with him, and told him all the things that happened while they were in Egypt. Then Israel said to them that is enough, "28 I will go and see him before I die" (Genesis 45:28).

Israel commanded that they all get ready to go to Egypt. They took their families, their servants, their livestock, their belongings, and they all started their journey southward. After a thirty-three mile journey, they reached Beersheba. There, Israel and his caravan stopped and offered sacrifices unto God the Creator; and in the night, God spoke to Israel in a vision. God said to him, "3 I am God, the God of thy father: fear not to go down into Egypt; for I

The Journeys of God the Creator

will there make of thee a great nation: 4 I will go down with thee into Egypt; and I will also surly bring thee up again: and Joseph shall put his hand upon thine eyes" (Genesis 46:3, 4).

Hearing God's assurance of his safety, the return to Canaan, the outcome and blessings of his children, while they were in Egypt, Israel got up in the morning and journeyed to Egypt with his household without any fear. And when they reached Egypt, Israel was one hundred and thirty years old. There, Israel sent his son Judah before them to go and talk to Joseph and to make the arrangements where Joseph wanted them to go and meet with him.

When Judah returned, he came to his father and said to him, "We will go to a place called Goshen and settle there. Joseph will meet us there." The land of Goshen is located west of the Suez Canal; and about one third of the way southward towards the Red Sea, from the Mediterranean Sea.

Emotionally, Joseph got into his chariot and made his way to Goshen. There he jumped off his chariot and ran to meet his father. He embraced his father, kissed him on his neck, and cried for a long time. Finally, Israel said to his son Joseph, "Now that I have seen you, and you are alive, let me die in peace."

After they had settled, Joseph came again unto his father's camp in Goshen and said to him, and to his brothers, Pharaoh wants to meet you. Therefore, I am come to bring you before him. But before we go, I want you to tell Pharaoh that you and all of your family's occupation is shepherding the flocks. If you do this, then, the Egyptians will not associate themselves with you because they believe that every shepherd is despicable to them.

Israel agreed. This was good for them. It would allow the children of Israel to be distinct in their culture and in their religion. This would prevent, to some degree, the influence of the heathen practices of the Egyptians upon them.

Israel agreed and so did his children. Joseph took five of his brothers before Pharaoh; and sure enough, Pharaoh did ask them of their occupation, and they all answered according to the advice that was given to them by their brother Joseph. Thus, Pharaoh did not tell his servants to employee his brothers into the offices of

The Journeys of God the Creator

Pharaoh.

Again, Pharaoh wanted to meet with Joseph's father. Israel appeared before Pharaoh and carried himself well in his presence. Pharaoh was pleased to meet with him, and told him whatever he needed all he had to do is ask. Israel blessed Pharaoh, and thanked him for his hospitality before he departed from him.

As the famine continued, the Egyptian citizen's money began to dwindle; and when that was gone, the people said to Joseph, "We have no money to buy food." And Joseph said to them, "I will buy the cattle, the horses, and your camels for a price; hence you can buy food." They agreed. When their cattle, horses, and camels were all gone, they came to Joseph again, and said, "Give us food before we perish." And Joseph said to them, "Sell your land unto Pharaoh and I will give you money to buy food." They sold their land and bought food, but when all of their commodities were gone, they had nothing to offer Pharaoh except their labor. They said that they were willing to work for their food. Pharaoh agreed, and they were given food for their labors. They were grateful for saving their lives, to work in the fields of Pharaoh, and in Pharaoh's projects. (See Genesis 47:13-26.)

Pharaoh was well pleased with the increased wealth in his coffers, and Joseph's administrative work. Pharaoh had secured the land unto himself.

Before the famine struck, the people that were working the land were giving Pharaoh one fifth of the product. Now, those who were not working in his fields, they were employed in building monuments, clearing the land, trading with other countries, and in all manner of Pharaoh's business.

Israel's children on the other hand, flourished and grew in numbers. They were left alone mainly because of the Egyptian's attitude towards shepherds in general, and because of their gratitude to Joseph for the direction he was leading the affairs of Egypt during the emergency the famine brought their country in. Although the Hebrew's were loathed as shepherds, they were not bothered to a large degree, as long as Joseph stayed in Egypt, and saw them through their crisis.

The Journeys of God the Creator

The Egyptians did not want to rock the boat, as the expression goes, because they had a good thing going in Joseph. Pharaoh and the citizens were more concerned about the provision of food than anything else at this point of their lives. Pharaoh and the people were grateful for Joseph's capable foresight and administration of the kings business. It was saving Pharaoh's citizen's lives, and at the same time, it was making Pharaoh rich. Israel was happy, right from the time he moved to Goshen, which was in the second year of the famine. He had with him all of his sons, and their families. During that time, Israel, his children, and their children's children prospered and multiplied. Israel lived peaceably for seventeen years in the land of Goshen.

There, in Goshen, one day Israel called his sons before him and said, "Bring before me Joseph." They did. And when Joseph arrived beside his father's bed, Israel said to him, "I am going to die, but before I die, I want you to put your hand under my thigh and swear that you will not bury me in Egypt. I want to be buried with my fathers in the land of Canaan in the field of Machpelah." Joseph swore to his father that he was going to do as he requested. Israel said to Joseph again, "Swear that you will do as I have requested." And Joseph swore again that he was going to comply as per his request.

Later on, Israel became very ill. He rallied enough strength, when Joseph came to visit him one day that he was able to call all of his sons together again and talk to them. He revealed to all of them the coming events in their lives, and their outcome. After he had finished telling them the outcome of their lives, he blessed them and died. Israel was one hundred and forty-seven years old when he died in the land of Goshen. Joseph fell upon Israel's face and wept for a long, long time.

Joseph called his physicians and asked to embalm his father. Because of his position and influence, it only took forty days for them to accomplish the task, and seventy days for morning.

Meanwhile because Joseph was in mourning, he sent representatives to Pharaoh and requested, if he could go and bury his father near Mamre, as he promised Him.

The Journeys of God the Creator

Pharaoh granted him his request.

Joseph took his father to bury him in the land of Canaan, as he promised. With him came the adults, from his household, his brother's household, his father's household, Pharaoh's dignitaries, and the elders of Egypt. And when the Canaanites saw the crowd gathered at Machpelah, they said, "11 This is a grievous mourning to the Egyptians" (Genesis 50:11).

Israel returned to Canaan, as God the Creator had promised him, seventeen years earlier that he was going to be buried with his forefathers.

Now that Israel was buried, Joseph's brothers were terrified of Joseph even more than before. They thought, the reason Joseph did not punish them before was due to their father's protection. But now, they thought, since their father was gone, Joseph was going to do them severe harm for what they did to him. In fear of retribution, Joseph's stepbrothers said to him, "16 Thy father did command before he died, saying, 17 So shall ye say unto Joseph, Forgive, I pray thee now, the trespass of thy brethren, and their sin; for they did unto thee evil; and now, we pray thee, forgive the trespass of the servants of the God of thy father. And Joseph wept when they spake unto him. 18 And his brethren also went and fell down before his face; and they said, Behold, we be thy servants. 19 And Joseph said unto them, Fear not: for am I in the place of God?" (Genesis 50:16-19).

And Joseph further responded by telling them not to worry. He was not going to do them harm. "God had a purpose in what you did," he said to them. In addition, he told them that he was going to take care of them. And he did.

Joseph was one hundred and ten years when he died in Egypt. Joseph was embalmed and placed in a coffin in Egypt.

After Joseph's death, the children of Israel continued to be fruitful in the land of Goshen. In fact, they "7 increased abundantly, and multiplied, and waxed exceeding mighty; and the land was filled with them" (Exodus 1:7).

After Joseph's death, the children of Israel lived in prosperity and tranquility in Goshen. Unfortunately, those happy times did not

The Journeys of God the Creator

last. Not too long after Joseph's death, an uprising came about by the native Egyptians, which toppled the residing Pharaoh who had conquered their land. Eventually, the new Dynasty, which came into power, did not recognize the previous government's policies, especially all of the foreigners who lived in their country. The new Pharaoh began to treat them as enemies and slaves.

On top of that policy, the new Pharaoh created a problem for himself with the Hebrews (the children of Israel). Instead of accepting the Hebrews as allies and work with them, as the previous administration had done, the new Pharaoh accused them as the enemy of Egypt. He was afraid that the children of Israel were going to side with other powers to over-through Egypt. To calm his fears, Pharaoh sent his soldiers to overpower the children of Israel and enslave them in his kingdom. He set over the Hebrews "11 taskmasters to afflict them with their burdens. And they built for Pharaoh treasure cities, Pithom and Raamses" (Exodus 1:11).

But Pharaoh ran into another problem. He thought that by overworking the Hebrews they would die off, and therefore, he would get rid of the excessive numbers faster from the land, which they occupied. But, the harder he made them work, the faster they multiplied. Pharaoh had a no win situation. What was he going to do next? If he allowed the Hebrew population to overtake theirs, sooner or later, they could easily over run them. So Pharaoh issued orders to have all of the male babies of the children of Israel killed and thrown into the Nile River, and the female babies saved.

During those perilous times, sixty-four years after Joseph's death, Moses was born. At that time many of the families tried to save their children. Some even contemplated leaving Goshen; but the majority preferred to stay there together. The Egyptian forces monitored the births of the Hebrew women, even though many women tried to conceal their pregnancy. Unfortunately, many died trying to save their babies.

One of many women who managed to save her son was a Levi by the name of "Jochebed." She managed to hide her baby for three months. But because she had too many close calls, she felt that it would be better if she sent the baby down the Nile, in a floating basket, with the hopes the baby survived its journey.

And that is what she did.

Pharaoh's daughter was in the Nile River with her servants. When the servants saw the baby in the basket, they told Pharaoh's daughter, and she said, "Bring the baby here." When she saw the baby she fell in love with it because she said that it was a beautiful baby. She named the baby "Moses" because he was found in the bushes.

There in Pharaoh's courts, Moses grew in knowledge of the sciences, administration, language, military, and more because Pharaoh's daughter, in agreement with her father, wanted Moses to be the next Pharaoh of Egypt.

But Pharaoh's daughter's wish was not fulfilled. One day, while Moses was observing the slaves at work, he saw one of the Hebrews beaten ruthlessly. In defense to the Hebrew, Moses went to separate the taskmaster and the Hebrew; in their heated brawl, Moses struck the Egyptian and killed him. Then, Moses took the body and buried it in the sand.

The next day, Moses came out to see more slaves at work. Again he observed few Hebrews in a heated argument. And when Moses rebuked them, one of them said to him, "Are you going to kill me also as you killed the Egyptian?"

Moses was stunned to find out that they knew of the incident! He was also surprised that the news had traveled throughout the camp so quickly! In his apprehension, he felt like an outcast. He quickly rationalized that since the Hebrews knew that he killed the Egyptian, surly by now, Pharaoh probably also knows of the incident!

One hundred and four years after Joseph's death, in fear, Moses escaped from Pharaoh. Quickly and discretely Moses moved past Pharaoh's men and past the slaves of Egypt. Moses decided to go eastward from Goshen and southeast around the Gulf of Suez until he reached a place called Midian, which was located in the Mount Sinai Peninsula.

Here is the account: "11 And it came to pass in those days, when Moses was grown, that he went out unto his brethren, and looked on their burdens: and he spied an Egyptian smiting an Hebrew, one of his brethren. 12 And he looked this way and that way, and when he saw that there was no man, he slew the Egyptian, and hid him in the sand. 13 And when he went out the second day, behold, two men of the Hebrews strove together: and he said to him that did the wrong, Wherefore smitest thou thy fellow? 14 And he said, Who made thee a prince and a judge over us? intendest thou to kill me, as thou killedst the Egyptian? And Moses feared, and said, Surely this thing is known. 15 Now when Pharaoh heard this thing, he sought to slay Moses. But Moses fled from the face of Pharaoh, and dwelt in the land of Midian" (Exodus 2:11-15).

By reading the above statement one would think that Moses fled all the way east of the Gulf of Aqaba, or in the Wilderness of Paran, as per some historical settings. But since the Midianites were nomads, one should consider Moses' account that these descendents of Abraham, many of them, had settled in the Mt. Sinai Peninsula, and in other parts of the land.

Having said that, where did Moses flee?

Moses fled to Mount Sinai area because Exodus 3:1 tells us that "Moses kept the flock of Jethro his father in law, the priest of Midian: and he led the flock to the backside of the desert, and came to the mountain of God, even to Horeb." And to further verify that Jethro and his daughters lived in the Sinai Peninsula, we are told, when Moses returned with the children of Israel from Egypt, and camped at "Rephidim," Jethro and Zipporah, Moses' wife, met Moses there with her two children. Therefore, when Moses fled from Egypt, Moses fled to the Sinai Peninsula.

What had happened, when Moses arrived in the land of Midian, he sat down near a well and observed seven women near the well of which some were drawing water out of the well. While the women were drawing the water, a number of shepherds came and started to chase the girls away because they wanted to use the water for themselves. When Moses saw what was taking place, he got up and chased the shepherds away. Then, he helped the girls to water their flock. After they finished watering the flock, the girls took Moses to their home and told their father what happened at the well. Reuel

The Journeys of God the Creator

(Jethro) said to his daughters, "Where is the Egyptian?" They brought him into their father's tent, and they talked. Moses decided to remain with Jethro; and during his stay, he married one of Jethro's daughters whose name was Zipporah.

Moses remained with Jethro for forty years before God the Creator called him to go down to Egypt. But Moses felt that he could not fulfill the task he was asked to do because this assignment required someone who was fluent in the Egyptian language. Not only that, but one had to be able to carry himself favorably before Pharaoh. Moses was acknowledging his inadequacies before his Creator. Although he was raised in the courts of Pharaoh, he had forgotten most of the language, and in general, how to speak. Moses was slow to speak due to the isolation he was living in. He hardly interacted with any one while he was shepherding the animals during the forty years he lived in the Sinai Peninsula. But, the Creator said to Moses that he was not to worry about his speech. God sent his older brother to him, from Egypt, to be his helper. Moses obeyed the LORD'S request; and when Aaron arrived, they discussed the mission and went to Egypt to bring the children of Israel out from that land.

Moses was eighty years old when he went to Egypt with his brother. There, Moses met with the leaders of the children of Israel and told them how it came about that he returned to Egypt. He told them how the LORD God of Abraham, the God of Isaac, and the God of Jacob (Israel) had spoken to him and told him to come to Egypt and ask Pharaoh to let all of God's people go. Moses also told them that he was to take them to the Promised Land. But many of the children of Israel preferred to stay in Egypt and serve Pharaoh. They were content with their lifestyle under Pharaoh's rule. In fact, many of the children of Israel did not know any other life because they were born and lived in that environment.

Nonetheless, Moses expounded to the children of Israel that the Promised Land was first given to Abraham; and then, to his seed who followed after him. And Moses told them that they were the seed of their father Jacob (Israel); and they were to go and possess the land, which God the Creator gave unto him.

The Journeys of God the Creator

They finally agreed to go with Moses and follow the Creator wherever He was to lead them. Then Moses said to them that there will be a number of plagues that will take place before Pharaoh finally lets them go; but they were to be patient and trust in the LORD God of their fathers. Eventually, Moses told them, they would leave Egypt with their families and with their belongings.

Moses pleaded with Pharaoh to let the children of Israel go out of Egypt, but he would not. Pharaoh's reaction was "Who is this God that I should obey Him?" Moses, by his brother, confronted Pharaoh with a number of plagues over and over again, as the LORD had revealed, but Pharaoh became more defiant and chose not to let God's people go. And to make matters worse, the more defiant Pharaoh became, the more abusive he was towards the children of Israel. And in turn, the children of Israel began to blame Moses for their hardships. But the LORD told Moses not to become discouraged because at the end, Pharaoh, by cursing the children of Israel, he will pronounce that curse upon the firstborn of Egypt. By his own volition, Pharaoh will place all of them under death. And when that curse is pronounced and accomplished, then he will let the children of Israel go.

And so it was, as God the Creator of Genesis 1:1 had revealed to Moses before he went to Egypt. When the final plague was at hand, Moses told the children of Israel to go home and prepare to leave the land of Egypt in the morning. But first they were to slay a lamb, paint the blood of the lamb on the doorposts of their homes, cook the lamb, eat it with bitter herbs, and wait for his command that was to arrive in the morning. But tonight, after they brushed the blood of the lamb on their doorposts, they were not to leave their homes. If they did, they will not be protected from the plague, which Pharaoh was going to bring upon the land.

The children of Israel said that they would do as Moses asked. They went in their homes and prepared themselves for the journey, the lamb, the unleavened bread, the bitter herbs, and for the plague that was to follow.

During the night, as the children of Israel were eating the lamb, a fearsome terror struck in that unforgettable night. The firstborn

The Journeys of God the Creator

males of all of the families in Egypt died who did not have the lamb's blood on their doorpost; and all the first-born Egyptian animals also died from large hailstones and lightning. The terror was so great that the bitter cry was heard throughout the land of Egypt. People and Pharaoh's advisors pleaded with him to let the children of Israel go. In his frustration and anger, finally Pharaoh sent his representatives to Moses and told Moses to take the children of Israel and get out of the land of Egypt as fast as they could go.

Moses and the elders of Israel had prepared for their departure from Egypt. In the morning, they and the children of Israel met at the fields of "Raamses"; and from there, they were going to be led by God the Creator, who appeared in the form of a Cloud above the children of Israel. Moses told the Children of Israel to follow the Cloud wherever He was to lead them. When the Cloud moved they were to move, and when the Cloud stopped, they to were to stop and camp. After they had organized themselves, the Cloud started to move from the fields of Raamses. After two hundred and fifteen years of stay in Egypt, God the Creator, who appeared in the form of a Cloud, started to guide the children of Israel eastward and northeast up above the banks of the Red Sea (Gulf of Suez).

But then, the Creator led the children of Israel southward to the fields of Succoth. The fields of Succoth are located east towards the Suez Cannel and southeast of "Raamses." There He (the Cloud) stopped; and the children of Israel rested after their thirty miles journey from the fields of "Raamses." During the night, the Creator, who was in a form of a cloud, turned into a blazing fire. The fire, above the camp, gave the children of Israel light, kept them warm during the night, and during the day the Cloud kept the children of Israel cool from the scorching sun.

From Succoth to Mount Sinai there were a number of stops and events, which took place. Many people are familiar with some of the events, which took place between the fields of Succoth and Mount Sinai. Therefore I am not going to go into detail regarding all of these events; but I will tell you about few incidences, which took place on their way to Mount Sinai.

The Creator of Genesis 1:1-Who is He?   By: *Philip Mitanidis*
The Journeys of God the Creator

One of the events occurred during the time when the children of Israel traveled southeast from Succoth to Etham, to a place called "Pihahiroth." The Creator said to Moses, "2 Speak unto the children of Israel, that they turn and encamp before Pihahiroth, between Migdol and the sea, over against Baalzephon: before it shall ye encamp by the sea" (Exodus 14:2). And, in verse nine, Moses states that the children of Israel camped "by the sea, beside Pihahiroth, before Baalzephon."

With the information, which Moses gives us, one can conclude that the children of Israel were pinned against the western shoreline of the Red Sea, in an area, which configured like a horseshoe. The Red sea, which Moses is referring to, is the modern name of Suez Canal. The children of Israel were in the area of "Baalzephon" near "Pihahiroth." These two places were located on either side of the horseshoe. In front of the horseshoe there was a place called "Migdol." "Migdol" was an Egyptian lookout tower. "Baalzephon" was a Canaanite deity. Therefore, it meant that the children of Israel were camped not too far from this pagan place of worship.

God the Creator brought the children of Israel to "Pihahiroth" to impress upon the children of Israel's hearts the difference between the heathen gods and Himself (the LORD God of their fathers). The children of Israel were to experience, first hand, the awesome power of God, so that they would not fear their enemies, which they were to encounter on their way to the Promised Land and in the Promised Land.

But before the children of Israel camped between the border towers of Egypt, which ran from the Mediterranean Sea towards the Red Sea, the Cloud led the Israelites between the tower of "Migdol" and "Pihahiroth," which is against the Gulf of the Red Sea. There, from the tower of "Migdol," the Egyptian guards, who were posted in that area to guard the borders of Egypt, saw the children of Israel coming their way. And when they saw the enormous crowd coming their way, they sent word to Pharaoh and told him of the illogical attempt of the children of Israel to cross over their borders. They said that they were headed towards the water of the Gulf of the Red Sea without rafts or boats!

The Journeys of God the Creator

In addition, the Egyptian guards wanted to know what to do with them, if they moved and attempted to cross their border?

Finally, the children of Israel settled close to "Pihahiroth" in an area, which was against the Gulf of the Red Sea. But while the children of Israel were settled in their camp, and relaxing from their journey, at one point, they heard the roar of 600 chariots coming their way. When they realized that Pharaoh's army was coming for them, they panicked! As Pharaoh's soldiers were almost upon the camp, the children of Israel said unto Moses: "11 because there were no graves in Egypt, hast thou taken us away to die in the wilderness? wherefore hast thou dealt thus with us, to carry us forth out of Egypt? 12 Is not this the word that we did tell thee in Egypt, saying, Let us alone, that we may serve the Egyptians? For it had been better for us to serve the Egyptians, than that we should die in the wilderness" (Exodus 14:11, 12).

Then Moses intervened and told the people not to fear the Egyptians. The Creator was going to deliver them as He delivered them from the hand of Pharaoh when they were in bondage. But how was the LORD going to deliver them when there was nowhere for them to flee? Again, Moses told the children of Israel that the LORD was going to fight for them, and therefore they should be at peace. But, how were they going to remain in peace when their lives were at stake?

Pharaoh's men were almost in the camp, and the fear of the people increased. Some were panic stricken because they could not run out from the enormous crowd and hide. Finally Pharaoh's army came near the camp of Israel and blocked the entrance to the camp. Pharaoh's soldiers regrouped and went forward to strike the camp of Israel. But at that moment something happened? As Pharaoh's army was closing in, and eagerly trying to enter in the camp that night, the Cloud went behind the camp of Israel and created gross darkness upon Pharaoh's army. At the same time, the Cloud provided light for the children of Israel, so that they could see where they were going. While the Cloud stopped the pursuers, Moses gave the command to the children of Israel to pick up their belongings and go forward towards the Sea. Many thought Moses lost it! Was

The Journeys of God the Creator

Moses expecting the children of Israel to swim across the sea? Then, Moses said to them, "The Egyptians will be no more."

Moses picked up his rod and stretched it over the water. The water of the Red Sea parted, creating a passage for the children of Israel to flee from Pharaoh's army. God the Creator who was in the form of a cloud caused the east winds to blow on the bottom of the passage and dried the soil between the towering watery walls. Then Moses told the children of Israel to start moving through the passage and cross to the other side of the sea. As the children of Israel were crossing to the other side of the sea, in between the overbearing walls of the sea, the Cloud shone upon them during the night, so that they could see where they were going. And when the children of Israel almost finished crossing, God the Creator removed the gross darkness from the Egyptian army and went over to the other side where the children of Israel were gathered. Seeing that the passage was clear to ride the chariots into, Pharaoh gave the command, and his chariots did pursue the children of Israel. But, when the chariots filled the passage, Moses stretched his hand over the sea, and the mighty walls of the sea came crushing upon chariot, man, beast, and drowned them all. The children of Israel saw many dead Egyptian bodies on the shore, in the morning that day.

Although the children of Israel thought that they could not escape from the Egyptian army, the Creator blinded the horsemen and the chariot rider until God the Creator parted the water of the sea and made a way for the children of Israel to escape the sword and the bow of the Egyptians. "31 And Israel saw that great work which the LORD did upon the Egyptians: and the people feared the LORD, and believed the LORD, and his servant Moses" (Exodus 14:31).

From the other side of the Gulf, God led the children of Israel southward in "Etham," a three days journey, to a place called "Marah." And from "Marah," God the Creator led the children of Israel southwards along the banks of the Red Sea, to avoid confrontation with the Amalekites.

After a number of stops on the way to Mount Sinai, about half of the way, there was confrontation between the children of Israel

The Journeys of God the Creator

and Moses. The children of Israel were in a place called the Wilderness of Sin. Their food and water became so depleted that it caused enormous stress within the Israelite camp. It got so bad that the people were wishing that they were dead. They said, "Would to God we had died by the hand of the LORD in the land of Egypt."

Don't you think that it is amazing how quickly the children of Israel forgot the plagues in Egypt, the parting of the Red Sea, the way the Cloud was leading them, and the rations that were supplied by the Creator thus far? Now that He had tested their trust in Him, they rebelled! They said, you "3 have brought us forth into this wilderness, to kill this whole assembly with hunger" (Exodus 16:3).

Can you imagine making that kind of accusation against God the Creator who was present? They said, "Ye have brought us forth into this wilderness, to kill this whole assembly with hunger."

Did the children of Israel forget why and how they were brought out of Egypt? Or, were they just complaining?

What do you think?

Needless to say, when the children of Israel moved towards Rephidim, to a place called Massah, the children of Israel started to complain again because there was no water in the camp neither was there water in the vicinity. They thought that this time they were going to perish for sure. So they said to Moses, "3 Wherefore is this that thou hast brought us up out of Egypt, to kill us and our children and our cattle with thirst?" (Exodus 17:3)

Moses went before God the Creator and said to Him, these people are ready to stone me; what shall I do with them? Then God the Creator of Genesis 1:1 said to Moses, "6 I will stand before thee there upon the rock in Horeb; and thou shalt smite the rock, and there shall come water out of it, that the people may drink. And Moses did so in the sight of the elders of Israel. 7 And he called the name of the place Massah, and Meribah, because of the chiding of the children of Israel, and because they tempted the LORD, saying, Is the LORD among us, or not?" (Exodus 17:6, 7)

Obviously, God the Creator was amongst them, but because they had not learned to trust Him, they made all kinds of derogatory remarks. The fact that God the Creator was there in a form of a

The Creator of Genesis 1:1-Who is He?   By: *Philip Mitanidis*

The Journeys of God the Creator

cloud to lead them, protect them, and feed them, on the way to the Promised Land, should have sufficed; but, for one reason or another, His presence wasn't enough for them?

Nonetheless, Moses did as God the Creator asked him. He went to the rock, and there, Moses struck the rock with his staff, and the water started to gush out of it. The water flowed like a river. And when the children of Israel saw the water, they quickly drank of it, and then, they gave water to their animals to drink.

In another incident, while the children of Israel were camped in "Rephidim," the Amalekites heard that the children of Israel were going to go onward to possess the land of Canaan. They did not like the Israelites going through their territory. They were worried about their land being overtaken by the children of Israel. Instead of dialoguing with the children of Israel, they fought with them. Although the children of Israel prevailed in "Rephidim," they did not get rid of the Amalekites. Over a year later, the Amalekites band together with the Canaanites and defeated the children of Israel at "Kadesh-barnea."

The Amalekites were the descendents of Esau, Jacob's brother.

The Journeys of God the Creator

Anyway because of the murmurings of the children of Israel, God the Creator permitted the Amalekites to attack the children of Israel at "Rephidim." This time, God the Creator defeated the Amalekites because the children of Israel obeyed His commands.

When Moses' father-in-law heard that the children of Israel had arrived at his back yard, as it were, he was very excited; he could not wait to go and visit Moses at the "mount of God" (Exodus 18:5). Jethro arrived at "Rephidim," in the camp of the children of Israel, with Moses' wife Zipporah, and their two children whose names were "Gershom" and "Eliezer."

While Moses was reunited with his family, Jethro could not get enough information regarding the events, which had taken place from the time he and his brother Aaron went to Egypt. Moses was glad to reveal to Jethro all the wonders God the Creator did on behalf of the children of Israel, and how He delivered them all from the hand of the oppressor. But, Moses had plenty of work to do, and therefore Moses could not spend the time with Jethro, as Jethro wanted him to. When Jethro saw the amount of time Moses was spending with the people, he said to Moses, "Delegate the less important work to others, and let them take the responsibility for it. The work that involves direct communication with God the Creator, you can spend the time doing that. If you do that," said Jethro, "you will have some time for yourself, and you will have time to spend with your family."

Moses heard the words of Jethro and saw the wisdom of his father-in-law. So, Moses delegated the work to others as Jethro suggested.

Jethro and Moses spent some time together discussing the work of the LORD, and at one point, Moses asked Jethro to join him and go with him to the Promised Land. Jethro thanked Moses, but he chose to stay where he was and continue in the LORD'S work there.

Finally, God the Creator brought the children of Israel from "Rephidim" to the foot of Mount Sinai. When the children of Israel were camped at the foot of Mount Sinai for less than a year, at one point, God the Creator revealed His will to the children of Israel. God the Creator said to Moses, "Prepare the people to meet with

The Journeys of God the Creator

Me at the border of mount Sinai." And Moses did as the LORD God of Israel asked of him. All the children of Israel and those who had joined the camp washed and cleaned themselves before they came near the mountain. No animal or man was to go pass the border of the mountain. As the children of Israel moved closer to the mountain, the awesome colors of flames, smoke, and thundering could be seen and heard in utter majesty coming from the top of Mount Sinai. As the children of Israel and those who joined the camp stood before the mountain, there, above and around the mountain of God, the angels of God the Creator hovered in orderly fashion. Then God the Creator came down upon the mountain and spoke to the children of Israel. As He spoke, the words rolled down the mountain, and out in the plains of Horeb, causing the ground to tremble.

God the Creator of Genesis 1:1 said to them,

"2 I am the LORD thy God, which have brought thee out of the land of Egypt, out of the house of bondage" (Exodus 20:2).

i

"You shall have no other gods before Me.

ii

"You shall not make for yourself an idol, or any likeness of what is in heaven above or on the earth beneath or in the water under the earth. You shall not worship them or serve them; for I, the LORD your God, am a jealous God, visiting the iniquity of the fathers on the children, on the third and the fourth generations of those who hate Me, but showing loving kindness to thousands, to those who love Me and keep My commandments.

iii

"You shall not take the name of the LORD your God in vain, for the LORD will not leave him unpunished who takes His name in vain.

iv

"Remember the sabbath day, to keep it holy. Six days you

shall labor and do all your work, but the seventh day is a sabbath of the LORD your God; in it you shall not do any work, you or your son or your daughter, your male or your female servant or your cattle or your sojourner who stays with you. For in six days the LORD made the heavens and the earth, the sea and all that is in them, and rested on the seventh day; therefore the LORD blessed the sabbath day and made it holy.

v

"Honor your father and your mother, that your days may be prolonged in the land which the LORD your God gives you.

vi

"You shall not murder.

vii

"You shall not commit adultery.

viii

"You shall not steal.

ix

"You shall not bear false witness against your neighbor.

x

"You shall not covet your neighbor's house; you shall not covet your neighbor's wife or his male servant or his female servant or his ox or his donkey or anything that belongs to your neighbor." Exodus 20:3-17 (NAS)

When the children of Israel "18 saw the thundering, and the lightning, and the noise of the trumpet, and the mountain smoking: and when the people saw it, they removed, and stood afar off." And when they heard the words of the Covenant (the Ten Commandments, Exodus 20:3-17), they trembled with fear because the Covenant revealed their sinful nature, and their past sins. They said to Moses, "19 Speak thou [you] with us, and we will hear: but let not God speak with us, lest we die. And Moses said unto the

The Journeys of God the Creator

people, Fear not: for God is come to prove you, and that His fear may be before your faces, that ye sin not" (Exodus 20:18-20).

By the way, the word "fear," as it is used in many verses, it means, "to hate evil." Here is the reference, "13 The fear of the LORD is to hate evil" (Proverbs 8:13).

After that awesome presentation, God the Creator allowed the event to sink into the minds of the children of Israel and encourage their willingness to adhere to the precepts of the Ten Commandments.

A number of days after the awesome audible presentation of the Covenant (Ten Commandments), by God the Creator of Genesis 1:1, the Creator's Associate asked Moses to take seventy elders, Aaron, and his two sons and go up the mountain to worship the Creator there. The Creator's Associate said to Moses: "1 come up unto the LORD, thou, and Aaron, Nadab, and Abihu, and seventy of the elders of Israel: and worship ye afar off. 2 And Moses alone shall come near the LORD: but they shall not come nigh; neither shall the people go up with him" (Exodus 24:1, 2).

Notice what the Creator's Associate said to Moses; he said to Moses that the seventy elders and the Levites were to go up with Moses and stand at a distance while Moses went and interacted with God the Creator. And the other thing the Creator's Associate said to Moses was that the elders and the Levites were to stand "afar off" and "worship" the Creator.

One of the reasons the seventy elders, Aaron, and his two older sons were asked to see the Creator was to give them strength and faith in the Creator, their LORD God of their fathers. They were to witness first hand that there was such an Individual. None were to assume that Moses was talking to the wind or pretend that he was interacting with the God of their fathers, every time he went up on the mountain. The elders and Levite priests were to see the Creator with their own eyes and witness in person His existence. And when these elders and Levites came down from the mountain, they were able to report to the children of Israel how they saw the God of their fathers and Moses interacting with Him. They were to encourage the children of Israel to trust in Him, as Moses did.

The Journeys of God the Creator

Isn't it strange, after seeing God the Creator face to face, later on, Nadab and Abihu practiced witchcraft before the Creator? Needless to say because of their unrestrained sinful acts, they were struck down by the Creator's presence and died. It must be remembered; sin cannot exist in the presence of the Creator. Nadab and Abihu knew this fact but they still sinned before Him.

Go figure?

By the way, can you comprehend why Nadab and Abihu would do such a thing before the presence of God the Creator?

Nonetheless, while Moses was interacting with God the Creator, before the elders of Israel and the Levites, the Creator gave Moses ceremonial laws and civil laws. And after they returned from the mountain, Moses took the time to write these ceremonial and civil laws in a book, which he called the "book of the covenant." The "book of the covenant" must not be confused with the Ten Commandments. Moses wrote the "book of the covenant," which contained the ceremonial and the civil laws; whereas the Ten Commandments were written by the "finger" of God the Creator on two tablets of stone

Regarding the ceremonial law, Moses "3 told the people all the words of the LORD, and all the judgments: and all the people answered with one voice, and said, All the words which the LORD hath said will we do. 4 And Moses wrote all the words of the LORD, and rose up early in the morning, and builded an altar under the hill, and twelve pillars, according to the twelve tribes of Israel. 5 And he sent young men of the children of Israel, which offered burnt offerings, and sacrificed peace offerings of oxen unto the LORD. 6 And Moses took half of the blood, and put it in basons; and half of the blood he sprinkled on the altar. 7 And he took the book of the covenant, and read in the audience of the people: and they said, All that the LORD hath said will we do, and be obedient. 8 And Moses took the blood, and sprinkled it on the people, and said, Behold the blood of the covenant which the LORD hath made with you concerning all these words" (Exodus 24:3-8).

The blood of the Covenant was ratified at the foot of Mount Sinai, between God the Creator of Genesis 1:1, and the children of

Israel in the first year of their arrival there.

Now, the children of Israel knew the difference between the Ten Commandments and the ceremonial law. The Ten Commandments are spiritual, whereas the ceremonial law is carnal. The ceremonial law stated when, how, and what was to be offered to God the Creator for a sin offering or for a thank offering. The ceremonial law was to be carried out until the Creator came in the "flesh" and offer Himself for the sins of the world. And when that was accomplished, the ceremonial law, with its offerings, washings, and the priesthood were to expire. But until then, the ceremonial offerings, the ceremonial laws, and the priesthood were to continue, as they had continued from the time of Adam.

> Please remember: *The ceremonial law was added to the Ten Commandments (Exodus 20:3-17) because of man's sin.*

You can learn more about the ceremonial laws, and about the offerings by reading the Torah, starting from Exodus twenty and onwards for the more detailed record.

In order to implement these laws, as a church, for the sacrificial offerings, washings, and all of the ceremonial procedures, God the Creator said to Moses,

> "8 let them make Me a Sanctuary; that I may dwell among them" (Exodus 25:8).

When Moses brought the request to build a Sanctuary for God the Creator, to live in, before the children of Israel, they responded cheerfully. The children of Israel pitched in with their offerings of fabric, wood, talents, gold, and silver, which they had received before they left Egypt. They all gave from their hearts. Anyone who gave begrudgingly, he or she was turned away with their offering. The end result was so successful that they had overabundance of material to complete the "House of God."

When all of the materials for the Sanctuary were finished, they erected the Sanctuary, as God the Creator commanded them, and

The Journeys of God the Creator

placed in the first and second compartments of the Sanctuary all of the furniture they had made for it.

In the first compartment (room) were the candlesticks, the table of incense, and the table with the 12 cakes on it, which represented the twelve tribes of Israel. The twelve cakes were often referred to as the showbread showbread in the Scriptures. The twelve cakes or "showbread" were replaced every Sabbath day (Saturday).

In the second compartment of the Sanctuary, which was identified as the "most holy place," the Ark of the Covenant, which contained the Ten Commandments (Exodus 20:3-17) within it, was placed there. And the writings of Moses, regarding the civil and ceremonial laws, were placed at the side of the Ark of the Covenant. Later on, Aaron's staff (rod), which budded, was placed in the "most holy place" of the Sanctuary while they were wandering in the wilderness.

There is a reason why Aaron's staff remained in the "most holy place" of the Sanctuary. It all started when Korah the Levite, a cousin of Moses, rebelled at Kadesh with his two hundred and fifty princesses. They wanted to overthrow Moses and Aaron from their positions by saying that God the Creator did not want them to be leaders any more. In order to settle the dispute, they sought God the Creator to give them a sign. So, they placed their rods in the Sanctuary to see, which staff was going to bud. The staff or staffs that budded indicated the Creator's choice of leaders.

Needless to say, the only rod that budded was Aaron's; the rest of the staffs that were put in the Sanctuary did not bud. That was a sign to the children of Israel that Aaron and Moses were still the appointed leaders by God the Creator, and not Korah or anyone else was to take over their leadership. And ever since that time, Aaron's rod, which budded, was placed in the "most holy place" of the Sanctuary as a reminder to the children of Israel that they should respect the leaders, in their respective positions, which God the Creator had set up.

Another important item in the "most holy place" was the "mercy seat" (a thick cover), which was made out of pure gold. It was placed on top of the Ark of the Covenant. And on top of the mercy seat, there were two cherubims. One cherub was placed at one end, on top of the "mercy seat," and the other cherub was placed at the other end on top of the mercy seat. These cherubims, which were made out of gold, were facing each other, and they looked downward towards the mercy seat with one wing extended upward, and the other wing folded downwards. And from the "mercy seat," God the Creator of Genesis 1:1 communicated with Moses. The LORD said to Moses, "22 And there I will meet with thee [you], and I will commune with thee from above the mercy seat, from between the two cherubims which are upon the ark of the testimony" (Exodus 25:22).

Although God the Creator did speak to Moses from the "mercy seat" throughout the years, (See Genesis 33:11) the high priest could see the Shekinah glory of God the Creator once a year above the "mercy seat," and that was during the Day of Atonement.

A huge curtain separated the rooms of the "most holy place" and of the "holy place." This long curtain, at the left of "the table of incense," also acted as a door, which allowed the high priest to enter into the "most holy place" once a year. The LORD said to Moses, "33 And the vail shall divide unto you between the holy place and the most holy" (Exodus 26:33).

The reason the Creator asked the children of Israel to build a Sanctuary and implement the ceremonial law and services was to meet the requirements of the Ten Commandments. In other words, the ceremonial law was added to the Ten Commandments because

The Journeys of God the Creator

of sin. And since the death penalty is imposed upon the offender of the Ten Commandments, as they are listed in Exodus chapter twenty, temporary provisions were made by the ceremonial law to let the sinner be forgiven by the offering of a sacrificial lamb on the alter, which was outside of the tent, in the eastern courtyard of the Sanctuary. It should be noted; this sacrificial lamb was a temporary provision for man's sins. The lamb and the ceremonial services pointed forward (1 Peter 1:7-12) to the supreme sacrifice of God the Creator, according to the "promise" (Galatians 3:16-19), when He was to come in the "flesh" to die for all of the penitent sinners of planet earth.

The Creator had to offer Himself as a sacrifice because He was the One who created the angels and man. He is responsible for their acts, and He was willing to pay for their sins, if they wanted to be saved from eternal death. Many of the angels who sinned did not

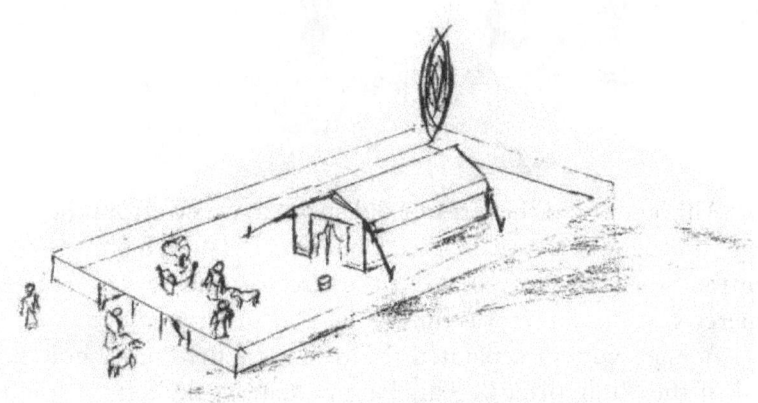

BY: PHILIP MITANIDIS

want to be saved because they thought they became stronger than their Creator through sin. For that reason, they did not want to be reinstated in His Kingdom. They assumed that eventually they would rule the universe. But Adam and Eve repented from their sins, and God the Creator said that He was going to save them and their progeny. I thank Him for His supreme sacrifice because there was no other way out for the human race to escape the death

The Journeys of God the Creator

penalty that is imposed upon it by the Ten Commandments.

Therefore, the ceremonial services of the Sanctuary centered on God the Creator of Genesis 1:1 whose presence was observed in the "most holy place" above the "mercy seat," and outside of the Sanctuary in a form of a cloud. God the Creator said to Moses, "8 let them make Me a sanctuary; that I may dwell among them [the children of Israel]" (Exodus 25:8). And God the Creator added,

> "45 I will dwell among the children of Israel, and will be their God. 46 And they shall know that I am the LORD their God, that brought them forth out of the land of Egypt, that I may dwell among them: I am the LORD their God" (Ex. 29:45, 46).

It should be remembered; the request to make the Sanctuary came after the children of Israel repented and forsook their sinful habits. Now that the camp of Israel was cleansed from their sins, God the Creator could move into His Sanctuary and dwell with the children of Israel.

The children of Israel did make a Sanctuary as God the Creator had requested. The task of building the Sanctuary, its drapes, and its furniture began in the first year of their arrival at the mountain of God. This event took place after the angels of God arrived and stationed themselves around and above Mount Sinai. It was after God the Creator spoke to the children of Israel from the top of the smoking mountain. It was after Moses went up the mountain and stayed for 40 days. It was after Moses, Joshua, Aaron, Aaron's two sons, and the seventy elders of Israel went up on the mountain, and saw the Creator's glory while Moses met with Him. It was after the covenant was ratified. It was after that event that the fence, drapes, altar, furniture, and the overall work of the Sanctuary were established. The completion of the Sanctuary took place at the end of the first year of their stay at the foot of Mount Sinai.

But, the assembly and dedication of the Sanctuary did not take place until the second year of their stay at the foot of Mount Sinai, which was the first month of the second year.

The record says, "17 And it came to pass in the first month in

The Journeys of God the Creator

the second year, on the first day of the month [April], that the tabernacle was reared up. 18 And Moses reared up the tabernacle, and fastened his sockets, and set up the boards thereof, and put in the bars thereof, and reared up his pillars. 19 And he spread abroad the tent over the tabernacle, and put the covering of the tent above upon it; as the LORD commanded Moses.

"20 And he took and put the testimony into the ark, and set the staves on the ark, and put the mercy seat above upon the ark: 21 And he brought the ark into the tabernacle, and set up the vail of the covering, and covered the ark of the testimony; as the LORD commanded Moses.

"22 And he put the table in the tent of the congregation, upon the side of the tabernacle northward, without the vail. 23 And he set the bread in order upon it before the LORD; as the LORD had commanded Moses. 24 And he put the candlestick in the tent of the congregation, over against the table, on the side of the tabernacle southward. 25 And he lighted the lamps before the LORD; as the LORD commanded Moses. 26 And he put the golden altar in the tent of the congregation before the vail: 27 And he burnt sweet incense thereon; as the LORD commanded Moses. 28 And he set up the hanging at the door of the tabernacle.

"29 And he put the altar of burnt offering by the door of the tabernacle of the tent of the congregation, and offered upon it the burnt offering and the meat offering; as the LORD commanded Moses.

"30 And he set the laver between the tent of the congregation and the altar, and put water there, to wash withal. 31 And Moses and Aaron and his sons washed their hands and their feet thereat: 32 When they went into the tent of the congregation, and when they came near unto the altar, they washed; as the LORD commanded Moses.

"33 And he reared up the court round about the tabernacle and the altar, and set up the hanging of the court gate. So Moses finished the work.

"34 Then a cloud covered the tent of the congregation, and the glory of the LORD filled the tabernacle. 35 And Moses was not able

The Journeys of God the Creator

to enter into the tent of the congregation, because the cloud abode thereon, and the glory of the LORD filled the tabernacle" (Exodus 40:17-35).

As per the above verses, when the dedication of the Sanctuary was finished and the Creator occupied the "most holy place" of the Sanctuary, by His presence, it meant that the Sanctuary was accepted by God the Creator as His dwelling place among the children of Israel.

The tribe of Levi was chosen to serve the needs of the Sanctuary and to also serve in the priesthood. Aaron was the high priest, and his two sons served under him. But, at one point, Nadab and Abihu, Aaron's sons died before the LORD because they offered strange fire before the LORD. By "strange fire" is meant that Aaron's sons were practicing witchcraft before God the Creator who dwelt in the camp of Israel. After their death, his other two sons, Eleazar and Ithamar ministered as priest before the LORD. Levi's sons, Gershon, Kohath, and Merari were given the task of dismantling the Sanctuary, erecting the Sanctuary, and carrying the Sanctuary from place to place. They were responsible for the general care of the Sanctuary's well being. (See Numbers chapters 3 and 4.)

In addition, after the dedication of the Sanctuary to God the Creator, the twelve tribes of Israel were organized in groups of threes around the Sanctuary. There were three tribes north of the Sanctuary, three to the south of the Sanctuary, three to the east of the Sanctuary, and three tribes west of the Sanctuary. The tents of Moses and the tribe of Levi were placed in close proximity around the periphery of the Sanctuary. The twelve tribes of Israel were located around the Levite tents. Those who were not Israelites, they were told to camp around the outside periphery of the tribes of Israel. After a number of years of faithfulness to God the Creator, these individuals who were in the outer camp, they were to be acknowledged as Israelites; up until that time, they were to continue taking part in the sin and thank offerings while they stayed in the outside circle. It was made very plain, by the Creator, to the children of Israel, and to individuals who wanted to join the camp of

The Journeys of God the Creator

Israel; they were to first join those individuals who were in the outer circle of the camp; and as long as they remained with the camp, they were to be counted as converts to the Creator. No human being who wanted to join in the worship of God the Creator was to be turned away. After a number of years of accepting the Creator as their LORD God and Savior, they and their descendents were counted amongst the children of Israel.

When the children of Israel were organized and counted, they were ready to depart from the foot of Mount Sinai, in an orderly fashion, to their destination. Now the children of Israel had leaders in every tribe, and soldiers from every tribe ready to defend the camp of Israel.

Finally, the day came, in the second year of their stay at the foot of Mount Sinai, God the Creator, whose presence was in the form of a cloud, lifted Himself from the Sanctuary above the Ark of the Covenant and began to go forward. That meant that the children of Israel had to dismantle their tents and the Sanctuary and prepare themselves to follow the Cloud in an organized manner wherever He led them.

Here is the account: "36 And when the cloud was taken up from over the tabernacle, the children of Israel went onward in all their journeys; 37 But if the cloud were not taken up, then they journeyed not till the day that it was taken up. 38 For the cloud of the LORD was upon the tabernacle by day, and fire was on it by night, in the sight of all the house of Israel, throughout all their journeys" (Exodus 40:36-38).

Early in the second year of their stay in Horeb, the children of Israel dismantled their tents and were ready to go. They waited for the priests of the Sanctuary to start their journey. The Ark of the Covenant was first carried out of the camp; and then, the Levites followed with the dismantled Sanctuary behind the Ark of the Covenant, about 300 meters apart. Behind the Sanctuary followed the three tribes from one sector of the camp, and then, the other three tribes followed from the adjacent area, and so on. One could see God the Creator hovering in a form of a cloud, ahead of the Ark of the Covenant, leading the priests who carried it. And behind the

The Journeys of God the Creator

Ark, in a distance, a person could see a long line of platoons marching orderly in front of each tribe. And behind each tribe one could see following their respective platoon, children, woman, animals, carts, and the elderly. It was quite a sight to see. It was disciplined and orderly, in comparison to their journey from the fields of Zoan to Mount Sinai.

When the children of Israel left Mount Sinai God the Creator led them northeast of Horeb to a place called Kadesh-barnea (Kadesh). Kadesh is located in the southern end of the Negeb; in David's time Kadesh was in the Wilderness of Paran. After a number of stops, three days here and seven days there, and so on, the children of Israel reached Kadesh. There they camped. And from there, as it was promised, the children of Israel were to go northeast between the Mediterranean Sea and the Dead Sea, better known as the Salt Sea, and possess the Promised Land (Canaan).

But before they went into the Promised Land, they sent spies into the land to see what the people and the land were like. They sent twelve spies in pairs. When they came back, a number of months later (more precisely 40 days), ten of these spies said that the people in the land are giants who live in cities that are well protected by huge walls. They said that the children of Israel were no match for them. Only Caleb and Joshua gave a positive report. They said that the cities and the people could be subdued, if only they would go in the land and possess it.

To the Creator's disappointment, the leaders of each tribe refused to go in and take the Promised Land as God the Creator had admonished them. They said that they and their little ones would perish, if they attempted to take the land. The children of Israel rebelled against God the Creator. They refused to go in and possess the land, even though they knew that it was promised to Abraham, Isaac, Israel, and to them. Instead, they wanted to make captains and guides to take them back to Egypt and live their lives in sin.

In response, God the Creator granted their desire. He told them, if they wanted, they could go back to Egypt! The prospect of going back sounded very good and many jumped at the opportunity. In their excitement, they said that they should select leaders and

The Journeys of God the Creator

organize themselves and go back to Egypt. But a cold reality set in; they remembered that there was no water or food in the desert! Who was going to supply their needs as they were going back to Egypt? There was no one to protect them from their enemies and the bands of thieves that roamed around the desert. Even worse, was Pharaoh going to take them back, or was he going to kill them?

After they assessed their situation, eventually they chose to stay with Moses and Aaron. After the camp settled down, they decided to go and posses the land without the help of God the Creator, and without His consent. This was done in order to show the Creator that they were willing to go and possess the land. At this point, the Creator told Moses to tell the children of Israel not to go to war without Him because they would lose their lives; but they in disobedience went anyway. The Amalekites, with the help of the Canaanites, slaughtered them as God the Creator predicted. Those that were left standing came into the camp and cried out to Moses of their defeat, and the loss of life.

God the Creator was displeased with their disobedience. He said to Moses, "35 Surely there shall not one of these men of this evil generation see that good land, which I sware to give unto your fathers, 36 Save Caleb the son of Jephunneh; he shall see it, and to him will I give the land that he hath trodden upon, and to his children, because he hath wholly followed the LORD." And the Creator added, "38 But Joshua the son of Nun, which standeth before thee, he shall go in thither: encourage him: for he shall cause Israel to inherit it. 39 Moreover your little ones, which ye said should be a prey, and your children, which in that day had no knowledge between good and evil, they shall go in thither, and unto them will I give it, and they shall possess it" (Deuteronomy 1:35, 36, 38, 39).

Moses, Aaron, Caleb, and Joshua wanted to go and possess the Promised Land, but the rest of the people refused to go. Because the children of Israel refused to go and possess the land, the Creator granted them their wish. He took all of them back into the wilderness. The reason God the Creator did not take them to the Promised Land was due to their unwillingness to follow the Creator as He guided them. If the Creator was to take them into the

The Journeys of God the Creator

Promised Land, they would fail miserably because they would not be willing to follow through with His instructions. And failing miserably means that they would be overthrown by the Canaanites. And if they were to be overthrown by the Canaanites that meant that God the Creator would fail to keep the promise that He made to Abraham.

To avoid the onslaught of the children of Israel by the Canaanites because they were not willing to obey God's leadership, in His mercy, God the Creator granted them to live their lives out in the desert, and later allowed their children to possess the Promised Land.

So, after they left Kadesh, the children of Israel wandered for thirty-eight years throughout the Wilderness of Paran and the Wilderness of Zin, before they journeyed to Moab country, which is east of the Salt Sea, and north of Edom.

Unless there is another Kadesh in the wilderness, in their fortieth year while wandering throughout the Wilderness of Sinai, the Desert of Paran, and the Wilderness of Zin, the children of Israel came about and camped at Kadesh-barnea again, in the Wilderness of Zin. Isn't it ironic, it appears from the record that the first time the children of Israel traveled from Mount Sinai to Kadesh-barnea, theoretically, it should have taken them eleven days; now it took them almost 38 years to come back to the same area? And when the children of Israel came to Kadesh from their wanderings in the desert; and there, in Kadesh, in the Wilderness of Zin, Miriam, the sister of Moses, died at the age of one hundred and thirty-two.

If you are wondering, why I said," while wandering in their fortieth year in the wilderness," when Moses states that they were wandering for thirty-eight years; it is simple. Moses said, "the space in which we came from Kadesh-barnea, until we were come over the brook Zered, was thirty and eight years; until all the generation of the men of war were wasted out from among the host" (Deuteronomy 2:14).

Please note: Moses calculates the thirty-eight years period from the time they first left Kadesh-barnea. He does not include the two-

The Journeys of God the Creator

years period as wandering, which they spent partly at Mount Sinai, and partly at Kadesh-barnea; that is why Moses mentions only 38 years of wandering.

The other point, which should be taken into account is the statement that it took the children of Israel, from the time they left Kadesh-barnea, thirty-eight years to cross the Brook of Zered, which is located at the southern tip of the Salt Sea (Dead Sea). That meant that the children of Israel crossed Brook Zered on their fortieth year.

Anyway, while the children of Israel were camped in the area of Kadesh, at one point after Miriam died, the children of Israel began to complain again to Moses and Aaron. They said, "3 Would God that we had died when our brethren died before the LORD! 4 And why have ye brought up the congregation of the LORD into this wilderness, that we and our cattle should die there? 5 And wherefore have ye made us to come up out of Egypt, to bring us in unto this evil place? it is no place of seed, or of figs, or of vines, or of pomegranates; neither is there any water to drink" (Numbers 20:3-5).

Moses and Aaron went to the Sanctuary and spoke to God the Creator regarding the complaints and demands of the children of Israel. The Creator said to Moses, "Go and speak unto the rock," and water will come out of it. Moses did as the LORD commanded, but in his anger, Moses said to the children of Israel, "10 Hear now, ye rebels; must we fetch you water out of this rock? 11 And Moses lifted up his hand, and with his rod he smote the rock twice: and the water came out abundantly, and the congregation drank, and their beasts also" (Numbers 20:10, 11).

Moses, the meekest man on planet earth got angry, not only at the children of Israel, but he also got angry with God the Creator for the awesome responsibility and burden he had to carry. The children of Israel were a rebellious lot. Their trust in the Creator and in the leadership of Moses was questioned throughout their journey, and under stress Moses had enough of their vicious abuses towards him. Unfortunately, Moses took his frustration upon God the Creator whom he loved, by striking the rock twice. As a reminder to Moses and to Aaron that He is not the One who is

The Journeys of God the Creator

abusing them, God the Creator said to them, "12 ye shall not bring this congregation into the land which I have given them," and because the children of Israel struggled with the Creator, and believed not in Him. (Numbers 20:12).

Moses and Aaron's deaths were sealed because they had rebelled in the wilderness, at a place called "Meribah." Now they are reminded that they are not permitted to go into the Promised Land with the Children of Israel.

After that ordeal, from Kadesh, Israel sent messengers to his brethren who lived in Edom. Edom was located east of Kadesh. Moses asked if "thy brother" (the children of Israel), could pass through their land by way of the King's Highway? The King's Highway ran from the tip of the Gulf of Aqaba northward through the land of Edom and through the land of Moab. If the king permitted them to pass, Moses assured the king that they would not touch anything of theirs; neither will they take anything from them. But, Moses added, if their livestock drank their water, he was willing to pay for it. All Moses wanted was to pass through Edom, on their way to Moab. The message was returned to Moses. The message of the king to Moses was simple; he told Moses that he and the children of Israel were not permitted to pass through their land. If he attempts to pass through their land, they will smite them by the sword.

Warned by the king of Edom, the children of Israel did not engage in any confrontation with Esau's descendents because the LORD told Moses not to. They dismantled the camp and journeyed southeast towards Mount Hor, which is located northeast of the Gulf of Aqaba. Having said that, the statement that the children of Israel went to Mount Hor might sound incorrect because Mount Hor ran within the borders of the Edomite kingdom. As you know the king of Edom did not permit Moses and the children of Israel to pass through his country. So! How can the children of Israel be camped at Mount Hor?

Consider the following: Moses said that God the Creator spoke to him "in mount Hor, by the coast of the land of Edom" (Numbers 20:23). The coast is identified as the "Red Sea"

The Journeys of God the Creator

(Numbers 21:4). Therefore, the camp of the children of Israel was located by the "coast of the land of Edom," which is the northern part of the Gulf of Aqaba? In fact the record states, "37 And they removed from Kadesh, and pitched in mount Hor, in the edge of the land of Edom" (Numbers 33:37). The statement "in the edge of the land of Edom" means just that; they were camped at the border (edge) of Edom. And while they were camped at the border of Edom, Moses, Aaron, and Eleazar went to the mountain of Hor.

When they arrived on top of the mountain, the Creator told them that Aaron was going to die there. But, before Aaron died, He asked that Aaron's position as a high priest be transferred to his son Eleazar. Moses took Aaron's priestly garments, he placed them upon Eleazar, and Eleazar became the high priest. After Aaron transferred his title to Eleazar, they said their good byes, and there, Aaron died in their fortieth year of their wanderings, as the LORD had predicted. There on Mount Hor, Moses and Eleazar buried Aaron. When they came down from the mountain, without Aaron, Moses explained to the children of Israel that Aaron their high priest had died; and he added, the Creator appointed Eleazar, his son, to the administration work of a high priest.

Here is the account: "22 And the children of Israel, even the whole congregation, journeyed from Kadesh, and came unto mount Hor. 23 And the LORD spake unto Moses and Aaron in mount Hor, by the coast of the land of Edom, saying, 24 Aaron shall be gathered unto his people: for he shall not enter into the land which I have given unto the children of Israel, because ye rebelled against My word at the water of Meribah. 25 Take Aaron and Eleazar his son, and bring them up unto mount Hor: 26 And strip Aaron of his garments, and put them upon Eleazar his son: and Aaron shall be gathered unto his people, and shall die there. 27 And Moses did as the LORD commanded: and they went up into mount Hor in the sight of all the congregation. 28 And Moses stripped Aaron of his garments, and put them upon Eleazar his son: and Aaron died there on the top of the mount: and Moses and Eleazar came down from the mount. 29 And when all the congregation saw that Aaron was dead, they mourned for Aaron thirty days, even all the house of

The Journeys of God the Creator

Israel" (Numbers 20:22-29).

There in the wilderness of "Araba," before they went and camped in "Zalmonah," the children of Israel continued to complain and point their finger at the Creator and Moses. "5 And the people spake against God, and against Moses, Wherefore have ye brought us up out of Egypt to die in the wilderness? for there is no bread, neither is there any water; and our soul loatheth this light bread" (Numbers 21:5).

It appeared that there was complaint after complaint throughout their journey; as if, they never stopped complaining! After nearly forty years of miraculous provisions of food, water, health, protection, and the containment of their raiment, one would think that the children of Israel would stop complaining and stop using derogatory language against the Creator. Instead of thanking Him for the privilege to be His people and help to spread His goodness and mercies to the surrounding pagan nations, the children of Israel rebelled against God the Creator again! It got so bad that their sins persisted, to a point, where the Creator removed Himself from the camp of Israel in order to avoid their destruction because of their sins. And He also removed His protection from the children of Israel and left them on their own to do as they pleased.

As the revolt increased against God the Creator, all of the sudden, horrifying cries swelled throughout the camp! One could hear cries of anguish here and there throughout the camp. Then, those cries of anguish amplified and turned into horror. As the terror increased throughout the camp, it was realized that the children of Israel were attacked by, what it seemed like, armies of fiery deadly serpents that were sprouting like vines from the soil. They were biting and coiling around their terrorized victims. Many serpents could be seen coming out from the sand and rocks attacking viciously the children of Israel. Terror was spreading throughout the camp. Cries of pain, agony, and torment could be heard emanating throughout the camp. Wailing and remorse increased. Because of the multiple snake bites, the children of Israel could be seen falling like cut trees to the ground, and on top of semi

The Journeys of God the Creator

dead and dead bodies. The dead were fast mounting up in numbers because help was nowhere in sight. Finally, a cold reality set in. God the Creator could not be seen above His Sanctuary. Help was not present. Failure to escape the multiple attacks and bites of the slithering unexpected fiery intruders, set in the children of Israel the desperation for deliverance and protection. The living with those who were dying screamed at Moses for help. Realizing their sinful acts towards the Creator, they said that they were sorry for their sins and asked for forgiveness.

As the children of Israel continued in their agony and pain, to fight of the deadly serpents, Moses inquired of the Creator as to what he should do? The Creator said to Moses that he was to make a bronze serpent and mounted on a pole and say to the children of Israel to look upon the bronze serpent, and they shall be saved. And the Creator added, "They must believe." And Moses did as the Creator suggested. Those individuals who looked at the bronze serpent and believed what God the Creator said, they were healed from the poisonous snakebites. Those who did not believe died. And those persons who believed and were not bitten by the scorpions and serpents, they were not attacked by the venomous serpents.

As the serpents slithered away from the people and crawled over the dead bodies, one could see the trauma in the people's faces. Some were crying for their dead loved ones. Others were burying their dead, and many were clinging to each other from fear. And many were clinging for their lives. Others found comfort in their loved ones arms. The trauma could be seen throughout the camp upon the thousands of living faces, and on the bodies of the dead, which had fallen in anguish, where they struggled for help and safety. An observer could catch sight of the children of Israel in their agonizing arena of grief, while they were sorting the dead bodies and giving them to their loved ones to bury. The whole surrounding area of the camp had turned into a massive graveyard.

The tragedy was so great that in one day twenty three thousand people died in the camp of Israel from the snakebites. A needless loss, don't you think? It was an awesome reminder that without

The Journeys of God the Creator

God the Creator there was no hope for their sinful lives. The children of Israel had a choice to make, they could abandon the Creator or fulfill the promise that was made to them and to their forefathers to go and inherit the Promised Land.

Just before the children of Israel reached the Brook of Zered, only three people remained alive from the original group that came out of Egypt and were counted. The original group that was counted, as warriors, died before they reached the land of Moab. The rest of the people were the offspring from that original group. Their offspring were more willing to go and possess the Promised Land than their parents. Because they were willing to go and possess the Promised Land, God the Creator veered the children of Israel northward over the Brook of Zered, northeast of the borders of Edom, and onwards to the territory of Moab, which is east of the Dead Sea. The country of Edom was located a number of miles northeast from the corner of Gulf of Aqaba. The kingdom of Edom extended all the way up to the southern tip of the Salt Sea and eastward from those points of reference. Gulf of Aqaba is the northern Gulf of the Red Sea.

After thirty-eight years of wandering throughout the wilderness, those individuals who were counted and had refused the first time to enter and possess the Promised Land died before they crossed the Brook of Zered. Only those individuals who were not counted, and the children of the parents who were counted crossed the Brook of Zered and entered into the Promised Land, which spanned on both sides of the Jordan River.

In addition, Moses, Joshua, and Caleb had also remained alive and entered the land of Moab. But in the case of Moses, his stay was short lived. Moses died in the land of Moab. He did not remain alive to inherit the Promised Land.

What happened, as you probably already know, before Moses died, they were camped in the land of Moab. During that time, the Creator took Moses on top of Mount Nebo on the east side of the River Jordan to see the rest of the Promised Land. Although Moses pleaded with God the Creator to let him remain in the Promised Land, he was not permitted. After Moses saw all of the Promised

The Journeys of God the Creator

Land, Moses died at the age of one hundred and twenty on top of Mount Nebo. The Creator took Moses' body and buried him in the valley of Moab,

> "6 over against Bethpeor: where no man knoweth of his sepulcher unto this day" (Deuteronomy 34:6).

After Moses died in the land of Moab, God the Creator set Joshua as the leader of the children of Israel.

The land of Moab is located on the east side of the Salt Sea, better known today as the Dead Sea.

Only Caleb, Joshua, the children, and those who were not counted were brought near the River Jordan. There, east of the River Jordan, at Shittim, the camp of Israel was erected, which was a short distance from the perverted mighty city called Jericho.

Jericho was located west of the camp of Israel, which was about five miles on the other side of the River Jordan. There, in the east side of Jordan, the children of Israel waited for Joshua to give the command to cross over the River Jordan and go to possess the rest of the Promised Land. But since the water of the river was too deep and too swift, the children of Israel thought that they had to wait for a long time before they could cross over the River Jordan. They said that the river was too dangerous to cross this time of year. The livestock, wagons, men, women, and children would easily be swept away in the turbulent spring currents of the river. But God the Creator called upon Joshua and instructed him to get the camp ready to move and go through the River Jordan and possess the rest of the Promised Land.

Joshua spoke to the leaders of Israel and told them that they should start preparing the camp to move. They were to make preparation to cross the River Jordan. Joshua also spoke to the Levites; they were to dismantle the Sanctuary, take the Ark of the Covenant, and lead the way through the River Jordan. Joshua told the priests that they should not worry about the massive and turbulent water of the River Jordan. He said to them that as soon as the soles of their sandals touch the water of the river, the water of

The Journeys of God the Creator

the river would part and the flow of water will be held back. And when the priests see the water stop flowing, then they were to go in the middle of the riverbed, with the Ark of the Covenant and wait there until such time the children of Israel and their livestock crossed to the other side safely. Thus, the priests prepared as Joshua commanded them.

The priests were to follow Joshua's command to the letter.

In addition, the leader of each tribe was told to pick up a big rock from the riverbed, while they were crossing the river. The leaders were told to take the rock with them and keep it until such time they combined all of the twelve rocks in one pile in memory of their crossing.

After the leaders and the priests were all instructed what to do, Joshua told them that in the following day, they were to dismantle the Sanctuary and prepare their tribes to cross the River Jordan in an orderly manner.

The next day the children of Israel did as Joshua had directed, and they all crossed into the rest of the Promised Land without encountering any resistance from the armies of Jericho, and from the other tribes of Canaan.

The spies of Jericho, who were sent by their king, observed how the river was dried up, while the children of Israel crossed to the other side of the River Jordan. They observed how the river literally stopped flowing downwards from the place of the crossing. The fish, frogs, bugs, and other wild life all of the sudden found their habitats gone. Many species were left stranded. The river bottom, from bank to bank, could be seen empty for miles upon

The Journeys of God the Creator

miles down its winding path. They also observed the water of the river heaped up like a towering wall across the river where the priests stood. The water of the river was backed up above the crossing for miles, and one could see the flooding of the low land. All of the sudden the people were wondering where the large amount of water was coming from? Their fields and groves were flooded? Their livestock ran away from the area, and some of the habitats were drenched with water? Some areas were turning into lakes!

When the spies saw what had taken place, they fled and told their commanders. In turn the commanders told the king of Jericho. For fear, they decided it was best that their army, and all their citizens stayed in the city. And the gates of the city's wall were to be kept closed. They said, "It is their God that dried the water of the river. He has gathered the water in to heaps." And they feared the God of Israel because they had heard what He had done to the Egyptians and to those who fought with Israel.

After the children of Israel crossed the River Jordan and went further into the Promised Land, they traveled towards the plains of the city of Gilgal, which was about three miles west from the River Jordan. They stayed there and organized themselves. And, while the children of Israel were camped at Gilgal, the children of Israel were circumcised and kept the Passover.

But something strange happened at the end of their first year's stay, while they were there in the plains of Gilgal; they noticed that it did not rain manna from the sky any more! It was explained to the children of Israel that there was not going to be any more food and water supplied by God the Creator for them. The reason the Creator, the LORD God of Israel, was not going to supply the rations for them any more, was due to the fact that on the land, which they were standing on, it was capable of providing ample food and water to sustain all of the children of Israel, and the needs of their livestock. The children of Israel accepted the explanation and went about gathering diverse food that was available in the vicinity.

Now, the task of reckoning was to fall upon the inhabitants of

The Creator of Genesis 1:1-Who is He?   By: *Philip Mitanidis*
The Journeys of God the Creator

Canaan for their debase sinful acts. The curse of Noah, upon the descendents of Ham, was upon them. The descendants of Ham refused to recognize God the Creator. They chose to seek after satanic orientated priests, seers, astrologers, idols, and gods, which they appeased by sacrificing their sons and daughters to them. They did not recognize the Creator as the God of the universe and hated those that did. That is one of the reasons why they wanted to eradicate the children of Israel to oblivion.

Although the Canaanites had heard what God the Creator did to the Egyptians and saw the proof in the drying up of the River Jordan, they hardened their hearts like Pharaoh, and were bound in unison to rid the Israelites from their land.

But, retribution was at hand. Like the antediluvians, the Canaanites did not want to repent. They chose to live in sin, and chose to spread sin wherever they went. Now they had a choice to make because God the Creator was moving in the area to live. And while God the Creator was in the area, like the camp of Israel, the land had to be clean from sin, sinful acts, and from unrepentant sinners. The Canaanites could stay if they repented; or they could move? If they repented, no harm would come to them; but if they stayed to fight, without repenting, they would die.

As you probably know, they became defiant against God the Creator, and stayed there to fight Him.

On their way inland, the first obstacle the children of Israel were confronted with was the mighty city of Jericho. The inhabitants of this towering fortress did not want to repent, move, or join God's people. They chose to fight the Creator to death.

Jericho was a vile fortress, which was not easily overcome by its former enemies. Although it seemed impenetrable to the human eye, with the help of God the Creator, this contemptible pagan city was going to be overthrown, as the Creator told Joshua.

One day, as Joshua was traveling in the vicinity of Jericho, which was about four miles south west of Gilgal, he wondered how he was going to overthrow this mighty fortress? Then, God the Creator spoke to Joshua and said, "2 I have given into thine hand Jericho, and the king thereof, and the mighty men of valour. 3 And

The Journeys of God the Creator

ye shall compass the city, all ye men of war, and go round about the city once. Thus shalt thou do six days. 4 And seven priests shall bear before the ark seven trumpets of rams' horns: and the seventh day ye shall compass the city seven times, and the priests shall blow with the trumpets. 5 And it shall come to pass, that when they make a long blast with the ram's horn, and when ye hear the sound of the trumpet, all the people shall shout with a great shout; and the wall of the city shall fall down flat, and the people shall ascend up every man straight before him" (Joshua 6:2-5).

Joshua did as God the Creator commanded, and the walls of Jericho came tumbling down to the ground. The armed men went in and destroyed everybody in the city with the exception of Rahab the prostitute. Her household was spared because she hid the two Israelite spies from the authorities of Jericho, before Israel crossed the River Jordan.

When the surrounding kings heard what happened to Jericho, fear was instilled in them. But in spite of the utter destruction of Jericho, and the revelation of the power of God the Creator, the kings of Canaan still remained defiant towards the Creator and towards the children of Israel.

So Joshua continued with the campaign, as Moses had written. Moses said,

"2 Ye shall utterly destroy all the places, wherein the nations which ye shall possess served their gods, upon the high mountains, and upon the hills, and under every green tree: 3 And ye shall overthrow their altars, and break their pillars, and burn their groves with fire; and ye shall hew down the graven images of their gods, and destroy the names of them out of that place" Deuteronomy 12:2, 3

Joshua went throughout the land destroying those who would not leave Canaan and those who would not repent. And when he had acquired enough land, He pitched the Sanctuary of the Creator in "Shiloh" and divided the land amongst the tribes of Israel.

Finally, the children of Israel did settle in the Promised Land.

The Journeys of God the Creator

Although they settled in the land, I must add, they did not eradicate all of their enemies as they were told to do so; therefore because of their stubbornness and complacency, the Creator allowed some of their enemies to remain in the land as a reminder of their disobedience to His admonition and to the Covenant.

It did not have to be that way?

The children of Israel could have retained all of the Promised Land, and its borders constantly expanding, if they only listened to the Creator's admonitions. Unfortunately, even the successors of Joshua did not comply with the LORD'S admonitions. Many times they abandoned the Creator, the LORD God of their fathers, and chose to serve the heathen gods, and the gods of their imagination. Consequently, their borders shrunk and the land was taken away from them a number of times; and the children of Israel, as you probably already know, even today, as it was written by Moses, they are scattered all over the planet without a country to call their own. (See Deuteronomy 28.)

This catastrophe was predicted by Moses, and by the prophets that followed. The prophets of old warned the children of Israel time after time what would happen if they rejected the Creator, the LORD God of their fathers, and His counsel.

The Creator's protection was removed from the children of Israel because they abandoned Him. Satan and his angels took over their lives and led them into ruin. All because they chose to abhor righteousness and love their evil living.

If only there were more people like Moses, Joshua, and Samuel. Today Israel would have been a beacon of light and forever expanding its borders, as it was promised, with converts for the Creator of the universe. If they did that, the plan of salvation for man would have been completed today. Sin and sinner would have been eradicated, and the Creator would have a clean universe today.

But, on a positive note, one of the many beautiful events, which took place in the Old Testament (OT), was during the time the children of Israel settled in the Promised Land. I find it so beautiful that it elates me every time I think of how it could have been with the children of Israel throughout their history, and even today.

The Journeys of God the Creator

This is what excites me: After the children of Israel settled in the Promised Land, the children of Israel were admonished to go to Shiloh and worship the LORD of hosts, who resided there in His Sanctuary, which Moses had built. Every year during the Passover, the Day of Atonement, and feast days, the children of Israel would go to Shiloh and worship there. They would take their families and come from all over the land to meet with the Creator who dwelt between the two cherubims, in the "most holy place." When the children of Israel left their homes unattended, there was no human agency to guard their homes, fields, orchards, livestock, and their belongings; they left their homes, by faith, unprotected and traveled to Shiloh. The record reveals that all who went to Shiloh to worship the Creator the LORD God of Israel did not worry about their enemies. They did not worry that their enemy would go in and take all that they had from their homes and farms. They did not worry that their homes would be burnt, robbed, or their livestock taken because past experience had shown that the Creator the LORD God of their fathers sent His angels and protected their property while they went to worship Him in Shiloh.

Can you picture thousands upon thousands of the children of Israel coming to Shiloh with their children to worship God the Creator without worrying about their homes and all of their possessions? When the children of Israel went back to their homes, after they had finished worshipping the Creator in Shiloh, they found all of their property as they had left it. There was no harm done to their livestock, homes, fields, or to their orchards. They found everything intact.

Isn't that beautiful?

Can you see the trust the children of Israel had in God their Creator during Joshua's days?

What a beautiful relationship!

Now, I am not going to go into a lot of details regarding the tribes of Israel and how they settled into the Promised Land; but I will briefly describe where the tribes of Israel settled, and what happened to the Sanctuary of God the Creator, which Moses built and the Sanctuary, which Solomon built, in order to show you the

The Journeys of God the Creator

duration of the Creator's residence in His Sanctuary.

The tribes of Israel settled in the Promise Land, commonly known as Canaan. Canaan encompasses the land from the Mediterranean Sea, and all the way eastward beyond the River Jordan. Canaan also covered the land south of the Sidonian territory, but more precisely, from the city of Dan, which is north of Damascus and all the way down to the land of the Amorites, and to Beer-sheba, which is in the Negeb. The children of Israel also settled east of the River Jordan. The Israelites settled in the land as follows: The tribe of Simeon settled in the lower part of Canaan, in an area, which is called the Negeb. The Negeb encompasses the Wilderness of Zin, which is southwest of the Salt Sea, and as far as the Mediterranean Sea. Judah settled north of Simeon, in between the Salt Sea and the Mediterranean Sea. Judah's territory went northward close to Jerusalem. The tribe of Dan settled north of Judah, west of Jerusalem, and as far as the Mediterranean Sea. Benjamin settled east of Dan, north of Judah, and as far as the River Jordan. The tribe of Benjamin occupied some of the familiar cities known as Jerusalem, Beth, Gibeon, Gilgal, and Jericho city. North of the tribes of Dan and Benjamin, the tribe of Ephraim occupied the territory. Their land spanned from the Mediterranean Sea to the River Jordan. And north of Ephraim one half of the tribe of Manasseh occupied a large chunk of land from the Mediterranean Sea to the River Jordan. The tribe of Issachar was located north of Manasseh and spanned from the valley of Megiddo to the River Jordan. Zebulon was sandwiched between the tribe of Asher and Naphtali. Asher occupied the land to the west of Zebulon and as far as the. Mediterranean Sea. Naphtali occupied the land east of Zebulon as far as the Sea of Galilee, and further north of Zebulon. The tribe of Reuben settled east of the Salt Sea and occupied the land from shortly above the tip of the Salt Sea to about half way down the Salt Sea, and eastward. The tribe of Gad and the other half tribe of Manasseh jointly occupied the land north of Reuben and all the way near the southern part of the Sea of Galilee. And their border spanned east of the River Jordan.

Now, I am not going to go into detail why there are thirteen

The Journeys of God the Creator

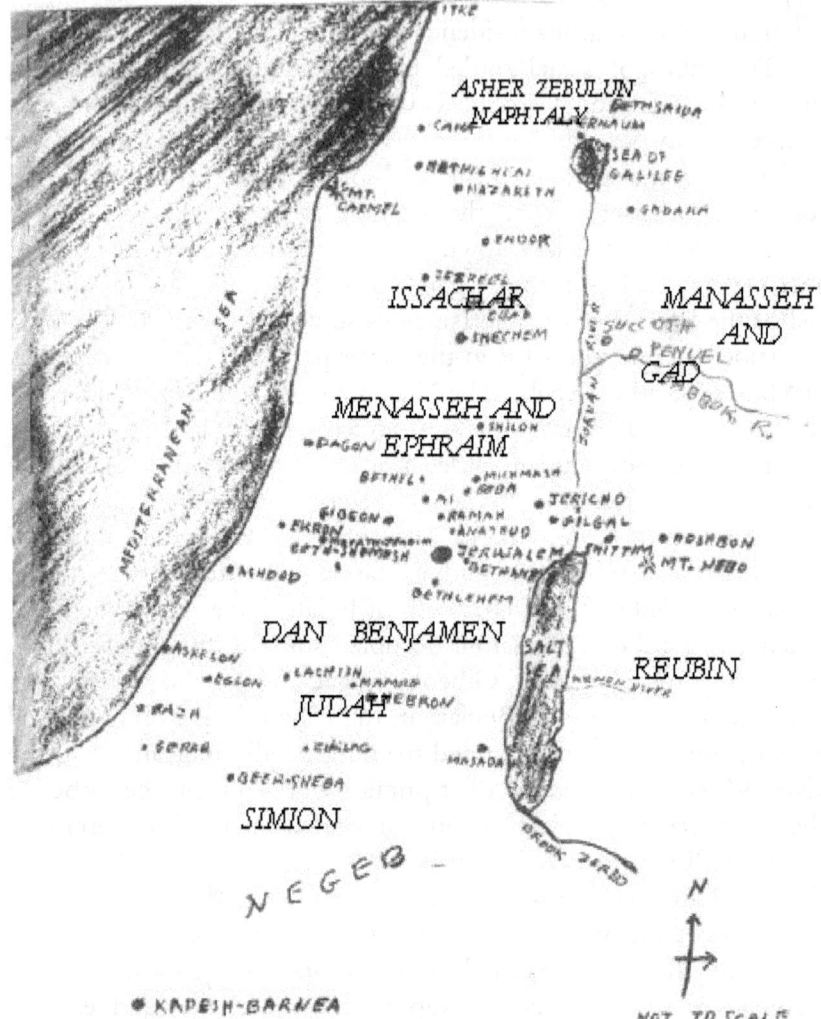

tribes and only twelve settlements, all of the sudden, but I will say this much, if you choose to do the research, consider what happened in Egypt before Israel and his sons went to Egypt; and during the time, when Joshua divided the land of Canaan and the land east of the River Jordan.

And, as far as the Sanctuary is concerned, which Moses had built, it remained in the middle of the tribes of Israel. It was erected

The Journeys of God the Creator

in a place called "Shiloh." As you probably already know, Shiloh is located west of Jericho and north of Bethel. If you are not familiar with Bethel, then, think north of Jerusalem. After Jerusalem is Gibeon; and after Gibeon is Bethel, and after Bethel is Shiloh. The distance from Jerusalem to Shiloh is approximately twenty-five miles.

As you already observed, the Sanctuary that was built, during the time of Moses, was made in the form of a tent. That tent, which was disassembled every time the children of Israel moved and assembled every time the Cloud stopped, was commonly referred to as the "House of God." That very same House of God (Sanctuary), which Moses built over forty years ago, the Levite priests carried it into the Promised Land. There, in Shiloh, they continued with its ceremonial services, after the children of Israel were circumcised and kept the Passover in the plains of Gilgal, when they first crossed over the River Jordan. When they divided the Promised Land amongst themselves, as I stated earlier, decision was made to let the Sanctuary rest in Shiloh, which is in the center of the tribes of Israel. This was done for accessibility and convenience for all of the children of Israel.

"29 And it came to pass after these things, that Joshua the son of Nun, the servant of the LORD, died, being an hundred and ten years old. 30 And they buried him in the border of his inheritance in Timnathserah, which is in mount Ephraim, on the north side of the hill of Gaash" (Joshua 24:29, 30).

After Joshua died, during the time of the Judges, the House of God remained in Shiloh. One major thing that happened to the House of God, during the judges, was the removal of the Ark of the Covenant from the House of God. This happened during the time when the children of Israel lost the war to the Philistines.

The Philistines declared war upon the children of Israel because God the Creator had removed His protection from Israel due to their sinful acts, which they practiced. More precisely, this event took place during the time when Eli the high priest was in office. The high priest Eli, and his sons, Hophni and Phinehas, mainly influenced the children of Israel to commit sinful acts. Eli's sons

The Journeys of God the Creator

polluted the Sanctuary and its services for such a long time that their evil acts were known all over the country. They, the children of Eli, even had sex with the women who came to the services of the Sanctuary. Although Eli, the high priest, did not like what his sons were doing in the Sanctuary, he, nonetheless, was not able to stop them from committing fornication. And the worse part was that Eli did not remove them from the Sanctuary, and from officiating over the services of the Sanctuary.

In the interim, Eli had a little boy given to him by his parents in order to serve the LORD. Eli took the child under his care and taught him the ways of the LORD and the services of the Sanctuary. And the little boy, whose name was Samuel, "18 ministered before the LORD, being a child, girded with a linen ephod. 19 Moreover his mother [Hanah] made him a little coat, and brought it to him from year to year, when she came up with her husband to offer the yearly sacrifice." "22 Now Eli was very old, and heard all that his sons did unto all Israel; and how they lay with the women that assembled at the door of the tabernacle of the congregation. 23 And he said unto them, Why do ye such things? for I hear of your evil dealings by all this people. 24 Nay, my sons; for it is no good report that I hear: ye make the LORD'S people to transgress" (1 Samuel 2:18, 19, 22-24).

As Eli and his sons continued to pollute the Sanctuary, the word of the LORD came one night to the little boy Samuel; and Samuel when he heard the voice he thought it was Eli the priest who was calling him. He got up from his bed, went to Eli, and said to him, "here I am!" Eli was stunned by Samuel's wakeup call! Eli knew that he had not called him. And when the little boy Samuel went to Eli the third time, Eli said to Samuel, "Go back to bed and when you hear the voice again say, 'Speak, LORD; for Thy servant heareth'." And sure enough the voice did call upon Samuel; and Samuel said, "10 Speak; for thy servant heareth. 11 And the LORD said to Samuel, Behold, I will do a thing in Israel, at which both the ears of every one that heareth it shall tingle. 12 In that day I will perform against Eli all things which I have spoken concerning his house: when I begin, I will also make an end. 13 For I have told him that I will judge his house for ever for the iniquity which he

The Creator of Genesis 1:1-Who is He?   By: *Philip Mitanidis*
The Journeys of God the Creator

knoweth; because his sons made themselves vile, and he restrained them not. 14 And therefore I have sworn unto the house of Eli, that the iniquity of Eli's house shall not be purged with sacrifice nor offering for ever." "19 And Samuel grew, and the LORD was with him, and did let none of His words fall to the ground" (1 Samuel 3:10 -14, 19).

But the children of Israel did not adhere to the words of God the Creator and did that which was not pleasing in His sight. God the Creator, therefore, removed Himself from His House in Shiloh, and when the children of Israel went to battle with the Philistines, the Philistines killed approximately four thousand men of Israel.

Here is the account: "3 And when the people were come into the camp, the elders of Israel said, Wherefore hath the LORD smitten us to day before the Philistines? Let us fetch the ark of the covenant of the LORD out of Shiloh unto us, that, when it cometh among us, it may save us out of the hand of our enemies. 4 So the people sent to Shiloh, that they might bring from thence the ark of the covenant of the LORD of hosts, which dwelleth between the cherubims: and the two sons of Eli, Hophni and Phinehas, were there with the ark of the covenant of God. 5 And when the ark of the covenant of the LORD came into the camp, all Israel shouted with a great shout, so that the earth rang again. 6 And when the Philistines heard the noise of the shout, they said, What meaneth the noise of this great shout in the camp of the Hebrews? And they understood that the ark of the LORD was come into the camp. 7 And the Philistines were afraid, for they said, God is come into the camp. And they said, Woe unto us! for there hath not been such a thing heretofore. 8 Woe unto us! who shall deliver us out of the hand of these mighty Gods? these are the Gods that smote the Egyptians with all the plagues in the wilderness."

But, the Philistine leaders said to their soldiers, "9 Be strong, and quit yourselves like men, O ye Philistines, that ye be not servants unto the Hebrews, as they have been to you: quit yourselves like men, and fight. 10 And the Philistines fought, and Israel was smitten, and they fled every man into his tent: and there was a very great slaughter; for there fell of Israel thirty thousand footmen. 11

The Journeys of God the Creator

And the ark of God was taken; and the two sons of Eli, Hophni and Phinehas, were slain" (1 Samuel 4:3-11).

And when Eli heard what happened to the army of Israel, he fell backwards from his chair, broke his neck and died. Eli was ninety-eight years old when he died. He had served Israel for forty years.

Meanwhile, the Philistines took the Ark of the Covenant and put it in the temple of their pagan fish god whose name was "Dagon." And when the priest and dignitaries came into the temple the following day, to see their coveted prize, they found the huge statute, Dagon, bowing down to the Ark of the Covenant! They could not figure out how that could have happened? Nonetheless, they repositioned Dagon back unto his place, and wondered about the meaning of the incident. The following day when they went into the temple, again, they found Dagon with its head and the palm of his hands cut off and bowing down before the Ark? Since the authorities could not find who or what had caused Dagon to prostrate himself before the Ark of the Covenant, they were scared and amazed at the event! In bewilderment, they put Dagon together again and set him back on his place. And when the Philistines did not return the Ark of the Covenant to the Israelites, God the Creator sent grievous sores upon the Philistines. And when they insisted on keeping the Ark of the Covenant, God sent severe plagues upon them.

Finally because the Philistines could not tolerate the anguish that was caused by the plagues upon them, they decided to move the Ark and place it into another city. Then, God sent the plagues there upon the people, in that city. And they intern tried to send the Ark into another city. The plagues were so bad and grievous that eventually nobody wanted the Ark of the Covenant in their temples or in their cities.

After seven months of terror and pain upon those who retained the Ark of the Covenant, the "2 Philistines called for the priests and the diviners, saying, What shall we do to the Ark of the LORD? tell us wherewith we shall send it to his place. 3 And they said, If ye send away the Ark of the God of Israel, send it not empty; but in any wise

The Journeys of God the Creator

return him a trespass offering: then ye shall be healed, and it shall be known to you why His hand is not removed from you" (1 Samuel 6:2, 3).

Finally, they put the Ark of the Covenant on a cart and placed gifts of precious stones and golden figurines upon it. These gifts matched the number of kings the Philistines had. The numbers of gods they worshipped, and according to the number of cities the Philistines had. When all of the gifts were loaded upon the cart, with the hope of appeasing the Gods of the Ark, they sent it on its way back to the Israelites without a driver.

The Philistines watched the cart intently to see if it was going to go to the Israelites or not because they feared that the animals might turn around with the cart and come back to them and receive more retribution for taking it in the first place.

As the cart continued on its way, they were relieved to see that the animals did not turn around and come back to them. The cart stopped at Joshua's field; and when the workers saw the Ark of the Covenant on the cart, they went and reported it to the Hebrew authorities. They in turn came and took the Ark of the Covenant, and let it stay in the house of Abinadab who lived in Gibeah.

The Ark of the Covenant remained in Abinadab's house for twenty years. After King Saul's demise, David became the king of Judah first and reigned for seven years in Hebron. After the seven years, David captured Jerusalem, and then, he became the king of Israel. When David moved to Jerusalem to live, he ordered the removal of the Ark of the Covenant from the house of Abinadab, and ordered the Ark to be brought to Jerusalem. Abinadab was already dead at this point of time. He had left the Ark of the Covenant in the keeping of his grandsons. Unfortunately, when King David ordered the Ark of the Covenant to be brought to Jerusalem, one of Abinadab's grandsons, whose name was Uzzah, died on the way to Jerusalem because he touched the Ark. For fear, King David diverted the Ark from its destination and placed it in another house that was located outside of Jerusalem. The Ark of

The Journeys of God the Creator

the Covenant rested in the house of Obededom the Gittite.

After realizing the blessing Obededom received because the Ark of the Covenant was in his home, King David thought of ways to secure the Ark and bring it in Jerusalem. So he had his trade's men build a tent, and told them to set it up in the city of Jerusalem. Finally, David had the Levite priests remove the Ark of the Covenant from Obededom's house and place it inside the tent, which he had built for it.

One day, as King David was sitting in his palace, which was made out of cedar wood, he became very troubled. He called Nathan the prophet of God and said to him, "2 See now, I dwell in an house of cedar, but the ark of God dwelleth within curtains. 3 And Nathan said to the king, Go, do all that is in thine [your] heart; for the LORD is with thee [you]. 4 And it came to pass that night, that the word of the LORD came unto Nathan, saying,

> "5 Go and tell My servant David, Thus saith the LORD, Shalt thou build Me an house for Me to dwell in? 6 Whereas I have not dwelt in any house since the time that I brought up the children of Israel out of Egypt, even to this day, but have walked in a tent and in a tabernacle. 7 In all the places wherein I have walked with all the children of Israel spake I a word with any of the tribes of Israel, whom I commanded to feed My people Israel, saying, Why build ye not Me an house of cedar?" (2 Samuel 7:2-7)

God the Creator asked a question; and that question was directed to King David. He said, "Shalt thou build me an house for me to dwell in?" God the Creator reminded King David that ever since Moses built the tent, He dwelt in it. And the Creator added even up until this day I "have walked in a tent and in a tabernacle."

So, was King David going to build God the Creator a house made out of cedar to live in?

Nathan said to David, "Go do all that is in thine [your] heart; for the LORD is with thee [you]."

The Journeys of God the Creator

David embarked upon the project of building a house for God the Creator, but the Creator told David that he could not build Him a house. David was disappointed. So he asked the Creator why he could not build the house for Him, and the Creator responded to David by telling him, "The reason you cannot build Me a house is due to the fact that you have too much blood on your hands." David was devastated; but the Creator added, you can help prepare the plans and the means to have the house build for Me by your son Solomon when he becomes a king after you."

David was overjoyed to hear that he could contribute to the "House of God." David gave enormous amounts of money, silver, gold, of his time, and preparing the blueprints for the building. At the same time, he also asked his subjects to contribute towards the building fund of what ever they were able to give. There appeared willing hands from all of the tribes of Israel, and a desire to erect a house for God the Creator in Jerusalem. David was pleased with the response and encouragement that he received from everyone.

David continued to prepare for the building of the House of God, and, at the same time, he continued to interact with his son Solomon regarding the plans and the design of the building. He also chose the sight where the House of God was to be built upon. It was on the threshing floor of Araunah the Jebusite, which was located near the north wall of Jerusalem. David chose that piece of land because the Creator appeared unto Abraham and his son there; and it was the same spot where God the Creator appeared unto David.

So, David went to see Araunah, and when Araunah saw David, he said to him, "21 Wherefore is my lord the king come to his servant? And David said, To buy the threshingfloor of thee, to build an altar unto the LORD, that the plague may be stayed from the people. 22 And Araunah said unto David, Let my lord the king take and offer up what seemeth good unto him: behold, here be oxen for burnt sacrifice, and threshing instruments and other instruments of the oxen for wood. 23 All these things did Araunah, as a king, give unto the king. And Araunah said unto the king, The LORD thy God accept thee. 24 And the king said unto Araunah, Nay; but I will

The Journeys of God the Creator

surely buy it of thee at a price: neither will I offer burnt offerings unto the LORD my God of that which doth cost me nothing. So David bought the threshingfloor and the oxen for fifty shakels of silver. 25 And David built there an altar unto the LORD, and offered burnt offerings and peace offerings, So the LORD was entreated for the land, and the plague was stayed from Israel" (2 Samuel 24:21-25).

The property was bought and it was ready for the commencement of building the House of God upon it. The project of building a house for God the Creator out of cut rock and of cedar wood became a passion for King David until his dying day.

King David died on his fortieth year of his reign. He reigned for seven years at Hebron, and thirty-three years in Jerusalem. He was buried in the city of David.

Just before David died, he called his son Solomon and gave him this beautiful advice. He said to him,

"2 I go the way of all the earth: be thou [you] strong therefore, and shew thyself a man; 3 And keep the charge of the LORD thy God, to walk in His ways, to keep His statutes, and His commandments, and His judgments, and His testimonies, as it is written in the law of Moses, that thou [you] mayest prosper in all that thou doest, and whithersoever thou turnest thyself: 4 That the LORD may continue His word which He spake concerning me, saying, If thy children take heed to their way, to walk before Me in truth with all their heart and with all their soul, there shall not fail thee (said He) a man on the throne of Israel." 1 Kings 2:2-4

Shortly before his father died, Solomon began his reign over Israel with few problems of which he quickly put an end to them. It took Solomon about four years to resolve his political problems, but after that, he concentrated on building the House of God on the threshing-floor of Araunah.

After all the pre-cut stones, beams, furniture, and preparation for the Sanctuary, King David and Solomon accomplished, it still took seven years to build the House of God. The erection of the Sanctuary was noiseless. In reverence to God the Creator and for His house, there were no tools used to build it. Finally, the House of God the Creator was completed in all its glory. But there was a snag! The builders could not figure out where to place one of the corner stones for the foundation? So, they rejected it.

When the House of God was finished, Solomon gathered all the children of Israel, to witness the dedication of the Sanctuary to God the LORD of hosts.

About nine hundred and fifty-six BC, God the Creator accepted His new dwelling place in Jerusalem. The Creator dwelt in between the two cherubims in the "most holy place" of His house, which was partly made out of cedar wood

After the dedication, God the Creator appeared to Solomon. This was the second time since Gibeon, the Creator appeared to Solomon. This time, the Creator said to Solomon,

> "3 I have heard thy prayer and thy supplication, that thou hast made before Me: I have hallowed this house, which thou hast built, to put My name there for ever; and Mine eyes and Mine heart shall be there perpetually. 4 And if thou wilt walk before Me, as David thy father walked, in integrity of heart, and in uprightness, to do according to all that I have commanded thee, and wilt keep My statutes and My judgments: 5 Then I will establish the throne of thy kingdom upon Israel for ever, as I promised to David thy father, saying, There shall not fail thee a man upon the throne of Israel" (1 Kings 9:3-5).

Unfortunately, Solomon with all his wisdom failed to stay the course. He started to apostatize in his twilight years. His apostasy was well visible. He went as far as to pacify his many pagan wives by building various idols for them, and altars to put their idols on them. He even put many of the idols in small temples, in the groves for his wives, so that they could go there and worship them.

Although the Creator had blessed Solomon with great wealth and success before his apostasy, soon his kingdom was going to be

The Journeys of God the Creator

divided.

After Solomon died, the children of Israel split the kingdom of Israel into two. There was a king over Judah and Benjamin, and there was a king who reigned over the rest of the tribes. And from there onward, these two kingdoms were recognized as the kingdom of Judah (Jews) and as the kingdom of Israel. Unfortunately, these two kingdoms, contrary to God's will, fought each other, on many occasions, for supremacy.

Eventually, the king was removed from Israel in 722 BC, and the ten tribes were dispersed from their homeland, only the king of Judah remained. The last king that reigned in Judah was terminated in 586 BC by the Babylonian Empire.

God the Creator lived on and off in His Sanctuary up until 586 BC. This was the time when King Nebuchadnezzar, in the third siege of Jerusalem destroyed the city, its walls, and even the Sanctuary of God the Creator. There in total ruins the House of God lay. It was not until after the seventy years of captivity of the children of Israel, by King Nebuchadnezzar that the House of God was rebuilt again. And when the Sanctuary was rebuilt, unfortunately, God the Creator did not reside in it again. He was absent from the "most holy place." The high priest could not see God's glory, during the Day of Atonement above the "mercy seat." In fact the "mercy seat" and the Ark of the Covenant were also absent from the "most holy place." No one seemed to know where the Ark of the Covenant went? Even today, no one knows for sure where it is; at least no one has authenticated and claimed proof of its existence.

Here are some of the references, which refer to the children of Israel when they returned to Jerusalem, after their seventy years of captivity, without mentioning the Ark of the Covenant: "14 And the elders of the Jews builded, and they prospered through the prophesying of Haggai the prophet and Zechariah the son of Iddo. And they builded, and finished it, according to the commandment of the God of Israel, and according to the commandment of Cyrus, and Darius, and Artaxerxes king of Persia. 15 And this house was finished on the third day of the month Adar, which was in the sixth

The Journeys of God the Creator

year of the reign of Darius the king. 16 And the children of Israel, the priests, and the Levites, and the rest of the children of the captivity, kept the dedication of this house of God with joy, 17 And offered at the dedication of this house of God and hundred bullocks, two hundred rams, four hundred lambs; and for a sin offering for all Israel, twelve he goats, according to the number of the tribes of Israel. 18 And they set the priests in their divisions, and the Levites in their courses, for the service of God, which is at Jerusalem; as it is written in the book of Moses" (Ezra 6:14-18).

After their seventy years of captivity, by King Nebuchadnezzar, the children of Israel were allowed to go back to rebuild the city of Jerusalem and to rebuild the Sanctuary of God the Creator. By reading the writings of Jeremiah, Ezekiel, Daniel, and the prophets who were present during the return to Jerusalem, at least three predominant points should be observed from the above presentation:

> 1). Although the Persian king gave the order to have all of the vessels returned to Jerusalem, the Ark of the Covenant was not found amongst the vessels. Ezra declares the king's command. He says; "5 And also let the golden and silver vessels of the house of God, which Nebuchadnezzar took forth out of the temple which is at Jerusalem, and brought unto Babylon, be restored, and brought again unto the temple, which is at Jerusalem, every one to his place, and place them in the house of God" (Ezra 6:5).
>
> If the Ark of the Covenant was amongst the vessels, Ezra would have stated somewhere in his writings that the Levite priests were summoned to go and take the Ark of the Covenant and carry it back to Jerusalem; but he does not give us that reference? In fact, I have not been able to find a reference to that fact in any of the Minor Prophets. Therefore, unless I have missed the reference, I am forced to conclude that the Ark of the Covenant was not there.
>
> 2). The other fact that is presented to us by Ezra, is the

The Journeys of God the Creator

failure in his writings to acknowledge when and if God the Creator accepted the Sanctuary as His dwelling place, during the dedication day, as God the Creator had done in the previous dedications (by Moses and by Solomon when they dedicated their Sanctuaries to God the Creator). One has to wonder how can such an important event, with all its glory, be absent from the writing of Haggai? Should not Haggai or any of his contemporaries have written about the Creator's acceptance of the Sanctuary during its dedication? Yes they should have. But instead, even though God the Creator was absent from the Sanctuary, He said that this inferior House (Sanctuary) would surpass the glory of the previous Sanctuaries that were built for Him. This is what the Creator said: "7 I will fill this house with glory, saith the LORD of hosts," "9 The glory of this latter house shall be greater than of the former, saith the LORD of hosts; and in this place will I give peace, saith the LORD of hosts" (Haggai 2:7, 9).

When was the above claim by the Creator the LORD of hosts fulfilled? For the answer read Matthew 21:10-16, as an example.

3). Although it appears that the Creator the LORD of hosts did not accept the Sanctuary as His dwelling place; it should be observed that He did not abandon the children of Israel. He acknowledged many times that He would be with them as long as they refrained from worshipping other gods. To Haggai the prophet, the Creator said, "2 Speak now to Zerubbabel the son of Shealtiel, governor of Judah, and to Joshua the son of Josedech, the high priest, and to the residue of the people, saying, 3 Who is left among you that saw this house in her first glory? and how do ye see it now? is it not in your eyes in comparison of it as nothing? 4 Yet now be strong, O Zerubbabel, saith the LORD; and be strong, O Joshua, son of Josedech, the high priest; and be strong, all ye people of the land, saith the LORD, and work: for I am with you, saith the LORD of hosts" (Haggai 2:2-4).

The Journeys of God the Creator

Although the children of Israel had rough time building the Sanctuary in Jerusalem, they did finish building it. When they finished building it, they had mixed feelings about it. On one hand, they were happy that they could rebuild the Sanctuary for the LORD of hosts; on the other hand, the Sanctuary paled in comparison to the former Sanctuary, which Solomon built. There was much discussion as to what should have been done, and what should be done to improve the house of God; but the structure was already up, and there was not much one could do at this point to bring it to the former figure.

Knowing what was in their hearts, the Creator the LORD of hosts said to Haggai "Who is left among you that saw this house in her first glory? and how do ye see it now? is it not in your eyes in comparison of it as nothing?" (Haggai 2:3).

In comparison to the former Sanctuary, which Solomon built, this Sanctuary was not in its extravagance. It was dim; but the LORD encouraged the children of Israel not to think in a demeaning manner about the Sanctuary, which they erected because the time is coming, the LORD said that He personally was going to glorify this Sanctuary; and when He does that, this Sanctuary will be more glorious than the previous Sanctuary.

> Here is the account: "7 I will fill this house with glory, saith the LORD of hosts," "9 The glory of this latter house shall be greater than of the former, saith the LORD of hosts; and in this place will I give peace, saith the LORD of hosts" (Haggai 2:7, 9).

With that kind of encouragement from the LORD of hosts, the children of Israel continued with the implementation of the ceremonial law and with the reading of the Torah.

But because the LORD of hosts did not accept the Sanctuary as His dwelling place, at the dedication, and His Shekinah glory could not be seen in the Sanctuary, it did not mean that He abandoned it, its services, or the children of Israel.

No, He did not!

138   The Creator of Genesis 1:1-Who is He?   By: *Philip Mitanidis*
The Journeys of God the Creator_____

The LORD told Haggai to encourage Zerubbabel; he said to him, "Yet now be strong, O Zerubbabel, saith the LORD." And the LORD adds by saying to the children of Israel "I am with you" (Haggai 2:4).

See! He did not abandon them.

If I may add, God the Creator the LORD of hosts has never left His people or a single individual who trusted or trusts in Him. It should be remembered; God the Creator does not leave a person. God will leave a person when that person chooses not to associate himself with God; and even then, the LORD is always waiting with open arms to welcome a person back to His kingdom.

God the Creator has chosen to fellowship with us. Look how many times He went back to the children of Israel. Unfortunately, many have chosen not to have anything to do with Him. All you have to do is to look at the historical overview of the children of Israel and observe how many times they chose to abandon Him. And so it is today, just look around you and observe how many people do you think truly do His will (stop sinning) and abide in Him?

In any case, in summation, the Creator's journeys took Him from Midia to Egypt, and from Egypt to Mount Sinai, and from Mount Sinai to Kadesh-barnea; and when the children of Israel did not want to go and possess the Promised Land, God the Creator of Genesis 1:1 traveled from Kadesh back into the desert for thirty-eight years. And in the fortieth year, the Creator took the children of Israel through Moab country to the east side of the River Jordan to a place called Shittim, which was near that mighty city called Jericho. From the east side of the River Jordan, God the Creator crossed the river last and entered into the rest of the Promised Land. There, in the west side of the River Jordan, the Creator traveled further into the Promised Land and stopped for a while in Gilgal. From Gilgal God the Creator traveled to Shiloh and stayed there for a long time. And from Shiloh He traveled to Kirjath-jearim, and after His 20 years stay in Gibeah, the Creator traveled to Jerusalem. And there in His city, which He had chosen, He dwelt for approximately 396 years before He abandoned His dwelling place

The Journeys of God the Creator

because the children of Israel fell into apostasy. He has not been seen in the "most holy place" of His Sanctuary ever since then.

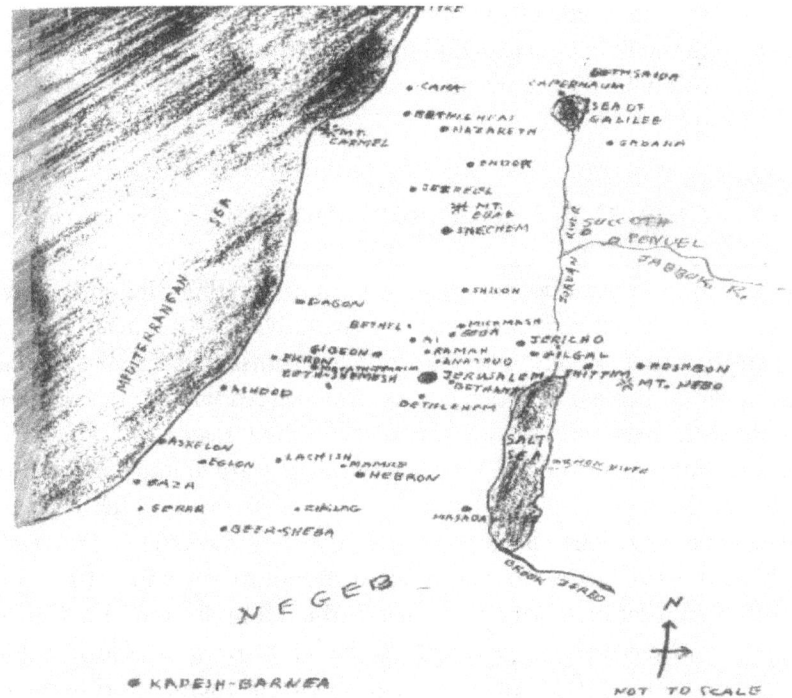

In fact, God the Creator of the universe, and everything that is in it has not been seen in His house, above the "mercy seat," ever since 586 BC. God's journey (1 Samuel 7:6, 7) ended in Jerusalem during the destruction of Jerusalem and the destruction of His house by the enraged army of King Nebuchadnezzar, which started about 606 BC and ended in 586 BC. To confirm what I am saying, today, go to Jerusalem and look for yourself inside the Sanctuary—if they let you—and see if the Shekinah glory of the LORD of hosts is there in the "most holy place" of the Sanctuary?

Please go and look!

Nonetheless, I have brought you this far in the historical sitting of the Creator's journey, from the Torah, as a prerequisite, in order to reveal that it was the Creator of Genesis 1:1 who:

1). Brought Abraham out of the land of Ur
2). Went with Moses and Aaron to Egypt
3). Brought the children of Israel out of Egypt
4). Led the children of Israel into the Promised Land
5). Dwelt in between the cherubims, in His Sanctuary
6). Is the LORD God and the King of Israel
7). Is "the LORD of hosts"
8). Is the sole Creator of Genesis 1:1; and
9). to reveal to you, in the forthcoming pages, who He is.

The Translator's Inconsistencies

Before I start quoting Bible verses from the Old and New Testaments, in order to reveal who is the Creator of Genesis 1:1, let us consider first the inconsistencies many translators create in their mistranslated Bibles, in order to give you an idea what you and I are dealing with, regarding the identity of God the Creator of Gen. 1:1.

Fortunately, in North America, you and I are able to find many Bibles in the market place that are translated from the Hebrew and Greek texts into various languages. But, the unfortunate part of all of these translations is the nightmarish thought that many, if not all, of these translations do not translate the Hebrew and the Greek Scriptures the same or identical to the Hebrew and Greek texts. Therefore you will find many inconsistencies in them. And because of these inconsistencies, the translators have created a big problem for their readers; and that problem is that many of these Bibles not only contradict each other, but, at the same time, they also contradict more severely the Greek inspired Scriptures of the New Testament (NT). These contradictions can readily be seen when you put these Bibles side by side, and compare their contents.

As an example, let me give you the translation of John 1:1, from Greek to English, from the following assortment of Bibles, and you can take the time, and observe for yourself the disagreements that exist amongst these translations.

"1 WHEN ALL THINGS BEGAN, the Word already was. The Word dwelt with God, and what God was, the Word was." John 1:1 (TNEB)

The Translator's Inconsistencies

"1 IN the beginning was the Word, and the Word was with God, and the Word was God." John 1:1 (OKJV)

"1 Originally the Word was, and the Word was with God, and the Word was a god." John 1:1 (NWTCGS)

"1 In the beginning was the one who is called the Word. The Word was with God and was truly God." John 1:1 (CEV)

"1 THE Logos existed in the very beginning, the Logos was with God, the Logos was divine." John 1:1 (Moffatt)

"1 IN THE beginning [before all time] was the Word (dChrist), and the Word was with God, and the Word was God Himself. [Isaiah 9:6]" John 1:1 (Amp.)

If you considered the above verses and compared each verse with the other verses, you should have noticed that each verse says something different from the other verses. And, if you were to further take the above verses and compare them to the Greek inspired Scriptures, you will find that all of these translations are saying something different about Christ the "Word." As you can see, there is no consistency in all of these translations.

These types of translation inconsistencies have created a lot of problems for the reader of the New Testament. In fact, they even have created problems for the majority of the theologians. And because of these discrepancies, many individuals have taken upon themselves to choose sides, as it were because one group believes one translation of the Bible, while another group believes another translation of the Bible, and so on.

These types of translation inconsistencies, it appears, have fragmented Christianity, to a large degree, into thousands of pieces. Just look at the number of religious groups that exist out there; you will find that it is a staggering number. It has been estimated by some reports that there are over twenty thousand religious doctrines out there, which many of them base their beliefs in the Bible. So,

The Translator's Inconsistencies

how is it that there are thousands upon thousands of church denominations out there when there is only one Bible doctrine? Should there not be one doctrine in these churches, which teaches the people to follow?

A person would think so? But that is not the case, when you look at the world and its worship practices.

On the other hand, there are those individuals who have read the Bible, but because of the discrepancies that are created by the translators of the Bible, many of these individuals do not believe in the Bible; therefore, they are not affiliated with any church. And those that are affiliated with various churches, you will find, many of these churches are not based upon the doctrine of the Bible. They have their own beliefs, which are erected upon some other writings or ideologies.

You cannot blame some of these individuals for excluding the doctrine of the Bible from their lives. They reason, how can the Bible be inspired when at one point the Bible says one thing, and in another verse, it contradicts itself?

How can a person say to those individuals, or to even one of those individuals that the Bible is inspired, when they can very easily point to the discrepancies amongst translations and within the various translated verses?

By reading the various Bible translations, you can't!

Therefore, you cannot really blame any or all of those individuals who do not believe the Bible or support any of the Bible doctrines.

In fact, you like myself probably have heard that the Scriptures of the Bible cannot be inspired because the Scriptures have been written by man, and have been rewritten by others, to a point, where the inspired truth has been lost. Or maybe you have heard or you have been told that the inspired Scriptures are contaminated. I have heard that kind of verbiage before many times; and you cannot blame people for thinking that way because of all the discrepancies that are found in the various Bible translations.

Nonetheless, Bible discrepancies of various translations and various objections have been shown and stated to me personally, a

The Translator's Inconsistencies

number of times. My response, to those individuals, has been that the Bible does not contradict it self; it is the translators who contradict the Bible by not translating the verses correctly. And I normally tell people that this fact can be proven by going directly to the Hebrew and to the Greek inspired Scriptures. If you were to go directly to the Hebrew and to the Greek Scriptures, these Scriptures would reveal the translator's mistakes, and the true meaning of the verse or verses.

Although you will find that there are a number of Bibles, which have been translated incorrectly, the problem does not always rest with the incorrect translation. I say that because a person can always verify the verse in the Greek Scriptures or in the Hebrew Scriptures in order to see if the translation is correct or not; but what many times happens is the fact that individuals will misquote the verse or verses in order to support his or her doctrinal beliefs. This not only robs the original contents of the verse, but it compounds the problem in the verse or verses that were translated incorrectly in the first place. Therefore the end result of the verses or verse is a serious disregard for the word of God the Holy Spirit.

Let me give you one example of many, from a familiar ground and show you how people misquote the inspired Scriptures of the Bible by adding words to it, or by changing the verse to read something else. But first, read the following verses and consider what the verses say, before you read my comments. The verses read, "4 Hear, O Israel: The LORD our God is one LORD: 5 And thou shalt love the LORD thy God with all thine heart, and with all thy soul, and with all thy might" (Deuteronomy 6:4, 5).

Have you considered the above verses? If you have, now consider my comments.

You will find Jews, Muslims, and many Christians who believe in the one God theory, as in the numerical one (1) God, will quote the above verses, and state that Moses is referring to one (1) God.

Did you know that?

If you did know, you probably also know what I am going to talk about next! But, if you were not aware of that fact, now that you have read the above verses, what do you say Moses said to the

The Translator's Inconsistencies

children of Israel before he died in the land of Moab? Is he saying to them that there is one (1) God or not?

If you said, Moses is saying that there is one (1) God, as in the numerical one, then ask yourself, where are the words "one God" in the above verses found?

Can you find them?

Obviously the answer is no!

You cannot find the words "one God" in those two verses—can you?

Hence, the comment that there is "one God" in the above verses is an added verbiage to Moses' words. These words do not exist in the above verses. Therefore one's belief that there is "one God," by the use of the above verses, is incorrect because that is not what Moses is saying.

On the other hand what Moses is stating is a simple fact that there is "one LORD." Check it out!

> Here is Moses' statement: "4 Hear, O Israel: The LORD our God is one LORD" (Deuteronomy 6:4).

Although the words "one LORD" do exist in the above verse, you will be surprised to know that there are a vast number of people, from various religious institutions, which I have interacted with, still misquote these verses to support their "one God" doctrine. Some of these religious institutions are quite large. Here are a handful of references: Jewish, Muslim, and yes, even a number of Christian churches.

It makes one wonder why some religious institutions refrain from acknowledging the fact of what Moses is saying? Moses says, "our God is one LORD." He does not say, "our God is one God." So! Why do people misquote the verse and say, our God is one God? Could it be because they do not want to acknowledge the fact that Moses is referring to Jesus Christ (Messiah), as we know Him now? Did you know Christ is addressed in the New Testament by the name of "one LORD" as He is addressed by His name of "one LORD" in the Old Testament (OT)?

The Creator of Genesis 1:1—Who is He? *By: Philip Mitanidis*

The Translator's Inconsistencies

Yes He is!

Nothing has changed. Even in the New Testament Christ is acknowledged and referred to as "One LORD." In reference to Jesus Christ the LORD of hosts, Apostle Paul says that we have "One LORD" (Ephesians 4:5). Paul agrees with Moses when he states, "our God is one LORD." Today, the "one LORD" of Deuteronomy 6:4 and of Ephesians 4:5 is commonly known by His character name of "Christ" (Messiah).

So, be careful when someone presents you with a "quote" from a verse or verses and tells you that this is what the verse says. Take the time and check it out, word for word because if it is wrong, and you accept it as truth, you will not only be deceiving yourself, but at the same time, you will deceive other people by telling them the same deceptive error.

Don't be like Eve.

By the way, there are severe warnings in the Old and in the New Testaments regarding willfully adding, deleting, and deceiving others by misquoting the word of God the Holy Spirit.

Here is one of the warnings from the Old Testament:

> "2 Ye shall not add unto the word which I command you, neither shall ye diminish ought from it, that ye may keep the commandments of the LORD your God which I command you" (Deuteronomy 4:2).

What the above verse says to you and to me is simply that if you and I misquote a verse or add to it, you and I will sin, break the Ten Commandments (1 John 3:4.). If you and I misquote or add to a verse or verses, we then become liars. And to make matters even worse, we will misrepresent God by our lies. But, if we do not misquote a verse, add, or delete words from it, then, we will abide within the Ten Commandments. In doing so, we will not sin and misrepresent God; we will be speaking the truth, as it is written by His prophets. When a person speaks, Apostle Peter advises, he or she "should do it as one speaking the very words of God," and not adding to or deleting the word of God (1 Peter 4:11). (NIV)

The Translator's Inconsistencies

Although you will find many warnings in the Old and in the New Testaments, regarding people who tamper with God's word, people will still choose to delete, add, or misquote the words of God the Holy Spirit.

Misquotations can be easily dealt with, but when it comes to deletions and additions to the word of God, you will find that they are harder to pinpoint in some Bible translations. Unless you know what the Hebrew and the Greek inspired Scriptures say, you will fall in the category of the many thousands upon thousands of individuals who rely upon their Bible translation for answers. And, if you do not know what the Hebrew and the Greek Scriptures say that will put you at a disadvantage. Therefore, somebody can take advantage of your ignorance and mislead you away from the facts as they are stated by the prophets of old. But, if you have some knowledge of the inspired Scriptures, you can always pick up your Bible and tell the individual that he or she is wrong because the Hebrew and the Greek Scriptures say something different than what he or she has quoted.

Having said all that, let us consider the various verses, which I have quoted for you at the beginning of this chapter and observe what they say about Christ the "Word" in comparison to the Greek text. Please compare the English text with the Greek text in John 1:1 so that you can observe all of the obvious discrepancies.

The ancient Greek text reads as follows:

"ΕΝΑΡΧΗΗΝΟΛΟΓΟΣΚΑΙΟΛΟΓΟΣΗΝΠΡΟΣΤΟΝΘΕΟΝΚΑΙΘΕΟΣΗΝΟΛΟΓΟΣ." ΙΩΑΝΝΗΝ 1:1

I will break down the above letters to their proper words; and when I do that, we will have the following:

"ΕΝ ΑΡΧΗ ΗΝ Ο ΛΟΓΟΣ ΚΑΙ Ο ΛΟΓΟΣ ΗΝ ΠΡΟΣ ΤΟΝ ΘΕΟΝ ΚΑΙ ΘΕΟΣ ΗΝ Ο ΛΟΓΟΣ." ΙΩΑΝΝΗΝ 1:1

And when I bring the above verse in the lower case, it will read as follows:

The Translator's Inconsistencies

"ΕΝ ΑΡΧΗ ΗΝ Ο ΛΟΓΟΣ ΚΑΙ Ο ΛΟΓΟΣ ΗΝ
"Εν αρχη ην ο Λογος και ο Λογος ην

"ΠΡΟΣ ΤΟΝ ΘΕΟΝ ΚΑΙ ΘΕΟΣ ΗΝ Ο ΛΟΓΟΣ."
"προς τον Θεον και Θεος ην ο Λογος."
ΙΩΑΝΝΗΝ 1:1

Now, let me fill in the direct English words as close as possible to the Greek text.

"ΕΝ ΑΡΧΗ ΗΝ Ο ΛΟΓΟΣ ΚΑΙ Ο ΛΟΓΟΣ ΗΝ
"Εν αρχη ην ο Λογος και ο Λογος ην
"In beginning is the Word, and the Word is

"ΠΡΟΣ ΤΟΝ ΘΕΟΝ ΚΑΙ ΘΕΟΣ ΗΝ Ο ΛΟΓΟΣ."
"προς τον Θεον και Θεος ην ο Λογος."
"with the God, and God is the Word."
ΙΩΑΝΝΗΝ 1:1. John 1:1 (Translation is mine.)

If we take the above English translation and separated it from the Greek text, we will have the following:

"₁ In beginning is the Word, and the Word is with God, and God is the Word." John 1:1 (Translation is mine.)

I do not want to get involved with the explanations of the Hebrew, Greek, and English grammatical rules and sentence structures because that is a subject in itself; but what I will do is to say the following in layman's words regarding John 1:1 with the support of the inspired Scriptures:

Simplistically, Christ the "Word," of v.1, just "is." He is from "everlasting to everlasting" (Psalms 90:2; Micah 5:2; Habakkuk 1:12, 1 Timothy 1:17). There is no time period or time element imposed upon Christ. Time is imposed upon the creation and its creatures there in. The word "beginning" of verse one applies to the creation of "all things" (John 1:3). Therefore time is associated with the

The Translator's Inconsistencies

universe and not with Christ the LORD. And because of this fact, the Greek inspired Scriptures of John 1:1 place Christ in the present tense and not in the past tense as many translators have done in the English language.

The verse will read as follows: "In beginning is the Word, and the Word is with God, and God is the Word." John 1:1 (Translation is mine.) John and the other prophets always place Christ the "Word," of v.1, in the present tense. The only time Christ is placed in past tense is when Christ came in the "flesh" and up until His death on Calvary's cross. But, mainly up until His resurrection on that Sunday morning. That's it! After the resurrection, time ceased to exist for Him, again.

Having said that, now take the time and compare the following Bible verses of John 1:1, with the above Greek verse, and observe the disagreements in the various Bible translations. At the same time, please keep in mind that the ancient Greek writings were not written in the lower case; they were written in the upper case setting without separating the words in order to enhance their speed reading. I am telling you that fact so that you will know that the punctuations, the upper case and lower case settings are used in today's Greek language. Therefore, don't become sidetracked or mislead by some of the grammatical theories that keep floating around about the Greek inspired Scriptures today.

Nonetheless, let us consider the previous verses briefly by comparing them to the Greek text.

The following verse is derived from the Old King James Version (OKJV) of the Bible. It reads as follows:

"1 IN the beginning was the Word and the Word was with God, and the Word was God" (John 1:1).

If you compare the above verse from the (OKJV) of the Bible, to the one I translated from the Greek Scriptures, you will find that it has been translated incorrectly. The definite article "the" in the beginning of the verse, in the phrase, "IN the beginnings," does not exist in the Greek Scripture. By adding the uninspired definite

The Translator's Inconsistencies

article "the" before the word "beginning," it conjures up the idea that that there was a beginning with the "Word" instead of the creation of "all things" in v.3. And since the definite article "the" does not exist before the word "beginning" it should not be used.

In addition, notice the last part of the verse—the predicate. It reads "and the Word was God," whereas the Greek Scripture reads, "and God is the Word" (ΚΑΙ ΘΕΟΣ ΗΝ Ο ΛΟΓΟΣ." ΙΩΑΝΝΗΝ 1:1). In other words, the "Word" (Christ) "is" still "God."

As you can see that is a big difference between the Greek Scriptures and the English translation.

Furthermore, by inserting the copulative verb "was" before the word "God," it places the word "God" in the pass tense. So, why would anyone add the word "was" before the word "God," when, as you can clearly see, the word "was" does not exist before the word "God" in the Greek Scriptures? By adding the word "was" to the verse, does that mean that at one point the "Word was God," and now the "Word" is not God? The question that emerges from that remark, is for one to ask, what happened to Him? Why does He not exist? Whereas, the Greek inspired Scriptures place the word "God" in the present tense (and God is the Word). This means that the "Word" (Christ) is still "God" today, tomorrow, and He is God forever.

Another translation of the Greek Scriptures is The New English Bible (TNEB). It reads as follows:

"1 WHEN ALL THINGS BEGAN, the Word already was. The Word dwelt with God, and what God was, the Word was." John 1:1 (TNEB)

Again, if you were to compare the above verse with the Greek Scriptures, you will find that the translation is not as the Greek text. In this verse the translators state, "WHEN ALL THINGS BEGAN, the Word already was." The remark in the (TNEB) does not state, "In beginning is the Word." The comment "WHEN ALL THINGS BEGAN, the Word already was" implies creation without

The Translator's Inconsistencies

identifying the Creator. That statement does not give credit to the "Word" (Christ) as the Creator. It leaves the creation and Christ the Creator of Genesis 1:1 out of the picture. The verse does not state who created "all things," as the Greek Scriptures indicate. The New English Bible states, "WHEN ALL THINGS BEGAN, the Word already was" (John 1:1). This remark can further imply or make one assume that somebody else, other than Christ the Creator of Genesis 1:1 was already creating. And that remark is not correct as per the Greek Scriptures because the Greek Scriptures state, "In beginning is the Word, and the Word is with God." Verse one identifies, in the Greek Scriptures, Christ the Creator and His Associate (God the Father). Verse one does not reveal the creation of "all things," verses three and ten, of John chapter one, do that.

The verse in the (TNEB) also sates that "the Word dwelt with God" (John 1:1). This implies that the "Word" resided in God's space, or something? And it also implies that the "Word" did not have His own dwelling place. Why would anyone want to say that the "Word" dwelt with "God," is a good question? Seeing that the translators chose to specify who dwelt with whom, why not say, "God" (Christ's Associate: God the Father) dwelt with the "Word" (Christ the Creator)?

Why do you think this translated verse undermines Christ the Creator of Genesis 1:1; John 1:1, 3, and 10?

In addition, the (TNEB) verse states, "what God was, the Word was" (John 1:1). This type of a statement conjures up the idea that the "Word" (Christ) is somehow a duplicate of "God" (His Associate)? The translation of this verse does not separate the "Word" and His Associate as two distinct Individuals who have the same name, as the Greek Scriptures do. The verse implies that the "Word" and "God" (the "Word's" Associate) are made from the same substance, or something because the verse reads, "and what God was, the Word was" (John 1:1). (TNEB)

And, if you were to consider the words "and what God was, the Word was," it will further implicate the "Word" (Christ) to be as one with His Associate, or He is part of His Associate. If that is the case, the words "and what God was, the Word was" will also mean

The Translator's Inconsistencies

that the "Word" and His Associate are in one body? Or it will mean that the "Word" was with Himself? And that brings us right into the Trinitarian theory, which teaches that Jesus Christ the LORD God of Israel is somehow one with His Associates. That kind of presentation of the "Word" is contrary to what the inspired Greek Scriptures are saying. The Greek Scriptures say, "the Word is with God" (Christ's Associate), and that is a huge difference.

Furthermore, please note, the Greek Scriptures, in John 1:1 state, "and God is the Word" (και Θεος ην ο Λογος). The verse does not state, "and what God was, the Word was." To confirm that Christ is not identical to God the Father, Christ the LORD of hosts asks, "To whom then will ye liken Me, or shall I be equal? saith the Holy One." Isaiah 40:25 (See Jeremiah 10:6, 7 also.)

So, the (TNEB) translation fails to address the "Word" (Christ) independently by His name "God" as the Greek Scriptures do. The Greek text says, "and God is the Word."

Another Bible identified as the (NWTCGS), reads as follows:

"1 Originally the Word was, and the Word was with God, and the Word was a god." John 1:1 (NWTCGS)

If you look at the Greek verse, which I have quoted previously for you, you will find the word "Θεος" (και Θεος ην ο Λογος.) is present in the predicate. This word "Θεος" (God) refers to the "Word" (Christ), who is identified by the Greek word "Λογος." (LOGOS). And, if you look in the above verse, the word "Θεος" is not translated in English to read "God" in the (NWTCGS) Bible; it reads, "was a god." Noticeably, if you look at the Word's Associate, whose name is also "Θεος" (τον Θεον), you will notice that his name is translated to read "God."

Since Christ's name in the Greek Scriptures is "God" and His Associate's name is also "God," should not their name in both cases be written "God" in the above verse?

In view of the fact that Christ's name ("God") is mentioned over 3,000 times throughout the Old Testament, and His name is capitalized there, don't you think that His name should also be

The Translator's Inconsistencies

capitalized in the New Testament?

Why, all of the sudden the translators chose to make Christ the Creator of Genesis 1:1 "was a god"?

Isn't that demeaning?

The Greek Scriptures do not read, "was a god." Look at the predicate again; the verse reads "and God is the Word."

"ΚΑΙ   ΘΕΟΣ   ΗΝ   Ο   ΛΟΓΟΣ
"and   God   is   the   Word."
ΙΩΑΝΝΗΝ 1:1. John 1:1 (Translation is mine.)

As you can plainly see, the Greek Scriptures identify Christ the Creator (the Word), and His Associate by the name "GOD." The Greek Scriptures do not elevate one Individual, and degrade the other Individual; out of respect, they are treated as equals.

But, in the (NWTCGS) Bible, the predicate is translated differently; it reads, "and the Word was a god." The words "God" and "Word" have been switched, and the indefinite article "a" has been added to the word "God" to make the predicate read, "and the Word was a god."

If you were to compare the verse from the (NWTCGS) Bible with the Greek Scriptures, you will find that the Greek Scripture is in total disagreement with the (NWTCGS) Bible. The predicate has been brutally altered to read, "and the Word was a god." The word "God" (Θεος) has not only been placed in the end of the verse, but at the same time, it has been dishonored to read "a god." So, why degrade the Greek word "God" to read "a god" when the prophets of the LORD do not?

And to make matters even worse, the translators have added the uninspired copulative verb "was" before the expression "a god" to read, "was a god." The words, "was a god" do not exist in the predicate, in the Greek Scriptures. So, why add them in the verse?

Obviously because they are self serving.

By the way, the (NWTCGS) Bible, in John 1:1 states that the "Word" (Christ), once upon a time, "was a god"; does that mean that the "Word" is not "a god" now? And, how could Christ the

The Creator of Genesis 1:1—Who is He? By: *Philip Mitanidis*
The Translator's Inconsistencies

Creator of Genesis 1:1 who is identified by the name "LORD" (יהוה) "God" (אלהים), now, it is said that He "was a god"? Was He "a god" once upon a time? And if He "was a god" once upon a time, when was that time period? I ask that question because I cannot find that time period, which is mentioned in the (NWTCGS) Bible, anywhere in the Greek inspired Scriptures. In fact, I cannot find a single verse in the entire 66 Books of the Bible, in the Hebrew or in the Greek Scriptures, where it states that Christ the Creator of Genesis 1:1 and of John 1:1, 3, 10 "was a god"?

Can you?

Remember, I said, "I cannot find a single verse in the Hebrew and in the Greek inspired Scriptures." I did not say in the translator's mistranslations of the Hebrew and of the Greek Scriptures!

Therefore, we can conclude that the verse of John 1:1, in the (NWTCGS) Bible, has been altered severely. The verse is nowhere near what the Greek text is saying about Christ the "Word." The Greek text says, "and God is the Word." The Greek text acknowledges that the "Word" (Christ) is "God"; whereas, the (NWTCGS) Bible departs from what the Greek inspired Scriptures are saying to us, by deleting words and by adding words and by altering the Greek text.

Another translation, which does not agree with the Greek inspired Scriptures, is the Moffatt Translation. It reads as follows:

"1 THE Logos existed in the very beginning, the Logos was with God, the Logos was divine." John 1:1 (Moffatt) (See Appendix, p.773 in the NWTCGS. 1950 Edition.)

The Moffatt translation, as you can see, removes the word "Θεος" (God) from the last part of the verse, and it replaces the word "God" with the word "divine." This translation is in complete error; I say that because the Greek word for "God" is "Θεος" in the above verse; "and God is the Word" ("ΚΑΙ ΘΕΟΣ ΗΝ Ο ΛΟΓΟΣ." ΙΩANNHN 1:1; John 1:1. Translation is mine). But, the Greek word for "divine" is totally different; it is "Θε-i-ος."

The Translator's Inconsistencies

Now, I ask you, where is the word "divine" (Θε-ι-ος) found in John 1:1 of the inspired Greek Scriptures?

Can you find the word?

As you can readily see, the word "Θε-ι-ος" (divine) does not exist in John 1:1 of the Greek inspired Scriptures.

How can anyone remove Christ's name, which is "God," and replace it with the non-existent word "divine," is mind boggling to me? That is adding to Scripture, and that is deleting Scripture, and no amount of words of gymnastics is going to justify the removal of the word "God," from John 1:1 and replace it with the word "divine."

This one fact remains, the word "God" has been removed in the Moffatt translation, and the word "divine" has been added to the verse, and that is an inescapable fact.

By the way, Christ's Associate is also identified by the name of "God," in John 1:1. Why was his name not changed to read "divine"? His name is identical to Christ's name; so, why pick on Christ the LORD God of Israel and bring His holy name to the level of "divine"?

Is it something about Christ the LORD of hosts that people do not like? Is it because He claims that He is God the Creator of the universe, and the LORD God of Israel that people do not like? Or is it because He came in the "flesh" to save man from his eternal death that bothers people? Or is it because Satan and his evil angels know that their dominion of planet earth was taken away from them at the cross? Or is it because they know that they have but a short time to live? Perhaps it is just a fad why people curse and blaspheme Christ's name. Or more evidently, is it because the prophet said, "Behold this child [Christ] is set for the fall and rising again of many in Israel; and for a sign which shall be spoken against"? Luke 2:34

What do you think?

Anyway, dear reader, if we can remove the words of God the Holy Spirit at will and replace them with our own words, why not replace all of the "God" words to read "divine"? There are plenty of verses like John 1:1 in the Old and in the New Testaments?

The Translator's Inconsistencies

What do you think of that proposal?

Does anyone want to set himself or herself above God the Holy Spirit and change His Scriptures in order to accommodate his or her doctrinal religious beliefs?

Does anyone really want to go down that road and do that?

Needless to say, the Moffatt translation is nowhere near the Greek inspired Scriptures of John 1:1. It not only removes Christ's name "God" (Θεος), but it also removes the coordinating conjunction "and" before the word God (and God is the Word).

Another translation reads:

"1 In the beginning was the one who is called the Word. The Word was with God and was truly God." John 1:1 (CEV)

In the Contemporary English Version Bible (CEV), the above verse states that the "Word" (Christ) "was truly God." This version acknowledges that the "Word" "was truly God" (John 1:1). Although the Contemporary English Version acknowledges that Christ is "God," they have placed Him in the past tense and added the words, "the one who is called."

The Amplified Bible (Amp) reads: "1 IN THE beginning [before all time] was the Word (dChrist), and the Word was with God, and the Word was God Himself. [Isaiah 9:6]" John 1:1 (Amp.)

The above verse, like the Greek inspired Scriptures, acknowledges that Christ (the Word) is "God" by saying that "the Word was God himself." (Amp.). It should be noted that, the word "Himself" does not exist in the Greek inspired Scriptures. But what the Amplified Bible does correctly is to separate the "Word" (Christ) from His Associate by saying, "and the Word was with God" (John 1:1). (Amp.)

As you can readily see in the above Bible translations, the translators vary their respective translation of the Greek inspired Scriptures in one form or another.

The (TNEB) Bible says, "The Word dwelt with God, and what God was, the Word was."

The (NWTCGS) Bible says, "and the Word was a god."

The Translator's Inconsistencies

> The Moffatt Bible says, "the Logos was divine."
> The (CEV) Bible states that Christ "was truly God."
> The (Amp.) Bible says, "and the Word was God Himself".
> The (OKJV) Bible says, "and the Word was God."
> The (Amp.) Bible, like the (OKJV), and the (CEV), acknowledges that Christ the "Word" is "God."

I am sure you can add other discrepancies to the above list; but, the point should be well taken by now that all of the above Bibles do not translate the Greek words the same in John 1:1. As you have read, the translators translate Christ the "Word" to read, "and what God was, the Word was." The "Word was a god." The "Word" was "divine," "was truly God," and so on.

Now, I ask you; by reading the above translations, who or what is the "Word" (Christ)? Is He "a god," "divine," "was God," "the same as God," "was truly God," or "the Word was God Himself"? Which one of these translations is correct?

Obviously, none of them are correct!

I make that remark because none of the above Bible translations say, "and God is the Word" (ΚΑΙ ΘΕΟΣ ΗΝ Ο ΛΟΓΟΣ.). All of these translations, to a degree have added to, or they have taken away from the Greek text.

So, you as a reader, how are you to know, which translation is correct, if you are unable to read and understand the Greek language? The only thing you will be able to discern is that the various Bibles, which you read or have read, do not agree with each other. Knowing that these Bibles do not agree with each other, it does not help you to know, which translation is correct; neither does it help you to choose the correct translation for your study?

Now you know why I made the statement earlier that it is harder to identify God the Creator of Genesis 1:1 in the New Testament. It is harder because of the inconsistencies the translator's create.

But, having said that, it does not mean that a concerned reader who is searching for the doctrine of the Bible is not able to know God's truth. You see, Jesus Christ the LORD stated that every person on planet earth would know the doctrinal truth of the Bible before He returns the second time to take His people home (Matthew 24:14). Therefore, regardless of all the incorrect translations of the Gospel of Jesus Christ, people will be able to receive the doctrinal truth and make a choice whether or not to accept Christ (Messiah), as their LORD God and Savior.

It should be noted, irrespective how the word of the LORD is mangled in a given translation of the Hebrew and of the Greek texts, God the Holy Spirit has made provisions for the reader, even in a mistranslated Bible, in order to reveal to a sincere person, the doctrinal truth of the Bible and refute all of the doctrines of men.

In closing, as you have noted, I have quoted the above handful of Bibles in order to show you how translators, and religious institutions have translated the Greek words to read something else in English. And, it should also be noted that the above remarks, and any other remarks in this book, are not intended to be malicious. The intent is simply to reveal the differences amongst these translations in the light of the Greek inspired Scriptures. In doing so, I hope it has sparked a desire in your heart to confirm what I have presented to you is the truth.

Therefore, if you compare the above or other Bible translations to the original Greek words, which I have quoted for you, you will notice that they all state something other than what the Greek words are saying. Compare my translation underneath the Greek words, and then, compare the other Bibles and see if they match my translation or not? Or better still; don't take my word, or anybody else's word as the truth. If you want to avoid the discrepancies between the Greek and the English of the various translations, do your own research; compare the English translations with the Greek inspired Scriptures, and see for yourself the outcome of the translated verses. You owe it to yourself to verify what I have presented to you, if it is correct or not? And you also owe it to yourself to verify if your own Bible translation is correct or not?

I encourage you, be like the "Bereans." (See Acts 17:10, 11.)

Misapplying Bible Verses____ As if mistranslated Bibles are not deceitful and misleading enough, a further cause for the rejection of Christ the LORD of hosts as the LORD God of Abraham, as the LORD God of Israel, and a way to exclude Jesus

Misapplying Bible Verses

Christ from the Old Testament, a common practice that is employed by religious institutions, theologians, laymen, and laywomen is to use the verses of the Old Testament, which refer to Christ the LORD God of Israel, and say, these verses refer to God the Father (Christ's Associate).

As an example, let me give you three overviews of the Torah (the 5 books of Moses) by the psalmist (Psalms 78), Nehemiah (Nehemiah 9), Apostle Paul (1 Corinthians 10:1-10), and few excerpts from the Torah.

Point no. 1). The psalmist's overview: "1 My friends, I beg you to listen as I teach. 2 I will give instruction and explain the mystery of what happened long ago. 3 These are things we learned from our ancestors, 4 and we will tell them to the next generation. We won't keep secret the glorious deeds and the mighty miracles of the LORD. 5 God gave his Law to Jacob's descendants, the people of Israel. And he told our ancestors to teach their children, 6 so that each new generation would know his Law and tell it to the next. 7 Then they would trust God and obey his teachings, without forgetting anything God had done. 8 They would be different from their ancestors, who were stubborn, rebellious, and unfaithful to God. 9 The warriors from Ephraim were armed with arrows, but they ran away when the battle began. 10 They broke their agreement with God, and they turned their backs on his teaching. 11 They forgot all he had done, even the mighty miracles 12 he did for their ancestors near Zoan in Egypt. 13 God made a path in the sea and piled up the water as he led them across. 14 He guided them during the day with a cloud, and each night he led them with a flaming fire. 15 God made water flow from rocks he split open in the desert, and his people drank freely, as though from a lake. 16 He made streams gush out like rivers from rocks. 17 But in the desert, the people of God Most High kept sinning and rebelling. 18 They stubbornly tested God and demanded from him what they wanted to eat. 19 They challenged God saying, "Can God provide food out here in the desert? 20 It's true God struck the

The Creator of Genesis 1:1—Who is He? By: *Philip Mitanidis*
Misapplying Bible Verses

rock and water gushed out like a river, but can he give his people bread and meat?" 21 When the LORD heard this, he was angry and furious with Jacob's descendants, the people of Israel. 22 They had refused to trust him, and they had doubted his saving power. 23 But God gave a command to the clouds, and he opened the doors in the skies. 24 From heaven he sent grain that they called manna. 25 He gave them more than enough, and each one of them ate this special food. 26 God's mighty power brought a strong wind from the southeast, 27 and it brought birds that covered the ground, like sand on the beach. 28 Then God made the birds fall in the camp of his people near their tents. 29 God gave his people all they wanted, and each of them ate until they were full. 30 But before they had swallowed the last bite, 31 God became angry and killed the strongest and best from the families of Israel. 32 But the rest kept on sinning and would not trust God's miracles. 33 So he cut their lives short and made them terrified. 34 After he killed some of them, the others turned to him with all their hearts. 35 They remembered God Most High, the mighty rock that kept them safe. 36 But they tried to flatter God, and they told him lies; 37 they were unfaithful and broke their promises. 38 Yet God was kind. He kept forgiving their sins and didn't destroy them. He often became angry, but never lost his temper. 39 God remembered that they were made of flesh and were like a wind that blows once and then dies down. 40 While they were in the desert, they often rebelled and made God sad. 41 They kept testing him and caused terrible pain for the Holy One of Israel. 42 They forgot about his power and how he had rescued them from their enemies. 43 God showed them all kinds of wonderful miracles near Zoan in Egypt. 44 He turned the rivers of Egypt into blood, and no one could drink from the streams. 45 He sent swarms of flies to pester the Egyptians, and he sent frogs to cause them trouble. 46 God let worms and grasshoppers eat their crops. 47 He destroyed their grapevines and their fig trees with hail and floods. 48 Then he killed their cattle with hail and their other animals with lightning. 49 God was so angry and

Misapplying Bible Verses

furious that he went into a rage and caused them great trouble by sending swarms of destroying angles, 50 God gave in to his anger and slaughtered them in a terrible way. 51 He killed the first-born son of each Egyptian family. 52 Then God led his people out of Egypt and guided them in the desert like a flock of sheep. 53 He led them safely along, and they were not afraid, but their enemies drowned in the sea. 54 God brought his people to the sacred Mountain that he had taken by his own power. 55 He made nations run from the tribes of Israel, and let the tribes take over their land. 56 But the people tested God Most High, and they refused to obey his laws. 57 They were as unfaithful as their ancestors, and they were as crooked as a twisted arrow. 58 God demanded all their love, but they made him angry by worshiping idols. 59 So God became furious and completely rejected the people of Israel. 60 Then he deserted his home at Shiloh, where he lived here on earth. 61 He let enemies capture the sacred chest, and let them dishonor him. 62 God took out his anger on his chosen ones and let them be killed by enemy swords. 63 Fire destroyed the young men, and the young women were left with no one to marry. 64 Priests died violent deaths, but their widows were not allowed to mourn. 65 Finally the Lord woke up, and he shouted like a drunken soldier. 66 God scattered his enemies and made them ashamed forever. 67 Then the Lord decided not to make his home with Joseph's descendants in Ephraim. 68 Instead he chose the tribe of Judah, and he chose Mount Zion, the place he loves. 69 There he built his temple as lofty as the Mountains and as solid as the earth that he had made to last forever." Psalm 78:1-69 (CEV)"

Like Moses, the psalmist admonishes his listeners not to forget, "4 His wonderful works that He hath done. 5 For He established a testimony in Jacob, and appointed a law in Israel, which He commanded our fathers, that they should make them known to their children: 6 That the generation to come might know them, even the children which should be born; who should arise and declare them to their children: 7 That they might set their hope in God, and not

Misapplying Bible Verses

forget the works of God, but keep His commandments: 8 And might not be as their fathers, a stubborn and rebellious generation" (Psalms 78:4-8). (See Psalm 106 for further details.)

Therefore we can ask, who is "the Most High" (v.56), Jesus Christ or Christ's Associate (God the Father)?

Who was tempted by the children of Israel; and identified Him as "the mighty Rock" (v.35), was it Jesus Christ or God the Father?

Who went to Egypt, and led the children of Israel into the Promised Land, was it Christ the LORD or God the Father?

Who is the Creator (v.69), Jesus Christ or God the Father?

Who dwelt in "Shiloh" (v.60), and later chose the Sanctuary on Mount Zion the place He loves (v.68) was it Christ or God the Father?

By reading the psalmist's above overview of what Moses wrote in the Torah (the five books of Moses), to whom do you think all of the above verses refer to (Psalms 78:1-69)? Do they refer to Jesus Christ the LORD or do they refer to Christ's Associate (God the Father)?

Likewise, Nehemiah, the Persian king's cupbearer, also provides an overview of what Moses said in the Torah about the God of Abraham and of Israel. And, if you look at the psalmist's account, and Nehemiah's account, you will observe, both of these prophets provide some additional information to Moses' writings (the Torah).

Here is <u>Nehemiah's overview of the Torah</u>.

Point no. 2). "6 Thou [You], even Thou, art LORD alone; Thou hast made heaven, the heaven of heavens, with all their host, the earth, and all things that are therein, the seas, and all that is therein, and Thou preservest them all; and the host of heaven worshippeth Thee. "7 Thou art the LORD the God, who didst choose Abram, and broughtest him forth out of Ur of the Chaldees, and gavest him the name of Abraham; 8 And foundest his heart faithful before Thee, and madest a covenant with him to give the land of the Canaanites, the Hittites, the Amorites, and the Perizzites, and the Jebusites, and the Girgashites, to give it, I say, to his seed, and hast performed

Misapplying Bible Verses

Thy words; for Thou art righteous: 9 and didst see the affliction of our fathers in Egypt, and heardest their cry by the Red Sea; 10 and shewedst signs and wonders upon Pharaoh, and on all his servants, and on all the people of his land: for Thou knewest that they dealt proudly against them. So didst Thou get Thee a name, as it is this day. 11 And Thou didst divide the sea before them, so that they went through the midst of the sea on the dry land; and their persecutors Thou threwest into the deeps, as a stone into the mighty waters. 12 Moreover Thou leddest them in the day by a cloudy pillar; and in the night by a pillar of fire, to give them light in the way wherein they should go. 13 Thou camest down also upon Mount Sinai, and spakest with them from heaven, and gavest them right judgments, and true laws, good statutes and commandments: 14 And madest known unto them Thy holy sabbath, and commandedst them precepts, statutes, and laws, by the hand of Moses Thy servant: 15 And gavest them bread from heaven for their hunger, and broughtest forth water for them out of the rock for their thirst, and promisedst them that they should go in to possess the land which Thou hadst sworn to give them. 16 But they and our fathers dealt proudly, and hardened their necks, and hearkened not to Thy commandments. 17 And refused to obey, neither were mindful of thy wonders that Thou didst among them; but hardened their necks, and in their rebellion appointed a captain to return to their bondage: but Thou art a God ready to pardon, gracious and merciful, slow to anger, and of great kindness, and forsookest them not. 18 Yea, when they had made them a molten calf, and said, This is thy God that brought thee up out of Egypt, and had wrought great provocations; 19 Yet Thou in Thy manifold mercies forsookest them not in the wilderness: the pillar of the cloud departed not from them by day, to lead them in the way; neither the pillar of fire by night, to shew them light, and the way wherein they should go. 20 Thou gavest also Thy good spirit to instruct them, and withheldest not Thy manna from their mouth, and gavest them water for their thirst. 21 Yea, forty years didst Thou sustain them in the wilderness, so

Misapplying Bible Verses

that they lacked nothing; their clothes waxed not old, and their feet swelled not. 22 Moreover Thou gavest them kingdoms and nations, and didst divide them into corners: so they possessed the land of Sihon, and the land of the king of Heshbon, and the land of Og king of Bashan. 23 Their children also multipliedst Thou as the stars of heaven, and broughtest them into the land, concerning which Thou hadst promised to their fathers, that they should go in to possess it. 24 So the children went in and possessed the land, and Thou subduedst before them the inhabitants of the land, the Canaanites, and gavest them into their hands, with their kings, and the people of the land, that they might do with them as they would. 25 And they took strong cities, and a fat land, and possessed houses full of all goods, wells digged, vineyards, and oliveyards, and fruit trees in abundance: so they did eat, and were filled, and became fat, and delighted themselves in Thy [Your] great goodness. 26 Nevertheless they were disobedient, and rebelled against Thee, and cast Thy law behind their backs, and slew Thy prophets which testified against them to turn them to Thee, and they wrought great provocations" (Nehemiah 9:6-26).

According to verse six, we can ask, who is the sole Creator, Jesus Christ or God the Father?

Who is "the host of heaven" worshipping (v.6), is it Jesus Christ the LORD or God the Father?

Who brough Abraham into the Promised Land (v.7), was it Christ the LORD or was it God the Father?

Who claims to be the God of Abraham and made a covenant with him (vs.7, 8), was it Jesus Christ or was it God the Father?

To whom do you think all of the above verses refer to (Nehemiah 9:6-26)? Do they refer to Christ or do they refer to God the Father?

Additionally, if you were to ask, to whom is Moses referring to, in the Torah, in the following verses, the majority of religious leaders (Jews, Muslims, Christians, theologians, laymen, and laywomen), will tell you that the following verses refer to Christ's

Misapplying Bible Verses_____

Associate (God the Father). But, to whom do you think the following verses are referring to?

Point no. 3). "4 And when the LORD saw that he turned aside to see, God called unto him out of the midst of the bush, and said, Moses, Moses. And he said, Here am I. 5 And He said, Draw not nigh hither: put off thy [your] shoes from off thy feet, for the place whereon thou [you] standest is holy ground. 6 Moreover he said, I am the God of thy father, the God of Abraham, the God of Isaac, and the God of Jacob. And Moses hid his face; for he was afraid to look upon God. 7 And the LORD said, I have surely seen the affliction of My people which are in Egypt, and have heard their cry by reason of their taskmasters; for I know their sorrows; 8 And I am come down to deliver them out of the hand of the Egyptians, and to bring them up out of that land unto a good land and a large, unto a land flowing with milk and honey; unto the place of the Canaanites, and the Hittites, and the Amorites, and the Perizzites, and the Hivites, and the Jebusites. 9 Now therefore, behold, the cry of the children of Israel is come unto me: and I have also seen the oppression wherewith the Egyptians oppress them. 10 Come now therefore, and I will send thee unto Pharaoh, that thou mayest bring forth My people the children of Israel out of Egypt" (Exodus 3:4-10).

Who called Moses' name from the burning bush (v.4)?
Who said, "I have surely seen the affliction of My people" (v.7)?
Who said, "I am come down to deliver them [the children of Israel] out of the hand of the Egyptians" (v.8)?
Who said, "I will send thee [you] unto Pharaoh" (v.10)?
Who called the children of Israel (Jacob) "My people" (v.10)?
Who said, "I am the God of thy [your] father, the God of Abraham, the God of Isaac, and the God of Jacob" (v.6)?
Who made all of the above statements to Moses? Was it Jesus Christ the LORD of hosts, or was it God the Father?

Misapplying Bible Verses

Point no. 4). "6 Wherefore say unto the children of Israel, I am the LORD, and I will bring you out from under the burdens of the Egyptians, and I will rid you out of their bondage, and I will redeem you with a stretched out arm, and with great judgments: 7 And I will take you to Me for a people, and I will be to you a God: and ye shall know that I am the LORD your God, which bringeth you out from under the burdens of the Egyptians. 8 And I will bring you in unto the land, concerning the which I did swear to give it to Abraham, to Isaac, and to Jacob; and I will give it you for an heritage: I am the LORD" (Ex. 6:6-8).

Who said, "I am the LORD, and I will bring you out from under the burdens of the Egyptians" (v.6)?
Who said, "I will take you to Me for a people, and I will be to you a God: and ye shall know that I am the LORD your God" (v.7)?
Who made all of the above comments to Moses, was it Jesus Christ the LORD of hosts, or was it God the Father?

Point no. 5). "21 And the LORD went before them by day in a pillar of a cloud, to lead them the way; and by night in a pillar of fire, to give them light; to go by day and night: 22 He took not away the pillar of the cloud by day, nor the pillar of fire by night, from before the people" (Exodus 13:21, 22).

Who led the children of Israel, from Egypt and all the way into the Promised Land "in a pillar of cloud," was it Christ or was it God the Father? (Answer: See 1 Corinthians 10:1, 2, 4.)

Point no. 6). "15 And the LORD said unto Moses, Wherefore criest thou unto Me? speak unto the children of Israel, that they go forward: 16 But lift thou up thy [your] rod, and stretch out thine [your] hand over the sea, and divide it: and the children of Israel shall go on dry ground through the midst of the sea" (Exodus 14:15, 16).

Who said to Moses to "stretch out thine [your] hand over the

Misapplying Bible Verses

sea, and divide it," was it Jesus Christ the LORD or God the Father?

Who said to Moses to tell the children of Israel to walk through the Red Sea, Christ or God the Father? (Answer: 1 Corinthians 10:1, 2, 4.)

Point no. 7). "11 And the LORD spake unto Moses, saying, 12 I have Heard the murmurings of the children of Israel: speak unto them, saying, At even ye shall eat flesh, and in the morning ye shall be filled with bread; and ye shall know that I am the LORD your God. 13 And it came to pass, that at even the quails came up, and covered the camp: and in the morning the dew lay round about the host. 14 And when the dew that lay was gone up, behold, upon the face of the wilderness there lay a small round thing, as small as the hoar frost on the ground. 15 And when the children of Israel saw it, they said one to another, It is manna: for they wist not what it was. And Moses said unto them, This is the bread which the LORD hath given you to eat. 16 This is the thing which the LORD hath commanded, Gather of it every man according to his eating, an omer for every man, according to the number of your persons; take ye every man for them which are in his tents" (Exodus 16:11-16).

Who said to the children of Israel "I am the LORD your God"?

What kind of food did the LORD their God provide for the children of Israel? (vs. 13 - 15)?

Who provided the food for the children of Israel, was it Christ or was it God the Father? (Answer: 1 Corinthians 10:3, 4.)

Point no. 8). "1 And all the congregation of the children of Israel journeyed from the wilderness of Sin, after their journeys, according to the commandment of the LORD, and pitched in Rephidim: and there was no water for the people to drink. 2 Wherefore the people did chide with Moses, and said, Give us water that we may drink. And Moses said unto them, Why chide ye with me? wherefore do ye tempt the LORD? 3 And the people thirsted there for water; and the people murmured

Misapplying Bible Verses

against Moses, and said, Wherefore is this that thou hast brought us up out of Egypt, to kill us and our children and our cattle with thirst? 4 And Moses cried unto the LORD, saying, What shall I do unto this people? they be almost ready to stone me. 5 And the LORD said unto Moses, Go on before the people, and take with thee of the elders of Israel; and thy [your] rod, wherewith thou smotest the river, take in thine hand, and go. 6 Behold, I will stand before thee [you] there upon the rock in Horeb; and thou [you] shalt smite the rock, and there shall come water out of it, that the people may drink. And Moses did so in the sight of the elders of Israel. 7 And he called the name of the place Massah, and Meribah, because of the chiding of the children of Israel, and because they tempted the LORD, saying, Is the LORD among us, or not?" (Exodus 17:1-7).

Who led the children of Israel through the wilderness of Sin?
Where did the children of Israel camp? (v.1)
Who told Moses to take his rod and stand before the children of Israel near one of the rocks? (v.5).
Who said to Moses "I will stand before thee [you] there upon the rock," while Moses was to "smite the rock," in order for the "water" to come out of it, "that the people may drink" (v.6)?
So dear reader, to whom do you think all of the above references refer to, Christ or God the Father?
For the answer, read 1 Corinthians 10:4 in the Greek text; and notice how it refers to Christ. It says, "πετρα [Rock] ητο ο Χριστος [Christ]."
And the (OKJV) reads, "4 and that Rock was Christ."

Point no. 9). "22 So Moses brought Israel from the Red sea, and they went out into the wilderness of Shur; and they went three days in the wilderness, and found no water. 23 And when they came to Marah, they could not drink of the waters of Marah, for they were bitter: therefore the name of it was called Marah. 24 And the people murmured against Moses, saying, What shall we drink?" (Exodus 15:22-24).

Misapplying Bible Verses

Likewise, after the above incident, "2 Moses said unto them, Why chide ye [all of you] with me? wherefore do ye tempt the LORD? 3 And the people thirsted there for water; and the people murmured against Moses, and said, Wherefore is this that thou [you] hast brought us up out of Egypt, to kill us and our children and our cattle with thirst? 4 And Moses cried unto the LORD, saying, What shall I do unto this people? they be almost ready to stone me."

"7 And he [Moses] called the name of the place Massah, and Meribah, because of the chiding of the children of Israel, and because they tempted the LORD, saying, Is the LORD among us, or not?" (Exodus 17:2-4, 7).

Who "murmured against Moses" (v.3), and who "did chide with Moses" (v.2)?
Who said, "Is the LORD among us, or not?"
Why were the children of Israel going to stone Moses?
What did Moses call the place where the children of Israel tempted the LORD of hosts? (v.7)
Why did the children of Israel tempt the LORD?
What LORD was tempted (vs. 2-4, 7) by the children of Israel; was it Christ or God the Father? (Answer: 1 Corinthians 10:4, 9.)

Point no. 10). "4 And they journeyed from mount Hor by the way of the Red sea, to compass the land of Edom: and the soul of the people was much discouraged because of the way. 5 And the people spake against God, and against Moses, Wherefore have ye brought us up out of Egypt to die in the wilderness? for there is no bread, neither is there any water; and our soul loatheth this light bread. 6 And the LORD sent fiery serpents among the people, and they bit the people; and much people of Israel died. 7 Therefore the people came to Moses, and said, We have sinned, for we have spoken against the LORD, and against thee; pray unto the LORD, that He take away the serpents from us. And Moses prayed for the people" (Numbers 21:4-7).

Who spoke against God and against Moses (v.5)?

Who was complaining that there was no water or bread and to whom?

Who "sent fiery serpents among the people, and they bit the people; and much people of Israel died" (v.6). In fact twenty-three thousand (23,000) of the children of Israel died in one day from the bites of the snakes and scorpions, which Satan and his evil angels amassed upon the children of Israel when Christ the God of Israel removed Himself and His protection from the camp of Israel.

Who is the God of Abraham and of Israel that was tempted by the children of Israel during their journey from Egypt and all the way to the Promised Land; was it God the Christ or was it God the Father?

For the answer, see 1 Corinthians 10:1-10. And notice vs.4 & 9 in the Greek text; they say, the children of Israel "tempted Christ [Χριστος]."

Therefore we can ask, since all three overviews of the Torah, according to Apostle Paul, in 1 Corinthians 10:1-10, refer to Christ, why are Muslims, Jews, and Christians teach and apply all of the above verses in this chapter, and the Torah, to God the Father?

The Creator's Name

As you have noted in the previous chapter, misapplication of Scripture is quite common, and so are the misapplications of Christ's Old Testament names, they are applied to God the Father by Jews, Muslims, theologians, and by the majority of Christians.

To clear that flawed belief, let us consider the Creator's name first.

As I have stated in the previous chapters, the Bible claims that the universe and "all things" were created by one omnipotent Spirit Being, who dwelt in His Sanctuary, which Moses built, traveled with the children of Israel in the wilderness for 40 years, and led them all the way into the Promised Land is none other than the Creator of Genesis 1:1 who is identified by Moses, the psalmist, Isaiah, and by the rest of the prophets by the name of "God". (אלהים)

Moses wrote: "1 IN the beginning God [אלהים] created the heaven and the earth" (Genesis 1:1).

The Creator of Genesis 1:1—Who is He?   By: *Philip Mitanidis*
The Creator's name

First, as you have read, Moses identifies the Creator by the name "God" (אלהים) in Genesis 1:1; and then, Moses identifies the Creator by His full name "LORD God." You will find the Creator's full name, "LORD God," appearing for the first time in Genesis 2:4.

Moses wrote: "4 These are the generations of the heavens and of the earth when they were created, in the day that the LORD God made the earth and the heavens" (Genesis 2:4).

As you can see in the above verse, Moses has provided more information about "God" the Creator of Genesis 1:1. He identifies God the Creator by His full name "LORD God." You will find the name "LORD God" used throughout the 66 books of the Bible. In fact, the Creator is often addressed by the name "LORD," "God," "LORD God," and sometimes He is addressed by His name "God the LORD."

To further confirm that the Creator of Genesis 1:1 is the same LORD God and Creator, of which the prophets of old often refer to Him by the name "LORD [יהוה], God [אלהים]," and the LORD God of Abraham and of Israel, let me direct you to the following verses:

The prophet of the LORD asks. "28 Hast thou [you] not known? hast thou not heard, that the everlasting God, the LORD, the Creator of the ends of the earth, fainteth not, neither is weary? there is no searching of His understanding" (Isaiah 40:28).

Isaiah, in the above verse, like Moses, refers to a single Individual by the use of the words "His" and "Creator." He does not use the word Creators. Likewise, Moses uses the singular pronoun "You" in the following verse to convey that there is only one Creator.

Moses said, "1 LORD, Thou [You] hast been our dwelling place in all generations. 2 Before the mountains were brought forth, or ever Thou hadst [has] formed the earth and the world, even from everlasting to everlasting, Thou [You] art God" (Psalms 90:1, 2).

The Creator's name

Moses in the above verse states that the Creator, the LORD God of Israel dwelt with the children of Israel "in all generation." And then he adds by saying that He is "from everlasting to everlasting Thou art God."

Thus far, the prophets of the Creator have identified the Creator, who created "the earth and the world" (v.2), by His name "LORD," "God," and "LORD God." The reason why they address the Creator by the name "LORD God" is due to the fact that the Creator Himself acknowledged to His prophets that His name is "LORD God."

As an example, when Moses was shepherding his father-in-law's sheep at the foot of Mount Sinai, he was confronted by what appeared to be a burning bush. During that time, Moses was asked by God the Creator to go on a mission for Him. The Creator asked Moses to go into Egypt and bring His people out of Egypt and into the Promised Land. In turn, Moses asked the Creator, if the children of Israel were to ask him who sent him, what was he to say to them?

> Here is His answer: "14 And God said unto Moses, I AM THAT I AM: and He said, Thus shalt thou say unto the children of Israel, I AM hath sent me unto you. 15 And God said moreover unto Moses, Thus shalt thou say unto the children of Israel, The LORD God of your fathers hath sent me unto you: this is My name for ever" (Exodus 3:14, 15).

The Creator personally acknowledges, in the above verses that His name is "LORD God" "for ever." That is the reason why all of the prophets address Him by the name "LORD [יהוה] God [אלהים]." God the Creator advised Moses to say to the children of Israel, "The LORD God of your fathers…hath set me unto you"; and then, God the Creator added, "this is My name for ever."

In the New Testament, the Creator's full name is the same. The only dissimilarity in the New Testament is the way the Creator's name is pronounced. In the Greek language, the Creator's name is transferred from "LORD [יהוה] God [אלהים]" to "LORD [Κυϱιος]

The Creator's name

God [Θεος]." And, if you were to pick up a Greek translation of the Old Testament, you will find the name of the Creator is addressed by the Greek words "Κυριος," "Θεος," and "Κυριος Θεος" throughout the Old Testament.

So, when you read the full name of the Creator in Hebrew, you will read it from right to left like this, ".יהוה אלהים" And when you read it in Greek, you will read it from left to right like this, "Κυριος Θεος." And when you read the Creator's name in English, you will read it like this, "Lord God." But some translators translate the Creator's name like this, LORD God. In the Old King James Version (OKJV), the majority of times, they have translated the Hebrew word "יהוה" to read "LORD" in the upper case. But when the Hebrew name "Adonay" is used to refer to the Creator, as the Masoretic scholars did in a number of verses, the (OKJV) uses the word "Lord" in the lower case, but then again, not in all cases?

Then, there are a variety of Bible translations in the market place, which translate the name of the Creator יהוה to read, "Lord," and other Bibles translate the name of the Creator יהוה to read "Jehovah," which is one hundred percent incorrect because the word "Jehovah" exists only seven times in the entire Bible, and not over six thousand times as some Bibles have done. And those seven references (Jehovah) refer to Christ the LORD of hosts. On the other hand, the majority of translations try to stay with the upper case and have the Creator's name read "LORD."

Therefore, by reading the Old and New Testaments, in the English language, you can easily observe the Creator's name, "LORD God," running like a thread throughout the sixty-six books of the Bible.

Although the Creator's name runs like a thread throughout the 66 books of the Bible, you should also be aware of the fact that He has over 20 different character names, which He uses to identify Himself with. If you are not familiar with His character names, read my book called "Moses Wrote About Me" *by Philip Mitanidis.* BEEHIVE PUBLISHING HOUSE INC.

One Creator or More?

Secondly, it is commonly believed by Jews, Muslims, and Christians, on one hand, there is only one Creator; on the other hand, some of these religious institutions believe that there was more than one Creator involved in the creation of the universe and everything that is in it. But, what do the prophets of old say on those two points?

To concur that God the Creator of Genesis 1:1, whose name is "LORD God," is referring to Himself as the sole Creator of "all things," and not to two or more Creators, consider the following presentation and please notice the claims that are made and the singular pronouns that are used in these verses to testify that there is only one Creator of "all things."

> Isaiah says: "26 Lift up your eyes on high, and behold who hath created these things, that bringeth out their host by number: He calleth them all by names by the greatness of His might, for that He is strong in power; not one faileth." Isaiah 40:26

When you lift your eyes up and look at the stars, black holes, quarks, galaxies, black dust, power balls, magnetic fields, black matter, and so on, do you know who created them? Isaiah declares, "behold who hath created these things…He calleth them all by names." Then Isaiah adds, "by the greatness of His might, for that He is strong in power."

Did you notice in the above verse the train of thought that is penned by the prophet Isaiah? Notice how he presents God the Creator. Isaiah uses the singular pronouns, when he is referring to the Creator of the universe. He uses the singular words "He" and "His." And, if you were to observe the Genesis account, you would also observe Moses wrote in the singular form, when he referred to God the Creator of Genesis 1:1.

Referring to God the Creator of Genesis 1:1, and of the creation week of Genesis chapter one, Moses penned these words:

> "1 THUS the heavens and the earth were finished, and all the host of them. "2 And on the seventh day [Saturday] God ended

One Creator or more?

His work which He had made; and He rested on the seventh day from all His work which He had made" (Genesis 2:1, 2).

Here to, in verse two, Moses is referring to God the Creator of heaven and earth in the singular form. Notice the words Moses is using to describe the Creator. They are "He," "He rested," "His," "His work," and "which He had made." These pronouns are identical to the pronouns Isaiah is using in Isaiah 40:26. These pronouns refer to one single Individual who is identified as the "Creator" (Isaiah 40:28) of the universe by Moses and by Isaiah.

Furthermore, the Creator of Genesis 1:1 also uses the singular pronouns, "I," "My," and "Mine" to express that He is the sole Creator of the universe and everything that is in it.

Moses states that the Man (Adam) was created first, and then, the woman (Eve) was created after Adam. In reference to the creation of the woman, Moses declares, "18 the LORD God said, It is not good that the man [Adam] should be alone; I will make him an help meet [helper] for him." "21 And the LORD God caused a deep sleep to fall upon Adam, and he slept: and He took one of his ribs, and closed up the flesh instead thereof; 22 And the rib, which the LORD God had taken from man, made He a woman, and brought her unto the man [Adam]. 23 And Adam said, This is now bone of my bones, and flesh of my flesh: she shall be called Woman, because she was taken out of Man" (Genesis 2:18, 21-23).

In the above verses, Moses is referring to the Creator in the singular form by the words "He" ("made He a woman"), and "I." ("I will make him help meet"). Moses clearly reveals that there is one Creator by the use of the words, "I will make him an help meet [helper]." The pronoun "I," in vs. 18 and 22, places the Creator in the singular form.

In another place, the Creator of Genesis 1:1 confirms that He is the One who created man and placed him upon the earth to live.

Referring to the time before the flood, Moses said, "6 And it repented the LORD that He had made man on the earth, and it grieved Him at His heart. 7 And the LORD said, I will destroy man whom I have created from the face of the earth;" (Genesis 6:6, 7).

The Creator of Genesis 1:1—Who is He? *By: Philip Mitanidis*

One Creator or more?

As you have observed, the above verses reveal that there is one Creator who is identified by Moses by the use of the pronouns "He," "Him," "His," and "I." And this Creator claims that it was He who created man and placed him upon the earth to live. The Creator says, "7 I will destroy man whom I have created from the face of the earth" (Genesis 6:7).

Did you hear that?

God the Creator is referring to Himself by the words, "I will" and "I have created." Please note; there is no claim by God the Creator of Genesis 1:1, at any time, where He says, "We created."

Moreover, the Creator used the same pronoun "I" when He had a dialogue with Job regarding the creation of the earth. Referring to the creation, God the Creator said to Job, "4 Where wast [were] thou [you] when I laid the foundations of the earth?" (Job 38:4).

Approximately seven hundred years later, God the Creator who spoke to Job said the same thing to Isaiah. God the Creator the LORD God of Israel of verses one and two of Isaiah 48, said to Isaiah; "13 Mine hand also hath laid the foundation of the earth, and My right hand hath spanned the heavens: when I call unto them, they stand up together" (Isaiah 48:13).

Here in these verses, God the Creator acknowledges that it was He who "laid the foundation of the earth." God the Creator of Genesis 1:1 first tells Isaiah, as He did to Job that it was He who "laid the foundation of the earth," and it was His right hand that "spanned the heavens." Then, the Creator described how He formed the earth and spanned the heavens. He said, "when I call unto them, they stand up together" (Isaiah 48:13).

Notice Isaiah's statement. He says that the Creator created by speaking (when I call unto them). Moses says the same thing in Genesis chapter one. He says, the Creator of Genesis 1:1 created "the heavens" and "all the host of them" by the word of His mouth. "And God said, Let there be…," and it was!

Prior to Isaiah's statement, the Creator of Genesis 1:1, the LORD God of Israel, revealed the same thing to King David. And under the inspiration of God the Holy Spirit, King David wrote:

One Creator or more?

"6 By the word of the LORD were the heavens made; and all the host of them by the breath of His mouth." "9 For He spake, and it was done; He commanded, and it stood fast" (Psalm 33:6, 9).

It is obvious from the above verses, King David makes it clear that "By the word of the LORD were the heavens made." And Moses' account agrees with King David's account that the Creator "spake, and it was done; He commanded, and it stood fast."

So, as per the above claims, is there more than one Creator?

Obviously, as per the above verses, the answer is a definite no!

In fact, I encourage you to take the initiative and read the entire sixty-six books of the Bible and study all of the creation verses in the Hebrew and Greek texts, and when you finish, you will observe that there is not a single creation verse, which claims or refers to more than one Creator. The verse or verses simply do not exist in the Bible! In fact, the prophet of old tells us that there is only one Creator.

Here are his words: "10 Have we not all one father? Hath not one God Created us?" Malachi 2:10

In confirmation to the above statement that the God of Genesis 1:1 is the only Creator of "all things," God the Creator proclaimed by the mouth of Isaiah; "24 Thus saith the LORD, thy Redeemer, and He that formed thee from the womb, I am the LORD that maketh all things; that stretcheth forth the heavens alone; that spreadeth abroad the earth by Myself" (Isaiah 44:24).

And the Creator of Genesis 1:1 adds by the pen of Jeremiah, "4 command them [the delegates who came to Jerusalem] to say unto their masters, Thus saith the LORD of hosts, the God of Israel; Thus shall ye say unto your masters; 5 I have made the earth, the man and the beast that are upon the ground, by My great power and by My outstretched arm" (Jeremiah 27:4, 5).

Can anybody dispute the Creator's claim that He created "all things," "the earth," "man," "beast," by His "great power"? And as

He says, He created "all things," "alone," and "by Myself" (Isaiah 44:24).

Try it; I encourage you!

The Identity of God the Creator

Thirdly, having written in the previous chapter a brief overview of the Individual who created "all things," by Himself ("by Myself"), "alone," and "by My great power," and identifies Himself by the name of "the LORD of hosts," and claims to be "the God of Israel" (Jeremiah 27:4, 5), I would like for you to keep the above thoughts in your memory because now, I have a question for you. Here is the question; who is the Individual, of Genesis 1:1, who dwelt between the two cherubims, led the children of Israel from Egypt and all the way into the Promised Land, claims to be the sole Creator of the universe and every thing that is in it, and identifies Himself by the name of "the LORD of hosts"?

Do you know who He is at this point?

Can you put on God the Creator of Genesis 1:1 an appearance, a face, a form, His activities, etc., etc., as Moses and the other prophets have done, in order to identify Him and have something tangible to relate to?

Can you?

If you can't, but went as far as to say that the Creator of Genesis 1:1 is the Individual who went to Egypt with Moses and Aaron, brought the children of Israel out of bondage, and dwelt between the two cherubims in His Sanctuary, which Moses built, and later, which Solomon built, I can agree with you. And if you said, He is the LORD God of Abraham and the God of Israel, I can agree. If you said, the Creator is the LORD of hosts, again, I can agree with you; but, you still have not identified the Creator of Genesis 1:1, all you have done is to give me His name and what He did!

So! How can I say that after I spent over one hundred and fifty pages telling you that the Creator of the universe, and everything that is in it, is the One who dwelt in the Sanctuary, which Moses built, and later on, in the Sanctuary, which Solomon built in Jerusalem?

I can say that because, you see, God the Creator of Genesis 1:1,

The Identity of God the Creator

who dwelt in the Sanctuary, which Moses built, has two Associates who have the same name as Himself. So, how do you know, which One of those three Individuals, who has the same name, is the Creator of the universe and everything that is in it and outside of it?

No! I am not making this up!

And yes, we are still in the Old Testament.

So! Who is the Individual who claims to be the God of Abraham, brought the children of Israel out of Egypt, dwelt between the two cherubims, and claims to be the sole Creator of the universe and everything that is in it?

Let me give you another hint.

When you look at a roomful of gods, which the world worships, and ask a Jewish rabbi, which One of those three Individuals, whose full name is "LORD God," is God the Creator of Genesis 1:1; he will tell you that there is only one God, as in the numerical number one (1). Therefore, he will claim that God the Creator of Genesis 1:1 is the LORD God of Abraham, Moses, Isaac, and of Jacob. He can quote to you any one of the Scripture references, which I have quoted for you, and may even quote some more Scriptures, in order to justify his claim; but will his efforts identify who is God the Creator of Genesis 1:1?

Likewise, the Muslim religious leaders will also tell you that God the Creator of Genesis 1:1 is the God of Abraham. But, like the Jewish religious answer, the teachers of the Qur'an cannot identify the God of Abraham, even though the Qur'an does reveal that Christ is the God of Abraham and the sole Creator of all things. On the other hand, in contradiction, the Imams and the Qur'an reject those revelations. Consequently, the most the Imams can acknowledge is to say, "The word *Allah*...has never been applied to anything other than the unimaginable Supreme Being." (See under the Tahrike Tarsile Qur'an, (MMP), 1992 Edition.

(For in-depth info on the character names of the God of Abraham, read my book called "Moses Wrote About Me." BEEHIVE PUBLISHING HOUSE INC.)

In addition, if you were to ask any Christians clergy who is the Creator, you will be told that God the Creator is the LORD God of

The Identity of God the Creator

Abraham and of Moses, but does that explanation identify who He is?

Does it?

Oh! Correction!

Many Christians will tell you that God the Father (Christ's Associate) is the Creator by quoting Ephesians 3:9 in their mistranslated Bibles; and some Christians will quote Romans 11:36 in their preferred translation of the Bible. Then again, the majority of Christians will tell you the opposite is true; they will tell you that God the Father created "through" Jesus Christ by quoting the "Apostle's Creed," and Colossians 1:16 in their favorite mistranslated Bibles. But are their claims correct?

Nonetheless, since the Jews, Muslims, and many Christian denominations cannot identify the Creator of Genesis 1:1 by Scripture, the question still stands; who do you think is God the Creator of Genesis 1:1?

Who do you think created the universe and everything that is in it outside of it?

Can you identify Him at this point?

I hope my previous hints helped you; but, if you are still unable to identify God the Creator at this point, do not feel bad because the Jews, the Muslims, and the majority of Christians, with all of their theology departments and prophets, have not identified God the Creator of the universe as per the Bible doctrine (2 John 9). All you have to do is to look at their diversified doctrinal beliefs, and you will see that they are unable to identify God the Creator of Genesis 1:1 as per the inspired Scriptures of the Bible. Please note: I said as per the inspired Scriptures (Hebrew and Greek texts of the Bible); I did not say as per man's interpretation of the Scriptures or by their favorite mistranslated Bibles.

These humongous religious institutions have a severe problem. How is it that Jews, Muslims, and Christians believe in the writings of Moses, and yet, they all believe in different Creators? How can that be? Should they not all believe in the same Creator? Should they not all believe in the God of Abraham who is identified in Nehemiah 9:6, 7 as the sole Creator? And should they not all

The Identity of God the Creator

believe in God the Creator of Moses who is identified in Genesis chapters one and two? And should they not all believe in God the Creator, the LORD God of Israel, who is identified throughout the writings of the Torah (5 books of Moses), and by the other prophets who were inspired to write about the Creator of Genesis 1:1?

What do you think?

What we have in the above presentation is the fact that the Jews, the Muslims, and the majority of Christians do not believe in God the Creator of Genesis 1:1.

They say they do, but do they?

Do you know why they do not believe in the same Creator?

Do you know why they do not believe in God the Creator of Genesis 1:1?

Take an educated guess and hold that thought!

Now compare your answer to the prophets of old.

Here is the answer. The Jews, Muslims, and the majority of Christians do not believe in God the Creator of Genesis 1:1 because the sole Creator of Genesis 1:1 is the "Messiah" (Christ, John 1:1, 14, 41, 3, 10).

Are you surprised!

As per the inspired Scriptures (Bible), Christ (Messiah) is the sole Creator of the universe and everything that is in it.

Although there are over twenty different ways we can identify that Christ is the sole Creator of the universe and everything that is in it (See my book "Moses Wrote About Me"); I will use couple of references to reveal that fact. Therefore let the prophets *first* identify Christ by the name of "the LORD of hosts," who dwelt in His Sanctuary above the "mercy seat," and *secondly*, let them confirm and identify the fact that Christ is the sole Creator of "all things" and the God of Abraham.

Having made the above comments let me take you back to the time when the God of Abraham went to Egypt with Moses and Aaron and took the children of Israel on a journey to the foot of Mount Sinai.

The Identity of God the Creator

Standing there on top of Mt. Sinai, the God of Abraham said to the children of Jacob (Israel), "2 I am the LORD Thy [Your] God who brought thee [you] out of Egypt, out of the house of bondage" (Exodus 20:2).

And after they accepted the God of Abraham as the LORD God of Israel, the ceremonial law, and the Ten Commandments, in agreement with their God, they ratified the blood of the Covenant at the foot of Mount Sinai. Once that agreement was acknowledged by the children of Israel, Moses was summoned to go up the mountain again. And when he did,

"1 the LORD spake unto Moses, saying...8 let them make Me a sanctuary; that I may dwell among them" (Exodus 25:1, 8).

And the children of Israel did.

And when the Sanctuary was completed, erected, and dedicated to the God of Israel (Exodus 40:33-35), He accepted the Sanctuary and dwelt there in the "most holy place" of the Sanctuary above the "mercy seat." And to reveal that His presence was there, a visible cloud could be seen hovering above the Sanctuary.

And in the first month of the second year of their stay at the foot of Mount Sinai, the camp of Israel was prompted by the God of Israel to move. "36 And when the cloud was taken up from over the tabernacle, the children of Israel went onward in all their journeys. 37 But if the cloud were not taken up, then they journeyed not till the day that it was taken up, 38 For the cloud of the LORD was upon the tabernacle [Sanctuary] by day, and fire was on it by night, in the sight of all the house of Israel, throughout all their journeys" (Exodus 40:36-38).

And when the children of Israel settled in the Promised Land (Canaan), after thirty-eight years of wandering, Joshua erected the Sanctuary, which Moses built, in a place called "Shiloh," which is located about twenty-five miles north of Jerusalem. There, the God of Israel was referred to and identified by the name of "Shiloh" and by the name of "the LORD of hosts." There He was worshipped by the children of Israel during special days and during their sin and

The Identity of God the Creator

thank offerings, which took place in the morning and at dusk in the eastern courtyard of the Sanctuary.

To confirm the fact that the Sanctuary of the God of Israel was pitched in "Shiloh," and the God of Israel dwelt in His Sanctuary, and was identified by the names of "the LORD of hosts" and "Shiloh," and the children of Israel worshipped Him there, here are few references from Samuel. He wrote: "1 NOW there was a certain man of Ramathaimzophim, of mount Ephraim…3 And this man went up out of his city yearly to worship and to sacrifice unto the LORD of hosts in Shiloh" (1 Samuel 1:1, 3), and that included his two wives who went with him to "Shiloh."

Did you notice? The God of Abraham and of Israel is identified by the name of "the LORD of hosts." They went "to worship and to sacrifice unto the LORD of hosts" in a place called "Shiloh."

And concerning one of his wives, whose name was Hannah, she did not have any children. And when she was there in "Shiloh," she prayed that the LORD of hosts would grant her children. (See 1 Samuel 1:9-18.)

And when she conceived, she dedicated the baby to God the LORD of hosts as she had promised Eli the priest. "24 And when she had weaned him [Samuel], she took him up with her, with three bullocks, and one ephah of flour, and a bottle of wine, and brought him unto the house of the LORD in Shiloh" and gave him to Eli the priest." Hannah said to Eli, "27 For this child I prayed; and the LORD hath given me my petition which I asked of Him: 28 Therefore also I have lent him to the LORD; as long as he liveth he shall be lent to the LORD. And he [Samuel] worshipped the LORD there" (1 Samuel 1:24, 27, 28).

Number of years later, during the war with the Philistines, we are told, "4 the people went to Shiloh, that they might bring from thence the ark of the covenant of the LORD of hosts, which dwelleth between the cherubims" (1 Samuel 4:4), to the battlefield because the children of Israel lost 4,000 solders during the first battle with the Philistines.

Contrary to "the LORD of hosts," the children of Israel did take the Ark of the Covenant to the battlefields and not only lost the

The Identity of God the Creator

war but at the same time they lost the Ark of the Covenant. The Ark was taken by the Philistines as a coveted trophy and placed it in the temple of "Dagon" their fish god.

So, as per the above verses, who did the children of Israel, Hannah, Eli, and Samuel "worship" in a place called "Shiloh"?

As per the above verses, it was "the LORD of hosts" who is also identified by the names of "Shiloh" and "the King of Israel" in the following verses. "4 Then all the elders of Israel gathered themselves together, and came to Samuel unto Ramah, 5 And said unto him, Behold, thou [you] art old, and thy [your] sons walk not in thy ways: now make us a king to judge us like all the nations. 6 But the thing displeased Samuel, when they said, Give us a king to judge us. And Samuel prayed unto the LORD.

> "7 And the LORD said unto Samuel, Hearken unto the voice of the people in all that they say unto thee [you]: for they have not rejected thee [you], but they have rejected Me, that I should not reign over them." 1 Samuel 8:4-7

As you have read above in verse seven, the children of Israel rejected "the LORD of hosts" their "King."

And so it was, to pacify the children of Israel, Samuel gave them Saul, a Benjamite, to be their king. (See also 1 Samuel 12:12.)

In addition, it should be noted that "the LORD of hosts" was also referred to by the name of "Shiloh," by the children of Israel.

Jacob before he died in Egypt said to his son Judah,

> "10 The sceptre shall not depart from Judah, nor a lawgiver from between his feet, until Shiloh come; and unto Him shall the gathering of the people be" (Genesis 49:10).

How was "Shiloh" going to come to the house of Judah and gather His people to Himself?

According to the above verse and the following verse, "Shiloh" (the LORD of hosts, the King of Israel) was going to come riding a donkey before He entered into Jerusalem; "11 Binding His foal unto

The Identity of God the Creator

the vine, and His ass's colt unto the choice vine [Judah]; He washed His garments in wine, and His clothes in the blood of the grapes" (Genesis 49:11).

Did you notice in verse ten above? Jacob personifies the word "Shiloh." Jacob refers to "Shiloh" by the pronoun "Him." He says, "unto Him shall the gathering of the people be." Therefore "Shiloh" who is identified by the name of "the LORD of hosts," by Samuel, is the One who was going to ride a donkey with a colt trailing into Jerusalem.

So! When will "the gathering of the people be" "unto Shiloh"?

The answer is given.

Jacob said that "the gathering of the people" will take place when "Shiloh" comes to them riding on a donkey with a colt trailing. Gen. 49:11

And so it was, eventually the tribe of Judah did inherit Jerusalem during the reign of King David; and after Solomon's apostasy, it became known as "the house of Judah" or "Jews" if you like. And during their Roman suppression, when the prophetic time clock struck, born out of a sinful woman (Galatians 4:4), "Shiloh" (the LORD of hosts), who dwelt in His Sanctuary, between the two cherubims, came in the flesh two thousand years ago to the house of Judah and revealed Himself to all of the children of Israel as their King, by riding a donkey into Jerusalem (Genesis 49:10, 11; Matthew 21:1-5); but the children of Israel "received Him not." The prophet of the LORD of hosts said, "11 He [Christ] came unto His own, and His own received Him not" (John 1:11); in stead, they crucified Him on Calvary's cross.

Here is Christ's personal claim that He is "the King of Israel: "1 AND when they [Christ and the apostles] drew nigh unto Jerusalem, and were come to Bethphage, unto the mount of Olives, then sent Jesus two disciples, 2 Saying unto them, Go into the village over against you, and straightway ye [all of you] shall find an ass tied, and a colt with her: loose them, and bring them unto Me. 3 And if any man say ought unto you, ye shall say, The LORD hath need of them; and straightway he will send them, 4 All this was done, that it might be fulfilled which was spoken by the prophet, saying,

185   The Creator of Genesis 1:1—Who is He?   *By: Philip Mitanidis*
The Identity of God the Creator_____

> "5 Tell ye the daughter of Sion [Zion], Behold, Thy [Your] King cometh unto thee [you], meek, and sitting upon an ass, and a colt the foal of an ass" (Matthew 21:1-5).

So, according to Christ's above own actions and words, He claimed openly to the public that He was "Shiloh" "the King of Israel," fulfilling Genesis 49:10, 11. This fact was well known throughout the land. In confirmation, when Christ was crucified, the pagan Romans put an inscription in three languages that Christ was the King of the Jews.

> Here is the reference: "38 And a superscription also was written over Him in letters of Greek, and Latin, and Hebrew, THIS IS THE KING OF THE JEWS" (Luke 23:38).

In view of the fact that the Roman authorities, the people of Judah, Galilee, and beyond—like the Magi, recognized Christ's claim that He was the King of the Jews, it follows, according to the above presentation and Isaiah 44:6, Christ the LORD of hosts is "Shiloh" "the King of Israel."

In addition, Isaiah tells us that the "the LORD of hosts" claims to be the "Redeemer" and the only "Saviour."

> He wrote: "6 Thus saith the LORD the King of Israel, and his Redeemer the LORD of hosts; I am the first, and I am the last; and beside Me there is no God" (Isaiah 44:6).

And adds, "11 I, am the LORD; and beside Me there is no Saviour" (Isaiah 43:11).

To reveal that there is only one "Savior," and that Savior is Jesus Christ, and therefore "the LORD of hosts," please note: the name "Jesus" means "Savior." The angel of the LORD said to Joseph, "21 And she shall bring forth a son, and thou [you] shall call His name JESUS: for He shall save His people from their sins"

The Identity of God the Creator

(Matthew 1:21).

And the name "Christ" means "Messiah." "41 He [Andrew] first findeth his own brother Simon, and saith unto him, We have found the Messias, which is, being interpreted, the Christ" (John 1:41).

Factually, there is only one Savior who can save a perishing sinner; and that Savior's name is Jesus Christ. Here is the account:

"12 Neither is there salvation in any other: for there is none other name whereby we must be saved" (Acts 4:12).

As per the above verses and as per the following verse, since salvation from our sins can only be given to us by Jesus Christ, we can conclude that Jesus Christ is the "Redeemer." He said to the children of Israel, "40 ye [all of you] will not come unto Me, that ye might have life" (John 5:40).

And since Christ is the only "Redeemer" (Acts 4:12), as per Isaiah's statement (Isaiah 44:6) it follows that Christ is the "LORD of hosts."

To further support the fact that Christ the "redeemer" is "the LORD of hosts," listen to Christ's claim: Christ identifies Himself as "the first and the last." Apostle John said, "17 And when I saw Him [Christ] I fell at His feet as dead. And He laid His right hand upon Me, saying unto me, Fear not; I am the first and the last; 18 I am He that liveth, and was dead; and, behold, I am alive for evermore. Amen" (Revelation 1:17, 18).

Now listen who claims to be the "the first and the last";

"6 Thus Saith the LORD the King of Israel, and his Redeemer the LORD of hosts; I am the first, and I am the last; and beside me there is no God" (Isaiah 44:6).

Did you hear who claims to be "the first and the last"?

That is right; "the King of Israel and his Redeemer" is Christ the LORD of hosts.

Christ "the first and the last" of Revelation 1:17, 18 is Christ "the first and the last" and "the LORD of hosts" of Isaiah 44:6.

The Identity of God the Creator

As a result, we can conclude, as per the above verses that the character names of "Shiloh," "the King of Israel," "Redeemer," and the "first and the last" all identify Christ by the name of "the LORD of host."

The *second* point the prophets make, about Christ the LORD of hosts, is the fact that they all identify Him as the sole Creator of "all things."

Simplistically, since Christ the King of Israel is the LORD of hosts, it follows in the following verses that Christ the LORD of hosts is the sole Creator of "all things." Here is the confirmation.

"4 command them [the delegates who came to Jerusalem] to say unto their masters, Thus saith the LORD of hosts, the God of Israel; Thus shall ye say unto your masters; 5 I have made the earth, the man and the beast that are upon the ground, by My great power and by My outstretched arm" (Jeremiah 27:4, 5).

"6 Thus Saith the LORD the King of Israel, and his Redeemer the LORD of hosts; I am the first, and I am the last; and beside me there is no God" (Isaiah 44:6).

Although the above two verses should suffice in confirmation that Christ the LORD of hosts is the sole Creator of "all things," here are few more excerpts to further help solidify Christ's claim in the above two verses that He created "alone," and as He says, "by Myself."

In the Torah, we are told by Moses that the LORD God of Abraham and of Israel said to Moses, "15 Wherefore criest thou [you] unto me? speak unto the children of Israel, that they go forward: 16 But lift thou [you] up thy [your] rod, and stretch out thine [your] hand over the sea, and divide it: and the children of Israel shall go on dry ground through the midst of the sea."

"21. And Moses stretched out his hand over the sea; and the LORD caused the sea to go back by a strong east wind all that night, and made the sea dry land, and the waters were divided. 22 And the children of Israel went into the midst of the sea upon the dry

The Identity of God the Creator

ground: and the waters were a wall unto them on their right hand, and on their left. 23 And the Egyptians pursued, and went in after them to the midst of the sea, even all Pharaoh's horses, his chariots, and his horsemen.

"24 And it came to pass, that in the morning watch the LORD looked unto the host of the Egyptians through the pillar of fire and of the cloud, and troubled the host of the Egyptians, 25 And took off their chariot wheels, that they drave them heavily: so that the Egyptians said, Let us flee from the face of Israel; for the LORD fighteth for them against the Egyptians.

"26 And the LORD said unto Moses, Stretch out thine hand over the sea, that the waters may come again upon the Egyptians, upon their chariots, and upon their horsemen. 27 And Moses stretched forth his hand over the sea, and the sea returned to his strength when the morning appeared; and the Egyptians fled against it; and the LORD overthrew the Egyptians in the midst of the sea. 28 And the waters returned, and covered the chariots, and the horsemen, and all the host of Pharaoh that came into the sea after them; there remained not so much as one of them. 29 But the children of Israel walked upon dry land in the midst of the sea; and the waters were a wall unto them on their right hand, and on their left. 30 Thus the LORD saved Israel that day out of the hand of the Egyptians; and Israel saw the Egyptians dead upon the sea shore. 31 And Israel saw that great work which the LORD did upon the Egyptians: and the people feared the LORD, and believed the LORD, and his servant Moses." Exodus 14:15, 16, 17-31

So! Who is this LORD God of Israel that brought the children of Israel out of the bondage of the Egyptians, divided the Red Sea, and went through the Red Sea to the other side safely?

The God of Abraham and of Israel gives the answer by saying,

"15 But I am the LORD Thy [Your] God, that divided the sea, whose waves roared: The LORD of hosts is His name." Isaiah 51:15

Did you hear that?

The Creator of Genesis 1:1—Who is He? By: *Philip Mitanidis*
The Identity of God the Creator

As per the above verse, the LORD God of Israel who "divided the sea" and made a way for the children of Israel to escape Pharaoh's army is "the LORD of hosts" (Isaiah 51:15). And "the LORD of hosts" who divided the Red Sea is identified by Apostle Paul, in 1 Corinthians 10:1-4, by the name of Christ (Hristos: Χριστος).

In confirmation, here are the cross references in 1 Corinthians 10:1-4, which reveal the events in the Torah, when the children of Israel traveled from Egypt to Mt. Sinai.

In verse one, Apostle Paul refers to "1 our fathers" who "were under the cloud [Exodus 13:20-22]." And adds; "all passed through the sea; 2 And were all baptized unto Moses in the cloud and in the sea [Exodus 14:21, 22]. 3 And did all eat the same spiritual meat [Exodus 16:14, 15]; 4 And did all drink the same spiritual drink: for they drank of that spiritual Rock that followed them [Exodus 17:4-6]: and that Rock was Christ [Χριστος]." 1 Corinthians 10:1-4

Therefore, given that Apostle Paul identifies "the LORD of hosts," who divided the Red Sea (vs. 2, 3; Is. 51:15), by the name of Christ (v.4), we can say with Apostle Paul and the Psalmist that it was Christ the LORD of hosts who "10 smote Egypt in their firstborn...11 And brought out Israel from among them...12 With a strong hand, and with a stretched out arm:

"13 To Him which divided the Red sea into parts...14 And made Israel to pass through the midst of it:...15 But overthrew Pharaoh and his host in the Red sea:" Psalms 136:10-15

And we can also agree with Apostle Paul and the Psalmist from above that the Individual who divided the Red Sea and identifies Himself by the name of Christ the LORD of hosts is none other than the sole Creator of the heavens, sun, moon, and the earth.

Here is the Psalmist's acknowledgement that Christ the LORD of hosts, who divided the Red Sea (Ps. 136:10-15), is the sole Creator by the use of the pronouns "Him" and "His" in the following verses. "5 To Him that by wisdom made the heavens...6 To Him that stretched out the earth above the waters...7 To Him that made great lights...8 The sun to rule by day...9 The moon and stars to rule by night: for His mercy endureth for ever." Psalms 136:3-9

The Identity of God the Creator

And here is Jeremiah's acknowledgement that Christ the LORD of hosts is the sole Creator of "all things."

> "4 Thus saith the LORD of hosts, the God of Israel; Thus shall ye [all of you] say unto your masters; 5 I have made the earth, the man, and the beast that are upon the ground, by My great power and by My outstretched arm." Jeremiah 27:4, 5

As you can readily see in the above verse, Jeremiah refers to Christ the LORD of hosts by the single pronouns "I" (I have made the earth), "My" (by My great power), "My" (by My outstretched arm), in order to convey to us that Christ the LORD of hosts is the sole Creator of "all things."

Therefore the Creator who created the earth, the man, and the beast that are upon the ground, by His great power and by His outstretched arm, is identified by the name of Christ the LORD of hosts. And Christ the LORD of hosts, in the New Testament, as per Moses and Apostle John, is the sole Creator of Genesis 1:1. Moses wrote,

> "1 In the beginning God created the heaven and the earth." Genesis 1:1

Likewise Apostle John agrees with the psalmist, Jeremiah, Apostle Paul, and Moses that the sole Creator of "the heaven and the earth" is Christ the LORD of hosts. John wrote:

> "10 He [Christ] was in the world, and the world was made by Him [Christ]" (John 1:10).

> "16 For by Him [Christ] were all thing created, that are in heaven, and that are in earth, visible and invisible, whether they be thrones, or dominions, or principalities, or powers; all things were created by Him [Christ] and for Him [Christ]" (Col. 1:16).

In addition, Christ the LORD of hosts says, "24 I am the LORD

The Identity of God the Creator

that maketh all things; that stretcheth forth the heavens alone; that spreadeth abroad the earth by Myself." Isaiah 44:24

Therefore, the Creator who created "alone" and as He says, "by Myself" (Isaiah 44:24) is identified by Isaiah and Jeremiah by the name of "the LORD of hosts." And the LORD of hosts is none other than Christ the Creator of Genesis 1:1; John 1:1, 14, 41, 3, 10; Romans 11:34-36, and Colossians 1:16, 17.

As you have witnessed, the inspired word of God the Holy Spirit identifies and testifies that Christ is the sole Creator of "heaven" and "earth" (Genesis 1:1; John 1:1, 3, 10). In fact, Christ the Messiah (Christ) personally made that claim when He was here on earth in the "flesh." Christ said, "15 All things that the Father hath are Mine" (John 16:15). Christ can say that because "16 all things were created by Him [Christ], and for Him [Christ]" (Colossians 1:16). Therefore, the universe as we know it was created by Christ the LORD of hosts; it was "16 created by Him [Christ], and for Him [Christ]" (Colossians 1:16).

Please note because there was no co-Creator involved, "all things" were created by Christ's "power" and by Christ's "discretion." They were not created by somebody else's "power" or "discretion" (Jeremiah 10:12).

Now you know why I said previously that the Jews, the Muslims, and the majority of Christians do not believe in God the Creator of Genesis 1:1. The reason why they do not believe in God the Creator of the Bible is due to the fact that they all claim that someone else, other than Jesus Christ (Messiah Daniel 9:26, 27; John 1:41), created the universe. They do not want to accept the Scripture references, which reveal that the sole Creator of the universe, and everything that is in it, is the Messiah (Christ), who was better known by the children of Israel, as the "God of Abraham," "the LORD God of Israel," "the LORD of hosts," "Shiloh," "the King of Israel," "the first and the last," "Redeemer," and of course, "the Creator" of Genesis 1:1; John 1:1, 3, and 10.

Please note, none of the above creation verses in the Hebrew or Greek texts refer to a co-Creator that is why Christ is identified in all of these verses as the sole Creator of "all things"; and that is an inescapable undisputed Scriptural fact.

The prophet of Christ the LORD of hosts sums up the above presentation this way; he says, "16 O LORD of hosts, God of Israel, that dwellest between the cherubims, Thou [You] art the God, even Thou {you} alone, of all the kingdoms of the earth: Thou [You] hast made heaven and earth." Isaiah 37:16

The Creator's Associates

Did you know, today, many Jews, Muslims, and many Christians do not believe that Christ the Creator of Genesis 1:1 has two Associates?

According to Scripture (Bible), yes He does!

Can you identify them by using the Old Testament references only?

Try it!

Don't despair if you cannot identify them by the use of the Old Testament.

But, if you said, "I know who they are," don't be too sure because the following presentation could very easily go against what you think is correct! So, take few minutes of your time, read the following pages, and compare these pages with what you believe. Don't be surprised if you find yourself in contradiction with the Bible prophets of old.

On the other hand, maybe you will not find the following presentation contradictory because you have studied the subject of Christ the Creator and His two Associates before; and you are aware of the fact that the Old and the New Testaments reveal three separate Individuals who have the same name—like your last name. But if you have not studied the subject of the Creator at all, or you have not studied it to the fullest, bear with me for few minutes while I present Jesus Christ the Creator of Genesis chapter one and two, John 1:1, 14, 41, 3, 10, and His two Associates (God the Father and God the Holy Spirit as we know them in the New Testament).

First let us consider the writings of the various prophets of the Bible, which will demonstrate that the inspired Scriptures of the Bible do not teach that there are three Individuals as in "one God" or of "one body" or of "one essence" in the universe, as in the

The Creator's Associates

mathematical number one (1). By studying other verses from the Bible, you will find that the Old and New Testaments reveal three separate Individuals who have the same name, and that name is "LORD God."

To confirm the above statements, here are few references from the Old and New Testaments, which reveal the fact that there are three separate Individuals (God the Christ, God the Father, and God the Holy Spirit) by the name "LORD God" who think independently and act independently.

In the Old Testament, we have the following revelation by Moses:

> "24 Then the LORD (יהוה) rained upon Sodom and upon Gomorrah brimstone and fire from the LORD (יהוה) out of heaven" (Genesis 19:24).

In the above verse, Moses identifies at least two Individuals by the name LORD .(יהוה) Moses says that the LORD, who visited Abraham with the two angels (see chapter 18 of Genesis), brought "brimstone and fire from the LORD out of heaven." Please note, the LORD who was on earth with the two angels brought fire "from" the LORD who was in "heaven." In the above verse, Moses depicts one LORD on earth and the other LORD in heaven, and that makes two Individuals who are addressed by the name "LORD" .(יהוה)

Likewise, here is a reference from the New Testament, which identifies more than one Individual by the name "LORD." The wording of the following verse is similar to the verse in Genesis 19:24.

> "18 The Lord grant unto him that he may find mercy of the LORD in that day [Rev. 6:16, 17]: and in how many things he ministered unto me at Ephesus, thou knowest very well" (2 Timothy 1:18).

Please note: I have placed one LORD (Christ) in the upper case, so that you can differentiate between Christ the Creator and His Associate (God the Father), which I placed his name in the

The Creator's Associates

lower case setting.

Notably, the apostle, like Moses, addresses two Individuals by the name "LORD" in the above verse. Apostle Paul desired that the "Lord grant unto him that he may find mercy of the LORD in that day" (Rev. 6:16,17). That means that one Lord (God the Father) grants mercy while the other LORD (Christ) will have mercy on that individual, in that day. So, one Lord grants mercy and the other LORD gives mercy. As you can see in this verse, there are two Individuals by the same name "LORD."

Now let me bring you to a verse, where the psalmist also makes reference to two separate Individuals. In this verse, the psalmist addresses Christ the LORD and His Associate (God the Father) by the same name, and that name is "God" .(אלהים)

Unfortunately, for whatever reasons, some translators have chosen not to translate the psalmist's verse to identify two Individuals by the name of God? The reason could very well be because of the translator's beliefs; they assume, the psalmist should have somehow referred to one God and not to two Gods. But the fact remains; the psalmist is referring to two separate Individuals by the name God. You can verify that fact by reading the verse in the Hebrew or in the Septuagint Greek Scriptures. As an example, one Greek text reads:

"Ο   ΘΕΟΣ   ισταται εν τη   συναξει   των δυνατων
"O   Theos   uctatai en ti   cinaxei   ton dinaton
 "   God   stands   in the gathering of   the mighty

"αναμεσον   των Θεον   θελει   κρινει."
"anamecou   ton Theon thelei   krinei."
"middle   of   God   He wants judge."
(Psalm 82:1). Βιβλικη Εταιρεια. (Translation is mine.)

In the above verse, the psalmist reveals two separate Individuals by the name, "God" (Θεος). In the Greek language the words "o Θεος" mean "the God" and "των Θεον" mean "to God." But the word "Θεος" means the same thing. The reason the Greek wording

The Creator's Associates

is different is due to the grammatical structure of the Greek sentence. Therefore, the Greek words (των Θεον) and (ο Θεος), in English refer to "God." The above verse translated into English will read, "God [Christ vs. 6-7] stands in the gathering of the mighty [the judges] in the middle of God [Christ's Associate] He wants to judge." (Translation is mine.)

The obvious inescapable fact, in the above verse, reveals that the psalmist, like Moses, agrees that there are two Individuals who are addressed by the name "God" .(אלהים)

If you look in the Septuagint Greek Scriptures, you will find that they confirm the fact that there are two Individuals mentioned by the name of "ΘΕΟΣ" (God) in Psalm 82:1. And, if you look in the Septuagint Bible, which was translated during the time of Alexander the Great from Greece, during the 3rd and 2nd Century B.C., you will notice that the two words "ΘΕΟΣ" are derived from the two Hebrew words "אלהים." And, if you go one step further and read the Hebrew text, you will find the word "God" is mentioned twice by the Hebrew word "אלהים." In English, the word "אלהים" translates as "El-o-him" or "El-o-km," if you like. Therefore, if you read the Hebrew verse, which is similar to the Greek verse, it will read in English as follows, "God stands in the center of God, He judges in the midst of the judges." (Translation is mine.)

Regarding the Hebrew and Greek verses, you will find some commentators and translators state that the second word "אלהים" cannot refer to another God because they believe that there is only one God, as in the numerical number "1" (one). Therefore, they say that the second word "אלהים" refers to the judges. But how can the second word refer to the judges when the word itself does not encompass the word judges. Both of the words, judges and God, are separate in the above verse. Thus these words have to be translated as such. In fact, the word judges cannot be found to be identified as being part of the Godhead in the entire Scriptures by the word "אלהים."

But, if we were to take the word judges and say that it refers to God, then we will have a big problem, and that problem will be that

The Creator's Associates

the verse will be identifying innumerable individuals by the name God! And, if we were to go down that road; we will end up identifying all of the judges as Gods.

Although historically the judges claimed that they were gods, by their own law, in order to avoid the angel of death to come upon them, does anybody want to address them as such?

So, why object to what the psalmist has written? He has identified two separate Individuals by the name "God." Should we not do the same? After all, the name "God" (אלהים) belongs to Christ the Creator and to His two Associates. We cannot apply Their name to someone else.

Nonetheless, let me clarify the Hebrew verse for you. If you recall, after Joshua died, the appointed judges administered the affairs of the children of Israel. The judges were individuals who preceded King Saul. These judges were residing in the tribes of Israel. During that time period of the judges, Christ the Creator was dwelling with the children of Israel in His Sanctuary, which was pitched in a place called "Shiloh." From Shiloh Christ the Creator, who was addressed by the children of Israel by His names "LORD," "God," "King of Israel," "LORD of hosts," and "Shiloh" was judging the judges of Israel. (See 1 Samuel 4:4.)

Therefore, the psalmist correctly states that Christ the Creator stood (in Shiloh) in the midst of the judges, and in the midst of God (His Associate), who is also addressed by the psalmist by his name "God," Christ the Creator judged the judges. You should remember, in the Old Testament, Christ the Creator of Genesis 1:1 was able to judge in the midst of the judges because He was a Spirit Being like His two Associates. He could be in two places at the same time. In fact He could be everywhere at the same time. His "whole creation could not contain Him"—remember?

Later on, the record tells us that Christ the Creator was judging Israel from His Sanctuary, which Solomon built for Him in Jerusalem.

There is no confusion in Psalms 82:1; the verse says that one God is standing in the midst of another God. That is straight forward, isn't it? So, why rewrite the verse to show only one

The Creator's Associates

"God"? Or why remove one God from the verse or change His name to read something else as some Bibles do? That is altering the word of God, and that is deleting the word of God. God does not approve of those types of insubordinate actions.

You know, there is a very strong condemnation placed upon those individuals who alter, delete, add, or wrongly preach the word of God the Holy Spirit.

> We are told: "8 though we, or an angel from heaven, preach any other gospel unto you than that which we have preached unto you, let him be accursed" (Galatians 1:8).

That is very strong language, isn't it? It says, "let him be accursed."

So, why would anyone alter the word of God under that type of condemnation? Shouldn't translators leave the presentation of the two words "God," in Psalm 82:1, intact?

What do you think?

Now, Let me take you to the New Testament and show you where Christ the Creator of Genesis 1:1, and His Associate are revealed by the name of "God." This revelation begins, in a setting, before Christ the Creator created the heavens and the earth.

> Apostle John the prophet says, "1 IN the beginning was the Word [Christ], and the Word [Christ] was with God [Christ's Associate], and the Word [Christ] was God" (John 1:1).

If you look at the words in the above verse "IN the beginning was the Word," the word "Word" (ΛΟΓΟΣ) in the predicate is identified by Apostle John by the name "God" (ΘΕΟΣ). John refers to the "Word" by the name "God" by saying, "and the Word was God." So, in essence what John says in the above verse is that the "Word," which John calls "God," was "with" His Associate whose name is also called "God." John says the "Word" (God) was with "God" (the Father). Here then, Apostle John identifies two

The Creator's Associates

Individuals by the name "God," just as the psalmist does in Psalms 82:1.

Now, let me bring, to your attention, another verse from the Old Testament, which reveals again Christ the Creator and His Associate; only this time, King David addresses Christ the Creator and His Associate by the name "LORD."

This is what King David said about Christ's Associate:

> "₁ THE LORD said unto My LORD, Sit Thou at my right hand, until I make Thine [Your] enemies Thy footstool" (Psalms 110:1).

In the above verse, unless a person is in full denial, it can readily be seen that there are two Individuals by the name "LORD" .(יהוה) Looking at future events, King David states that the "LORD" (God the Father) will say to David's "LORD" (Christ the LORD God of Israel) to "Sit Thou [Christ] at my [God the Father's] right hand, until I [God the Father] make Thine [Christ's] enemies Thy [Christ's] footstool."

As you can see in the above verse, David reveals two Individuals by the name of "LORD." And in the New Testament, Christ the LORD acknowledges what King David said. (See Mark. 12:35-37; Matthew 22:42-45.)

In the following verses, you can plainly see that there are two separate Individuals who are addressed by the name "God." In verse one of Hebrews chapter one, the apostle is referring to Christ's Associate (God the Father) by the name "God." On the other hand, God the Father is addressing Christ the Creator by the name "God," in v.8.

Here is the verse in the New Testament where God the Father makes reference to Christ the Creator after Christ came in the "flesh."

> "₈ But unto the Son [Christ] he [God the Father] saith, Thy [Your] throne, O God [Christ], is for ever and ever: a scepter of righteousness is the

The Creator's Associates

sceptre of Thy kingdom" (Hebrews 1:8).

As you can see, in the above verse, God the Father is referring to Christ by the name of "Son" and "God." As you well know, this verse refers to Christ the Creator after He came in the "flesh." And in this verse, although Christ the Creator of Genesis 1:1 is in the human form, Christ's Associate (God the Father) personally acknowledges Christ the Creator as his "God." Christ's Associate states unequivocally, "Thy [Your] throne O God is for ever and ever."

Another acknowledgement that is made by Christ's Associate (God the Father) is the fact that he acknowledges Christ's Kingdom. Christ's Associate says to Christ the Creator, "a sceptre of righteousness is the sceptre of Thy [Your] kingdom."

In addition, if you were to look at verse one of Hebrews, you will find Christ's Associate, in this verse, is identified by the name "God."

> It reads, "1 GOD, who at sundry times and in diverse manners spake in time past unto the fathers by the prophets" (Hebrews 1:1).

Here then, in verse one and in verse eight, again, we see two separate Individuals revealed to us by the name "God." God (the Father) is addressed "God" in v.1 and God (the Christ) is addressed "God" by God (the Father) in v.8.

Let me bring you one more reference, in order to show you where Christ's Associate (God the Father) personally addresses Christ the Creator, again, by the name "LORD". (יהוה)

Approximately five hundred BC, the prophet Zechariah revealed, in one of the incidences, where God the Father personally addressed Christ the Creator by His name "LORD". (יהוה)

> Zechariah said, "1 AND he shewed me Joshua the high priest standing before the angel of the LORD [יהוה], and Satan standing at his right hand to resist him. 2 And the LORD [יהוה] said unto Satan, The LORD [יהוה] rebuke thee, O Satan; even

The Creator's Associates

the LORD [יהוה] that hath chosen Jerusalem rebuke thee" (Zechariah 3:1, 2).

Let me clarify the verses. "And he [the angel] shewed me [Zechariah] Joshua the high priest standing before the angel [Gabriel] of the LORD [Christ's Associate], and Satan standing at his right hand to resist him.

"And the LORD [Christ's Associate] said unto Satan, The LORD [Christ] rebuke thee, O Satan; even the LORD [Christ] that hath chosen Jerusalem rebuke thee."

Who had chosen Jerusalem for His dwelling place?

It was Christ the Creator, the LORD God of Israel, who chose Jerusalem—remember? Christ the Creator said to King Solomon "I have chosen" Jerusalem (1 Kings 11:13). And to King David, Christ said, "I have chosen Jerusalem, that My name might be there" (2 Chronicles 6:6).

So, who was the LORD who said, "The LORD rebuke thee, O Satan"?

It was none other than Christ's Associate, who is better known in the New Testament by the name of God the Father. God the Father acknowledges Christ the Creator by the name "LORD [יהוה]"; and he (God the Father) also acknowledges the fact that Christ the Creator was the One who chose Jerusalem as His dwelling place.

Likewise, as you have observed, in the above verse, the Associate of Christ the Creator, who is mentioned by the prophet Zechariah, is revealed to us by the name of "LORD." Therefore, in these verses, like the previous verses, which we have read, reveal two separate Individuals by the name "LORD" (יהוה) and that is an inescapable fact.

Let me say again, as you can readily observe in the Greek and Hebrew Scriptures, Christ's Associate and Christ the Creator have the same name, and that name is "LORD God" (יהוה אלהים). In fact, Christ's Associate (God the Father) personally acknowledges Christ the Creator, of Genesis 1:1, by the name "LORD God" (יהוה אלהים). We should do the same, don't you think? Or are we above Christ's Associate (God the Father)?

The Creator's Associates

Thus far, I have taken you to verses where you have observed two Individuals by the name of "LORD" and "God"; now, let me introduce to you the second Associate of Christ whose name is also "LORD God."

Please don't say, what!

And yes, we are still in the Old Testament.

Bear with me for few moments while I explain, and reveal Christ's second Associate whose name is also "LORD God."

As you have learned, Christ the Creator of Genesis 1:1 was the One who brought the children of Israel out of the land of Egypt. He said, "I am the LORD Thy [Your] God, which have brought thee [you] out of the land of Egypt" (Exodus 20:2). And this same LORD God who brought the children of Israel out of Egypt made a request to Moses while they were staying at the foot of Mount Sinai. Christ the Creator said to Moses, "8 let them [the children of Israel] make Me a Sanctuary; that I may dwell among them." And then, Christ the Creator added, you will make the Sanctuary "9 According to all that I shew thee, after the pattern of the tabernacle, and the pattern of all the instruments thereof, even so shall ye make it" (Exodus 25:8, 9).

Obviously the pattern was revealed to Moses while he was on Mount Sinai in the presence of Christ the Creator. In that pattern there were curtains, posts, furniture, and many more items, which Moses had to make. Some of these items needed special talent to make them. Since Moses could not find anyone to make certain pieces, in a highly skilled workmanship, God the Creator provided a helper for the people that were to do the skilled work. The name of that helper is "God."

Please notice in the following verses, Christ the LORD of hosts is addressing His second Associate by the name of "God."

Here is the confirmation, "1 And the LORD [Christ the LORD of hosts] spake unto Moses, saying, 2 See, I have called by name Bezaleel the son of Uri, the son of Hur, of the tribe of Judah: 3 And I have filled him with the spirit of God, in wisdom, and in understanding, and in knowledge, and in all manner of workmanship" (Exodus 31:1-3).

The Creator's Associates

As you can see in the above verses, it is Christ the LORD who filled Bezaleel with the Spirit of "God." He did not fill Bezaleel with His own Spirit; He filled him with someone else's Spirit. It was His second Associate's Spirit that filled Bezaleel; and when Bezaleel was filled with God the Holy Spirit, he was able to produce the desired artwork on the furniture that they were preparing for the Sanctuary.

Here then, in Exodus 31:1-5, Moses refers to two separate Individuals who have the same name, and that name is "God." In these verses, distinctly and separately, Moses refers to Christ the God of Israel and to "God" the "Holy Spirit." Moses' comments reveal to us that he is talking about two separate Individuals who have the same name.

By the way, you should remember that "God the Spirit," "Spirit of God," "Holy Spirit," or "Holy Ghost," are translated contrary to the inspired Scriptures, by some translators, to read as some kind of an "active force." The words "active force," or "force" if you like, which replace the above names of God the Holy Spirit cannot be found anywhere in the inspired Hebrew and Greek Scriptures. Therefore the words "active force" cannot be used to refer to the Creator's second Associate because the Creator's Associate's name is not some kind of "active force." His name is "God" and "LORD." To replace his name "LORD God" by the words "active force" is not only demeaning and disrespectful; but at the same time, a person is further adding sin upon self by adding to Scripture and deleting Scripture; and that is an outright blasphemy.

Nonetheless, as in the Old Testament, we have the same testimony in the New Testament that Christ the Creator has a second Associate. And this second Associate (God the Holy Spirit) is distinctly identified separately from the Creator's first Associate (God the Father), which we have already studied.

In the following verse, the Creator's two Associates are identified for us this way:

> "35 And the angel [Gabriel] answered and said unto her [Mary], The Holy Ghost shall come upon thee [you], and

The Creator's Associates

the power of the Highest shall overshadow thee: therefore also that holy thing which shall be born of thee shall be called the Son of God" (Luke 1:35).

As you have noticed, there are three separate Individuals mentioned by Luke, the physician, in the above verse. He states that one of Christ's Associates, who is identified by the name "Holy Ghost," was to come upon Mary. And we are also told that the other Associate of Christ, who is identified as the "Highest" (God the Father) was to "overshadow" Mary, and when these two Associates of Christ the Creator were to come upon Mary, they were to transfer, or "send" Christ the Creator of Genesis 1:1 from an awesome Spirit Being, in her seed, to become flesh and blood. And when confirmation took place; we are told, "35 that holy thing which shall be born of thee [Mary] shall be called the Son of God" (Luke 1:35).

Now, I am not going to expand on Christ's second Associate who is identified by the name "the Holy Ghost," but I will say this much, if you want to research Christ's second Associate, you will find Him mentioned in the Old and in the New Testaments by His names "God," "LORD," "Holy Ghost," "Spirit," and "Holy Spirit."

By the way, I am not going to give you the references, but, if you are going to do the research on God the Holy Spirit, you will find God the Holy Spirit, God the Christ, and God the Father are also mentioned in a similar setting, as in Luke 1:35, in the Old Testament.

If you are still wondering about the name of the three Individuals who go by the name LORD God, let me explain it this way: Simplistically, the name "LORD God," "LORD," "God the LORD," or "God" is similar to your last name. Your last name not only refers to you, but it also encompasses the other members of your family. If you were to refer to one of your family members, by your last name, I would not know to whom you are referring to because they all have the same last name. A quick way to identify any one of your family members would be, if you used their given names. You know as well as I do, without their given names, it will

The Creator's Associates

be very difficult to identify them, especially if they are not in view.

So it is with the three Individuals who go by the name "LORD God." In order for us to know who is who, we must identify them by their character names or by their given names, if you like. Without the revelation of their character names, we will have difficult time identifying them independently. That does not mean that we cannot identify them; we can by observing what each Individual did or is doing right now. As an example, we have followed Christ's activities thus far, and we found out that Christ the Creator of Genesis 1:1 was the One who took Abraham out of Ur (Iraq) and sent him to Canaan (Palestine). We also found out that it was Christ the Creator of Genesis 1:1 who went to Egypt with Moses and Aaron to bring His people into the Promised Land. We also learned that Christ was the One who dwelt in His Sanctuary in the midst of the children of Israel. We also found out that Christ the Creator of Genesis 1:1; John 1:1, 3, 10, 14, and 41 came in the "flesh" to save man from his eternal death, and so on. We can do the same thing with the Creator's two Associates. But, needless to say, it is much easier when we use their character names to identify them.

Therefore, if you are looking for Christ the LORD God of Israel, only in the Old Testament, you will find Him by the following character names: "the King of Israel," "the first and the last," "the Rock," "Creator," "the LORD of hosts," "the God of Israel," "the Most High," "Shiloh," etc., etc., and of course, dwelling in between the two cherubims and leading the children of Israel from Egypt all the way into the Promised Land. And when you read these verses, which refer to Christ the LORD of hosts, please observe in all of these verses, Christ the LORD and the prophets use the single pronouns, "I," "Me," "My," "Him," etc., etc., to denote Christ's distinctiveness and individuality from His two Associates (God the Father and God the Holy Spirit). And to drive the point home that Christ is distinct from His two Associates, Christ the LORD of hosts says, "25 To whom then will ye [all of you] liken Me, or shall I be equal? saith the Holy One" (Isaiah 40:25). Or, "6 who in the heaven can be compared unto the

The Creator's Associates

LORD?" (Psalms 89:6).

"6 there is none like unto Thee, O LORD." Jeremiah 10:6

"2 There is none holy as the LORD: for there is none beside thee [You]: neither is there any Rock like our God" (1 Samuel 2:2).

So! To whom should we "compare" Christ the "Rock"? Or, to whom should we make Him "equal"?
Obviously to no one because Christ the LORD of hosts adds,

"9 I am God, and there is none like Me" (Isaiah 46:9).

By making the above statements, Christ the LORD of hosts makes Himself distinct from His two Associates (God the Father and God the Holy Spirit). And, as you have read in this chapter, Christ's Associates are also distinct from Christ and from each other. And that is where the inspired Scriptures leave us. Scripture does not reveal what they are made of or how they came to exist? When Moses asked Christ the LORD to reveal Himself, Christ replied, "I AM THAT I AM" (Exodus 3:14).

Therefore a person cannot speculate. All he or she can say, as per the revelation of Scripture that there are three separate distinct Individuals who think and act independently, treat each other as equals, and have the same name (LORD God). In fact, Christ and His two Associates who go by the name LORD God, sometimes, they use their name "LORD God" collectively. They do that because they do not discriminate amongst each other. Each one of them can say, "I am the LORD God," and they would be right because according to Scripture that is their "name" (Matthew 28:19). And notably, by having the same name, it is hard to distinguish who is who, especially, if you don't know their character names.

Note: If you are not too familiar with the character names of Christ the LORD of hosts, read my book called "Moses Wrote About Me" By: *Philip Mitanidis*. BEEHIVE PUBLISHING HOUSE INC.

The Creator's Transformation

The transformation of Christ the LORD of hosts, the Creator of Genesis 1:1; John 1:1, 3, 10, from an awesome Spirit Being into a human being, is identified by the character name of "Christ," which means (Messiah: John 1:41).

But, how was He transferred from an awesome Spirit Being, whose creation could not contain Him (1 Kings 8:27), into a helpless little baby, born in the little town of Bethlehem approximately 2,000 years ago?

First, let Christ the Creator of Genesis 1:1; John 1:1, 3, and 10, who dwelt with the children of Israel in the Promised Land, and is identified as the God of Abraham, the God of the children of Israel, and the Savior of the world, reveal to us the promise He made prior to His coming in the "flesh," by the use of the forthcoming verses.

About 740 BC, the children of Israel accused Christ their God of abandonment. They said,

"$_{14}$ The LORD hath forsaken me [Israel], and my LORD hath forgotten me" (Isaiah 49:14).

In response to their unwarranted allegation, prophetically, Christ the LORD God of Israel said to them,

"$_{15}$ Can a woman forget her sucking child, that she should not have compassion on the son of her womb? yea, they may forget, yet will I not forget thee [you]." Isaiah 49:15

Christ the LORD God of Israel did not "forsake" or "forget" the children of Israel. He made the "promise" to Adam, Noah, Abraham, Isaac, Jacob, King David, etc., etc., that He was going to come in the "flesh" (Galatians 4:4) to save them and their descendents from their eternal death. And, in order to put the children of Israel at ease, He reminded them of the above "promise," and the horrible torture, and death He was going to

The Creator's Transformation

endure for their sakes. Christ the Creator the LORD God of Israel foretold His own agony and death upon the cruel cross by saying,

> "16 Behold, I have graven thee [you] upon the palms of My hands; thy [your] walls are continually before Me" (Isaiah 49:16).

So! When was Christ the LORD God of Israel going to come to planet earth, be crucified, and receive those scars on His hands?

According to Daniel the prophet, we are told in Daniel 9:25, 26 that the "Messiah" (Christ the God of Israel) was to come in the "flesh" in a certain time-line during the Roman Empire. Here is Daniel's time-line.

```
457 BC      408 BC           27 AD     34 AD
!------7 wks--!-------62 wks----!-----+------!------------------------2300 yrs
Decree      City             Messiah  Midst of   Gospel to Gentiles
            Rebuilt          Anointed wk cut off
```

Although Daniel gives us the time period of Christ's coming in the flesh, other prophets reveal to us how Christ the Messiah was going to come, from what tribe He was going to come, and where He was going to be born. As an example, Micah said,

> "2 But thou, Bethlehem Ephratah, though thou be little among the thousands of Judah, yet out of thee shall He [the LORD God of Israel] come forth unto me [His Associate] that is to be ruler in Israel; whose [the LORD God of Israel] goings forth have been from of old, from everlasting" (Micah 5:2).

And Isaiah adds, "14 the LORD Himself [Christ the Creator the LORD God of Israel] shall give you a sign; Behold, a virgin shall conceive, and bear a son, and shall call His name Immanuel" (Isaiah 7:14).

As you have read, Immanuel (Christ) was going to be born out of a "virgin," from the tribe of Judah, in a place called "Bethlehem."

The Creator's Transformation

Here is the cross reference of the above verse, and the actual occurrence about 2,000 years ago:

> "22 Now all this was done, that it might be fulfilled which was spoken of the LORD [Christ the LORD God of Israel] by the prophet [Isaiah], saying, 23 Behold, a virgin shall be with child, and shall bring forth a son, and they shall call His name Emmanuel, which being interpreted is, God with us" (Matthew 1:22, 23).

This very same God of Israel, "whose goings forth have been from of old, from everlasting" (Micah 5:2), says that He was going to provide "a sign." Isaiah writes, "the LORD Himself" (the LORD of hosts) was going to provide that "sign." And He did. He gave that sign by Himself during the time period when Mary, from the tribe of Judah, carried Him; and He gave a sign that a Virgin was going to give birth to Him. And at His birth, the sign of a star (angels) was to appear above Him, as Balaam from Mesopotamia predicted about 1400 BC when he was overlooking at the beautiful and orderly camp of Israel from the mountain. Christ the Creator, the LORD God of Israel not only foretold of His coming in the "flesh" around 740 BC, He also gave the sign that He was going to be born in the little town of Bethlehem. And when Christ the Creator, the LORD God of Israel arrived in the "flesh," He was to be recognized as the One who was "Immanuel" (God with us).

In those days (2,000 years ago), many did recognize Christ to be "God with us" (Matthew 1:23), and many abhorred the idea that He was the "Messiah" (Christ: John 1:1, 14, 41); but that is another story.

Anyway, where was this Virgin going to conceive a "son" who was to be identified by the name "Immanuel" (God with us)?

As per the prophecy, which the prophet Micah penned for us, it states that Christ (Messiah) was to be born in Bethlehem, which is in Judaea. Notably Micah the prophet did not say that Christ was going to be born in Bethlehem, which is in Galilee. He could have, but he did not say that. In fact, since Mary and Joseph lived in the

The Creator's Transformation

province of Galilee, one would think that Christ would be born in Bethlehem of Galilee? But that is not what the prophet stated! Isaiah had stated that a Virgin was to conceive "Immanuel" (God with us); and Micah the prophet tells us where "Immanuel" (God with us) was going to be born. He said that the birth of "God" was going to take place in the town of "Bethlehem," in the province of "Judea."

But Mary lived in the province of Galilee, which is north of Judea, in a little town called Nazareth. She did not live in Judea! So, why was she going to give birth to the LORD God of Israel in Judea? And how was she going to give birth to the LORD God of Israel in the little town of Bethlehem, in order to fulfill the prophecy, which Micah predicted?

Bethlehem was over eighty miles away. In those days traveling by foot and carrying few rations meant a very arduous long journey. After all, why would anyone who is pregnant travel such an enormous distance and take the chance of being robbed or beaten or even have a miscarriage?

Actually, she did not have a choice. Well, she did, but if she did not go to Bethlehem, she would have a severe problem with the Roman authorities. You see, Mary's husband, Joseph, who was from the line of King David, had to go to Bethlehem in Judaea to register for the taxes, which they were to be levied upon them according to the Roman law. Foreseeing this event, God the Holy Spirit inspired Micah, about 735 years earlier, to write that the birth of Christ the Creator, the LORD God of Israel, was going to take place in Bethlehem in the province of Judaea.

> He said: "2 But thou, Bethlehem Ephratah, though thou be little among the thousands of Judah, yet out of thee shall He [the LORD God of Israel] come forth unto me [His Associate] that is to be ruler in Israel; whose [the LORD God of Israel] goings forth have been from of old, from everlasting" (Micah 5:2).
>
> And here is the cross reference: "1 NOW when Jesus was born in Bethlehem of Judaea in the days of Herod the king, behold,

The Creator's Transformation

> there came wise men from the east to Jerusalem, 2 Saying, Where is He that is born King of the Jews? for we have seen His star [angels] in the east, and are come to worship Him. 3 When Herod the king had heard these things, he was troubled, and all Jerusalem with him. 4 And when he had gathered all the chief priests and scribes of the people together, he demanded of them where Christ [Messiah] should be born. 5 And they said unto him, In Bethlehem of Judaea: for thus it is written by the prophet, 6 And thou Bethlehem, in the land of Juda, art not the least among the princes of Juda: for out of thee shall come a Governor, that shall rule my people Israel" (Matthew 2:1-6).

All of these predictions that were given to the children of Israel were fulfilled in Mary and her husband Joseph. I included Mary's husband as being part of the prophecy because he was from the lineage of King David.

Many individuals knew the fulfillments of the above prophecies, and many of those individuals believed in the coming of the Messiah (Christ). In fact, we are told that there were people who studied the prophecies of the coming "Messiah" who lived thousands of miles away from the hub of the Jewish center, which was Jerusalem. That is not to say that there were no believers in Jerusalem, there were many who believed in the prophecies, but few accepted the manner of the coming of the God of Israel as "Christ" the Messiah. What the leaders of Israel expected was a Messiah who was going to come in awesome power that was going to deliver the Jewish nation from the Roman yoke and set up a kingdom, which was not going to be moved by any earthly power. They did not want their Messiah to die, as it is revealed in Isaiah chapter fifty-three; they wanted their Messiah to lead them to victory over their enemies and give them worthy position in His Kingdom.

Prophetically, as per Daniel's prophecy, they were correct to expect the God of their fathers to appear as the "Messiah" (Christ) during the time of the Roman power; but they were delusional because on one hand, they believed that the "Messiah" was going to be born in Bethlehem, and on the other hand, they did not want to

The Creator's Transformation

accept the prophecy because of the thought of the birth and death of a man did not fit their expectation of power, which was capable of delivering them from the Roman suppression.

On top of those demeaning thoughts, there was another problem with the leaders of Judah. Many of the priests and leaders of the Sanhedrin paid homage to Herod the Great, the heathen king. In fact, the Sadducees and the Pharisees were split on their political agenda and in their religious beliefs; therefore, they could not all agree upon a simple statement of "thus saith the LORD," in order to guide them into victory over their enemies. Most of the individuals who held high positions were more interested in keeping their positions alive and advancing in power at the expense of others.

But, if you recall, their bubble was burst when a number of wise men came into Jerusalem, from the east, with their caravan, seeking the King of the Jews. And as they went about asking directions for the location of Bethlehem, in order to go and worship the newborn King, Jerusalem went into uproar! Many did not know that they had a new King over them? Through the commotion, the wise men found themselves standing before King Herod to explain their actions. "But, we have seen His star," the wise men explained to the pagan king. Then the king said to the wise men, "8 Go and search diligently for the young child; and when ye have found Him, bring me word again, that I may come and worship Him also" (Matt. 2:8).

But when Herod and his advisors looked outside to see the star, which the wise men claimed to have followed, the star (angels) was nowhere to be seen? The Creator's Associates advised the angels not to be visible until further notice. The Creator's Associates did not want Herod to give the command to his soldiers to go with the wise men and kill the baby Jesus. So Herod said to the wise men, "Go and search diligently for the young child; and when ye have found Him, bring me word again, that I may come and worship Him also."

The wise men were allowed to go and find the King of the Jews; but how were they going to find Him? They could not see the star (angels) shining over the newborn King any more? They had to go and ask for directions again because they did not know the way

The Creator's Transformation

to Bethlehem, and under whose roof baby Jesus was staying under?

Nonetheless, the wise men gathered their caravan and started going southwest to Bethlehem. When they were a distance away from Jerusalem, the star (angels) reappeared in a dazzling brilliance, only this time, the wise men and their caravan were led by the band of angels (star) directly to baby Jesus. When they arrived, they gave gifts and worshipped Him. And when they were ready to return to their country, the angel of the LORD came and warned them not to return to Jerusalem again and tell Herod where the baby was located.

After eight days of His birth, baby Jesus was circumcised and dedicated in His House (Sanctuary) by the residing priest. There a man by the name of Simeon came into the temple looking for Jesus. This "25 man was just and devout, waiting for the consolation of Israel: and the Holy Ghost was upon him. "26 And it was revealed unto him by the Holy Ghost, that he should not see death, before he had seen the Lord's Christ. 27 And he came by the Spirit into the temple: and when the parents brought in the child Jesus, to do for Him after the custom of the law, 28 Then took he Him up in his arms, and blessed God, and said, 29 Lord, now lettest Thou thy servant depart in peace, according to Thy word: 30 For mine eyes have seen Thy [Your] salvation, 31 Which Thou [You] hast prepared before the face of all people; 32 A light to lighten the Gentiles, and the glory of Thy people Israel. 33 And Joseph and his mother marveled at those things which were spoken of Him. 34 And Simeon blessed them, and said unto Mary His mother, Behold, this child is set for the fall and rising again of many in Israel; and for a sign which shall be spoken against" (Luke 2:25-34).

Yes, many will speak against Christ, and some in vengeance, like King Herod the Great, who decided to eliminate the newborn King of Israel because he did not want to lose his throne. When he saw that the people were expecting a new King, and the wise men did not return to tell him where the new born King was, Herod ordered his soldiers to go in Bethlehem, and kill all of the male children under two years old. Here is the account: "16 Then Herod, when he saw that he was mocked of the wise men, was exceeding wroth, and sent forth, and slew all the children that were in Bethlehem, an in all

The Creator's Transformation

the coasts thereof, from two years old and under, according to the time which he had diligently enquired of the wise men. 17 Then was fulfilled that which was spoken by Jeremy the prophet, saying, 18 In Rama was there a voice heard, lamentation, and weeping, and great mourning, Rachel weeping for her children, and would not be comforted, because they are not" (Matthew 2:16-18).

The prophet's of God foretold the killing of all of those babies in that area, many years before this incident took place.

But, before Herod's soldiers engrossed themselves in the revolting evil act of killing the little innocent children, the angel of the LORD spoke to Joseph and told him that he should take his family and go to Egypt until such time he was told to return again into his own country. Joseph obeyed the angel and went to Egypt.

Joseph was able to go to Egypt and sustain his family by selling some of the expensive gifts, which the wise men gave to Jesus. And when Herod died, and was replaced with another king, the angel of the LORD came to Joseph and told him that it was safe to return to his own country.

Joseph did return and lived with his family in the town of Nazareth in Galilee instead of Judah. Jesus Christ lived and worked in Nazareth until the time He left for His ministry, at the age of about thirty.

So, how was Christ the Creator of Genesis 1:1, the LORD God of Israel, who dwelt between the cherubims, changed from an all-powerful Spirit Being, whose "creation cannot contain Him," into a fragile little baby?

Christ's transformation took place with the help of His two Associates (God the Father and God the Holy Spirit). The prophet Isaiah says, "7 The zeal of the LORD of hosts [Christ] will perform this" (Isaiah 9:7). The prophet Isaiah states that Christ the God of Israel was going to be changed into a human form by the "zeal [eagerness] of the LORD of hosts [Christ]." In addition, the Creator's two Associates were enthusiastic, passionate, fervent, and eager to help "send" Christ the Creator from His awesome Spirit state and power into a human "flesh" in order to accomplish His mission, which was to redeem man from eternal death.

The Creator's Transformation

Here is how it happened: "30 And the angel [Gabriel] said unto her, Fear not, Mary: for thou [you] hast found favour with God. 31 And, behold, thou shalt conceive in thy womb, and bring forth a son, and shalt call His name JESUS. 32 He shall be great, and shall be called the Son of the Highest: and the LORD God shall give unto Him the throne of His father David: 33 And He shall reign over the house of Jacob for ever; and of His kingdom there shall be no end. 34 Then said Mary unto the angel, How shall this be, seeing I know not a man? 35 And the angel answered and said unto her, The Holy Ghost shall come upon thee, and the power of the Highest shall overshadow thee: therefore also that holy thing which shall be born of thee shall be called the Son of God" (Luke 1:30-35).

The two Associates of Christ the Creator, the LORD God of Israel, are God the Holy Spirit, and God the Father (Highest), as we know them by their character names in the New Testament. The prophets of the New Testament, as in this case, use these character names in order to avoid confusion of who is who?

The transformation of Christ the Creator, the LORD God of Israel, was accomplished with the help of His two Associates. By the "zeal" of Christ "the LORD of hosts" (Isaiah 9:7), they helped to transform Him, from an awesome Spirit Being, whose creation could not contain Him, into a little baby. The angel Gabriel said to Mary, "The Holy Ghost shall come upon thee, and the power of the Highest shall overshadow thee." After that, the Angel added, "therefore also that holy thing which shall be born of thee shall be called the Son of God."

So, Christ the Creator of Genesis 1:1, the LORD God of Israel was to be transformed into a helpless little baby by the help of His two Associates; and He was to be called the "Son of God." But before He could be transformed into a little baby, He had to submit Himself to His two Associates by stripping Himself from His awesome powers in order for His two Associates to be able to accomplish the task of transformation. If Christ the Creator, the LORD God of Israel, did not submit Himself to His two Associates,

The Creator's Transformation

His transformation would not have been accomplished. But because of His love for the human race, Christ the Creator submitted to His two Associates and emptied Himself from His awesome powers and came in the form of a "sinful flesh." I say sinful flesh because His mother Mary was under the law, which means that she was a sinner, and therefore Christ the Creator, the LORD God of Israel was born from the "sinful flesh" of Mary.

> Here is the reference "4 But when the fullness of the time was come, God sent forth His Son, made of a woman, made under the law" (Galatians 4:4). And Paul adds: "3 For what the law could not do, in that it was weak through the flesh, God sending his own Son in the likeness of sinful flesh, and for sin, condemned sin in the flesh" (Roman 8:3).

Paul states; when "the fullness of time was come" (when the prophetic clock of Daniel struck), God (the Creator's Associates) "sent forth" (transformed) Christ the Creator, the LORD God of Israel, from an awesome Spirit Being into the "flesh," "by the zeal of the LORD of hosts"(Isaiah 9:7). And when Christ the God of Israel was transformed into "flesh," He became, to His Associate, a "Son" called "Christ."

Please note, I am not saying that God the Christ was a sinner, by saying that He came in a "sinful flesh." Neither is the apostle saying that God the Christ is a sinner. Scripture is clear on that point. God the Christ did not sin while He was on earth as some suggest. The only thing I am saying, like Apostle Paul, is that Christ was born out of a sinful woman, "in the likeness of sinful flesh," and that is a big difference. Stop and think for a moment; you and I have inherited from our mother's a sinful flesh, a body that decays, and eventually, it will grow old and perish, if it does not break down before it gets old. You and I did not receive a perfect body of flesh at our birth; and neither did Christ the LORD of hosts that is why Apostle Paul says that Christ was born from "sinful flesh."

In addition, as I stated before, before Christ the Creator the LORD God of Israel could become a man, born out of a woman,

The Creator's Transformation

He had to empty Himself from all of His powers and submit Himself to His two Associates for the transformation to take place.

Here is the account where Christ the Creator, the LORD God of Israel emptied Himself in order to become a man:

> "5 Let this mind be in you," Paul writes, "which was also in Christ Jesus "6 Who, being in the form of God, thought it not robbery to be equal with God [the Father]: 7 But made Himself of no reputation, and took upon Him the form of a servant, and was made in the likeness of men: 8 And being found in fashion as a man, He humbled Himself, and became obedient unto death, even the death of the cross" (Philippians 2:5-8).

In the above verses, the prophet identifies "Christ" by the name of "God." And Paul states that "God" (Christ) emptied Himself from His awesome powers and was "fashioned as a man." And the apostle adds, "and became obedient unto death, even the death of the cross."

This awesome Spirit Being, Christ the Creator of Genesis 1:1, John 1:1, 3, 10, who is the LORD God of Israel came into this world in the form of a little baby, so that He could die for the sins of the human race, as He had promised Adam, Eve, and to His prophets that followed. He came to save those that want to be saved from their eternal death. Christ the Creator of Genesis 1:1, John 1:1, 3, 10, came into the world in the "flesh" for your benefit and mine. His scars on His back, on His hands, on His feet, on His head, and on His left side of His chest, from Calvary's cruel cross will remain for eternity. And when little children will see those scars on His hands, they will inquire;

> "6 What are these wounds in Thine [Your] hands?" Christ the Redeemer will answer, "Those with which I was wounded in the house of My friends" (Zechariah 13:6).

Christ stooped to the level of human flesh and permitted evil men and women to treat Him with the utmost cruelty, so that we can be treated with everlasting love, as His sons and daughters.

A person cannot help but wonder? What is man that caused Christ the Creator of Genesis 1:1 to leave His lofty heavenly throne and stoop down to the level of man, in order to save man from his eternal destruction?

No wonder, the prophets of old exclaimed, "God is love"!

God the Creator in the New Testament

Thus far, from the previous chapters, we have learned that the Creator of Genesis chapter one is Christ the LORD of hosts who is the God of Abraham and of Israel. We also learned that Christ the Creator is the Individual who dwelt in between the two cherubims in the "most holy place" of His Sanctuary, and walked with the children of Israel from Egypt all the way into the Promised Land (Exodus 20:2; Isaiah 51:15; 1 Corinthians 10:1-9). And, we also learned, the Individual who dwelt in between the two cherubims in His Sanctuary in "Shiloh," and later in "Jerusalem," is none other than Christ the Creator of Genesis 1:1; John 1:1, 3, 10.

In confirmation, Christ the LORD of hosts, the God of Israel, claims that He is the sole Creator of "all things" by saying,

> "4 command them [the delegates who came to Jerusalem] to say unto their masters, Thus saith the LORD of hosts, the God of Israel; Thus shall ye say unto your masters; 5 I have made the earth, the man and the beast that are upon the ground, by My great power and by My outstretched arm" (Jeremiah 27:4, 5).

In agreement with the psalmist, Isaiah, Jeremiah, Moses, and Apostle Paul, Apostle John takes the above information one step further, in the New Testament, and identifies "the LORD of hosts" "the God of Israel" by saying, the "Creator," who created "all things" is "Christ." He wrote,

> "3 All things were made by Him [Christ the "Word" of v.1]; and without Him [Christ] was not anything made that was made." "10 the world was made by Him [Christ]." John 1:3, 10

God the Creator in the New Testament

Did you hear that?

It is unanimous; the sole Creator of "all thing," the "heavens," "man," "earth," etc., etc., is Christ the LORD of hosts who dwelt in between the two cherubims in the "most holy place" of His Sanctuary, and led the children of Israel to the Promised Land.

You can read the Old and New Testaments from the beginning to the end, and you will find, the answer will always come out that the Creator of the heavens and of the earth is Christ the LORD God of Israel. The only difference between the Old Testament and the New Testament is the fact that even though the Creator is addressed by His name LORD God, throughout the Bible; in the New Testament, the prophets go one step further, in order to avoid confusion as to who is who, they address God the Creator of Genesis 1:1, most of the time, by His character name of Christ (Messiah). That is one of the reasons why Apostle John first states that the Creator of Genesis 1:1 is God and Creator of John 1:1, 3, 10; and then, Apostle John identifies the Creator of Genesis 1:1 by His character name of "Christ" (John 1:1, 14, 41).

In fact, Christ the Creator, of the Old Testament, can be seen in all of the New Testament creation verses. These New Testament creation verses reveal that "Christ" is the sole Creator of Genesis chapter one. And to confirm that fact, in the New Testament, John states in his writings, as Moses did in Genesis chapter one, by saying,

"10 the world was made by Him [Christ]" (John 1:10).

As you have read, John agrees with the Old Testament prophets by saying, "the world was made by Him [Christ]." That statement and the use of the pronoun "Him," makes Christ the LORD of hosts, the sole Creator of the whole universe and everything that is in it. Likewise, Moses said the same thing. He said,

"God created...the earth" (Genesis 1:1).

John's remarks, like Moses' comments, refer to pre-creation of the ecosystem, when planet earth was void (Genesis 1:2), and after the creation of the earth, when the ecosystem of the earth was created. In other words, Apostle John, in John chapter one, is saying the same thing Moses is saying in Genesis chapter one.

In fact, you will find, theologians also agree that verses (John 1:1, 3, 10, 14, 41) of John chapter one refer to Christ the Messiah; but more importantly, the rest of the prophets agree with Apostle John that these verses identify and refer to Christ, as the Messiah, and as God the Creator of "all things" (vs. 1, 3).

To further confirm the above facts that the Creator of Genesis chapter one is the same God and Creator of John chapter one, let us consider the "Word" (Christ) of John 1:1 first, as the "Messiah," and then, we will view the Creator and the translators discrepancies in the majority of the creation verses, in the New Testament, in the light of the Greek text.

But, before we begin, let me make a suggestion; please consult the Old King James Version (OKJV) of the Bible as we study Christ the Creator of Genesis 1:1 in the New Testament. And let me also make a recommendation to please memorize John 1:1 from the (OKJV) Bible, in order to avoid confusion between the "Word" (Christ) and "God," Christ's Associate (God the Father).

Here is the verse from the (OKJV).

"1 IN the beginning was the Word, and the Word was with God, and the Word was God." John 1:1

And, here is the above verse in the Greek text as close a possible into English:

"Εν αρχη ην ο Λογος και ο Λογος ην
"In beginning is the Word, and the Word is

"προς τον Θεον και Θεος ην ο Λογος."
"with the God, and God is the Word."
ΙΩΑΝΝΗΝ 1:1. John 1:1 (Translation is mine.)

Christ (Messiah)_____ Having made the above comments, here is a brief review, which identifies God the Creator of Genesis chapter one as Christ the "Messiah" in the New Testament, just as He is identified in the Old Testament as the

Christ (Messiah)

"Messiah."

First, Apostle John, in chapter one, testifies that the "Word" of John 1:1 "was with God" (God the Father). *Secondly,* he testifies that the "Word" is Christ the "Messiah." Simplistically, in reference to Christ the "Word" (v.1), John explains his statement this way; he says,

> "1 In the beginning was the Word, and the Word was with God, and the Word was God." "14 And the Word [of v.1] was made flesh, and dwelt among us" (John 1:1, 14).

And the "Word" who became "flesh" is identified by the name of Christ. Andrew said, "41 We have found the Messias, which is, being interpreted, the Christ." John 1:41

As you can see, the "Word," of v.1, was transformed into "flesh"—a human being (v.14). And that human being (flesh) is identified by the name of "Messiah," which is interpreted "the Christ" (John 1:1, 14, 41).

In confirmation, at one point, after watching Christ performing various miracles and listening to His Gospel message, John testifies of Christ's coming in the "flesh." He gives evidence that Andrew went and looked for his brother Peter, and when he found his brother, Andrew said to him, "41 We have found the Messias, which is, being interpreted, the Christ." John 1:41

The interpretation for the word Messiah is as follows: The Hebrew word "Messiah," from the Old Testament (Daniel 9:25-27), is identified by the Greek word "Messias," in John 1:41. And the Greek word "Messias," when it is interpreted, it means "Χριστος" (Hristos). And the Greek word "Χριστος" means "Christ" in English.

Paul also agrees with John and Andrew that it was Christ the Creator of Genesis 1:1, John 1:1, 3, and 10 who came in the "flesh." Paul says, "2 For the law of the Spirit of life in Christ Jesus hath made me free from the law of sin and death. 3 For what the law could not do, in that it was weak through the flesh, God [Christ's Associates] sending His own Son in the likeness of sinful flesh, and for sin, condemned sin in the flesh [Christ's death on Calvary's

Christ (Messiah)

cross]" (Romans 8:2, 3). After all, when Christ the Creator of Genesis 1:1; John 1:1, 3, 10 came in the "flesh," whose Son would He claim to be?

As you have read, the above verses agree with the (OT) prophets that it was God the Creator of Genesis 1:1; John 1:1, 3, 10 who was transformed, with the help of His two Associates, from an awesome Spirit Being, whose creation cannot contain Him, into a human being (flesh: John 1:1, 14, 41; Luke 1:35). In fact, if you were to further research, the Old and New Testaments, you will find the evidence overwhelming that it was Christ the Creator, the King of Israel (John 1:49; 1 Samuel 12:12), who came in the "flesh" to His own people (the children of Israel); but His own people "received Him not."

The prophet of old testifies to that fact and says,

"11 He [Christ the Word of v.1] came unto His own [the children of Israel (Jacob)], and His own received Him not" (John 1:11).

As per the above verses, it follows that Christ the "Messiah" of John 1:1, 14, and 41 is none other than God the Creator of Genesis chapter one and John 1:1, 3, and 10, who came in the "flesh" to His own people, as He "promised," but His own people "received Him not."

But because Christ (the Messiah) was not received by the majority of the children of Israel (Acts 13:44-46), 2,000 years ago, the apostles, after Christ was crucified, went everywhere to the Gentiles telling them that Christ died for them also. And when they heard that Christ (the Messiah) died for them also, they accepted Christ as their LORD God and Savior; and took the task to help spread the Gospel message throughout the world that "Christ," as per the Old and New Testaments, is the sole Creator, "Messiah," and the Savior of the world (Daniel 9:25, 26; John 1:1, 14, 41).

As you can readily see, according to Daniel the prophet [Daniel 9:25-27], and according to Apostle John the prophet, the "Word" (John 1:1) is identified by His character name of Christ, which means "Messiah" (John 1:1, 14, 41). In fact, Jesus Christ the LORD of hosts personally acknowledges that He is the Messiah (Christ). He said to the Samaritan woman, "I that speak unto thee [you] am He."

> Here is His acknowledgement: "25 The woman saith [said] unto Him [Christ], I know that Messias [Messiah] cometh, which is called Christ: when He is come, He will tell us all things. 26 Jesus said unto her, I that speak unto thee [you] am He." John 4:25, 26

Can anyone dispute Christ's claim?

Christ "with God"_____ In addition, Apostle John clearly states that "Christ" the "Word," of John 1:1, was "with" His Associate (God the Father) whose name is "God."

> John says, "1 IN the beginning was the Word, and the Word was with God" (John 1:1).

As you have read, Apostle John states that Christ the "Word" (of v.1) "was with God" (His Associate) "IN the beginning," when "all things" (v.3) began to be created by Christ the LORD of hosts.

As it was stated before, Apostle John identifies the "Word" to be none other than Christ (the Messiah) of verses 1, 14, 41; and then, he explains that the "Word" (Christ) "was with God" (God the Father). If you were to read the Greek inspired Scriptures you will find John emphasizes the fact that the "Word" (Christ), "was with God."

Thus, Apostle John, like the Old Testament prophets, identifies two Individuals in John 1:1 by the name of "God" when he says, "IN the beginning was the Word [Christ], and the Word [Christ] was with God [God the Father]" (John 1:1). Therefore, you can equate John's statement by saying, Christ the Messiah "was with God," His Associate (God the Father). Christ was not with Himself as many would have you believe."

God the Christ_____ Moreover, you will find, Apostle John identifies Jesus Christ the "Word," of John 1:1, by the name of "God."

John says, "1 IN the beginning was the Word, and the Word was with God, and the Word was God" (John 1:1).

In order to identify who is the "Word," in John 1:1, Apostle John first isolates the "Word" from "God" (the Father), by saying, "and the Word was with God." After revealing that the "Word" and "God" (the Father) are two separate Individuals, John says, "14 the Word [of v.1] was made flesh, and dwelt among us" (John 1:1, 14). And this "Word," who became flesh (v.14), and "dwelt among us," the apostles, is identified by the name of "Christ."

So! Who is the "Word" that dwelt with the apostles?

We are told, the Individual who came in the "flesh" and dwelt amongst them, is none other than "Christ" John 1:1, 14, 41.

Having identified the "Word," you will notice, the "Word" is further revealed in the Greek text by the name of "God" in the predicate of John 1:1. John says, in the Greek text, "and God is the Word."

Consequently, the end result of John's statement is that "God" was with "God." But to avoid confusion of what John is saying, John identifies the "Word" first by the name of Christ (the Messiah) in vs.1, 14, 41, and then he identifies Christ the "Word" by the name of "God" in the predicate by saying, "and the Word was God" (v.1).

Therefore, as per John's testimony, Christ the "Word" is "God." John says, in the Greek Scripture, "and God is the Word." (Translation is mine.) John's testimony cannot be disputed; it does not matter how hard a person tries. Like the Old Testament Hebrew verses, the Greek inspired Scriptures state that Christ is "God," "and God is the Word" (ΚΑΙ ΘΕΟΣ ΗΝ Ο ΛΟΓΟΣ). And that is an inescapable fact.

Christ the Creator _____ Furthermore John identifies the "Word" (Christ), of John 1:1, as the sole Creator of "all things" in John 1:1, 3, 10.

John says, "1 IN the beginning was the Word, and the Word was with God, and the Word was God" (John 1:1).

It should be noted in the above verse, the definite article "the" does not exist in the Greek text of John 1:1; therefore the words

Christ the Creator _____

"IN the beginning" do not reflect upon Christ the "Word"; these words reflect upon the event when the creation of the universe began. I say that because verses one, three, and ten, of John chapter one, are identified by the word "beginning," of John 1:1. Time applies to the movement of the universe and its creatures. Christ the Creator did not have a beginning. He is from "everlasting to everlasting"—remember?

> In reference to Christ the Creator, Moses said, "1 LORD, Thou [You] hast been our dwelling place in all generations. 2 Before the mountains were brought forth, or ever Thou [You] hadst formed the earth, and the world, even from everlasting to everlasting, Thou art God" (Psalm 90:1, 2)

As per the above words of Moses, we are told that Christ the LORD God of Israel, who created the earth and dwelt with the children of Israel in His Sanctuary, "in all generations," is from "everlasting to everlasting." Therefore, the words "IN the beginning" cannot and do not refer to Christ the LORD God of Israel, in John 1:1; they refer to the time when Christ the "Word" began to create "all things" (John 1:3).

> Furthermore, as per the above verses John can claim, "3 All things were made by Him [Christ the Word of v.1]; and without Him [Christ] was not anything made that was made." John 1:3

The above presentation by the prophet John is plain and simple, John says, "All things were made by Him," the "Word" (Christ) of v.1. In fact, the above verse states that there was nothing made unless Christ the "Word" made it. Did you hear that dear reader? John says that there was nothing made unless Christ made it. That means, there was no pre-creation or a co-Creator involved in the above verses or in any of the creation verses in the entire Bible. Please go and look, I strongly encourage you!

John, like the Old Testament prophets, says, "1 IN the beginning was the Word, and the Word was with God [the Father],

The Creator of Genesis 1:1—Who is He?   By: *Philip Mitanidis*

Christ the Creator _____

and the Word was God. 3 All things were made by Him [Christ the Word]; and without Him [Christ the Word] was not anything made that was made." John 1:1, 3

What John is acknowledging in the above verses is the simple fact that Christ (the Word), of v.1, is the One who is God the Creator of "All things" (v.3). And then, later on, John adds that Christ (the Word), of v.1, who created "all things" (v.3), is the same God who created the "world" (v.10). John says, "10 He [Christ the "Word"] was in the world, and the world was made by Him [Christ]" (John 1:10). There is no confusion in John's statement; he says,

"and the world was made by Him [Christ the Word of v.1]" (John 1:10).

Please note; the Greek text does not say, "the world was made *through* Him [Christ]" as many mistranslated Bibles do. The Greek text says, "10 He [Christ] was in the world, and the world was made by [δι'] Him [Christ]" (John 1:10). And that, as per the Greek text, is an undisputed statement.

Although the above statements are self-revealing, there are religious institutions, which use John 1:10 to state that there is more than one Creator involved in the creation of the earth by the use of their mistranslated Bibles. Grammatically, there is no way that anyone can change the single pronoun "Him" to read Them or the word "by" [δι'] to read "through" in vs. 3, 10. John is referring to one single Individual, and not to two or more Individuals. Notably, John's statement is identical to the Old Testament's statements. Apostle John agrees with the Old Testament prophets that there is only one Creator who created the "heaven and the earth," "alone" (Isaiah 44:24). Moses also testifies that there is only one Creator, and he states it as such in Genesis chapter one. Read the entire chapter for yourself and observe that there is only one Individual who was involved in the creation of "all things." Moses, under the inspiration of God the Holy Spirit, starts his chapter by saying, "IN the beginning God created the heaven and the earth." And then, Moses says that this God, from Genesis 1:1, began to speak the creation of the earth's ecosystem into existence, all by Himself.

Likewise, there is no dispute by God the Holy Spirit who also inspired Apostle John to write, "3 all things were made by [δι'] Him [Christ]; and without Him [Christ] was not any thing made that was made" (John 1:3). Both Moses and Apostle John refer to the Creator in their writings by the pronouns "I," "He," "His," and "Him." That means that there was only one Creator who created "all things" "alone," and as He says, "by Myself" (Isaiah 44:24). And, as per John chapter one that Creator is God the Christ (Messiah) John 1:1, 3, 10, 14, 41.

Although the above verses clearly state that Christ the "Word" is "God" (v.1) and sole Creator of "all things" (v.3), people still reject Him as the sole Creator of the universe. Noteworthy, the rejection of Christ the LORD of hosts, as the sole Creator of "all thing," does not end in John chapter one. People and religious institutions still try to muster up their objections and the rejection of Christ the Creator of "All things," not only by the creation verses, which we have studied thus far, but also by the creation verses, which we are going to study next.

Creating "through" Christ?_____ Another way people and religious institutions try to discredit Jesus Christ the LORD of hosts, as God and Creator of His universe, and as the LORD God of Israel, is to say or make somebody do the creating "through" Christ. And that is what many Bible translators have done in the creation verses of the Greek inspired Scriptures of John 1:3 and 10. They have inserted the uninspired word "through" in the creation verses of John 1:3 and 10. Therefore because of this seemingly innocent added word, many individuals reject Jesus Christ the LORD, as the sole Creator of Genesis 1:1; John 1:3, 10, and as the sole Creator of His universe.

Can you imagine laymen, men of the cloth, and theologians clinging to and anchoring their beliefs on the uninspired added word "through" that is injected in John 1:3 and 10 in the various Bible translations? They not only base their faith on the uninspired added word "through," but, if you stop and think about it, they also base their salvation and their doctrines upon the uninspired word "through." In fact, these individuals go as far as to defend their faith

Creating "through" Christ?

and their church doctrines that are based upon the added uninspired word "through." In doing so, they reject Apostle John's writings and Jesus Christ the LORD God of Israel as the sole Creator of His universe and everything that is in it and outside of it.

Don't you think that is awesome?

Nonetheless, if you were to look at all of the creation verses in the Hebrew text of the Old Testament, you will observe, they all claim that there was one Individual who created "all things." And that Individual is Christ the LORD of hosts.

As an example, here are a handful of Hebrew creation verses, which reveal that Christ the LORD of hosts is the sole Creator of "all things."

> "28 the everlasting God, the LORD, the Creator of the ends of the earth" says, "11 Ask Me…concerning the work of My hands…12 I have made the earth, and created man upon it…My hands, have stretched out the heavens, and all their host have I commanded." Isaiah 40:28; 45:11, 12

> "24 I am the LORD that maketh all things; that stretcheth forth the heavens alone; that spreadeth abroad the earth by Myself." Isaiah 44:24;

> "4 Thus saith the LORD of hosts, the God of Israel; Thus shall ye [all of you] say unto your masters; 5 I have made the earth, the man, and the beast that are upon the ground, by My great power and by My outstretched arm." Jeremiah 27:4, 5

And by the psalmist's pen, Moses confirms the above statements by saying, "16 Thou [You] hast made heaven and earth." Psalms 90:2

As you have read in the above Hebrew verses, there is only one Individual who was involved in the creation of "all things," and that Individual is Christ the LORD of hosts. These creation verses like the rest of the creation verses in the Old Testament do not speak of another Creator or a co-Creator involved with Jesus Christ the King

Creating "through" Christ?

of Israel. And neither does the Greek text in the New Testament speak of a co-Creator involved with Christ the God of Israel.

Here are few references to testify to that fact.

"1 IN the beginning was the Word, and the Word was with God, and the Word was God."

"3 All things were made by Him; and without Him was not any thing made that was made." "10 He was in the world, and the world was made by Him" (John 1:1, 3, 10)

As you have noticed, all of the above verses refer to Jesus Christ the LORD (the "Word") from John 1:1; and they all state that the Creator of "all things" is Christ (the "Word") from verse one. None of these verses, as you can see, refer to or involve a second, third, or more Creators or co-Creators with Christ the LORD. Apostle John clearly states, "all things were made by Him" (Christ) (v.3). And "the world was made by Him" (v.10) Christ of verse one. How much plainer can Apostle John be?

To further confirm the fact that "all things" (v.3) were made by Christ the LORD of hosts, here are the two verses of John 1:3 and 10 from the Greek text, which testify of the fact that Christ the King of Israel (John 1:49) is the sole Creator of "all things" by the use of the inspired Greek word δι' [by].

"3 Παντα δι' [by] αυτου εγειναν και χωρις αυτου δεν εγειναν ουδε εν το οποιον εγεινεν."

"10 Ητο εν τω κοσμω, και ο κοσμος εγεινε δι' [by] αυτου." Ιωαννην 1:3, 10 (Βιβλικη Εταιρεια)

Given that Apostle John identifies Christ as the sole Creator in the Greek text, by the use of the Greek inspired word "δι' " (by), in John chapter one, and tells us that Christ created "All things," and the "world," by Himself, we should accept his testimony. And we should also accept Christ's personal acknowledgement that He

Creating "through" Christ?

created "all things," "alone," and as He says, "by Myself." Isaiah 44:24

So, let me ask you, in view of these overwhelming testimonies that Christ is the sole Creator, why are many people and religious institutions adamant and continue to say that God the Father, as we know him now by his character name, is the one who created "through" Christ?

They do because many translators have translated the Greek word δι' (by), in the creation verses, of the New Testament, incorrectly to read "through," and because they believe in the man-made "Apostles Creed."

Having said that, at this point, let me make a recommendation. As a result of the uninspired use of the added word "through" in the New Testament creation verses by the Bible translators, theologians, and clergy, I strongly recommend that you make a mental note of the word "through" (Greek: δια or δια μεσου). And I strongly recommend that you also take the time to remember that the word "through" (δια μεσου) does not exist in any of the creation verses, in the New Testament and when the prophets of God speak about creation and about Christ the Creator.

On the other hand, please also remember the single Greek word "δι'." The Greek word "δι'," when it is translated into English, it means "by." Please also note that the word "δι' " (by) <u>does</u> exists <u>in all</u> of the New Testament creation verses.

Here are the Greek verses, from John 1:3 and 10, which reveal to us the use of the Greek word "δι' " (by):

"3 Παντα δι' [by] αυτου εγειναν και χωρις αυτου δεν εγειναν ουδε εν το οποιον εγεινεν."

"10 Ητο εν τω κοσμω, και ο κοσμος εγεινε δι' [by] αυτου." Ιωαννην 1:3, 10 (Βιβλικη Εταιρεια)

As you can readily see, in the Greek text, the word "δι' " (by) is present in the above two verses (John 1:3, 10). And, as you can observe, the uninspired added word "through" (δια or δια μεσου)

Creating "through" Christ?

does not exist in the above creation verses of the Greek inspired Scriptures.

These verses, in the Greek Scriptures, state without a doubt that Jesus Christ the LORD God of Israel is the sole Creator of "all things."

Confirmation to that fact comes by the pen of Apostle John in John 1:1, 3, 10. Apostle John plainly states in these verses that Christ the God of Israel is the One and only Creator who created "all things" by Himself.

Listen to what Apostle John is saying about Christ the Creator; he said: "3 All things were made by Him; and without Him was not any thing made that was made." "10 He was in the world, and the world was made by Him" (John 1:3, 10).

Did you hear what Apostle John said about Christ the "Word"?

Like the Old Testament Prophets, Apostle John, in the above two verses, confirms the fact that Christ the God of Israel is the sole Creator of the "world" and of "all things" by the use of the inspired Greek word "δι'" (by).

Unfortunately for many, the rejection of Jesus Christ the LORD God of Israel as the sole Creator of Genesis chapter one, John 1:1, 3, and 10 is based upon their belief on the various mistranslated Bibles and not upon the Hebrew and Greek texts.

For that reason, you will find some Bibles make Jesus Christ the sole Creator of the universe, as in the (OKJV) Bible, which says, "3 All things were made by Him; and without Him was not any thing made that was made." "10 He was in the world, and the world was made by Him" (John 1:3, 10). And in a number of mistranslated Bibles, they imply that someone else created "through" Jesus Christ the LORD as in "The Amplified Bible" (AMP). It says, "3 All things were made and came into existence through Him; and without Him was not even one thing made that has come into being." "10 He came into the world, and though the world was made through Him, the world did not recognize Him [did not know Him]." John 1:3, 10 (Amp.)

As you have read in "The Amplified Bible," it states in verses 3 and 10 that somebody created "all things" and the "world"

The Creator of Genesis 1:1—Who is He?   *By: Philip Mitanidis*

Creating "through" Christ?

"through" Christ.

But, if you were to look at the Greek creation verses, of John 1:3, and 10, you will find that a reference to the word "through," or an identity of another Creator, besides Christ, do not exist in these creation verses.

Therefore, the fact that Christ the Creator of Genesis 1:1 is the same God and Creator of John 1:1, 3 and 10, it makes it impossible to say that Christ the Creator created "through" Himself! Neither is it possible to say that Christ the Creator (the Word of John 1:1) created through someone else, or through God the Father. Neither is it credible to say that God the Father created through Jesus Christ because Jesus Christ (the Word) of v.1 is the sole Creator who is identified by the prophets of old by the use of Genesis 1:1; John 1, 3, and 10. And, since Jesus is identified in the Greek text of John 1:1, 3, and 10, as the sole Creator, how can God (the Father), or anyone else, create anything "through" Christ?

To make matters even worse, people who believe in the added uninspired word "through," in these creation verses, they implicate others to do the same. In doing so, these individuals who have been implicated to accept the added word "through," as being God sent; in turn, they too place their faith in the uninspired word "through." Therefore, they also reject Jesus Christ the LORD of hosts as the sole Creator of His universe.

But, we can further ask, why do people accept and place their faith in the uninspired word "through"? Don't you think a person should be more willing to reject the uninspired added word "through," especially when it deals with God the Creator?

Logically, a person would think so!

But, to make matters even worse, more deceiving, and more devastating than the added uninspired word "through," some translators of the New Testament creation verses, take the liberty to compound the problem by adding the word "God" to the uninspired word "through" in some of the creation verses in the New Testament. For example: we are told, "[3] Through him God made all things; not one thing in all creation was made without him." "[10] The Word was in the world, and though God made the

Creating "through" Christ?

world through him, yet the world did not recognize him." John 1:3, 10 (TEV)

As you can see, by injecting the uninspired added word "God" in the above New Testament creation verses, the translators make the reader to assume that the added word "God" refers to God the Father. Therefore, contrary to the Greek text, the added word "God" reinforces the thought that it was God the Father who created "through" Jesus Christ the LORD.

By adding and using the uninspired words "God" and "through" in the creation verses of John 1:3, and 10, a person can make a statement that "God the Father created all things through Jesus Christ." But that statement is not correct because it is based upon an assumption that it was God the Father who created "through" Jesus Christ, and not because the Greek text said so. As an assumption, you can insert any name you want in these verses. You can say for example, God the Holy Spirit created "all things" through Christ. Or, the man on the moon created "all things" through Christ? Or, inject any other name you want in these altered creation verses. Try it! Read the creation verses in the various translations, which contain the added word "through," and notice how the word "through" leaves the door wide open to inject any name you want as the Creator who created "all things" through Jesus Christ. By injecting a name or names, and words in these verses, remember, the added name, names, or words belong to the person who injects them there. As a result of these misleading opinionated acts, a serious consideration should be given to the added words "God" and "through" and their use, by the various Bible translations, in the New Testament creation verses.

Don't you find it strange, after the clear cut statements that Jesus Christ the LORD of hosts is the sole Creator who created "all things," "alone," and as He says, "by Myself" (Isaiah 44:24), people still point their finger on some of the mistranslated creation verses of John 1:1, 3, and 10, in their chosen Bibles, and emphatically state that it was God the Father who created everything "through" Jesus Christ, even though the words "God the Father," and the uninspired added words "God" and "through" do not exist in these creation

Creating "through" Christ?

verses to show us that "God" (the Father) is the Creator or co-Creator?

On the other hand, since God the Holy Spirit's name is also "God," why not say, God the Holy Spirit created through Christ? Why exclude him from the creation verses?

Although we can add, delete, and inject at will any name we want in these creation verses, one thing is for sure, you cannot find a single verse in the entire Bible, in the Hebrew or in the Greek inspired Scriptures, where it says, God the Father created all things through Jesus Christ; or God the Holy Spirit created through Jesus Christ. The verse does not exist

But, contrary to popular opinion of the assumption that God the Father created through Jesus Christ, inspired Scriptures are not divided between the Old Testament and the New Testament creation verses.

In view of the above facts that Christ the Creator of Genesis 1:1, John 1:1, 3, and 10 is the only Creator who created "all things" by "Himself," "alone," and "by His power" (Isaiah 44:24; Jeremiah 10:12), church doctrines and translators should not translate the New Testament creation verses contrary to the Greek Scriptures and say that there was more than one Creator by the use of the added words "God" and "through."

Remember the following fact; the Old Testament does not speak of two Creators or more, and neither does the Greek inspired Scriptures of the New Testament reveal more than one Creator. So, why are translators and church doctrines bent of portraying two Creators by the use of the uninspired added words "God" and "through" in the creation verses of John chapter one?

Why are they posturing the New Testament creation verses against the Old Testament creation verses in error by the use of the uninspired added words "God" and "through"?

Do you know?

As I stated before, they do because their church doctrine, which is based upon the man-made "Apostles Creed," says so!

Therefore, contrary to the Greek text, they accept the uninspired words "God" and "through" in their favorite Bible

Creating "through" Christ?

translation as being the inspired words of God the Holy Spirit. In doing so, a person would think that a warning would ensue within not to let the various inaccurate church literature and Bible translations of the Greek inspired Scriptures dictate and fool them to believe what they say is the truth, regarding the creation verses of the New Testament, by the added words "God" and "through."

Therefore you will find because of the inaccurate Bible translations from Greek to English and diverse church doctrines,

it is harder to prove from the various Bible translations of the New Testament that Jesus Christ the LORD God of Israel is the sole Creator of Genesis 1:1 and of John 1:1, 3, and 10.

On the other hand, let me also say that it is easier to prove that Jesus Christ the LORD of hosts is God the Creator of Genesis 1:1 by using the Old Testament. I say that because the Old Testament has been translated more accurately from the Hebrew language into English; whereas the New Testament has been translated poorly from the Greek language into English in a number of Bible translations regarding the creation verses. This fact will become quite apparent when I bring few more quotations into view from the New Testament regarding the subject matter of Christ the Creator, and the creation verses.

For your edification, here are a handful of Bibles, which the translators have translated the creation verses in variance to the Greek inspired Scriptures of John 1:1, 3, and 10.

"₁ IN THE beginning [before all time] was the Word (d Christ), and the Word was with God, and the Word was God Himself. [Isa. 9:6]" "₃ All things were made and came into existence through Him; and without Him was not even one thing made that has come into being." "₁₀ He came into the world, and though the world was made through Him, the world did not recognize Him [did not know Him]." John 1:1, 3, 10 (Amp)

"₁ In the beginning the Word already existed; the Word was

Creating "through" Christ?

with was with God, and the Word was God." "3 Through him God made all things; not one thing in all creation was made without him." "10 The Word was in the world, and though God made the world through him, yet the world did not recognize him." John 1:1, 3, 10 (TEV)

"1 In the beginning was the one who is called the Word. The Word was with God and was truly God." "3 And with this Word, God created all things. Nothing was made without the Word." "10 The Word was in the world, but no one knew him, though God had made the world with his Word." John 1:1, 3, 10 (CEV)

"1 WHEN ALL THINGS BEGAN, the Word already was. The Word dwelt with God, and what God was, the Word was" "3 and through him all things came to be; no single thing was created without him." "10 He was in the world; but the world, through it owed its being to him, did not recognize him." John 1:1, 3, 10 (TNEB)

"1 In the beginning was the Word, and the Word was with God, and the Word was God." "3 All things came into being by Him, and apart from Him nothing came into being that has come into being." "10 He was in the world, and the world was made through Him." John 1:1, 3, 10 (NAS)

And here is how the Old King James Version (OKJV) of the Bible depicts Apostle John's statements:

> "1 IN the beginning was the Word, and the Word was with God, and the Word was God."
>
> "3 All things were made by Him; and without Him was not any thing made that was made."
>
> "10 He was in the world, and the world was made by

Creating "through" Christ?

Him" (John 1:1, 3, 10) (OKJV)

Now, take the time and compare the above Bibles with the Greek verses and with the Old King James Version, and notice what they say regarding who created the "all things," and the "world." Consider also the use of the words "by," "God," "through," and "apart from" in the above verses in the various Bible translations.

Notice what the above five Bible translations say, with the exception of the (OKJV) Bible, regarding Christ the Creator. The majority of the above translations say that somebody created "All things" (v.3) and the "world" (v.10) "through" Jesus Christ? These presentations are totally in contradiction with the Old Testament prophets, and with the Greek Scriptures of the New Testament. The prophets of the Old Testaments wrote that the Creator of Genesis 1:1 created "all things" by Himself and "alone" (Isaiah 44:24). None of the Bible verses in the Old Testament state that someone created "all things" "through" the Creator of Genesis 1:1. Neither will you find verses, which will state that God the Creator of Genesis 1:1 created something "through" someone else. You cannot find a single verse, which makes those types of remarks in the Old Testament; and yet, in the New Testament those types of statements are very common in a number of Bible translations, as you already have observed thus far.

Therefore because these mistranslated New Testament creation verses are in total contradiction with the Old Testament creation verses, I am going to briefly review the above creation verses in order to reveal few discrepancies that are in them, just in case you missed them. By reviewing these verses, my intent is not to put the above translations down or any other translation, but to cause you to further review these verses in the Greek inspired Scriptures so that you can verify what I have been saying to you is correct or not?

You should know; the translators have translated the above verses differently from each other's verses for various reasons. But, most of all, they translated the verses as such, probably, due to copyrights; and because of these copyrights, these translations

Creating "through" Christ?

cannot say the same thing as the other translations. If they did, they will all read the same; therefore, what will be the point of producing another similar Bible under a new publisher?

Therefore the above Bibles should not be viewed in a derogatory manner because of few mistranslated verses; it does not mean that the rest of the verses are not translated correctly. Be thankful that you and I have access to these Bibles so that we can read these Bibles and compare them to the Hebrew and to the Greek inspired Scriptures for the final results of what the prophets of old are saying.

Having said that, let us consider the above Bible verses in the light of the Greek Scriptures.

The Greek text reads; "All things" were created "by" (δι') Him (Christ).

"3 Παντα δι' [by] αυτου εγειναν και χωρις αυτου δεν εγειναν ουδε εν το οποιον εγεινεν."

"10 Ητο εν τω κοσμω, και ο κοσμος εγεινε δι' [by] αυτου." Ιωαννην 1:3, 10 (Βιβλικη Εταιρεια) John 1:3, 10

Here are the contradictions made by the various Bibles.

The Amplified Bible (Amp.) uses the word "through" in verses 3 and 10 to imply that somebody—who ever that is—created "through" Christ the "Word." But, as you can see, the Greek Scriptures do not agree that somebody created "All things" "through" Christ (the Word). The Greek Scriptures state unequivocally, the Creator of verses 3 and 10 is Christ (Messiah). Verses three and ten use the Greek word "δι' " (by) to specify the fact that "3 All things were made by Him [Christ]; and without Him [Christ] was not any thing made that was made." "10 He [Christ] was in the world, and the world was made by Him [Christ]" (John 1:3, 10). These verses, in the Greek Scriptures, state without a shadow of doubt that "All things" were made "by" Christ; and the "world" was made "by" Christ. Therefore, as in the Old Testament, there was no other Creator involved in the creation of the universe and

Creating "through" Christ?

everything that is in it.

On the other hand, the Today's English Version (TEV) Bible tells us that "Through him" (Christ) "God made all things" (v.3), and in v.10, it says, "God made the world through him" (Christ) (John 1:3, 10). (TEV).

Like the Today's English Version (TEV) Bible, the Contemporary English Version (CEV) says, "And with this Word" (Christ), "God created all things" (v.3); and in v.10, we are told, "God had made the world with his Word" (Christ). John 1:3, 10. (CEV).

By reading the above verses, a person can very easily be persuaded to believe that God created by speaking things into existence, as in Genesis chapter one because the (CEV) Bible states "God had made the world with his Word." On the other hand, by reading the above verses, a person can also very easily be persuaded to believe that it was "God" who created "through" Christ. Or, as the (CEV) puts it, "And with this Word" (Christ), "God created all things" (John 1:3). (CEV). If we were to accept the notion that it was "God" who created "through" Christ, a person has to wonder who was speaking in Genesis chapter one when everything was spoken into existence? Was God speaking through Christ? Or was Christ speaking the ecosystem into existence? But, if it was God (Christ's Associate) who was speaking through Christ, what was the point of doing that? Was Christ so incompetent that He could not utter the words, "Let there be light" or make the light appear; and therefore God (Christ's Associate) had to say the words for Him? Or was Christ used as a puppet?

Is that what happened in Genesis 1:3 and onward?

I have to ask again, what was the purpose of God (Christ's Associate) speaking through Christ the LORD of hosts, in order to create the ecosystem of the earth, if He was so incompetent?

There is something wrong with the above scenario, don't you think?

Of course there is something wrong. The inspired Greek Scriptures never said, "Through him" (Christ) "God made all things" (v.3). Or "God made the world through him" (Christ) (v.10)

The Creator of Genesis 1:1—Who is He?   By: *Philip Mitanidis*

Creating "through" Christ?
_____

(John 1:3, 10) (TEV). Or, "And with this Word" (Christ), "God created all things" (v.3). Or "God had made the world with his Word" (Christ) (v.10) (John 1:3, 10) (CEV).

The word "God" does not exist in verses 3 and 10 in the Greek text—go and look! Therefore the word "God" should not be added in these verses to state that "God" created: "through" Christ, or "with this Word," or "with his Word," as the (TEV) and (CEV) Bibles allude to.

But on the contrary to the above, the Greek Scriptures state, "3 All things were made by [δι'] Him [Christ]; and without Him was not any thing made that was made." "10 He [Christ] was in the world, and the world was made by [δι'] Him [Christ]" (John 1:3, 10); and that is a big difference. As you can see the above verses make Christ the sole Creator of His universe.

On the other hand, The New English Bible (TNEB) does not translate the Greek word "αυτου" to read Him in v.10. It reads, no pun attended, "it." The word "it" does not identify Christ the Creator in these verse, as it should. The word "it" does not exist in v.10 in the Greek Scriptures. The word is "αυτου," and this word translates into English to read "Him."

Moreover, as you can see, verse ten in the (TNEB) does not state, "the world was made by [δι'] Him," as per the Greek Scripture. The New English Bible eradicates the notion that Christ is the sole Creator of the world. It reads; "but the world, through it owed its being to him." By the way, if we accept that the word "Him" refers to (Christ), I have to ask, who or what is "it"? And where did "it" come from?

Do you know?

On the other hand, The New English Bible does translate the word "χωρις," in v.3, correctly. It reads "without."

On the overall, The New English Bible has translated the Greek Scriptures of verses 3 and 10 in disagreement. This translation does not capture what the Greek Scriptures say about Christ the Creator. These two verses imply that somebody created the "all things" through Jesus Christ (and through him all things came to be). Whereas the Greek inspired Scriptures state, and identify that "all

Creating "through" Christ?

things were created by Him [Christ]," "and the world was made by Him [Christ]." As you can readily see, the Greek Scriptures identify Christ as the sole Creator of Genesis 1:1; Isaiah 44:24; John 1:1, 3, and 10, where as (TNEB) does not.

If you look in the New American Standard (NAS) Bible, you will notice that the word "δι' " is translated to read, "by" in v.3; but in v.10, it reads "through." And, if you look in v.3, for the Greek word "χωρις," you will find the English words "apart from."

As we have studied earlier, the Greek word "δι' " means "by." The Greek word "δι' " does not mean "through," The Greek words "δια μεσου" mean "through." If you look at verse three and verse ten, in the Greek Scriptures you cannot find the Greek words "δια μεσου." Therefore the Greek word "δι' " cannot be translated to read "through" in these verses.

In addition, if you look at verse three in the Greek Scriptures, the word "χωρις" is present; but in the (NAS) Bible, you will find the words "apart from." Again these words do not reflect the meaning of the Greek word "χωρις." The words "apart from," in Greek mean "χωριστα απο." Take a good look at the Greek verses, and you will observe that these two Greek words cannot be found in v.3, in the Greek inspired Scripture.

Therefore, the words "through" (v.10) and "apart from" in verse three do not reflect the Greek meaning of the words "δι' " and "χωρις."

Verse three should read: "3 All things were made by [δι'] Him [Christ]; and without [χωρις] Him was not any thing made that was made." And verse ten, as per the Greek Scriptures should read, "10 He [Christ] was in the world, and the world was made by [δι'] Him" (John 1:3, 10).

Contrary to the Greek text, conceder what the verses say in the (NAS) Bible:

> "3 All things came into being by Him, and apart from Him nothing came into being that has come into being." "10 He was in the world, and the world was made through Him." John 1:3, 10 (NAS).

The Creator of Genesis 1:1—Who is He? *By: Philip Mitanidis* 241
Creating "through" Christ? _____

As you can see without difficulty in the above verses, verse ten of the (NAS) Bible uses the word "though" (v.10), but in v.3, it uses the words "apart from." Therefore, when you read John 1:3 in the (NAS), you will notice that it states "apart form" God the Word (Christ), of v.1, "nothing came into being that has come into being." (NAS).

By using the words "apart from," does that mean only Christ (the Word of v.1) was created? If that is the intent, I ask you, how can "all things" be created "by Him" (Christ) (v.3), if "apart from Him nothing came into being that has come into being"? John 1:3 (NAS). If nothing has been created except ("apart from") Christ, how did planet earth, you, me, and the rest of the galaxies out there came into existence? Who made them? And if somebody, other than Christ, claims to have created the universe, I have to ask, who is this anonymous being?

Do you know?

Secondly, since verse ten of the (NAS) Bible implies that someone else created "All things," "through" God the Word (Christ) of v.1, I have to ask, this someone else, assuming it was God the Father (Christ's Associate), who supposedly created through Christ, was he unable to create the universe by himself, and for that reason he needed Christ to help do it for him?

And, if God (Christ's Associate) was unable to create the universe by himself, how was he able to empower Christ to help him create the universe? And, if Christ's Associate was able to empower Christ, as per some beliefs, to help him create the universe, why was God (the Father) not able to empower himself to create the universe?

On the other hand, Christ claims that He is from "everlasting to everlasting," and that He is the Creator of "all things." So! How can Christ be used as a tool by God (the Father) to create "through" Him, as many assume? Was Christ more powerful than God the Father; is that why he had to create "through" Him (Christ) or something?

What do you think? Need I go on asking questions?

On a more serious note; when you read John 1:3 and 10, in the

Creating "through" Christ?

(NAS) and like Bible verses, ask yourself, why does v.3 state, "All things came into being by Him" (Christ); and in v.10, it says, "the world was made through Him" (Christ). Those two statements are in total contradiction. One verse says, "All things came into being by Him" (Christ), and the other verse says, "the world was made through Him" (Christ). So, if "All things" were created "by" Christ (v.3); how can the "world" be created "through" Christ (v.10)? Is not the "world" included in the "All things"?

Moreover, if we were to accept that somebody created "through" Christ, I have to ask, who is this individual who created "through" Christ? Can you identify him? I cannot find him mentioned anywhere in the New Testament or in the Old Testament? What I do find in the Torah is Christ the Creator of Genesis chapter one and two. And the Creator, according to the Old Testament prophets, is none other than Jesus Christ the LORD God of Israel. And Christ the LORD God of Israel says that He created "all things" "alone." See! He did not need any help. He created everything "alone," and He says, "by Myself" (Isaiah 44:24).

Did you hear that?

Christ said, I created "all things"; and then, He added "by Myself."

And to further clarify His statement, Christ the Creator said that He created "all things" without the help of any one else by the use of the word "alone" (Isaiah 44:24).

So I ask, does anyone misunderstand Christ's words? If so, please consult your dictionary for the meaning of the words "alone" and "by Myself."

Thus according to Christ's statements, there was no one else involved with Him in the creation of the universe and everything that is in it. John confirms that fact in the Greek text by saying, "He [Christ] was in the world, and the world was made by [δι'] him [Christ]" (John 1:10).

Therefore God (the Father), or any one else for that matter, is not the Creator or co-Creator with Christ in the creation of His universe. I say that because if you believe God the Father created through Christ, what you are saying, or alluding to that there are two

The Creator of Genesis 1:1—Who is He?   By: *Philip Mitanidis*
Creating "through" Christ?

Creators. And that cannot be true because according to the inspired word of God the Holy Spirit, God the Father did not create anything. That is the reason why you cannot find a single verse in the entire 66 books of the Bible where it states God the Father is the Creator. The verse does not exist. But, if you were to deny the fact that there is no verse or verses to be found in the entire Bible, which state that God the Father created something, then you are in denial of the facts that Christ the God of Israel is the sole Creator of His universe.

But, if we deny the fact that Christ the LORD God of Israel is the sole Creator of His universe, and go down that road, then the Creator's claim that He created "alone" is totally incorrect. It is a lie. But since Christ does not lie; He is sinless; He is holy—remember? And given that His prophets do not lie; we can take the writings of the Greek Scriptures and accept the fact that "all thing were made by Him [Christ]" (John 1:3). And as the (NAS) Bible puts it, "All things came into being by Him" (John 1:3) (NAS).

As you have read a number of times, in John 1:3, and 10, we have the untainted acknowledgement, in the Greek inspired Scriptures that "by" (δι') Christ "all things were made." They were "made by Him." These verses, one, three, and ten of John chapter one state unequivocally, in the inspired Greek Scriptures that the "Word" (Christ) of v.1 was the One who created everything by Himself and for Himself.

Here are the references: "All things were made by [δι'] Him [Christ], and without [χωρις] Him [Christ] was not any thing made that was made."

"He [Christ] was in the world, and the world was made by [δι'] Him [Christ]" (John 1:3, 10).

Can anyone make a clearer statement than that? Personally, I don't know how anyone can? If there was another means of making a clearer statement, don't you think God the Holy Spirit would have made it?

Jesus Christ the LORD of hosts is the sole Creator of "all things." There is no other Creator mentioned besides Christ in the New Testament, in fact there is no other Creator mentioned besides

Creating "through" Christ? _____

Christ in the entire 66 books of the Bible.

So, why add personal words to the word of God the Holy Spirit, and make these creation verses disagree with the prophets of old and with Christ the Creator? Don't people know when they add, delete, or alter the word of God the Holy Spirit; they are setting themselves above God the Holy Spirit?

That is an outright blasphemy!

And do you know, any person who blasphemes willfully God the Holy Ghost will not be forgiven? Did you know that? Jesus Christ the LORD God of Israel warned and said, people can blaspheme His name, and be forgiven; but, if people blaspheme willfully God the Holy Spirit, they shall not be forgiven.

> Christ the Creator warns, "28 Verily I [Christ] say unto you, All sins shall be forgiven unto the sons of men, and blasphemies wherewith soever they shall blaspheme: "29 But he that shall blaspheme against the Holy Ghost hath never forgiveness, but is in danger of eternal damnation" (Mark 3:28, 29).

So! Why tempt God the Holy Spirit, when Christ the God of Israel gives such a severe warning? Anyone who will not take seriously Christ's warning that individual will die in his or her sins.

Consequently, why not leave the Greek inspired word of God the Holy Spirit intact, in John 1:1, 3, and 10, and translate the Greek word "δι' " to read "by," and avoid the condemnation, which Jesus Christ the LORD of hosts warns about?

Do you think people do not take Christ's warning seriously dear reader, is that why people and religious institutions add, delete, and misquote the Hebrew and the Greek Scriptures?

By the way, did you memorize all of the contradictions the translators have created in their Bibles thus far?

I strongly recommend that you fortify yourself with the doctrinal truth of the Bible so that people and satanic agencies will not be able to deceive you. (See 1 Timothy 4:16)

By not translating the Greek words of John chapter one correctly into English, as you can see, it confuses the reader? And the worst part of these mistranslated Bibles is the fact when a person is reading the above mistranslated Bibles, it makes a person wonder if the Bible is inspired?

But, people don't have to wonder, the uninspired words "through," "apart from," and "God made the world through him" (Christ) do not exist in the above verses of the inspired Greek text. Therefore we do not have to labor the point any further on the creation verses of John chapter one. The verses, in John 1:1, 3, 10 of the Greek Scriptures, speak clearly for themselves; like the Old Testament creation verses, they make Christ the sole Creator of the universe. These verses say, "3 All things were made by [δι'] Him [Christ]; and without [χωρις] Him [Christ] was not any thing made that was made." "10 He [Christ] was in the world, and the world was made by [δι'] Him [Christ]" (John 1:3, 10). As you have read, none of these creation verses, in the Hebrew text or in the Greek text, say that somebody created the "all things" "through" Jesus Christ.

In Christ's defense, need the inspired words of God the Holy Spirit say more?

Romans 11:33-36 and Colossians 1:16, 17 _____ In addition to John 1:1, 3, and 10, which we have discussed, I want to bring to your attention to a handful of other verses, which have been translated incorrectly. These translated verses also contradict the Greek inspired Scriptures regarding Jesus Christ the Creator, and the creation of "All things." The incorrect translations of these verses can be found in Romans 11:36 and Colossians 1:16 and 17 in a number of Bibles.

It should be noted that a number of translators who have translated these Greek verses into English, like the previous verses, which we have reviewed, contradict the Greek inspired text, the Old Testament writers, and Christ the Creator who has claimed all along that He created "all things," "alone," "by Myself," "by My outstretched arm," and as He said, "by My great power" (Jeremiah 27:5).

I am going to quote, Romans 11:33-36 and Colossians 1:16, 17, from the (OKJV) Bible and from the (NWTCGS) Bible in order to show you the inconsistencies these Bibles create, not only with the Greek Scriptures, but also between each other's translations. If you like to view other Bibles for your edification, I recommend it because just like the (OKJV) Bible and the (NWTCGS) Bible, without a doubt, you will find discrepancies in those Bibles. And when you do, you should be conscious of these discrepancies so that you will build confidence in your new possessed knowledge. If you are conscious of these discrepancies, no one will be able to deceive you; and, at the same time, you will be able to lead your objectors to a simple truth, which says, "thus said the LORD."

The advice that was given to Timothy, by Apostle Paul, I like to pass on to you at this point. I do hope that you will take Paul's admonition just as Timothy did. Paul's counsel reads as follows:

> "16 Take heed unto thyself [yourself], and unto the doctrine; continue in them: for in doing this thou [you] shalt both save thyself, and them that hear thee [you]." 1 Timothy 4:16

So, dear reader, take heed to the Hebrew and to the Greek inspired Scriptures, and be not misled by outside interpretations, which are injected in the statements of the prophets of God. The prophet's statements were inspired by God the Holy Spirit. It was God the Holy Spirit who moved his prophets to write Christ's Gospel message for you and for me.

> Paul said, "16 All scripture is given by inspiration of God, and is profitable for doctrine, for reproof, for correction, for instruction in righteousness. 17 That the man of God may be perfect, throughly furnished unto all good works." 2 Timothy 3:16, 17

> And Apostle Peter adds, "20 Knowing this first, that no prophecy of the scripture is of any private interpretation. 21 For the prophecy came not in old time by the will of man: but holy men of God spake as they were moved by the Holy Ghost." 2 Peter 1:20, 21

So! Take heed to the prophets of God, dear reader; do not despair, whenever you find yourself without an answer to an

The Creator of Genesis 1:1—Who is He? *By: Philip Mitanidis*
Romans 11:33-36 and Colossians 1:16, 17

objection, remember, the answer is always in the Bible. God the Holy Spirit foresaw man's objections; therefore, he made sure that the answers to all objections were written in the Bible for your benefit, and for the benefit of the Gospel of Jesus Christ the LORD God of Israel (Mark 1:1).

Having said that, let us look at the verses in Colossians 1:16, 17, and in Romans 11:33-36, and observe the various translated discrepancies that are found in these New Testament verses.

First, here are the verses from the Old King James Version:

"16 For by Him were all things created, that are in heaven, and that are in earth, visible and invisible, whether they be thrones, or dominions, or principalities, or powers: all things were created by Him, and for Him: 17 And He is before all things, and by Him all things consist" (Colossians 1:16, 17).

"33 O the depth of the riches both of the wisdom and knowledge of God! How unsearchable are His judgments, and His ways past finding out! 34 For who hath known the mind of the LORD? or who hath been His counsellor? 35 Or who hath first given to Him, and it shall be recompensed unto Him again? 36 For of Him, and through Him, and to Him, are all things: to whom be glory for ever. Amen" (Romans 11:33-36).

Here are the above verses as they are presented to us by the New World of the Christian Greek Scriptures (NWTCGS) Bible.

"16 because by means of him all other things were created in the heavens and upon the earth, the things visible and the things invisible, no matter whether they are thrones or lordships or governments or authorities. All other things have been created through him and for him. 17 Also he is before all other things and by means of him all other things were made to exist" (Colossians 1:16, 17). (NWTCGS)

"33 Oh the depth of God's riches and wisdom and knowledge!

The Creator of Genesis 1:1—Who is He? By: *Philip Mitanidis*
Romans 11:33-36 and Colossians 1:16, 17

How unsearchable his judgments are and past tracing out his ways are! 34 For "who has come to know Jehovah's mind, or who has become his counsellor?" 35 Or, "Who has first given to him, so that it must be repaid to him?" 36 Because from him and by him and for him are all things. To him be the glory forever. Amen" (Romans 11:33-36). (NWTCGS)

And here are the two verses in the Greek text, which reveal the Greek word "δι' "; and when it is translated into English, it will read "by."

"16 επειδη δι' [by] αυτου εκτισθησαν τα παντα...τα παντα δι' [by] αυτου και εις αυτον εκτισθησαν." Κολοσσαεις 1:16 (Βιβλικη Εταιρεια)

"36 Επειδη εξ αυτου, και δι' [by] αυτου, και εις αυτον ειναι τα παντα αυτω η δοξα εις τους αιωνας. Αμην." Ρομαιους 11:36 (Βιβλικη Εταιρεια)

If you compare the verses of Colossians 1:16, 17 and Romans 11:33-36 of the (OKJV) Bible to the verses of the (NWTCGS) Bible, you will find that the (OKJV) Bible and the (NWTCGS) Bible do not agree with each other. In fact, both of these Bibles disagree with the Greek inspired Scriptures in number of places. Please note: The Old King James Version of the Bible (OKJV) tells us in Colossians 1:16 that Christ is the sole Creator of "all things." But, in contradiction, the (NWTCGS) Bible says, "all other things" were created "through" Christ.

As you can see, the (NWTCGS) Bible, not only disagrees with the Greek inspired Scriptures and with the (OKJV) of the Bible, but it also deletes and adds words to the Scriptures.

Listen to what the (NWTCGS) Bible says contrary to the Greek inspired Scriptures in Colossians 1:16; "because by means of him all other things were created." And this is what the (OKJV) Bible says, which is the closest to the Greek rendering. It says, "For by Him [Christ] were all things created."

As you can see, there is a big difference between these two

The Creator of Genesis 1:1—Who is He?   By: *Philip Mitanidis*
Romans 11:33-36 and Colossians 1:16, 17

Bibles.

If we were to consider the word "means" in the (NWTCGS) Bible, in the above verse as a noun, it means, "way" and "resources." The above verse, then, will read as follows "because by" resources "of him all other things were created." In other words: By His (Christ's) resources all other things were created. But, a person has to ask, what "other things" were created? Did Christ really create "other things"? Like what? And, we can further ask, how many "other things" were there created? And where do we find these "other things" mentioned or revealed in the entire Bible?

I have not been able to find them.

Can you?

If you can, write to me, or e-mail me, and tell me of the "other things" Christ created?

In any case, I don't think you can.

Do you know why, you will not be able to find those "other things"?

You will not be able to find those "other things" because as we have learned, *one,* Christ the Creator of John 1:1 and 3 created "all things." Therefore there are no "other things" created, as the (NWTCGS) Bible states. Christ the Creator says, "I am the LORD that maketh all things" (Isaiah 44:24). Moreover, Apostle John, like Apostle Paul, confirms what Christ the Creator has claimed in the above verses. John, like Isaiah and Apostle Paul says, "3 All things were made by Him [Christ]" (John 1:3). Therefore there are no "other things" created. In fact, in the Greek inspired Scriptures, John 1:3 says, "3 All things were made by Him: and without Him was not any thing made that was made." John says, "3 All things were made by Him [Christ]." And then, John adds, "without Him [Christ] was not any thing made that was made" (John 1:3). In other words, there was not a single thing made or created unless Christ made it.

So, since "all things were made by" Christ, and nothing was made "without Him" (Christ), how can "other things" be made or created?

Therefore, one has to ask, is Apostle Paul disagreeing with

Christ the Creator and with Apostle John?
Is Apostle Paul lying to us?
What do you think?
But, do you know what? Apostle Paul says, "I do not lie" (Romans 9:1). In fact, Paul states that his conscious "is clear" because he does not lie. If he willfully did lie, Apostle Paul would not be an apostle of Jesus Christ the LORD of hosts.

Nonetheless, as we have read, according to the Greek inspired Scriptures, there are no "other things" created. And since there are no "other things" created, it means Christ the Creator, Apostle John, and Apostle Paul are telling us the truth.

And, the *second* reason why you will not be able to find those "other things" is due to the fact that the word "other" was added by the translators of the (NWTCGS) Bible before the word "things" to make the verse read "other things." In fact, if you were to read verses 16 to 20 in Colossians chapter one, in the (NWTCGS) Bible, you will find the word "other" has been added five times in these verses. The word "other" does not exist in the inspired word of God in these verses. In fact, even the words "means of" do not exist in the Greek inspired text. These words have been added to the verses in Colossians chapter one.

It should be noted; the word "other" changes the meaning of the verses from its intended message by the prophet of old.

The message of verse sixteen in the Greek Scriptures is simple. It says, "16 For by [δι'] Him [Christ] were all things created, that are in heaven, and that are in earth, visible and invisible, whether they be thrones, or dominions, or principalities, or powers: all things were created by [δι'] Him [Christ], and for Him [Christ]" (Colossians 1:16).

Although I have been saying that the word "other" does not exist in the Greek inspired Scriptures before the word "things," I want you to consider the verses in the Greek and in the English setting of the (OKJV), of the Bible, and see for yourself if the word "other" (αλλη, αλλον, or αλλος) is present or not?

First, here is the verse (Colossians 1:16) from the (Βιβλικη Εταιρεια) Greek Bible.

The Creator of Genesis 1:1—Who is He? *By: Philip Mitanidis*
Romans 11:33-36 and Colossians 1:16, 17

"16 επειδη δι' [by] αυτου εκτισθησαν τα παντα, τα εν τοις ουρανοις και τα επι της γης, τα ορατα και τα αορατα, ειτε θρονοι, ειτε κυριοτητες, ειτε αρχαι, ειτε εξουσιαι, τα παντα δι' [by] αυτου και εις αυτον εκτισθησαν." Κολοσσαεις 1:16 (Βιβλικη Εταιρεια)

And the Old King James Version reads:

"16 For by [δι'] Him were all things created, that are in heaven, and that are in earth, visible and invisible, whether they be thrones, or dominions, or principalities, or powers: all things were created by [δι'] Him, and for Him" (Colossians 1:16).

Did you find the word "other" (αλλη, αλλον, or αλλος) anywhere in v.16 in the Greek text or in the English translation of the (OKJV) Bible? Of course not! The word "other" does not exist in the above verse. In fact, the word "other" does not exist in any of the verses, in Colossians 1:16-20. And yet, you will find the word "other" has been added five times in the (NWTCGS) Bible to mislead the reader. The added uninspired word "other" contradicts the rest of the creation verses, which contain the words "all things."

I do not know if you know, but there is a strong warning to individuals and religious institutions that add or take away words from the word of God.

> Moses said, "2 Ye [all of you] shall not add unto the word which I command you, neither shall ye diminish ought from it, that ye may keep the commandments of the LORD you God which I command you" (Deuteronomy 4:2).

> Solomon cautions: "6 Add thou [you] not unto His words, lest He reprove thee, and thou [you] be found a liar." Proverbs 30:6

> And Paul warns: "8 But though we, or and angel from heaven, preach any other gospel unto you than that which we have preached unto you, let him be accursed" (Galatians 1:8).

The Creator of Genesis 1:1—Who is He?   By: *Philip Mitanidis*
Romans 11:33-36 and Colossians 1:16, 17

So, why is man deleting and adding his own words to God's words under these kinds of severe warnings?

Do you know?

Consequently, if you were to further consider verses 16 and 17, in the (NWTCGS) Bible, you will find more discrepancies because the translators are using the word "through" and "by means of" in these verses.

> "16 because by means of him all other things were created in the heavens and upon the earth, the things visible and the things invisible, no matter whether they are thrones or lordships or governments or authorities. All other things have been created through him and for him.
>
> "17 Also he is before all other things and by means of him all other things were made to exist," Colossians 1:16, 17 (NWTCGS).

In the beginning of v.16 and in v.17, the word "by" is used, in the above verses. By writing "means of" after the preposition "by" is like double talk. I say that because the synonym for the preposition "by" is "by means of." So, in essence the (NWTCGS) Bible acknowledges that Christ is the only Creator in the beginning of v.16, when it says, "because by means of him all other things were created in the heavens and upon the earth." But at the end of v.16 the translators decided to use the uninspired word "through," and this makes v.16 to contradict itself because the last part of the verse reads, "All other things have been created through him and for him."

So, the beginning of the verse makes Jesus Christ the LORD of hosts the sole Creator of "all things," but the verse at the end says that somebody created "through" Christ. Needless to say, that is a total contradiction. These types of contradictions leave the reader in perplexity because the reader does not know what to believe?

Does a person believe that "all things" were created "by" Christ; or were "all things" created "though" Christ?

The Creator of Genesis 1:1—Who is He? By: *Philip Mitanidis*
Romans 11:33-36 and Colossians 1:16, 17

In order to make sense of the verse, a person has to remove the added uninspired words from the verse in the (NWTCGS) Bible. Consequently, if you remove the added words "other" and "means of," in the beginning of v.16, the verse will read, "by him" Christ "all things were created in the heavens and upon the earth," which is correct according to Genesis chapter one and two and elsewhere. And verse seventeen will read, "by him" Christ "all things were made to exist" (v.17).

But even by the removal of the added words "other" and "means of," the verses in Colossians 1:16 and 17 are still made to contradict the apostle's statements. These verses, in the (NWTCGS) Bible, are still made to contradict the Greek Scriptures because the translators have used the uninspired word "through" at the end of v.16. If you read the latter part of v.16, you will notice that it contradicts the beginning of v.16. And it also contradicts the beginning of v.17.

Therefore the word "through" cannot be used because, as we have studied before in John 1:3 and 10, the Greek word "δι'" (by) is used in the Greek inspired Scriptures, and not "δια μεσου" (through). And so it is in Colossians 1:16, the Greek word "δι'" is used. The Greek word "δι'" translated into English will read "by."

Thus, if you were to remove the added words "other," "means of," and "through" from verses 16 and 17, of the NWTCGS Bible, you will find that these verses will read almost like the Old King James Version of the Bible, which has the Greek word "δι'" translated correctly to read "by."

Here are verses sixteen and seventeen, of Colossians one, taken from the (NWTCGS) Bible without the added uninspired words "other," "means of," and "through." The verses will read, "because by him all things were created in the heavens and upon the earth, the things visible and the things invisible, no matter whether they are thrones or lordships or governments or authorities, All things have been created by him and for him. 17 Also he is before all things and by him all things were made to exist" (Colossians 1:16, 17). (NWTCGS) (Modified)

By removing the added words "other," "means of," and

The Creator of Genesis 1:1—Who is He? *By: Philip Mitanidis*
Romans 11:33-36 and Colossians 1:16, 17

"through," the above verses in the (NWTCGS) Bible make Jesus Christ the LORD God of Israel the Creator of "all things," just as the Old Testament prophets have done, just as Apostle John has done in John 1:1, 3, 10, and just as Christ the LORD God of Israel reveals that He is the sole Creator:

> Listen, "24 Thus saith the LORD, thy Redeemer, and He that formed thee from the womb, I am the LORD that maketh all things; that stretcheth forth the heavens alone; that spreadeth abroad the earth by Myself" (Isaiah 44:24).

As you can clearly see in the above verse, Christ the Creator of Genesis 1:1; John 1:1, 3, and 10 says, "I am the LORD that maketh all things; that stretcheth forth the heavens alone; that spreadeth abroad the earth by Myself." And the Apostle Paul agrees. He says,

> "16 For by Him [Christ] were all things created, that are in heaven, and that are in earth, visible and invisible, whether they be thrones, or dominions, or principalities, or powers: all things were created by Him [Christ], and for Him [Christ]: 17 And He is before all things, and by Him [Christ] all things consist" (Colossians 1:16, 17).

If you look at verse sixteen and verse seventeen in the (OKJV), you will notice, the translators have used the correct word "by" in their translation. Therefore there are no discrepancies between the (OKJV) Bible and the Greek Scriptures, and the Creator's claim when the inspired word "by" (δι') is used. These verses like the previous verses in the Old and in the New Testaments reveal one Creator who created "all things" by Himself and for Himself; and as we have learned, the sole Creator who is revealed by the prophets of old is Christ the LORD of hosts.

Therefore, the verses in Colossians do not reveal somebody creating "all other things" "through" Christ, but what you will find in the Greek Scriptures is the fact that it was Christ who created "all things" by Himself (by Him) and for Himself (for Him).

The Creator of Genesis 1:1—Who is He? By: *Philip Mitanidis*
Romans 11:33-36 and Colossians 1:16, 17

In addition to the above verses, if you were to make the comparison in Romans chapter eleven, between the (OKJV) Bible and the (NWTCGS) Bible, you will find that these Bibles further contradict each other again.

If you look at Romans 11:34, you will notice that the (OKJV) says, "For who hath known the mind of the LORD?" And if you look at the verse in the (NWTCGS), it says, "who has come to know Jehovah's mind."

It should be noted that some translators mistranslate the word "יהוה" (LORD) to read "Jehovah" and apply it to God the Father only. But, as we have seen in the Old and in the New Testaments, the word "יהוה" (LORD) refers to God the Father, to God the Holy Spirit, and to God the Christ, as we know them now by their character names, in the New Testament.

The mistranslated word, "Jehovah," which is extracted incorrectly from the Hebrew word "יהוה" (YHWH), is used only in a handful of mistranslated Bibles. The word "יהוה" (YHWH) is addressed by the New Testament prophets to read "Κυριος" (Kerios) in the Greek inspired Scriptures. Thus the translators, in the majority of the Bible verses, have translated the Creator's name in the Old and in the New Testaments to read "Lord" or "LORD." But some translators have chosen to translate the Creator's name to read incorrectly, "Jehovah," throughout the Old Testament, and only in few verses in the New Testament.

So, as per the prophets of old, in the majority of the verses, Christ the Creator the LORD God of Israel is addressed by the name of "LORD" and in some Bibles by the mistranslated word "Jehovah."

Having said that, let us consider what the (NWTCGS) Bible, which uses the mistranslated word "Jehovah," says about Jesus Christ the Creator in Romans 11:33-36.

"33 Oh the depth of God's riches and wisdom and knowledge! How unsearchable his judgments are and past tracing out his ways are! 34 For "who has come to know Jehovah's mind, or who has become his counselor?" 35 Or, "Who has first given to him, so that it must be repaid to him?" 36 Because from him and by him and for him are all things. To him be the glory forever. Amen" (Romans 11:33-36). (NWTCGS).

If we were to consider the above verses in the (NWTCGS) Bible, we will notice that Christ the Creator in v.33 is addressed by the name "God" (Θεου). And in verse thirty-four, Christ the Creator is addressed by the name of "Jehovah." Christ the Creator is identified by His name Jehovah, just as He is identified in the Old Testament by the name of Jehovah over 6,000 times in some Bibles. And in verse thirty-six, we are told that Christ the Creator, whose name is Jehovah, was the One who created "all things." The verse reads, "36 Because from him and by him and for him are all things" (NWTCGS). What these verses reveal to us is the fact that Christ the Creator, of v.33 and v.34 is the sole Creator of the universe, just as the other earlier creation verses have stated by the use of the word "by" (δι'). The verse says, "from him and by him and for him are all things" (Romans 11:36). (NWTCGS).

As you can see, as per the above verses, nothing has changed. Christ the LORD of hosts is the sole Creator of "all things" because verse thirty-six states, "all things" are created "from him," "by him," and "for him" (NWTCGS) Bible. This verse, like the other creation verses, which we have been studying, says the same thing. Verse thirty-six says that there is only one Creator who created "all things" from Himself, by Himself, and for Himself. And according to the previous creation verses, which we have studied, God the Creator is none other than Jesus Christ the God of Israel.

The above statements in verse thirty-six, as you can see, are in the singular form. These statements claim that Jehovah (Christ), of v.34, created "all things" by Himself and for Himself. And that makes Him the only Creator of "all things." The verse does not involve another Creator, as the translators have done in Colossians 1:16, by the use of the added words "other" and "through." Contrary to Colossians 1:16, the translators state in Romans 11:36, in their (NWTCGS) Bible that there is only one Creator who has created "all things" by Himself.

The Creator of Genesis 1:1—Who is He?   By: Philip Mitanidis
Romans 11:33-36 and Colossians 1:16, 17

So, are "all things" created "by him" (Christ) or not?

As per verse thirty-six, the answer is obviously "by him" because that is what Apostle Paul has written in the Greek Scripture. He says, "from him and by him and for him are all things" (Romans 11:36), and the (NWTCGS) Bible confirms that fact. There is no mistake in Paul's wording. Verse thirty-six refers to Christ the Creator of verses 33 and 34 whose name is "God" and "Jehovah." As you can see, verse thirty-six does not state or imply that there is another individual who was involved in the creation of "all things."

Check the Greek Scriptures.

But, contrary to the above Scripture, the verses of Romans 11:33-36 are applied to God the Father by the (NWTCGS) Bible translators and by some church doctrines. These verses do not apply to God the Father because you cannot find God the Father identified in any of the above creation verses. And, as we have already learned from all of the previous Scriptures, the sole Creator of "all things" is Jesus Christ the LORD God of Israel. Therefore, these verses apply to Christ the Creator of Genesis 1:1; Isaiah 44:24; John 1:1, 3, 10; Colossians 1:16, and 17. They apply only to Christ because there is no second Creator or a co-Creator mentioned anywhere in these verses, and in the entire inspired Scriptures (Bible). Please note: I said, "In the entire inspired Scriptures."

Having said that, now, I have a question for you.

Since the translators of the (NWTCGS) Bible apply the verses in Colossians 1:16 and 17 to Christ the LORD, and claim, presumably that God the Father created everything "through" Jesus Christ, why do they apply Romans 11:36 to God the Father and state that everything was created by God the Father without Christ?

Does that make since to you?

If God the Father is the sole Creator who created "all things" for himself and by himself (v.36) that means that there is no other Creator except himself! So why do they use the uninspired word "through," in Colossians 1:16, to imply that God the Father created "through" Jesus Christ?

That is a total contradiction.

Since they use verse thirty-six of Romans 11 to state that God

Romans 11:33-36 and Colossians 1:16, 17

the Father created "all things" by himself, why not claim the other creation verses and say, all of these verses refer to God the Father? Then again, that will create a bigger problem in people's manmade doctrines. If they do that, they would have to stop saying that God the Father created "all things" or "all other things," "through" Jesus Christ. And that would mean that Jesus Christ never created anything. And if Jesus Christ never created anything, and that He was never involved with the creation of the universe, men's doctrines will have to stop saying that somebody was creating "through" Christ. These doctrines will have to admit that Jesus Christ the LORD God of Israel is not the Creator of the universe, and that He was never involved in the creation of the universe. And if that is acknowledged, the contradictions would get even bigger because all of the verses, which state that Christ is the sole Creator, will have to be eliminated. And if we cut these creation verses out of the Bible, which refer to Christ the LORD, we would end up with more man-made doctrines.

Does anybody want to do that?

The translators of the (NWTCGS) Bible believe that God the Father is identified as the sole Creator in Romans 11:36. Apostle Paul states in the Greek Scriptures that Christ is the sole Creator in Romans 11:33-36 and in Colossians 1:16 and 17.

So, who is right? Is Apostle Paul right; or is the translator's doctrine of the (NWTCGS) Bible right?

Obviously, Apostle Paul is right because he acknowledged in the Greek Scriptures, by the inspiration of God the Holy Spirit that Christ is the sole Creator who is identified in Romans 11:36 and in Colossians 1:16, 17 by the use of the words "from Him" and "by Him." Paul, like the other prophets of old, does not recognize the involvement of another Creator in the creation of the universe and everything that is in it.

Please go and look; I strongly encourage you.

On the other hand, if the translators wanted to reveal another Creator or a co-Creator in their (NWTCGS) Bible, they would have translated Romans 11:36 to read like the verses they translated in Colossians 1:16. If they did that, they would have added the

The Creator of Genesis 1:1—Who is He?   By: *Philip Mitanidis*
Romans 11:33-36 and Colossians 1:16, 17

uninspired words "other," "means of," and "through" to Romans 11:36, as they did in Colossians 1:16. And, if we were to translate Romans 11:36 as the (NWTCGS) Bible has translated Colossians 1:16, we will have something like the following in Romans 11:36, "Because by means of him and through him and for him are all other things."

By reading verse thirty-six with the altered and added words, as they have done in Colossians 1:16, 17, we can easily see that somebody is creating through someone. And since the translators of the (NWTCGS) Bible believe that God the Father is portrayed in Romans 11:33-36 that means somebody was creating the "all other things" through God the Father. If that is the case, one would wonder who created the "all other things" through God the Father? Was it God the Holy Spirit?

What do you think?

Let me say again, if verse thirty-six is applied to God the Father, the discrepancies will continue to compound. Stop and think for a moment; if the translators translated the word "δι' " to read "through," in v.36, it will mean that somebody created "all things" "through" God the Father. And if the added word "through" was used, the obvious question that will suddenly surface again is who created the all things "through" God the Father?

Was it God the Christ?

Oh! I can't say that because the (NWTCGS) Bible states in Colossians 1:16 that somebody was creating "through" Christ. So, if somebody was creating the "all things" "through" Christ in Colossians 1:16, and somebody was creating the "all things" "through" God the Father in Romans 11:36, the only alternative that is left for us is to conclude that it was God the Holy Spirit who created "through" God the Father and "through" God the Christ!

What do you think about that scenario?

See the chaos that is created by not translating the word of the LORD correctly?

Furthermore, if we were to apply Romans 11:33-36, to God the Father, we will continue to run into disagreements with God's prophets because Apostle Paul, in the Greek Scriptures, in

The Creator of Genesis 1:1—Who is He?   By: *Philip Mitanidis*
Romans 11:33-36 and Colossians 1:16, 17

Colossians says, "17 He [Christ] is before all things, and by Him all things consist." And Paul adds, "16 all things were created by Him [Christ], and for Him [Christ]." These statements, by Apostle Paul, are clear and concise in the Greek inspired Scriptures. There is no room for misunderstanding of what he wrote. He says that it was Christ who created "all things" from Himself, by Himself and for Himself. So, how can Romans 11:33-36 apply to God the Father?

But you know what? Let me take these verses one step further and consider the following: If we were to accept that God the Father is referred in Romans 11:33-36, and Jesus Christ is referred in Colossians 1:16-17, then we have a big problem because the verses in Romans 11:33-36 and the verses in Colossians 1:16, 17 claim the same thing in the Greek text. In fact, if you were to look at the words in Romans 11:36 "from him, by him and for him are all things" in the (NWTCGS) Bible, and in Colossians 1:16 "all things were created by Him, and for Him" in the (OKJV) Bible, you can see that both of these verses say the same thing almost word for word.

Therefore, it appears that the translators, in their (NWTCGS) Bible, have made God the Father in Romans 11:36 to claim the same thing as Jesus Christ is claiming in Colossians 1:16 (OKJV). God the Father claims that he created "all things" from himself, by himself, and for himself. And God the Christ claims the same thing. Christ claims that He created "all things" by Himself and for Himself in Colossians 1:16.

Now what?

And to make matters even worse, it was Paul who wrote the verses in Romans 11:33-36 and in Colossians 1:16, 17. That being the case, one has to ask, why is Apostle Paul saying one thing to the Church in Rome and another thing to the Church in Colossians?

Do you thing the apostle is lying to these Churches?

Obviously, the answer is no!

Paul said, "1 I say the truth in Christ, I lie not, my conscience also bearing me witness in the Holy Ghost" (Romans 9:1).

You see, if Apostle Paul is lying, he is condemning himself because he has stated to the Church in Galatia:

The Creator of Genesis 1:1—Who is He? By: *Philip Mitanidis*
Romans 11:33-36 and Colossians 1:16, 17

> "8 though we, or an angel from heaven, preach any other gospel unto you than that which we have preached unto you, let him be accursed." Galatians 1:8

Paul does not lie. He has testified to that fact. Paul, like the other prophets of old recognize only one Creator, and that Creator is Jesus Christ the LORD God of Israel; therefore the verses in Romans 11:33-36 apply to Jesus Christ the LORD, as do the verses in Colossians 1:16, 17.

Don't be sidetracked by the mistranslated word "Jehovah" in Romans 11:34 just because some people only apply it to God the Father. It does not mean that they are right. Remember, it is their claim that the name "Jehovah" applies to God the Father. Paul does not make that claim; and neither do the other prophets of God the Holy Spirit. In fact, there are seven references of the word "Jehovah," which only apply to Christ the LORD; and Romans 11:34 is not one of them because the word Jehovah does not exist in the Greek scriptures. The word is "Κυριος" (LORD); and that word applies to Jesus Christ the LORD of hosts.

Like Moses' statement in Deuteronomy 6:4, Apostle Paul acknowledges that Christ is the LORD (Κυριος).

He said; "5 One LORD [Κυριος], one faith, one baptism" (Ephesians 4:5).

Furthermore, in the Greek Scriptures, Paul claims that the sole Creator of Colossian 1:16 and of Romans 11:36 is Jesus Christ the LORD God of Israel. Apostle Paul does not contradict himself. As we have read, it is the translators who make the contradictions in their (NWTCGS) Bible, and the application of these verses.

Therefore, what the translators have done unawares or by intent, in Romans 11:33-36, contrary to their belief, is to acknowledge, in their Bible (NWTCGS) that Jesus Christ the LORD God of Israel is "Jehovah," as they have done in 1 Corinthians 10:9. Here is their statement: "9 Neither let us put Jehovah [Χριστον: Christ] to the test, as some of them put him to the test, only to perish by the serpents." 1 Corinthians 10:9 (NWTCGS)

And here is the verse in the Greek Scriptures where Apostle

The Creator of Genesis 1:1—Who is He? By: Philip Mitanidis
Romans 11:33-36 and Colossians 1:16, 17

Paul confirms the fact that the word Jehovah refers to Christ (Χριστον):

> "9 Μηδε ας πειραζωμεν τον Χριστον [Christ], καθως και τινες αυτων επειρασαν, και απωλεσθησαν υπο των οφεων." Α Κορινθιους 10:9 (Βιβλικη Εταιρεια) 1 Corinthians 10:9

As you can readily see in the above verses, the verses identify Jesus Christ the LORD by the name "Χριστον" (Christ). And if you were to look in the (NWTCGS) Bible, the translators identify Christ (Χριστον) by the name of "Jehovah," just as they have done in the related verses in Numbers 21:4-6.

> These verses read, "4 While they continued trekking from Mount Hor by the way of the Red Sea to go around the land of Edom, the soul of the people began tiring out because of the way. 5 And the people kept speaking against God and Moses: "why have you brought us up out of Egypt to die in the wilderness? For there is no bread and no water, and our soul has come to abhor the contemptible bread.
>
> "6 So Jehovah sent poisonous serpents among the people, and they kept biting the people, so that many people of Israel died." Numbers 21:4-6 (NWTCGS 1961 Edition)

So, for the translators of the (NWTCGS) Bible to claim that the name "Jehovah" applies to God the Father is a total contradiction on their part because as you can see, they do address Jesus Christ by the name "Jehovah" in 1 Corinthians 10:9, in Numbers 21:4-6, and in Romans 11:34, and throughout the Torah in their Bibles.

Remember, the name "יהוה" or "YHWH," if you like, is Christ's name in the Hebrew tongue. In fact, you will find Christ's name "יהוה" (YHWH: LORD) mentioned well over six thousand times in the Old Testament alone. Consider for a moment, how many times Moses addressed Christ the Creator, by the name of ".יהוה" (LORD) during His journey with the children of Israel. And then,

The Creator of Genesis 1:1—Who is He?   *By: Philip Mitanidis*
Romans 11:33-36 and Colossians 1:16, 17

consider the other references by the other prophets of God, that will give you an idea how often Christ is addressed by His name ".יהוה." And since Jesus Christ the LORD God of Israel is the Creator of "all things" (Isaiah 44:24, John 1:3, Colossians 1:16), the words "God" and "Jehovah," as per the (NWTCGS) Bible, in Romans 11:33 and 34, refer to Jesus Christ the LORD of hosts who is the Creator of "all things" (v.36).

Furthermore, in the Greek text, we are told by Apostle Paul that "all things" were created "of Him" (Christ), "by Him" (Christ), and "for Him" (Christ) in Romans 11:36. And we are also told by Paul that "all things" were created "by Him" (Christ) and "for Him" (Christ), in Colossians 1:16. And, since we are told by the prophets Moses, King David, Isaiah, Jeremiah, Apostle John, and Apostle Paul that it was Jesus Christ the LORD God of Israel who created "all things" of Himself, by Himself, and for Himself, we can accept that as a fact, not only because the prophets of old have said it, but because Jesus Christ the Creator has said it also.

In fact, before Jesus Christ the LORD of hosts was transformed from an awesome Spirit Being into a human being, Christ left His creation in the keeping of His Associates (God the Father and God the Holy Spirit). And while Christ the Creator was on earth as a human being, He claimed, everything that the Father has "are Mine."

Here is Christ's acknowledgement:

"15 All things that the Father hath are Mine:" John 16:15

Christ the Creator of Genesis 1:1; John 1:1, 3, and 10 makes that claim because He is the Creator of "all things"—remember? "All things" were created "of Him," "by Him" (Christ) and "for Him" (Christ).

Can anyone else make that claim?

By using the inspired Scriptures of the Bible, the answer is no!

And, if somebody does make that claim, then, you can be sure, their claim will contradict all of the creation verses, which refer to Christ in the Old and in the New Testaments. Just remember at least one thing; "all things" were created "of Him" Christ or "from Him" Christ, if you like. And since "all things" are "from Him" Christ (εξ αυτου), how can it be said that the "all things" are from someone else or "all things" are "through" Christ? And since "all things" are "from Him" Christ and "by Him" Christ, it cannot be said that "all things" were created "through" Christ.

As I have stated before, I have brought to your attention a handful of Scriptures from different Bible translations to show you that many translators have not translated a number of the Greek creation verses correctly, and because of that fact, these translations have created a lot of inconsistencies in the word of God the Holy Spirit. In doing so, these translations cause a reader to wonder which translation is correct? And the worst part of these translations is that people who see these discrepancies question the reliability of the Bible and its claims. In fact, there are people out there who do not believe that the Bible is inspired, like the Mormons and Muslims, to mention a few. And the reason they give, why they do not believe in the Bible, is due to their belief that the Bible is contaminated. When they say, "The Bible is contaminated," what they mean is that the original writings of the prophets, in the Hebrew and in the Greek languages, have been lost due to various translations. Therefore, they do believe in other writings, which they think are not contaminated. And because of that ideology, in many cases, they end up getting sympathizers for their cause.

So, in essence, a bad translation, as in Romans 11:33-36 and Colossians 1:16 and 17, of the Greek inspired Scriptures can create a lot of damage to the word of God if you let it.

Just think about it. If one soul (person) was lost because of one incorrect translation would that not be bad enough? Especially, if it was your daughter, son, or any other loved one who was or is deceived into perdition by this one incorrect translation. It would be a great loss to you and to Christ the Creator who died for that individual.

So, be careful, which Bible translation you use as a guide for your salvation, and for the knowledge of the Bible doctrines. I

The Creator of Genesis 1:1—Who is He? *By: Philip Mitanidis*
Romans 11:33-36 and Colossians 1:16, 17

strongly recommend that you look at the verses in Romans 11:33-36 and in Colossians 1:16-17 in your Bible, and observe if the uninspired words "other" and "through" are used. If the added uninspired words "other" and "through" are used in some or all of the creation verses, then you will know that the words "through" and "other" do not exist in these verses because if you look in the Greek Scriptures you will fined the Greek word δι' (by) is used by the prophets of God. And once you have confirmed the fact that the Greek word δι' (by) is used in all of the creation verses in the Greek Scriptures, you will also notice that the Creator of "all things" is Christ the LORD God of Israel who created "all things" of Himself, by Himself, and for Himself (Isaiah 44:24; Romans 11:36; Colossians 1:16). And since the Greek words "εξ αυτου" (from or of) and δι' (by) are used in these verses, you can also conclude that there is no co-Creator involved with Christ the LORD God of Israel. You can be sure of that fact because both Apostle John and apostle Paul state, "Because from him and by him and for him are all things" (Romans 11:36). (NWTCGS). "All things were made by [δι'] Him [Christ]" (John 1:3); "by [δι'] Him [Christ] were all things created…all things were created by [δι'] Him [Christ], and for Him [Christ]," and "by [δι'] Him [Christ] all things consist" (Colossians 1:16, 17).

The fact that "all things" are "from Him [εξ αυτου]" (Christ), "by Him" (Christ), "by His power," "by His wisdom," and "by His discretion," how can "all things" be created "through" Christ?

Therefore there is no co-Creator involved with Christ the Creator! The above inescapable statements, of Romans 11:36, John 1:3, 10, Colossians 1:16, and 17, in the Greek inspired Scriptures, and Jeremiah 10:12 in the Hebrew text make Christ the LORD of hosts the sole Creator of His universe and everything that is in it.

By the pen of Jeremiah, Christ the LORD of hosts confirms that fact by saying, "4 Thus saith the LORD of hosts, the God of Israel; Thus shall ye say unto your masters; "5 I have made the earth, the man, and the beast that are upon the ground, by My great power and by My outstretched arm" (Jeremiah 27:4, 5).

Can anybody dispute Christ's above words?

Summation of the word "through"_____ If you recall, I stated earlier that there are verses, like the above creation verses, which have been translated very poorly, and these verses do pose a huge challenge to individuals who are looking for the doctrinal truth in the inspired Scriptures of God the Holy Spirit. But, a person should not be discouraged. The answers are found in the Hebrew and in the Greek Scriptures.

Having said that, please keep in mind the following two facts: God the Holy Spirit does not contradict himself in these verses, or in any other verses of the Bible; it is the translators who contradict what God the Holy Spirit has written by the hands of his prophets.

Also, keep in mind; whenever you are confronted with the creation verses, which we have studied in the New Testament, the Greek words "δια" or "δια μεσου" (through) do not exist in these verses. And when you are confronted with these verses, you can reveal to your objectors that they are unable to find the Greek words "δια" or "δια μεσου" (through) anywhere in the creation verses. They do not exist. What they will find in these verses is the Greek word "δι' " (by), and that makes Jesus Christ the LORD God of Israel the One and only Creator of "all things," and that means, the entire universe and everything that is in it and outside of it. Stop and think for a moment, since "all things" came into existence "from Him" (Christ) (Romans 11:36), how can they be created "through" Christ?

For your edification, I have compiled all of the creation verses, which we have studied, in order to show you where the Greek words "δι' " (by) and "χωρις" (without) are used consistently by the prophets of God in the inspired Greek Scriptures. These creation verses are found in John 1:3, 10; Romans 11:33-36; and Colossians 1:16, 17. If you were to look at these verses in the (OKJV) Bible, you will observe that in all of these verses, John 1:3, 10, and Colossians 1:16, 17, the word "by" (δι') is used with the exception of Romans 11:36. The verse in Romans 11:36 has been translated incorrectly in the (OKJV) Bible. By translating verse thirty-six incorrectly, it has become in odds with the other creation verses, which have been translated to read "by."

But, notably, in verse thirty-six of the (OKJV) Bible, the translators chose to insert the word "through" even though the Greek word "δι' " (by) is present in the Greek text. If we replace the added uninspired word "through" with the correct word "by," (δι') in Romans 11:36, the verse will read, "For of Him, and by Him, and to Him, are all things: to whom be glory for ever. Amen."

For your consideration, I have removed the word "through" from Romans 11:36, in the (OKJV), and I have used the correct word "by" in order to show you that there are no discrepancies amongst all of these Greek creation verses, and with the Old Testament creation verses. They all agree that God the Creator of Genesis 1:1, John 1:1, 3, 10, Colossians 1:16, 17, and Romans 33-36 is Jesus Christ the LORD of hosts.

Here are the results from the (OKJV):

"1 IN the beginning was the Word, and the Word was with God, and the Word was God." "3 All things were made by Him; and without Him was not anything made that was made." "10 He was in the world, and the world was made by Him" (John 1:1, 3, 10).

"16 For by Him were all things created, that are in heaven, and that are in earth, visible and invisible, whether they be thrones, or dominions, or principalities, or powers: all things were created by Him, and for Him: 17 And He is before all things, and by Him all things consist" (Colossians 1:16-17).

"33 O the depth of the riches both of the wisdom and knowledge of God! how unsearchable are His judgments, and His ways past finding out! 34 For who hath known the mind of the LORD? or who hath been His counsellor? 35 Or who hath first given to Him, and it shall be recompensed unto Him again? 36 For of Him, and by Him, and to Him, are all things: to whom be glory for ever. Amen" (Romans 11:33-36).

By the way, have you memorized all of the discrepancies in all of the creation verses, which we have reviewed thus far and the use of the Greek word δι' (by)?

Ephesians 3:9_____ As you have observed from our previous discussions, the diverse Bible translations have created a number of contradictions amongst each other. These translations

Ephesians 3:9

have contradicted Christ's personal statements and His prophets of old; and they have contradicted what the prophets have written in the Hebrew and in the Greek Scriptures concerning Christ the Creator, and the creation of "all things."

Sadly, the contradictions do not stop in only the few verses, which we reviewed. No! The contradictions are spread throughout the other verses in the New Testament, which speak about Christ the Creator of Genesis chapter one, John chapter one, and the creation of the heavens and of the earth.

Even though the Greek inspired Scriptures clearly dispute the various Bible translations, and unmistakably reveal that "All things were made by Him [Christ]" (John 1:3), there are those who still assume and support the idea that God the Father created through Christ by ignoring the Greek inspired Scriptures, and the personal statement of Christ when He says that He created "all things," "by My power," "alone," and "by Myself." Jeremiah 27:5; Isaiah 44:24.

Then, as if mistranslations are acceptable, there are individuals who will quickly point to the verse in Ephesians chapter three to support their stand that it was God the Father who created "all things by Jesus Christ."

Here is what verse nine says in the (OKJV) of the Bible:

> "9 And to make all men see what is the fellowship of the mystery, which from the beginning of the world hath been hid in God, who created all things by Jesus Christ" (Ephesians 3:9).

Very convincing isn't it?

The verse says that, "God…created all things by Jesus Christ."

So, if this verse is correct, then, all of the creation verses, which we have studied, and the Creator's statements are all a big lie.

Stop and think for a moment, if the above verse is correct, it also means that all of the Old Testament writers, and the creation verses of John chapter one are wrong! And that means that Christ the Creator of Genesis 1:1, the LORD God of Israel, is lying to us when He says that He created "all things" "alone" and as He says, "by Myself." Isaiah 44:24

The Creator of Genesis 1:1—Who is He?   By: *Philip Mitanidis*
Ephesians 3:9 _____

Now what?

What are your thoughts at this point?

You know, the first time this verse was quoted to me, it kind of buckled my legs for a moment because I thought; finally, there is a verse that actually contradicts the rest of the Scriptures.

Well, don't despair. The Bible does not contradict it self.

Remember, it is the translators who contradict the word of God by their inaccurate translations. Thus, when you see discrepancies in some form or another, in some of the translations, go and consult the Hebrew and the Greek Scriptures for clarification.

Therefore, let us do that. Let us look at other translations, and then, the Greek text, so that we can see the outcome of Ephesians 3:9.

This is what the New American Standard says,

"9 and to bring to light what is the administration of the mystery which for ages has been hidden in God, who created all things" (Ephesians 3:9). (NAS)

And the last part of the verse in The New English Bible reads as follows:

"9 was hidden for long ages in God the creator of the universe" (Ephesians 3:9). (TNEB).

The New American Standard reads:

"9 God, who created all things;" Ephesians 3:9 (NAS)

The above translations, as you can see, do not agree with the (OKJV) of the Bible, which says, "hath been hid in God, who created all things by Jesus Christ." And neither does the Greek text agree with the (OKJV) of the Bible. It reads,

"9 God, He all things created." (Translation is mine.)

As you have read, the other Bibles and the Greek Scriptures do

Ephesians 3:9 _____

not have the words "by Jesus Christ" added at the end of verse nine. These words do not exist in the Greek text. So, why did the translators of the (OKJV) Bible add the words "by Jesus Christ" to the verse when they stated in John 1:3, and 10 that: "3 All things were made by Him [Christ]: and without Him was not any thing made that was made"; and "10 He [Christ] was in the world, and the world was made by Him" (John 1:3, 10)? Could it be because the translators, who were translating that portion of the Scriptures, believed that the Creator was someone other than Jesus Christ the LORD, in Ephesians 3:9? Could be? Some translators do have the tendency to translate verses according to their preconceived beliefs! It is not uncommon. But, one would think that one of the translators, of the (OKJV) Bible, would have noticed the error?

Nonetheless, reading the verse in Ephesians 3:9 in all of the above Bibles, with the exception of the (OKJV), they all agree that it was "God who created all things." And as per the inspired hand of Apostle John, he writes in John chapter one that the Creator, who created "all things," is "God" the "Word [Christ]." Or as the (TNEB) states it, "God" (Christ) is the "creator of the universe" (Ephesians 3:9). Does that ring a bell? It should because that is exactly what Moses wrote in Genesis 1:1. Moses said, "God created the heaven and the earth."

Another way a person can identify that it was Jesus Christ the LORD God of Israel who is mentioned as the Creator in Ephesians 3:9 is to go and read the verse in the Greek Scriptures. But, if you are not able to read the Greek Scriptures, you can identify that it is Jesus Christ who is mentioned by Apostle Paul in Ephesians 3:9 by cross-referencing the related verses to get your answer as to who created "all things," in Ephesians 3:9.

For example, verse nine says, "9 and to bring to light what is the administration of the mystery which for ages has been hidden in God, who created all things;" Ephesians 3:9 (NAS). If you refer to another verse, which Apostle Paul also wrote, you will notice the following about Christ: "2 with a view to an accurate knowledge of the sacred secret of God, namely, Christ" (Colossians 2:2). (NWTCGS)

The Creator of Genesis 1:1—Who is He? *By: Philip Mitanidis*

Ephesians 3:9

As you can readily see in Colossian 2:2, Paul is referring to Jesus Christ. Paul says, "the sacred secret," or the Mystery, is "of God." And who is this "God," to whom Paul is referring? The answer is given. We are told, the "mystery," is "of God, namely Christ." So, the mystery that is mentioned by Apostle Paul in Ephesians 3:9 and in Colossians 2:2, is "2 of God, namely, Christ." Therefore, the "God" of Colossians 2:2 is the same "God" of Ephesians 3:9. The only difference between the two verses, which Paul wrote, is the fact that in Ephesians 3:9 Paul gives us little more information. He says, "God [Christ] created all things." Here then, Paul agrees with John that it was God the Christ who made "3 All things," "10 the world was made by Him [Christ]" (John 1:3, 10). Paul is also in agreement with Moses who said, "1 God created the heaven and the earth" (Genesis 1:1); and added, "2 Thou hadst formed the earth" (Psalms 90:2).

As you have read in Ephesians 3:9, Apostle Paul agrees with Apostle John that God the Creator is none other than God the "Word" (Christ) of John 1:1, 3, 10. Paul further agrees with Apostle John that "God" did not create the universe "through" someone. He did it all by Himself. Paul says, "9 and to bring to light what is the administration of the mystery which for ages has been hidden in God, who created all things"
(Ephesians 3:9). (NAS)

Paul not only addresses Christ the Creator by His name "God," but he also acknowledges that Christ is the sole Creator who "created all things" by Himself.

See! There is no contradiction between the two prophets of God. They both agree that God the Christ created "all things." The Creator of Genesis 1:1: John 1:1, 3, 10; Romans 11:33-36; Colossians 1:16, 17; and Ephesians 3:9 is Christ (Messiah). There is unity in the writings of the prophets. Again, they all claim that there is only one Creator, and that Creator is Jesus Christ, as we know Him now by His character name.

These verses, as you can readily observe in the Greek Scriptures, do not identify another Creator, as some of the translations presumably imply in Ephesians 3:9. Therefore you should ask the question, where is the literal verse, in the Greek text, which literally says word for word, "God the Father or God created through Jesus Christ"?

Can you find such a verse in the Hebrew or in the Greek text?

Go ahead and look! I encourage you; and when you exhaust your search, would you then, as per the inspired Greek Scriptures, accept the fact that God the Christ is the sole Creator of His universe?

Revelations 3:14 _____ If you recall, I stated earlier that it was a harder undertaking to reveal who is the Creator of Genesis 1:1 by the use of the New Testament. Now perhaps, you can understand why I made that statement. I made it because as you have witnessed, various Bible translations are in conflict with the inspired Greek Scriptures and with each other.

Although, I have covered a handful of verses for you, in the New Testament, regarding Christ the Creator of Genesis 1:1; John 1:1, 3, 10; Romans 11:34-36; Ephesians 3:9, Colossians 1:16, and 17, I want you to know there are other verses, which I have not covered that are translated just as bad. In some cases, they are translated even worse than the ones we have sighted thus far.

Let me give you one example from the book of Revelation; we have verse fourteen reads as follows:

> "14 And unto the angel of the church of the Laodiceans write; These things saith the Amen, the faithful and the true witness, the beginning of the creation of God" (Revelation 3:14).

So, who is "the Amen, the faithful and the true witness" that is mentioned by John in the above verse? To answer the question, we have to go to Revelation 1:5, and let John give us the answer.

> Here is the answer: "5 And from Jesus Christ, who is the faithful witness, and the first begotten of the dead, and the prince of the kings of the earth. Unto Him that loved us, and washed us from our sins in His own blood." Revelation 1:5

As per the above verse, the "Amen" and the "true witness" is "Jesus Christ."

The Creator of Genesis 1:1—Who is He?   By: *Philip Mitanidis*
Revelations 3:14

By the way, you will find the word "Amen" used in the Old and in the New Testaments quite frequently.

The word "Amen," it appears, is used loosely and ignorantly by the populous around the word, mainly because most people do not know the meaning of the word; if they did, most likely, they would not use it so loosely. Jews use the word "Amen" in their prayers, and so do Christian churches use the word "Amen" in their prayers. But, the majority of the people in our society do not know that they are referring to Jesus Christ's character name when they say "Amen," or when they close their prayer by saying "Amen." Or when they say, "Amen to that" flippantly or seriously. In fact most people think it is a Christian practice or tradition to close a prayer by saying "Amen." That of course is not true. The practice of closing one's prayer by saying Amen existed in the Old Testament times. The children of Israel use to say "Amen to that" or "Amen" at the end of their prayers. Or they would say "Amen" after a reading.

Here is an example of many: "14 And the Levites shall speak, and say unto all the men of Israel with a loud voice, 15 Cursed be the man that maketh any graven or molten image, an abomination unto the LORD, the work of the hands of the craftsman, and putteth it in a secret place. And all the people shall answer and say, Amen. 16 Cursed be he that setteth light by his father or his mother. And all the people shall say, Amen. 17 Cursed be he that removeth his neighbour's landmark. And all the people shall say, Amen." Deuteronomy 27:14-17

As you can see, the children of Israel associated the word "Amen" to the Creator, the LORD God of Israel.

Later on when Christ the Creator (Messiah) came in the "flesh" on planet earth, He started many of His statements with the word "Amen." I do not know why many translations have failed to translate the word "Amen" in their translations to read "Amen"? What many translators have done, is to translate the word "Amen" to read "verily," "truly," or "in truth," in their Bibles.

As an example: "3 Jesus answered and said unto him [Nicodemus], Verily, verily, I say unto thee, Except a man be born again, he cannot see the kingdom of God" (John 3:3).

The Creator of Genesis 1:1—Who is He? By: *Philip Mitanidis*
Revelations 3:14 _____

The word "verily" in the above verse is translated from the Greek word "Amen." So, why don't the translators translate the Greek word "Amen" to read "Amen" in English?

A good question isn't it?

Anyway, Jesus Christ the "Amen" did admonish His followers to end their prayers with His character name "Amen." And rightly so because we are told,

> "12 Neither is there salvation in any other: for there is none other name [Christ] under heaven given among men, whereby we must be saves" (Acts 4:12).

As per the above verse, salvation is through the Messiah (Christ). No one else can give you salvation. Therefore, if a person wants to be saved from eternal death, and enter into Christ's holy Kingdom, he or she has to acknowledge Jesus Christ the LORD as his or her LORD God and Savior. Jesus said that no person could go to God the Father for salvation (John 14:6). As in the Old Testament times, salvation is by Jesus Christ and no one else (Isaiah 43:11).

But, if an individual wants to have his or her prayer heard that person has to pray to God the Father in the name of Jesus Christ the LORD, and end his or her prayer by the use of the character name of Jesus Christ by saying "Amen."

Remember Jesus Christ the LORD God of Israel said, "no man cometh unto the Father, but by Me" (John 14:6). You see there is exclusion here. If Jesus Christ is rejected as the LORD God and Savior in one's life, and Christ is not acknowledged first, in one's prayer that individual's prayer is not acknowledged or forwarded by God the Holy Spirit to Christ and by Christ to God the Father. It is as simple as that.

Nonetheless, as per Christ's admonition, the majority of Christians have kept the practice of saying Amen for the past two thousand years. Christians do claim, when they pray, they pray in Christ's name. So, every time you say, "Amen," you in essence are referring to the Creator, Jesus Christ the LORD God of Israel. As

The Creator of Genesis 1:1—Who is He? By: *Philip Mitanidis*
Revelations 3:14

you observed, Christ is acknowledged by His character name "Amen," in the Old and in the New Testaments.

On the other hand, since it is revealed in Revelation 1:5 and 3:14 that Jesus Christ the LORD is the "Amen," some Christian institutions claim that Christ is a created being by referring to Revelation 3:14. That is the teaching by few religious institutions. And that teaching is the furthest thought from the truth. One of these religious institutions, which uses Revelation 3:14 to show that Christ is a created being, uses their (NWTCGS) Bible to support their doctrine.

This is what their (NWTCGS) Bible says in v.14,

"14 And to the angel of the congregation in Laodicea write: These are the things that the Amen says, the faithful and true witness, the beginning of the creation by God:" Revelation 3:14 (NWTCGS)

And here is the same verse in the (OKJV) Bible.

"14 And unto the angel of the church of the Laodiceans write; These things saith the Amen, the faithful and the true witness, the beginning of the creation of God." Revelation 3:14

And here is the last part of the verse in the Greek Scriptures:

"14 Η   ΑΡΧΗ   ΤΗΣ   "ΚΤΙΣΕΩΣ   ΤΟΥ   ΘΕΟΥ."
"the [she]   beginning of the [she] "creation of [to] God."
                            Revelation 3:14 (Translation is mine.)

If you look at the end of the verse, in the (NWTCGS) Bible, you will see the words "the beginning of the creation by God." What the translators have done in this verse is to remove the preposition "of," which is the closest word to the Greek word "του," before the word "God," and replaced it with the preposition " by." By removing the preposition "of" and replacing it with the preposition "by," the verse in the English translation is made

Revelations 3:14

to imply that the "Amen" is "the beginning of the creation by God." And that is the furthest thought from the truth for a number of reasons.

For instance, as you can see, the preposition "by" (δι') does not exist before the word "God" in the above text. The Greek word before the word "God," in v.14 is "του" (to). And the Greek word for "by" as we have already learned is "δι'." And that is a big difference. Therefore, one can say that the verse in the (NWTCGS) Bible has been translated incorrectly; and the conversation should stop right now because the preposition "by" (δι') does not exist in v.14 in the Greek inspired Scriptures. But since the verse in the (NWTCGS) Bible is in error on a number of counts, we can continue to consider few of these other points for your acknowledgement.

Another reason why you cannot say, the "Amen" is "the beginning of the creation by God," is due to the fact that the added words "was" or "is," in one's doctrine or in one's vocabulary, do not exist between the word "Amen" and the words "the beginning of the creation by God," in Revelation 3:14. One cannot add the words "was" or "is" and say, "The Amen," was or is "the beginning of the creation by God" because the words "was" and "is" do not exist before the words "the beginning of the creation by God," in v.14.

Please keep in mind that the following words, "saith the Amen, the faithful and the true witness, the beginning of the creation of God" are broken down into three separate remarks, in the Greek Scriptures.

The three separate comments are:

One, *"These things saith the Amen."*
The second statement says, *"the faithful and the true witness."*
And the third remark says, *"the beginning of the creation of God."*

Although these three statements are not separated by spaces, in the Greek text, you cannot couple the "Amen" with the "beginning of the creation." The reason why you cannot couple "the Amen"

The Creator of Genesis 1:1—Who is He? *By: Philip Mitanidis*
Revelations 3:14

with the "beginning of the creation," or say, the "Amen" was or is "the beginning of the creation by God" is due to the fact that the words, "the beginning of the creation," are placed in the feminine gender in the Greek text.

Let me explain: In English, we say, "The woman, the man, and the creation." In all of the three statements, we use the definite article "the" to identify the "woman," the "man," and the "creation" without specifying the gender for "woman," "man," and "creation." In English we assume to understand what gender the "woman," the "man," and the "creation" are. And therefore we do not specify their gender.

In the Greek language one does not assume the gender of the "woman," "man," and "creation." A person has to specify what gender the "woman," "man," and "creation" fall in. One has to say, "η" woman, "o" man, "της" creation, and "του" God. In the Greek, the genders are identified of "η" woman and "της" creation. These two references are in the feminine gender. The "o" man and "του" God are identified in the male gender. Therefore, the reader in the Greek language is presented with the gender identity of "the creation of God." In this case, "the creation" is in the feminine gender. These words read like this in the Greek: "η αρχη της κτισεως του Θεου." The feminine gender of the word "της" refers to the creation; the feminine creation refers to the male gender word to (του), and the male word to (του) refers to the male gender "God." Thus in the Greek, these words state that the feminine creation was of "God."

The closest translation for the Greek word "του" is "of." But more precisely one has to say, "to [του] God," as in "the coat belongs to John." But, if one uses the word to (του), the English grammatical construction of the sentence will not be correct. Therefore one is forced to make a choice in the translation of the Greek word "του."

But one thing is for sure, the Greek word "του" does not translate "by"; the preposition "by" is translated in the Greek to read "δι'." And since the Greek word "δι'" does not exist in v.14, one cannot use the word "by" to say, "by God." Therefore one has to use "of" or "to."

Furthermore, since the Greek words "the creation" are in the feminine gender, and refer to God, a person cannot refer the words "the beginning of the creation" back to the word "Amen." For anyone to state that Christ is "the beginning of the creation by God" is placing Jesus Christ in the feminine gender. Does anybody want to go down that road?

Do you really want to call Christ a "She"?

Obviously the answer should be no because that will be an outright blasphemy.

Therefore, the translation in the (NWTCGS) Bible of Revelation 3:14 is incorrect by at least four counts.

> 1). People and religious institutions that want to make Christ a created being, have the tendency to remove the second remark "the faithful and the true witness" from the verse, and add the words "is" and "was" to the third remark of v.14, which is "the beginning of the creation of God." Many individuals use the words, "was" and "is," verbally and in their literature, to state that the "Amen" was or is "the beginning of the creation by God." The words, "was" and "is" are not found in the Greek inspired Scriptures. These words are added to the verse. Therefore, they are unacceptable as proof that Christ is a created being.
>
> 2). The added preposition "by" (δι') does not exist before the word "God." It is an added word to v.14 in the (NWTCGS) Bible. The Greek word before the word "God" is "του," which means "of" or "to." Therefore the uninspired added word "by" is unacceptable as proof that Christ is a created being.
>
> 3). The Greek letter "η" refers to the word "beginning." And the feminine word "της" refers to the word "creation." Therefore the words "the beginning of the creation," refer to the Greek word "του," and the word "του" brings the feminine creation to God the Creator (Christ) of Genesis 1:1; John 1:1, 3,

The Creator of Genesis 1:1—Who is He?   By: *Philip Mitanidis*
Revelations 3:14 _____

and 10.

4). Since the creation is in the feminine gender, religious institutions, which say Christ is a created being by the use of the added preposition "by," place the "Amen" (Christ) in the feminine gender. And that is an outright blasphemy because Jesus Christ the LORD is a male and not a female. Christ said "I am He" (John 8:24), and that should suffice as proof that He is a male.

The closest rendering of the Greek words "η αρχη της κτισεως του Θεου" is found in the (OKJV) Bible. It reads, "the beginning of the creation of God;" I say that it is the closest to the Greek because the preposition "of" is used before the word "God." Although the (OKJV) of the inspired Scriptures uses the definite article "the" before the word "creation," the translators did not have any choice. If the translators wrote, "she creation," the structure of the grammatical wording would not be proper in the English language. Therefore translators had to use the definite article "the" before the word "creation." By using the definite article "the" before the word "creation," the reader in English does not know that the creation is identified in the feminine gender in the Greek Scripture. That puts a reader at a disadvantage. Unless, you read and understand the Greek language, you cannot confirm the true meaning of the verse. Therefore, many readers who cannot confirm the verse in the Greek Scriptures, unfortunately, are at the mercy of the translators.

Nonetheless, "the beginning of the creation of God" is the closest translation possible in the English language, and that makes the "Amen" (Christ), God the Creator of His feminine creation.

A lot more can be said about the above verse, and the difficulty some translations present to the reader of the Bible. That difficulty is not only with some of the Bible translations, but the difficulty also exists because the Greek in some instances cannot be translated directly or very accurately in the English language, or in some of the other languages.

Having said that, and the information, which I have given you earlier, you should be able to deal with further issues on the above difficult verse and verses like it. And when you sort out these difficult verses, you will find that the "Amen" (Christ) is God the sole Creator of His universe, after all.

Hasn't it been testy?

Three Religious Doctrines

1). The Trinitarian Theory The Trinitarian theory does not exist in the inspired Scriptures of the Bible, and neither can it be explained by Scripture. A man called Athanasius made the Christian Trinitarian theory popular shortly after the death of the apostles. Later his theory was accepted in one form or another, by the Protestant reformers.

The Christian Trinitarian theory was placed in a form of Catechism or Creed as in "The Apostles Creed." It was invented for the sole purpose of explaining the God of the Bible by going beyond Scripture references.

Having said that, please remember, this theory is the invention of man. You cannot find it in the inspired Scriptures of God the Holy Spirit.

We are probably in disagreement already!

Anyway, the reason the Trinitarian theory does not exist in the Bible is simply because there are no Bible verses to support the conclusion of the theory. What the Trinitarian theory does is to place the emphases on the word "one" in one of the Bible verses. The most frequent explanation to support the Trinitarian doctrine comes from the following quoted verse. Jesus said to the Jews, "I and My Father are one" (John 10:30).

The Trinitarian doctrine proposes that God the Christ and God the Father are "one," by explaining that the word "one" means "one substance." But, the word "one," as it is used in the Greek inspired Scriptures, is in the plural form. The word "one" is not in the numerical form. Therefore, the word "one" refers to more than one individual, just as the word "one," in some verses, refers to more than one individual in the Old Testament. The word "one," as it is used in John 10:30, is in the form of unity and purpose. And this

The Creator of Genesis 1:1—Who is He?   By: *Philip Mitanidis*
The Trinitarian Theory

unity of purpose refers to the name "LORD God." (See John chapters 16 and 17.) Therefore Christ the Creator and His two Associates are not confined in one shell; and neither do they split Themselves into three separate Individuals, and then, reassemble Themselves in one unit. Therefore, let me say, as per the inspired Scriptures, there is no mention in the entire 66 book of the Bible of one God with three heads bobbing around in the universe in one body.

Nonetheless, let me give you one reference of many where the word "one" is in the plural form when it is used in reference to the name "LORD God." Consider the following comments that were made by Christ the LORD of hosts. Referring to His disciples, Jesus said, "21 That they all may be one; as thou [[you], Father, art in Me, and I in thee, that they also may be one in us: that the world may believe that thou hast sent Me. 22 And the glory which thou gavest Me I have given them; that they may be one, even as we are one: 23 I in them, and thou in Me, that they may be made perfect in one" (John 17:21-23).

By reading the above verses, should we conclude that Christ, the Father, and the twelve disciples are all in one body? As per the Trinitarian theory, if we follow that logic and insert our own ideology, one has to say, yes! But, Scripture opposes that answer. Scripture obviously answers no! So, why add to the inspired word of God by saying that Christ and the Father are "one" person or one unit? Why teach people that Christ and the Father are the same person? Oh! I should have said, why teach people that Christ, the Father, and the Holy Spirit are the same person? Some might say, "Well that is not quite right what the Trinitarians believe?"

In response, I say, yes, there are some who believe in the above Creed, and there are others who do not! You see, dear reader, if you were to go and ask a handful of people who believe in the Trinitarian theory, you will find a number of opinionated variations of their Trinitarian faith.

For example, in many Christian "Creeds," you will find that many of the Protestant Christian believers believe in one breath that they worship one God in three persons, and visa versa. In general,

The Trinitarian Theory

the Trinitarian Christian Creed states that there are three persons in one God, and of "one substance." And contrary to that statement, they add that there is one person of the Father, another person of the Son, and another person of the Holy Spirit.

So, the question that rises from the above, we can ask, how can the Father, the Son, and the Holy Spirit be three Individuals when some of the Creeds state that They are all "One" and of "one substance"? These two statements are in total contradiction with each other. And to make matters even worse, Christian Creeds go on to argue, contrary to the inspired Scriptures that there are not three Gods, but one God.

So, which is it?

Are there three Gods, or are They one God of "one essence"?

Now here is the hard part. Where do we find the verse or verses in the inspired Scriptures of the Bible, which state that God the Father, God the Christ, and God the Holy Spirit are of "one essence"?

Do you know?

I cannot find the verse?

So! Why make a statement like that?

Moreover, the Trinitarian theory cannot decide which way to go in their explanations? Does the Trinitarian theory teach that there are three Gods in one body; or does it teach that there is only one God who is made up of three Individuals of "one substance"? The bottom line is, as hard as it tries; it cannot have both. Some explanations, or rather the majority of the explanations, which I have come across, on the long run, claim that there is "one God in three persons."

You know, I might offend some people by what I am going to say next, but consider my opinion for what it is worth. If, we were to accept the Trinitarian theory that God the Christ, God the Father, and God the Holy Spirit are one, as in one body, or that they are made up of "one substance," logically, we can conclude that Christ did not die on Calvary's cross! How can I say that? I can say that because rationally what the Trinitarian doctrine makes me conclude is the fact that only an extension of God died on Calvary's cross

The Creator of Genesis 1:1—Who is He?   By: *Philip Mitanidis*
The Trinitarian Theory

2,000 years ago. Their one God, as the Trinitarian theory teaches, is comprised of God the Father, God the Christ, and God the Holy Spirit.

Agreed?

Therefore, in order for God (God the Father, God the Christ, and God the Holy Spirit) to die, and pay for the sins of the world, They all had to die at the same time on Calvary's cross, otherwise God did not die; only an extension of God died on the cross. And that extension as per the Trinitarian theory is God the Christ. That means that there was no atonement for the sins of the world. And the death of Christ on Calvary's cross is a big pretence. Please remember, I said, "As per the Trinitarian theory, a person could conclude, only an extension of God died on Calvary's cross."

On the other hand, if God the Father, God the Christ, and God the Holy Spirit are "one," as in one "essence," as the Trinitarian theory teaches, then a person can also conclude that They all physically died on Calvary's cross! But that cannot be true also because God the Father and God the Holy Spirit are not in a physical form; they are Spirit Beings, just as Christ was before He came in this world of ours in the "flesh." Therefore, only the extension of God physically died on Calvary's cross; and that extension was Christ.

And another question, of many, can be asked, if They are all of "one substance," just before Christ died, to whom was Christ praying when He said, "Father forgive them for they know not what they do"?

Was He praying to Himself?

Why?

Should I continue asking questions?

Therefore, the interpretation of God, as per the Trinitarian theory, is in disarray. It cannot explain nor does it explain the God (God the Father, God the Christ, or God the Holy Spirit) of the Bible because it imposes interpretations on the inspired Scriptures by going beyond the inspired Scriptures; and that makes the conclusion of the theory an opinion. In doing so because of these opinionated interpretations, and lack of Scripture, we can conclude

The Trinitarian Theory

that the Trinitarian doctrine does not exist in the inspired Scriptures.

By the way, can I ask one more question; why are the Trinitarians using John 10:30 to prove that God the Holy Spirit, God the Father, and God the Christ are "One" and of "one substance" when the verse does not include God the Holy Spirit as being "One," or of "one substance," with God the Father and with God the Christ?"

You know, if the Trinitarians went as far as to stick to Scripture and say that God the Father, God the Christ, and God the Holy Spirit are three separate Individuals who think and act independently, and treat each other as equals, as they have done, and stopped right there, the Trinitarians would have ample support to sustain their claim, from the Old and New Testaments; but, by going beyond the Scriptures and by adding to their theory that God the Father, God the Christ, and God the Holy Spirit "are one" and of "one substance," it puts their opinion in contradiction with the inspired Scriptures because Christ the LORD of hosts says, "9 I am God, and there is none else; I am God, and there in none like Me" (Isaiah 46:9).

And to further refute the idea that there is somebody "like" Christ, and of "one substance" or "essence," Christ the LORD of hosts asks, "25 To whom then will ye [all of you] liken Me, or shall I be equal? saith the Holy One" (Isaiah 40:25). "2 There is none holy as the LORD: for there is none beside thee [You]: neither is there any Rock like our God" (1 Samuel 2:2). "6 Forasmuch as there is none like unto Thee [You], O LORD; Thou art great...there is none like unto Thee" (Jeremiah 10:6, 7). "6 who in the heaven can be compared unto the LORD?" (Psalms 89:6), obviously, as per the above claims, to no one!

But, if we claim that we know what Christ the Creator and His two Associates are made of, and how they came to exist, we can ask with the prophet of old, "34 who hath known the mind of the LORD?" in order to explain Him to us; "or who hath been His counseller"?

And Isaiah adds, "28 there is no searching of His understanding" (Romans 11:34; Is. 40:28).

So! The question is simple, who does know the mind of Christ the LORD of hosts, and can explain Him beyond Scripture? Do His Associates, do angels, does man, or can somebody else explain Him?

***2). The One God Theory*_____** The one God theorists (Jews, Muslims, and some Christians) excludes Christ as being "the Creator," "the LORD of hosts," "the God of Abraham," "the God of Israel," "the King of Israel," "the Messiah," and the One who dwelt in between the cherubims in the "most holy place" of His Sanctuary in "Shiloh" and later in "Jerusalem." It teaches that the Messiah (Christ) is still to come.

Although the claim's of the "One God Theory" are nowhere to be found, in the inspired Scriptures (Bible), consider the following scenario, on behalf of the "One God Theory," which claims that Christ (Messiah) is still to come in the "flesh" to die for sinful men and women.

Contrary to the inspired Scriptures, it is claimed by the one God theorists that the God of Abraham is not Christ the LORD of hosts! They claim that the God of Abraham is God the Father, as he is known in the Christian circles. Therefore, by making that claim, they state that God the Father is the Creator and the almighty God of the universe. And it is also claimed by the one God theorists that the writings of the Torah refer to their one God (the Father). Therefore, since the one God believers apply the Scriptures of the Torah to God the Father, a person has to conclude that it was God the Father who promised Adam, Noah, Abraham, Moses, and King David that he was going to come in the "flesh," through their lineage, and die for the sinners of planet earth. From that statement, a question appears immediately before us; we can ask, did God the Father come and die as per the "promise" and as per the Messianic prophesies? Historically, the answer, as per the inspired Scriptures, is a definite no! Therefore, we can conclude that he did not keep his promise to Adam, Eve, Noah, Abraham, Isaac, Israel, Moses, King David, etc., etc.

But, if we were to assume that God the Father came and died, we can further ask, when did he die? And, who resurrected him from his death, since there is no other God like him? I ask those questions because, you see, Scripture teaches that the "wages of sin is death" (Romans 6:23). If God the Father became sin or a curse

The Trinitarian Theory

for the sinners of planet earth, he would have died; then, somebody had to resurrect God the Father from his death; otherwise, he would remain dead. So, who did or who was going to resurrect him? The answer, obviously, would be no one because the one God theory teaches that there is only one God the Father, as in the numerical number one (1). And since that is their belief, you and I, and the rest of the universe should not be here and would not be here because everything would have vanished with the death of God the Father. The universe and everything that is in it would vanish because there would be no living God to sustain it.

Needless to say, we are still here!

Furthermore, if we were to accept the "One God Theory" that God the Father will die in the future for the sins of the world, we have a great contradiction because Scripture teaches us that, "only God hath immortality" (1 Timothy 6:16). That being the case, we can also conclude that God the Father cannot really die because he is immortal! In other words, he cannot be killed.

Therefore, this one God the Father could not die on Calvary's cross, or anywhere else for that matter, for the sins of the world. And, if he portrays his death that means that his death would be only a charade, sham, fake, and pretence because he cannot be killed due to his immortality. As pretence, the promise by God the Father to die for Adam and Eve, and their offspring cannot be fulfilled by him.

Thus, if we were to accept the one God religious doctrine, God the Father has lied to Adam, Eve, Noah, Abraham, Moses, Isaac, Israel, and to King David. And he has lied to you and to me because as per the one God theory, it makes him the one who has promised Adam and Eve that he would die for their offspring and save them from their eternal death.

But, since he cannot be killed, as a Spirit Being, the only way for God the Father to die is to strip himself from all of his powers, stop existing as a Spirit Being, and become a man. When he does that, then man can take him and kill him. Then he will die? But the big question stands, is he willing to do that for Adam and Eve, and for you and for me?

The Creator of Genesis 1:1—Who is He? By: *Philip Mitanidis*

The Trinitarian Theory

Well, as per the one God theory, and the applications of the Scriptures of the Torah to God the Father, one would expect him to strip himself from his powers, transform himself into human flesh, and die for the sinners of planet earth, as he promised; but will he?

By the way, don't hold your breath!

Given that there are only seven rapid and short prophetic events to be fulfilled, before the second coming of Christ the LORD of hosts takes place, and if I may add; they have already started, a person can ask, when is God the Father going to die for the sins of the world, as he promised Adam, Noah, Abraham, Isaac, Israel, Moses, and King David? Personally, it will never happen because these seven last prophetic events do not deal with a coming Messiah who is going to offer himself for atonement. Therefore, as per the inspired Scriptures (Bible), we can conclude; since God the Father is not going to die for the sinner; the sinner will eventually perish forever. I make that statement because there is not a single verse in the entire Bible where it tells us that God the Father has died or he is going to die for the repentant sinners of planet earth.

That being a Scriptural fact, as you can see, the one God doctrine brings no hope to the sinner. But more importantly, it does not exist in the inspired Scriptures. The one God doctrine does not exist because *one,* ninety-six percent of the Torah speaks about Christ the Creator of Genesis 1:1 (John 5:45-47). *Two,* the Torah and the rest of the prophets acknowledge that Christ the Creator was going to come in the "flesh" and die for the sins of the world. These Messianic verses do not apply to God the Father. As per the inspired Scriptures, they apply to Christ the Creator of Genesis 1:1; John 1:3, 10. And these prophecies, especially the ones in the book of Daniel, state that God the Messiah will die during the time the Roman Empire occupies the Middle East. As per the historians, and as per the Greek inspired Scriptures, the only Individual that died in that period of time, 2,000 years ago, was God the Christ of Genesis 1:1; John 1:1, 3, 10. There is no record of the death of God the Father during that time period historically or Scripturally.

Therefore, the application of the "One God Theory" and the application of the Torah, to the one God the Father, are in total contradiction with the inspired Scriptures.

By the way, the one God theory cannot make its mind up whether or not the God of Abraham, when he comes, is going to be the "Messiah" (Christ) or is the "Messiah" (Christ)?

3). The Arian Theory

In addition, to the above theory, you will find that there is another one God theory, as in the numerical one (1) God, which tries to get around the above problems; and if I may add, very unsuccessfully, by stating that God the Father created a little god called Christ (Messiah). And this big God the Father sent the created poor little god called Christ (Messiah) to planet earth to die for the sins of the people.

Can you imagine the above scenario?

No! I am not making this up!

There are millions upon millions of people out there who believe in this one God Arian man-made religious doctrinal theory. Like the previous theories, this one God Arian man-made theory, with its created little god, has many big problems also. It to is in confusion. A man called Arius made the one God Arian theory popular after the death of the apostles. His theory is often called the Arian doctrine. It became popular after the Nicaean council disputes, in 325 A.D. It teaches that there is only one God (the Father, as he is known in the Christian circles). And, it teaches that Christ (Messiah) is only a created being.

Having said that; let me emphasize this one Scriptural fact before we continue with the Arian doctrine. There is not a single verse in the entire 66 books of the Bible, which states that Christ is a created being. The verse or verses do not exist in the inspired Scriptures of the Bible. But what you will find, in reference to Christ the Messiah, is the fact that He is the sole Creator of "all things" (John 1:3; Colossians 1:16; Isaiah 44:24; Jeremiah 27:4, 5) and not the created.

On the other hand, as per the one God Arian theory, we have the following scenarios. I do not know why God the Father used this poor created little man called Christ, as atonement for the sins of the world; and why he chose Him from all of the created beings up there (3rd heaven) and not from the entire universe, but this much I do know, these points are not explained by the Arians, neither do they know?

The Creator of Genesis 1:1—Who is He?   By: *Philip Mitanidis*

The Arian Theory

But, we can ask, did he (God the Father) intimidate, frighten, harass, and bribe this poor helpless little created being called Christ (Messiah) by saying to Him, if you succeed in surviving the temptations, the abuse, the ridicule, the torture, and die without sinning, I will resurrect you from your death, and I will let you be second in command, and I will let you sit on my throne? But, if you fail, I will create another Messiah (Christ), and I will send Him to accomplish the mission. Does that mean, if this helpless created little god called Christ (Messiah) failed in His mission to save man, the big God would create another little god, and he would send Him to planet earth to die for the sins of the people of planet earth? And, if this feeble little god called Christ (Messiah) failed in His mission to save man, the big God would create another little god, and he would send Him to planet earth to die for the sins of the people of planet earth. And if this powerless little god called Christ (Messiah) failed in His mission to save man, the big God would create another little god, and he would send Him to planet earth to die for the sins of the people of planet earth. And, if this weak little god called Christ (Messiah) failed in His mission to save man, the big God would create another little god, and he would send Him to planet earth to die for the sins of the people of planet earth. And if this vulnerable little god called Christ (Messiah) failed in His mission to save the human race, the big God would create another little god, and he would send Him to planet earth to die for the sins of the people of planet earth. And so on would the scenarios go until the mission was successful.

So! The question is, is that what happened?

Has this bully, one God (the Father), pulled wool over our eyes and over the eyes of the individuals who dwell throughout the universe, and in the third heaven, by creating one or many little gods called Christ until one of them finally succeeded to die sinless on Calvary's cross?

If the above scenario did occur, there is, nor has there been any remission for man's sins. Consequently, man will perish in his sins, and is perishing without the hope of salvation because there is no accountability whatsoever by this one God (the Father).

The Arian Theory

On the other hand, if there was accountably by this one God (the Father), he should have died for the sins of the world because the Arian theory, like the one God theory, applies the Scriptures of the Torah to God (the Father) and not to Jesus Christ. By applying the Torah (the five books of Moses) to God the Father, it makes God the Father the Creator of the world and of man. It also makes him the one who interacted with Adam, Abraham, Isaac, Jacob, Moses, Samuel, King David, etc, etc. Furthermore, it makes God the Father as the one who dwelt in between the two cherubims in his Sanctuary, and as the one who led the children of Israel from Egypt and all the way into the Promised Land. It also makes him the "Messiah" (Christ). And, it makes him the one who made a promise to Adam and to Eve that he would die for the sins of the world, and not some poor little created being called Christ.

Thus, a person would expect God the Father to fulfill his promise.

Of course he should!

But, since he has not fulfilled his promise to die, on behalf of the human race, we can conclude that the plan of salvation as per the one God Arian theory, which teaches that a created being came to die for the human race, is a total mockery. It is a mockery because Scriptures tell us, "7 None of them," in other words, nobody "can by any means redeem his brother, nor give to God a ransom for him" (Psalms 49:7).

Since no created being can atone for the sins of the world, the one God Arian theory, which states that there is a created being, called "Christ" (Messiah), who atoned for the sins of the world, is a pretense, a mockery a deception. Therefore there is no salvation for the human race.

On the other hand, if you are wondering how the Arian so-called Christians reject Christ as the God of His universe, as the God of Abraham, as the God of Israel, and make the claim that Christ is a "created being," here are a handful of references for your consideration, which they commonly use to support their two Gods man-made religious doctrine.

The first reference _____ is found in Proverbs 8:22. It reads: "22 The LORD possessed me in the beginning of His way, before His works of old" (Proverbs 8:22) in the OKJV.

What the Arian believers claim and do, in the above verse, is to first remove the Hebrew word "possessed" (qana קאנא) from the above verse and replace it with their own uninspired word "produced" (qarab קאראב) in their Bible (NWTCGS).

Secondly, they take the word "LORD" and apply it to God the Father; and then apply the word "me" (wisdom) to Jesus Christ. In doing so, they say and claim that Christ is acknowledging that the LORD (God the Father) "produced me" (Christ) "in the beginning of his way"!

And they also claim that Christ is the Individual who was used by God the Father to create the universe. To support their theory, they use verse thirty, and say, "30 Then I [Christ] was by him [God the Father], as one brought up with him [God the Father]: and I [Christ] was daily his delight, rejoicing always before him [God the Father]" (Proverbs 8:30).

Can you imagine the above twisted claims?

Very convincing, isn't it? That is, if you are gullible enough to accept their uninspired word "produced" and the application of verse 30?

Now consider my claim. Solomon is claiming and is acknowledging that the "LORD" (Jesus Christ) "possessed me" (God the Father); or "produced me" (God the Father)—if you want to accept the Arian uninspired word "produce"—"in the beginning of his [Christ's] way" (Proverbs 8:22).

And, I also claim that God the Father is the Individual who was used by Jesus Christ the LORD to create the universe. To support my statement, I use verse thirty, which reads, "30 Then I [God the Father] was by him [Christ]: as one brought up with him [Christ]: and I [God the Father] was daily his [Christ's] delight, rejoicing always before him [Christ]" (Proverbs 8:30).

So! What do you think of the above scenarios?

Who is right, the Arian claims or my claims?

Obviously, according to Scripture, none of us are right.

The reason why the Arian claims are wrong and my claims are wrong is due to the fact that we both have made personal statements to convince you, as to who "possessed" or who

The Arian Theory

"produced" whom without Scriptural evidence. As you have observed, we simply added our personal choice of names in the verses. In fact, you can do the very same thing. You can put any name you want as the Arian Christians have done and as I have done in the above verses (22 & 30); and then, you to can claim that you are right. But needless to say, at this point, all of our claims are wrong because we all added our own preferred names and opinions in the verses.

But, contrary to our claims, now listen to what King Solomon claims.

King Solomon claims that "The LORD," of verse twenty-two, is identified, as the Creator "of His works of old" (Proverbs 8:22).

And who is the Creator of "His works of old"?

As we have studied thus far, we have found out that the Creator of the universe and of "all things" is Jesus Christ the LORD God of Abraham and not God the Father.

In addition, Solomon says that it was "the LORD" who "possessed" (qana) something "before His works of old" (v.22).

So! What did "the LORD" of verse twenty-two possess?

According to verse twenty-two He "possessed me."

Who is "me"?

According to the whole chapter (Proverbs eight), it is "wisdom."

Please read the whole chapter and notice how "wisdom" is personified by the pronouns "she," "I," "Me," "My," etc., etc.

As a result, what Christ the Creator of verse twenty-two possessed, "in the beginning of His way," was "wisdom."

Here are few references to the fact that the LORD possessed "wisdom" and not as per the added word "produced," as the Arians would like us to believe. The psalmist says, "24 O LORD, how manifold are Thy [Your] works! In wisdom hast Thou [You] made them all: the earth is full of Thy riches" (Psalms 104:24). "3 In whom [Christ] are hid all the treasures of wisdom and knowledge" (Colossians 2:3).

Thus, according to the above verses, "the LORD" of verse twenty-two is identified as the Creator of "His works of old," which

The Creator of Genesis 1:1—Who is He?   *By: Philip Mitanidis*   293
The Arian Theory

He created by His "wisdom," and "wisdom" is identified as a "she" (Proverbs 8:1-3).

In addition, we are told "wisdom" is from "everlasting" (v.23), just like Christ the Creator. Moses testifies to that fact. He says, "1 O LORD, Thou, [You] hast been our dwelling place in all generations. 2 Before the mountains were brought forth, or ever Thou hast formed the earth and the world, even from everlasting to everlasting, Thou art God" (Psalms 90:1, 2).

Therefore, according to the above verses, Christ the Creator and "wisdom" are from "everlasting."

And, as per verse twenty-three, "wisdom" is not and it cannot be said that "wisdom" is "produced" or "created" and then "possessed." Neither can we say that "wisdom" is Christ because Christ is the Creator of "all things" (Colossians 1:16; Isaiah 44:24). And, neither can we say that God the Father created the universe through Jesus Christ the LORD by saying that "wisdom" refers to Christ. If we do that, all I can say, we are adding to Scripture, deleting Scripture, and that is an offence to God the Holy Spirit.

Furthermore, we cannot say that "wisdom" was a co-Creator or helped to create the universe because "wisdom" claims that Christ the LORD of Proverbs 8:22 was the sole Creator by saying, "26 While as yet He had not made the earth," "27 When He prepared the heavens," "28 When He established the clouds above," "29 When He gave to the sea His decree," "30 I [wisdom] was with Him [the LORD v.22]." Proverbs 8:26-30

As you can see, wisdom acknowledges that she did not create anything. In fact, none of the above verses (vs. 26-30) claim "wisdom" created something. All of the above references state that it was "He," the Creator of verse twenty-two, who created, and that is an inescapable fact.

But, if we choose to believe that the words "the LORD" of verse twenty-two refer to God the Father, and the words "possessed me" refer to Christ the LORD, then you will have a bigger problem to deal with because Solomon claims that "wisdom" is a "she" (Proverbs 8:1, 2, 3)!

In fact, King Solomon says, "4 Say unto wisdom, Thou [you] art my sister" (Proverbs 7:4).

Now what?

Do you still want to claim, "wisdom" is Christ?

If you do, then, you will have to acknowledge that Christ is a "she"!

Do you really want to make that blasphemous claim?

If you do, please remember, you will willfully blaspheme Christ the LORD God of Israel because Christ the LORD said, "24 I said therefore unto you, that ye shall die in your sins; for if ye believe not that I am He, ye shall die in your sins" (John 8:24).

Christ the LORD God of His universe claims that He is a "He" and not a "she."

Do you still want to disclaim Christ as the sole Creator of "all things" and call Him a "she"?

It's your move.

The second point _____ to consider is found in a verse that is used quite extensively by the Arians, in order to claim that Christ is a created being and not the sole Creator of "all things."

The verse reads, "15 Who [Christ] is the image of the invisible God [the Father], the firstborn of every creature" (Colossians 1:15).

Did you notice; there is nothing in the above verse where it states Christ is a created being? And yet, the Arian believers continue to use the above verse by saying, "Christ is a created being."

So, I ask, where are the words in the above verse, which state "Christ is a created being"?

Can you find them?

Of course not! They simply do not exist. These words are added to the verse.

What the Arian believers do is to explain away the word "firstborn," in contradiction to the empirical meaning of the word.

Apostle Paul says "firstborn."

The Arians say, "created."

Who are you going to believe?

Nonetheless, it is this word (firstborn) that the Arian believers

The Arian Theory

use to support their religious man-made doctrine. They claim that the word "firstborn" means created. Now I ask you; what dictionary says that the compound word "firstborn" means created? But, contrary to their claim, the word "firstborn" means to have the first baby expelled from a woman's body at birth. In other words; the baby is the first one to be born from a woman; and not the second-born, third-born, etc., etc.

On the other hand, the word "created" has the opposite meaning from the word "firstborn." The word "created" means to make something out of nothing; whereas, the word "firstborn" means to make something from something already in existence. In this case a woman's egg and a man's sperm make a baby.

To confirm the fact that Christ was the "firstborn" of Mary, here is the reference: "24 Then Joseph being raised from sleep did as the angel of the LORD had bidden him, and took unto him his wife: 25 And knew her not [had no intercourse] till she had brought forth her firstborn son: and he called His name JESUS" (Matt. 1:24, 25).

Having stated the above Scriptural fact that Christ is the "firstborn" of Mary, now I have a question for you. Why has Apostle Paul stated that Christ is the "firstborn of every creature," or "creation" if you like, when He was only born about two thousand years ago? Others have been first-born way before Him? For example, many of Adam's children were born four thousand years before Christ. So! Why is Apostle Paul placing Christ birth before Adam's children?

Actually, he does not physically place Christ first as the "firstborn."

How can I say that when Apostle Paul explicitly states in Colossians 1:15 that Christ is the "firstborn of every creature." I can say it because Apostle Paul explains his statement in verse eighteen. In verse eighteen Paul makes Christ the LORD the "firstborn of every creature" by "preeminence." In other words, although Christ's birth of Mary was not the "firstborn of every creature," He is made first by "preeminence." In fact, in verse eighteen, Apostle Paul even makes Christ the "firstborn" raised from the dead. As you know Christ was not the first to be raised from the dead. There were many individuals raised from the dead, in the Old Testament, way before Christ died on the Calvary's Cross. In fact, Christ resurrected many individuals during His Gospel ministry.

For example, Christ the LORD of hosts raised Lazarus from his death; so how can Christ be the "firstborn" (πρωτοτοκος) raised from the dead? He was not! (See John 11.) Paul does not contradict himself and neither does he contradict the other prophets who have made others preeminent, like King David; what he does claim is the fact that Christ is raised first from the dead in "preeminence" (πρωτευων), and that is a big difference. Paul's statement confirms that fact by saying,

"18 And He [Christ] is the head of the body, the church who is the beginning the firstborn from the dead: that in all things He might have the preeminence [πρωτευων]" (Colossians 1:18).

Did you notice? In the above verse, Christ the LORD of hosts is made "preeminent" (πρωτευων) in "all things." He is made first (preeminent) "in all things" even though He is not. Therefore for the Arian Christian believers, or anyone else for that matter, to use Colossians 1:15 to prove that Christ is a created being is futile.

Third point _____ In addition, you will find that there is not a single verse in the entire inspired Bible, which says that God the Father created a little god called Christ. Go and look; I encourage you.

But on the contrary to the one God   Arian beliefs, which has removed the word "God" from John 1:1 and added the words "was a god" in their (NWTCGS) Bible, the inspired word of God the Holy Spirit testifies that God the Father did not create a little god. So! How can Christ be a created being?

In confirmation to the fact that Christ is not a created being comes in the form of the following testimony:

"10 Ye [the children of Israel] are My witnesses, saith the LORD, and My servant whom I have chosen: that ye may know and believe Me, and understand that I am He: before Me there was no God formed, neither shall there be after Me" (Isaiah 43:10).

The Creator of Genesis 1:1—Who is He?   By: *Philip Mitanidis*

The Arian Theory

Since the Arian believers apply the above verse to God the Father, God the Father testifies by saying, "there was no God formed" (OKJV). And, as the (NAS) puts it, "Before Me there was no God formed. And there will be none after Me" (Isaiah 43:10) (NAS). The (NIV) Bible says, "Before me no god was formed, nor will there be one after me" (Isaiah 43:10) (NIV).

So, if we apply the Arian one God theory to the above verse, we find the above verse in total contradiction with the one God Arian religious doctrine. It is in total contradiction because God the Father says that he did not create "a god" at any time. In fact he says, "there was no God formed." Therefore Christ is not "formed" or "created."

Now what? What kinds of spin or excuses are the Arians going to create in order to further support their man-made Arian religious doctrine?

Looking at the above testimony by Isaiah, I have to ask, who are you going to believe? Are you going to believe the one God Arian religious man-made doctrine, which says that Christ is a little god who was created by a big God (the Father)? Or are you going to believe Isaiah 43:10, and like verses, which say, "no god was formed" by God the Father?

By the way, why would God the Father want to have another "god" beside him to be worshipped when he, as per the Arian doctrine, explicitly, on numerous occasions, has said, "You shall have no other gods before me," or worship created gods beside him? And yet, contrary to the first commandment, and verses like the first commandment, the Arian believers worship God the Father through their created little god called "Christ"!

Go figure!

Let me say again, contrary to the one God Arian theory, as we have read many times in the inspired Scriptures, and I do emphasize the word "inspired," and not in man's favorite mistranslated Bibles, the Scriptures testify that Christ is God the Creator of Genesis 1:1, John 1:1, 3, 10, and not the created. And because of that fact, I thank God (that includes all three Individuals) that the Arian one God doctrine does not exist in the inspired Scriptures of the Bible.

But, what does exist in the inspired Hebrew and in the Greek Scriptures is the fact that Christ the Creator of His universe, was willing to strip Himself from His awesome powers, from His form (a Spirit Being), and come down to planet earth in the "flesh" (Philippians 2:5-8), to save man, as He had "promised" Adam, Eve, Noah, Abraham, Moses, King David, Isaiah, etc., and not some poor little helpless created being.

Do I hear an Amen?

The fourth point. _____ In further disagreement with the one God Arian theory and its claim of a created little god (Christ), now consider few of many verses, where the beloved Apostle John and Apostle Paul acknowledge Christ the LORD, as the "God" and "Saviour," who died on Calvary's cross.

Here is their testimony, which states that God the Christ died for the penitent sinners and not some poor little created being called "a god."

> "16 Hereby perceive we the love of God, because He laid down His life for us" (1 John 3:16).

> "3 For I delivered unto you first of all that which I also received, how that Christ died for our sins according to the scriptures" (1 Corinthians 15:3).

> "5 They are the descendants of our great ancestors, and they are the earthly family into which Christ was born, who is God over all. Praise him forever! Amen." Romans 9:5 (NCV)

> "16 And without controversy great is the mystery of godliness: God was manifest in the flesh, justified in the Spirit, seen of angels, preached unto the Gentiles, believed on in the world, received up into glory." 1 Timothy 3:16

In confirmation that Christ the King of Israel (John 1:49) died, Isaiah writes; "6 Thus saith the LORD the King of Israel, and his Redeemer the LORD of hosts; I am the first, and I am the last, and beside Me there is no God" (Isaiah 44:6). And Matthew the apostle agrees with Isaiah by saying the following about the "King of

The Creator of Genesis 1:1—Who is He?   By: *Philip Mitanidis*
The Arian Theory

Israel," who is identified by the name of "Christ." "5 Behold thy King cometh unto thee [the children of Israel]" (Matthew 21:5). And when the King of Israel came to His own people (John 1:11), He was taken to be crucified. Matthew said, "1 AND it came to pass, when Jesus had finished all these sayings, He said unto His disciples, 2 Ye know that after two days is the feast of the Passover, and the Son of man [Christ] is betrayed to be crucified. 3 Then assembled together the chief priests, and the scribes, and the elders of the people, unto the palace of the high priest, who was called Caiaphas, 4 And consulted that they might take Jesus by subtilty, and kill Him" (Matthew 26:1-4). And when they took Him, "35 they crucified Him, and parted His garments, casting lots: that it might be fulfilled which was spoken by the prophet [King David], They parted My garments among them, and upon My vesture did they cast lots" (Matthew 27:35).

As per the above verses, and like verses, it is obvious that it was Christ the Creator who died for us. He (God the Christ, Romans 9:5; 1 Timothy 3:16) was the One who "washed us from our sins in His own blood" (Revelation 1:5); and has "purchased" you and me "with His own blood" (Acts 20:28). As you can observe from the above verses, it was Christ the Creator of Genesis 1:1; Isaiah 44:24; John 1:1, 3, and 10 who came in the flesh and died for us (Philippians 2:5-8).

So! The question is, as per the inspired Scriptures, did God the Christ of Genesis 1:1 die, or did He not die?

As we have read, and, as per the following verses, 1 John 3:16; Romans 9:5; Revelation 1:5; 1 Corinthians 15:3; Matthew 26:1-4; 27:35, and like verses, the answer is yes! God did die; but it was not God the Father. It was God the Christ. God the Christ was crucified, as He promised Adam, Noah, Abraham, Isaac, Israel, David, Isaiah, Micah, etc.

Christ the Creator of His universe is a responsible God after all. He is responsible for His universe, and He is responsible for the outcome of man's sins. And being responsible, He stripped Himself (Ephesians 2:5-8) and did die (1 Peter 1:18, 19) for the penitent sinner, as He promised Adam, Noah, Abraham, Isaac, Jacob, King

David, Daniel, etc., etc.

God the Christ did die as He "promised," and not some poor little created being as some would like us to believe.

Point number five _____ Let me make few more important observations about God and say that God does not tempt man to serve Satan, to sin, to torture, to blaspheme, to kill, to abuse, to lie, etc.

Scripture tells us that God does not tempt anyone. But, the one God Arian theory demonizes God the Father. The one God Arian doctrine tells us that God the Father not only created Christ but he also sent Him to planet earth to be tempted, persecuted, beaten, whipped, tormented, tortured, hung on the cross, and killed Him!

What kind of a monster is God to do that to a created being?

He is not the God of the Bible that I know of!

As you can see, the one God Arian doctrine makes their one God the Father a tyrant because according to the Arians, he sent this poor little created god called Christ to be tempted, spit upon, beaten, tortured, and at the end, he had Him killed. And that scenario is in total contradiction with what Apostle James has written (James 1:13). In fact the one God Arian theory is in total contradiction with the entire inspired Scriptural doctrine.

On the other hand, Christ, the God of the Bible that I know of, is "love." He proved it on Calvary's cross. Christ does not abuse or tempt His created beings. He does not tempt or abuse man; neither does He desire for man to perish. In fact, He stripped Himself (Ephesians 2:5-8) from the awesome Spirit Being that He was and came in the "flesh" to save man (Luke 9:56). He did not come to tempt, torture, and to destroy man. He came to save the human race. Therefore, He does not tempt anyone.

We are told: "13 God cannot be tempted with evil, neither tempteth He any man" (James 1:13).

Did you hear that?

Christ, the Creator of His universe, is not the cause of all the horrors that are imposed upon the human race; it is Satan and his satanic agencies who have continued to abuse and tempt man into untold sinful horrors. Just take a look around you, and observe the unending inhumane suffering! Satan is the one who tempted Adam and Eve, remember? It was not God. God does not tempt man to sin or promote sin.

So! Why blame Christ the Creator of Genesis 1:1, or His two Associates, for the woes of this sin filled feverish world of ours? God the Christ is not the Author of the horrors of this world of ours. Satan and his satanic agencies are.

Christ the LORD God of Israel is "love." He proved it on the cross; how can He be a villain?

Point number six. _____The one God Arian theory, as you probably already know, ridicules the Trinitarian believers by saying that when Christ was praying on the cross, He must have been praying to Himself. Ironically, this same ridicule comes flying right back on the faces of the one God Arian believers because the one God Arian believers state that God the Holy Spirit is only God the Father's "active force." And because the Arians believe that God the Holy Spirit is only God's (the Father's) "active force," they have changed many references of God the Holy Spirit to read "active force" in their (NWTCGS) Bible.

Can you imagine that?

How can anyone go and change the words God the Holy Spirit, purposely, is mind boggling to me. See Genesis 1:2 of many references, as an example, in the (NWTCGS) Bible.

Anyway, since the Arians believe that God the Holy Spirit is God's (the Father's) "active force," like the Trinitarian belief, their one God the Father prays to himself also because we are told, "26 the Spirit itself maketh intercession for us with groanings which cannot be uttered" (Romans 8:26). That being a fact, we can conclude that God's "active force" intercedes for us "with groanings which cannot be uttered" by us. Therefore, this one God the Father talks to himself. So, according to the above scenario, God's "active force" takes all of your prayers, your thanks giving, and petitions them with "groanings which cannot be uttered," by you, to himself!

Can you imagine that?

That is belittlement and that is an outright blasphemy!

So, as per the above Arian theory, God the Father grunts and groans with noises to himself that cannot be uttered by us, when we pray to him. Wooo! Does he not know what you and I are praying about without the "active force"? Does the "force" think for God the Father, is that why he does not know what we pray for? And

The Arian Theory

does he not know your thoughts without making all of those noises to himself, in order to make your prayer more affective and convince himself that he should accept your prayer? And, if he cannot convince himself whether to accept your prayer or not, does he then grunt and groan even harder to himself in order to convince himself that he should answer your prayer? And, if that does not work, does he then abandon your prayer? He just gives up! Or, is it because he cannot make his mind about you? Or is it because he needs the "active force" to make his decision on your behalf?

Woooh! Let me put on the brakes right about now, dear reader; it looks like I have been duped into the same vein of thought as the Trinitarian doctrine by the Arian one God the Father doctrine.

If you and I were to accept the Arian one God the Father doctrine, we have to accept the fact that God the Holy Spirit is only an "active force" because that is the Arian Christian teaching. As an "active force," however you want to play around with these uninspired words, the bottom line is that a person has to conclude, contrary to the one God Arian doctrine that the "active force" of God the Father is personified. How can I make a statement like that? I can make a statement like that because as per the Arian one God doctrine the "active force" picks up your prayers and your petitions and takes them before God the Father "with groanings which cannot be uttered" by you (Romans 8:26). The fact that the "active force" takes your prayers directly to God the Father in utterances of expressions, which you cannot utter, it means that the "active force" acts independently from the thought processes of God the Father. And since these thought processes are independent from God the Father, it means that the "active force" is personified and independent from the thought processes of God the Father. Therefore, the thought processes of the "active force" and the thought processes of God the Father are distinct and separate from each other.

On the other hand, if we do not want to accept what Apostle Paul is saying in Romans 8:26 and cling to the one God Arian doctrine, then, we have to accept the fact that the personified "active force" is part of God the Father because the one God (the Father) Arian doctrine states that the "active force" is God's "active force." If we accept that as a fact, then we have to conclude that God the Father, when he takes your prayers and brings them to himself, by his "active force," he is talking to himself, "with groanings which cannot be uttered" by you. That being the case, a person has to further conclude that the "active force" is part of God's make up. And, if we go down that road, as per the one God Arian theory, a person also has to conclude that God the Father is made up of two individuals, the personified "active force" and himself. And that being the case, a person also has to further conclude that there are two individuals in one body with two heads bobbing around the universe. And that dear reader brings us right into the same vein of thought as the Trinitarian doctrine. The only difference between the Trinitarian doctrine and the one God Arian doctrine is that the Trinitarians have three Gods bobbing around the universe in one body whereas the one God Arian doctrine has two Gods in one body bobbing around the universe.

So! Why do the Arian believers ridicule and bash the Trinitarian believers when they mutually fall into the same deceptive pit?

Why do the one God Arian believers pick on the Trinitarian theory (doctrine), when their man-made one God Arian theory (doctrine) does the very same thing as the Trinitarian doctrine?

Therefore the one God Arian theory becomes just that, a theory. But more importantly, the one God Arian theory, like the Trinitarian theory, does not exist in the inspired Scriptures of the Bible.

Please note; I said, "In the inspired Greek Scriptures." I did not say, in the altered Scriptures of the Arian Bible (NWTCGS), which has been altered by the Arian translators and incorporated to support their religious man-made doctrine.

Point number seven_____ Now, let me bring before you the name "Jehovah" for your consideration from the Arian doctrine.

"In North America and probably elsewhere, people like myself have been confronted with the Arian doctrine in one point of time or another. My experience has been when Arian representatives come knocking on my door, normally they try not to disclose who

The Arian Theory

they are because they fear that they would be turned away before they give their little canvass. But irrespective of the outcome, they try to leave their magazines for me to read; that way, they feel that I will receive their doctrinal Arian message, which predominantly states throughout their writings that God the Father is Jehovah.

Paradoxically, although they claim that God the Father is Jehovah, if you were to confront them to show you one single verse from the entire Bible where it states that God the Father is Jehovah, they are not able to produce a single verse to support their Arian belief!

Are you surprised!

No! I am not making this up. If I was, I would be lying to you; and that I would not knowingly do because if I did lie to you, I would re-crucify my LORD Jesus Christ and put Him into open shame. (See Hebrew 6:6)

Nonetheless, the Arians insist that God the Father is Jehovah? And to prove their point, their first response is to claim that they can show you over 6,000 verses, from their Bible, where God the Father is identified by the name of Jehovah. The reason they make that claim is due to the fact that they have been taught to believe that the word LORD (יהוה) means Jehovah, which is one hundred percent in error. As I have stated before, the word LORD (יהוה) does not translate into English or any other language—and that includes the Hebrew language—to read Jehovah. Let me say again; the Hebrew word "יהוה" translates into all languages to read LORD. But, regarding the Hebrew word Jehovah, you will find the word appearing only seven times. And then again, some will tell you that the word Jehovah appears eight times in the entire Bible; but that is another study.

Here are some of the references out of the seven: Jehovah-jireh (Genesis 22:14); it means, Jehovah will provide. Jehovah-nissi (Exodus 17:15, 16); it means, Jehovah is my banner. Jehovah-shalom (Judges 6:23, 24); it means Jehovah is peace. See also Exodus 6:3; Isaiah 12:2, and the rest, I will let you search for them.

Therefore, since there are only seven references with the word Jehovah, they cannot claim that the word Jehovah appears over

The Creator of Genesis 1:1—Who is He?
The Arian Theory

6,000 times in their Bible or any other Bible that has translated the Hebrew word "יהוה" to read incorrectly, Jehovah.

But, if you were to dispute their claim that the Hebrew word "יהוה" does not translate to read Jehovah, they will quickly go to one of their favorite verses (Psalms 83:18) and point out to you that the verse contains the Hebrew word Jehovah and it refers to God the Father.

Well, if you do go to your Bible and look at the verse, you will definitely find the Hebrew word Jehovah there, which is one of the seven references, and not the word "יהוה" (LORD); but does the verse and the word Jehovah refer to God the Father?

They claim that it does, but can they show you the words God the Father in that verse? Or prove that the verse refers to God the Father?

Obviously not because the words God the Father have been added to the verse; these words do not exist in the verse. Therefore all they have done is to reveal to you that One of the Individuals from the Godhead is identified by the name of "Jehovah."

So! Who is identified in Psalms 83:18 by the name of "Jehovah"?

To answer according to the inspired Scriptures, Jehovah is none other than Christ the Creator of Genesis 1:1.

How do we know?

Consider the following; the verse reads as follows:

"18 That men may know that Thou [You], whose name alone is JEHOVAH, art the Most High over all the earth" (Psalms 83:18).

So, who is the Most High? And "whose name alone is Jehovah"?

As you have read in the above verse, the answer is given; Jehovah is "the Most High."

"The Most High" is one of Christ's character names; and in the New Testament, "the Highest" is God the Father's character name.

To confirm the fact that the character name "the Most High"

The Arian Theory

refers to Jesus Christ the Creator, as we know Him now in the New Testament, here are the references, which reveal that the children of Israel tempting Christ the "Most High God" during His travel with them towards the Promised Land and in the Promised Land.

> "56 Yet they tempted and provoked the Most High God, and kept not His testimonies; 57 But turned back, and dealt unfaithfully like their fathers: they were turned aside like a deceitful bow. 58 For they provoked Him to anger with their high places, and moved Him to jealousy with their graven images. 59 When God heard this, He was wroth, and greatly abhorred Israel; 60 So that He forsook the tabernacle of Shiloh, the tent which He placed among men; 61 And delivered His strength into captivity, and His glory into the enemy's hand. 62 He gave His people over also unto the sword; and was wroth with His inheritance. 63 The fire consumed their young men; and their maidens were not given to marriage. 64 Their priests fell by the sword; and their widows made no lamentation. 65 Then the LORD awakened as one out of sleep, and like a mighty man that shouteth by reason of wine. 66 And He smote His enemies in the hinder parts; He put them to a perpetual reproach. 67 Moreover He refused the tabernacle of Joseph, and chose not the tribe of Ephraim: 68 But chose the tribe of Judah, the mount Zion which He loved. 69 And He built His sanctuary like high places, like the earth which He hath established for ever" (Psalms 78:56-69).

Briefly, as you have read in the above verses "the Most High God" was tempted by the children of Israel (v.56). The Most High God abandoned His dwelling place in the Sanctuary, which was pitched in "Shiloh" by Joshua (v.60). In other words, the Most High God refused the tabernacle of Joseph, and chose not the tribe of Ephraim (v.67). The Most High God "chose the tribe of Judah, the mount Zion which He loved" (v.68). Who chose to dwell in the Sanctuary in Jerusalem? Why it was none other than Jesus Christ the LORD of hosts—remember? We have studied this point earlier.

The Creator of Genesis 1:1—Who is He? *By: Philip Mitanidis*

The Arian Theory

And then, the psalmist acknowledges that the Most High God is the Creator by saying: "And He built His sanctuary like high places, like the earth which He hath established for ever" (v.69).

To further confirm the fact that Christ the LORD of hosts is the Most High God, read the chapters of the three overviews in Psalms 78; Nehemiah 9; and 1 Corinthians 10 to refresh your memory that Jesus Christ the Creator is the God of Israel, is the One who took the children of Israel out of Egypt and led them into the Promised Land, is the One who gave the children of Israel water to drink from rocks, is the One who fed them, is the One who protected them, is the One who dwelt in His Sanctuary in Shiloh and in Jerusalem, is the Creator, and is the Most High God who was tempted (Psalms 78:56-58) by the children of Israel, etc., etc.

And when you finish reading "The Three Overviews," you would have noticed according the Psalmist, Nehemiah, and Apostle Paul, the Individual who was temped was Christ the LORD of hosts. Christ is identified by the psalmist in verse fifty-six by the name of "the Most High God" and Creator of the "earth" (v.69). And since Christ is the One who was tempted by the children of Israel and is the sole Creator, the words "the Most High God" can only refer to Christ the LORD of hosts.

But, simplistically, Christ identifies Himself as the "first and the last," in Revelation 1:17, 18, to Apostle John. And in Isaiah 44:6 Christ also identifies Himself as the "first and the last," as "the LORD of hosts," and as "the King of Israel." Therefore Christ the LORD of hosts who is "the King of Israel" identifies Himself by the character name of "the Most High" in Psalms 47:2. The verse reads as follows: "For the LORD Most High is terrible; He is a great King of all the earth." (See also Matt. 21:5; Luke 23:38; John 1:49 where Christ is revealed as the King of Israel.)

Consequently, since Christ is the King of Israel (John 1:49), it follows that the words "the Most High" refer only to Christ the LORD of hosts. The verse reads: "18 That men may know that Thou whose name alone is JEHOVAH, art the Most High over all the earth" (Psalms 83:18).

But more simplistically, compare Psalms 78:56 with Psalms

The Arian Theory

78:35 and notice how Christ the "Rock" and "Redeemer" is identified by the name of "the Most High God." See also where Christ is identified by the name of "Rock" 1 Corinthians 10:4, and in 2 Samuel 22:32. And notice how Christ the "Rock" of Psalms 92:15 is identified as the Creator in v.5 and by the name of "the Most High" in vs.1, and 8 of Psalms 92; and notice how Christ "the Most High" is further identified by the Psalmist by the name "Jehovah" in Psalms 83:18.

Therefore, for anyone to use Psalms 83:18 to prove that God the Father's name is Jehovah is futile because, as we have seen, according to Scripture, especially in the other six references, which contain the name of Jehovah, they all refer to Christ the LORD of hosts "whose name alone is Jehovah" (v.18).

By the way, did you know that the Arians, today, contrary to their belief, identify Christ (Χριστος) the LORD by the name of "Jehovah" over 6,000 times in their Bible—the "New World Translation of the Christian Greek Scriptures" (NWTCGS) 1961 Edition and onward—and yet, they refuse to call Christ by His name Jehovah!

Go figure?" * 1

A lot more can be said about the one God Arian religious doctrine; but just like the Trinitarian doctrine, and the one God doctrine, it continues to contradict it self and the inspired Scriptures.

In conclusion, please remember, since these three man-made religious doctrines do not exist in the inspired Scriptures, you should give them a serious consideration. I make that statement because if, you were to accept the Trinitarian doctrine, the one God doctrine, or the Arian one God doctrine, as per their doctrinal theories, God did not die because the Trinitarian theory implies only an extension of God died; and the Arian one God theory states that some poor little created guy called Christ died; and the one God doctrine teaches that the Messiah is yet to come. If that is your belief,

---

* 1. Mitanidis, Philip *"Moses Wrote About Me"* pgs. 163-168 BEEHIVE PUBLISHING HOUSE INC. 2011

according to the inspired word of God, there is no atonement for your sins.

Even though men and women can argue about their above doctrines and each one can claim that their doctrine is correct, till the tides come in; and even then, they will not finish arguing because when we argue doctrines that are based on man-made theories and outside interpretations of the Bible doctrine, a person can argue or discuss the objections, almost forever.

But, contrary to the above theories, what you do find, as we already found in the inspired Hebrew and Greek Scriptures, are verses, which disclose the fact that there are three separate Individuals who treat themselves equally, think independently, act separately, and have the same name; and that name is "LORD God." And that is not the Trinitarian theory, the one God theory, or the one God Arian theory.

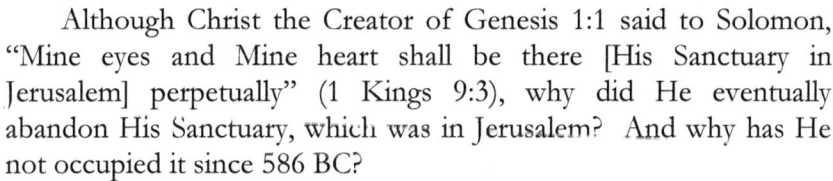

A Question

Although Christ the Creator of Genesis 1:1 said to Solomon, "Mine eyes and Mine heart shall be there [His Sanctuary in Jerusalem] perpetually" (1 Kings 9:3), why did He eventually abandon His Sanctuary, which was in Jerusalem? And why has He not occupied it since 586 BC?

Christ the LORD of hosts abandoned His Sanctuary because His stay in Jerusalem was conditional, just as His stay was conditional in "Shiloh."

> Christ the Creator said to Solomon, " 6 "But if you or your sons turn away from me and do not observe the commands and decrees I have given you and go off to serve other gods and worship them, 7 then I will cut off Israel from the land I have given them and will reject this temple I have consecrated for my Name. Israel will then become a byword and an object of ridicule among all peoples. 8 And though this temple is now imposing, all who pass by will be appalled and will scoff and say, 'Why has the LORD done such a thing to this land and to this temple?" 9 People will answer, 'Because they have forsaken

the LORD their God, who brought their fathers out of Egypt, and have embraced other gods, worshiping and serving them— that is why the LORD brought all this disaster on them.' " (1 Kings 9:6-9). (NIV).

The condition that was set by Christ the Creator was not new. Similar warnings and conditions were given to Moses, and to the leaders that followed after him. If the children of Israel did not meet those conditions (of verses 3-5) the Creator's warning to Solomon was: 6 "But if you or your sons turn away from me and do not observe the commands and decrees I have given you and go off to serve other gods and worship them, 7 then I will cut off Israel from the land I have given them and will reject this temple I have consecrated for my Name. Israel will then become a byword and an object of ridicule among all peoples." (1 Kings 9:6, 7) (NIV).

> The OKJV puts it this way, "7 Then will I cut off Israel out of the land which I have given them; and this house, which I have hallowed for My name, will I cast out of My sight; and Israel shall be a proverb and a byword among all people." 1 Kings 9:7

The first fact, why Jerusalem and the Sanctuary were eventually destroyed, was due to the rejection of Christ the God of Israel. After King Solomon died, his kingdom was divided into two kingdoms. Like Solomon, after his death, the children of Israel fell into apostasy, prior to Christ's coming in the flesh, a number of times, during the 900 years period. During that turbulent time, the house of Israel and the house of Judah fought with each other for dominance. That unstable period was well known to the children of Israel throughout their generations because during that time period, (a), the last king of the house of Israel was removed in 722 BC. (b). It was confirmed and apparent that Christ the Creator dwelt in His Sanctuary for approximately 345 years after Solomon's death. The reason the Creator dwelt for 345 years more in His Sanctuary was due to the destruction of the Sanctuary, which took place by the

The Creator of Genesis 1:1—Who is He? By: *Philip Mitanidis*

A Question

Babylonian army. And the reason why the Sanctuary was destroyed was due to the rejection of Christ the Creator by the children of Israel. They would not listen to Him or to His prophets. They, like their forefathers went and did their own thing, which was contrary to the Creator's advice. And   (c), finally, Christ the Creator left the children of Israel unto their own devises. They continued to serve other gods. And when the Creator's protection was removed from Jerusalem, the Babylonian army came, and during the first siege, overthrew Jerusalem, and took many of the leaders, or princesses if you like, into captivity. And, after the second siege took place, by the Babylonian army, King Zedekiah tried to get help from the Egyptians, in order to jointly attack the Babylonian Empire. When King Nebuchadnezzar heard what was taking place, in his fury, he unleashed his troops and defeated the combined forces of Judah and Egypt. Nebuchadnezzar was so mad at King Zedekiah for trying to overthrow his kingdom, during the third siege, he captured Zedekiah, put his eyes out, and took him captive to Babylon. In 586 BC, during the third siege, the Babylonian army demolished Jerusalem literally to the ground; even the Temple of Solomon was flattened. The whole city and its walls were left in utter ruins; only a handful of people, including Jeremiah the prophet of the LORD of hosts, were left behind to work the farmland for the Babylonian king.

The second fact occurred after the Medo-Persian Empire overthrew the Babylonian kingdom. When Cyrus, the Persian king, captured the city of Babylon, he was confronted by the overwhelming prophetic evidence, which referred to him (Isaiah 43:28; 45:1-4). He was told that it was God the Creator who set his kingdom up. Convinced by the word of God, he co-operated with the children of Israel in their endeavor to go back to their homeland. During that time, after their seventy years of captivity, all of the children of Israel were given the liberty, by the Persian king, to return to their homeland. The king also gave them aid to rebuild Jerusalem and the House of God.

Contrary to God the Creator's advice, only a small number of people responded and returned to Jerusalem. The majority of the

A Question

children of Israel, who were dispersed throughout the Babylonian kingdom, did not return to their homeland.

Later on, Nehemiah, the Persian king's cupbearer, came and helped to speed up the restoration of Jerusalem, and the House of God. During that period of time, the Ark of the Covenant could not be found; therefore, it was absent from the House of God, when the children of Israel dedicated the Sanctuary to God. During the dedication of the House of God, the Creator's glory could not be seen in the Sanctuary. This meant that God the Creator did not dwell in the rebuilt Sanctuary.

The third fact is the destruction of the House of God in 70 AD. In addition to the 484 years of absenteeism from His Sanctuary, for approximately another two thousand years, Christ the Creator has not been seen in His Sanctuary in Jerusalem. The Creator's Shekinah glory, in the "most holy place," has not been seen; neither has it been seen in all of that time period. Even today, if you were to go into the House of God the Creator, in Jerusalem, you will not see the Shekinah glory of Christ the Creator residing in the "most holy place" between the two cherubims.

Today, as in the previous years, Christ the Creator, the LORD God of Israel, cannot be seen dwelling in His Sanctuary. How do I know? I know because His Shekinah glory cannot be seen in the "most holy place," neither can anyone see Him as a cloud hovering over the "most holy place." Go to Jerusalem today; and look for yourself, if God the Creator resides over or in the "most holy place" in the form of a cloud? Or go inside the "most holy place," if they let you, and see for yourself, if the Shekinah glory of Christ the Creator is present? The fact that the Shekinah glory cannot be seen in the "most holy place" of the Sanctuary, and a none Levitical Priest can stand in the "most holy place" of the Sanctuary, with out being killed, is proof enough that Christ the Creator does not reside there any more.

Again, how do I know? I know because Christ the LORD of hosts personally said to the children of Israel, "Your house is left unto you desolate." He has abandoned it. Notice, He not only abandoned the Sanctuary, but He also disclaimed it. Referring to the

The Creator of Genesis 1:1—Who is He?   By: *Philip Mitanidis*
A Question_____

Sanctuary in Jerusalem, Christ said to the Jews, "Your house." Prior to that statement, Christ the Creator, the LORD God of Israel use to refer to the Sanctuary as "His House." In fact, He use to call it "My house," but not any more!

As you probably already know, the Roman army destroyed the Sanctuary in Jerusalem in 70 AD. After the Romans occupied the city, they gradually rebuilt Jerusalem and the Sanctuary. But because the Jews would not stop terrorizing and fighting the Romans, the Romans issued a decree, in 135 AD, to remove the Jews from Jerusalem, and at the same time, enacted the death penalty upon any Jew who returned or entered Jerusalem intentionally or covertly. Although the Jews were happy to learn that the Sanctuary was rebuilt, the joy of the house of Judah did not last because they received word that the Romans placed their gods in the Sanctuary and occupied it. Later the Ottoman Empire had control over the region. Eventually the majority of the Jews were dispersed from the area, and they were not able to return to Jerusalem. It was not until the late nineteen forties (1948), the Jews were permitted to return to Jerusalem. But, before they returned, the English government decided to place a border between the Jewish state and the Palestinian state. This border divided the Sanctuary, between the Palestinians and the Jews.

Today, as in the past fifteen hundred years, there has been, and there still is a great irritant dispute over the Sanctuary's ownership. The "most holy place" of the Sanctuary is in the Palestinian territory, and the "holy place" is in the Jewish territory. The Jews want to claim the Sanctuary for their god; and like wise, the Muslims want to claim it for their god. But you know what? Christ the Creator does not reside in there any more. He has not dwelt there for nearly 2,500 years. He has rejected it, so why bother claiming it for Him? Christ the Creator of Genesis 1:1 stated very emphatically to the priests, Pharisees, and to the Sadducees, "your house is left unto you desolate" (Luke 13:35). He does not want it any more. Its ceremonial services are not needed any more. That is one of the main reasons why He has abandoned it.

Today, it can be seen that the Sanctuary in Jerusalem is

The Creator of Genesis 1:1—Who is He?   By: *Philip Mitanidis*
A Question

inoperative. In fact, today, the so-called Solomon's Temple is guarded by the Palestinians and by the Jews. The Sanctuary is under lock and key, in order to avoid unauthorized persons entering in it. That means that the Sanctuary is not open to receive the repentant sinner with his or her sacrificial sin offering or thank offering.

That being the case, let me leave this sobering thought with you. If Christ the Creator who made it a point to dwell in the Sanctuary, in Jerusalem, still has use for it and for its services, would He not raise a prophet or a people to make sure that its ceremonial laws and services continued in full force today, and throughout its existence?

Why has He not done that throughout these past 2,000 years?

Why has He not claimed it again?

Don't you think that there is something wrong with the above picture?

I say that because originally the ceremonial law and the services of the Sanctuary were implemented for the benefit of the sinner. The sinner was given the opportunity to repent for his or her sins. If sinners truly repented for their sins, they were to take an animal in the eastern part of the courtyard of the Sanctuary, and offer it for their sin offering. There the individual would place his or her hand on top of the animals head; and looking towards the "most holy place" of the Sanctuary, the sinner would confess his or her sins over the animal; after that, he or she would slay the animal by cutting its throat with a knife, and then, the priest would take over from there onward in the ceremonial service.

Scripture states: "without the shedding of the blood, there is no remission of sins." That is why individuals had to bring an animal to the altar of sacrifice. In addition, this sacrificial act was also done to remind the individual of "the shedding of the blood," which was going to take

The Creator of Genesis 1:1—Who is He?   By: *Philip Mitanidis*
A Question

place, in the future, by the supreme sacrifice of God the Creator. Until then, the sacrificial services had to continue.

So! Why haven't they?

Having stated the above, I hope you do not get annoyed or mad at me for asking the following questions; and for giving you the answers from the Bible. But, as you ponder over the questions, please remember, the Sanctuary in Jerusalem is closed. It is not in service. Today's padlocks on the doors of the Sanctuary speak very loudly of this fact

Here are the questions; since sinners have not sacrificed animals for their sins in the eastern courtyard of the Sanctuary in the city of Jerusalem, according to the Law of Moses (the ceremonial law), how were the sinners forgiven and saved in the past 2,000 years; and how are the sinners forgiven and saved today? The big question is, have all of the people, who have lived and died for the past two thousand years, died in their sins because they were unable to offer a sin offering?

What do you think?

If a person says, they have been forgiven, how is it possible to forgive them without the sacrificial offering for their sins? And how is it possible to cleanse the Sanctuary without the ceremonial service by the high priest? Especially without the service of the Day of Atonement when the cleansing of the Sanctuary took place once a year from all of the accumulated yearly sins of the people? These services, for most of the time, in the past 2,000 years have not been implemented in the Sanctuary. So, how are the sins of all the people who have died in the past 2,000 years forgiven without their sacrificial offerings for their sins, and without the implementation of the Day of Atonement taking place every year?

If you recall, Christ the Creator, the LORD God of Israel, sent prophets throughout the ages to guide and direct the children of Israel in the way that they should go. And He always managed to bring His people back to Himself. But, if you were to look in the Scriptures of the Bible, you will observe, the last prophets that were sent to the house of Judah, with the written and verbal words, after the prophet Malachi (420 BC), were the apostles of Christ the

A Question

LORD. But, after them, where are the prophets that were sent or are sent to the house of Judah and to the house of Israel? Has anyone seen them or heard from them?

If salvation was by the implementation of the ceremonial law, where is or where are the prophets of God who have been sent to the children of Israel to tell them to go and take the Sanctuary, and start the sacrificial services for the sins of the people? Why hasn't Christ the LORD God of Israel, in the past 2,000 years, sent a prophet or prophets to tell the Jews or anyone else for that matter, to go and reclaim or claim the Sanctuary? Since the sacrificial services for sin offering was or is so crucial to save an individual from eternal death, why has Christ the Creator, the LORD God of Israel, not given the Sanctuary to His people to implement the sin offerings in all of these thousands of years?

Do you know?

He hasn't because He has no use for it any more! And the reason why Christ the Creator has no use for the Sanctuary in Jerusalem any more is due to the fact that He has become the sacrificial lamb who takes away the sins of the world. John the Baptist said, "29 Behold the lamb of God, which taketh away the sin of the world" (John 1:29). Christ has fulfilled the sacrificial offering, which pointed to Him. The Sanctuary services, priesthood, and the ceremonial law have ended on Calvary's cross (Ephesians 2:15). Christ the Creator has fulfilled the "promise," which He made to Adam and Eve six thousand years ago. In fact, this same "promise" was made to Abraham, Isaac, Jacob, Moses, David, Isaiah, Daniel, Micah, etc.

> The record states: "16 Now to Abraham and his seed were the promises made. He saith not, And to seeds, as of many; but as of one, And to thy seed, which is Christ [Messiah].
>
> "17 And this I say, that the covenant, that was confirmed before of God [the Father] in Christ, the law [ceremonial law], which was four hundred and thirty years after, cannot disannul, that it should make the promise of none effect" (Galatians 3:16, 17).

The Creator of Genesis 1:1—Who is He? By: *Philip Mitanidis*
A Question

It should be remembered that the "promise" has been fulfilled. Christ the Messiah the LORD God of Israel had come in the "flesh" (John 1:1, 14, 41), and paid the penalty for man's sins. We are told, "13 Christ hath redeemed us from the curse of the law [Ten Commandments, as they are listed in Exodus chapter twenty], being made a curse for us" (Galatians 3:13). Therefore, since Christ fulfilled the sacrifice for the sins of the world, we do not need to bring an animal for a sin offering in the eastern courtyard of the Sanctuary any more.

Today, as in the past two thousand years, a sinner can come to Christ (Messiah) without a sacrificial sin offering because "28 Christ was once offered to bear the sins of many" (Hebrews 9:28). Therefore a person's sins can be forgiven without bringing a lamb to the altar of sacrifice in the eastern courtyard of the Sanctuary in Jerusalem because Christ is the sacrificial lamb (John 1:29).

Today, all a person has to do is to bring self before Christ, and ask forgiveness for his or her sins. It does not matter how great or horrid one's sins are; all of his or her sins will be forgiven. The promise is there. Christ says that He will not turn away anyone who has repented for his or her sins, and comes to Him. The repentant sinner will be justified freely by His grace and be accepted as His child, and be bound for Christ's eternal Kingdom. Scripture says: "8 while we were yet sinners, Christ died for us. 9 Much more then, being now justified by His blood, we shall be saved from wrath through Him" (Romans 5:8, 9).

Do I hear an Amen!

Salvation, like before—in the Old Testament—is by Christ. Christ said, "4 I am the LORD thy God from the land of Egypt, and thou [you] shalt know no god but Me: for there is no Saviour beside Me." Hosea 13:4

And today we are told, "12 Neither is there salvation in any other: for there is none other name under heaven given among men, whereby we must be saved." Acts 4:12.

Remember, Christ has paid the penalty for your sins. Christ our Creator died for us, "while we were yet sinners." Now, we are "justified by His blood," and because we are justified by His blood,

A Question

"we shall be saved from wrath through Him [Christ]" (Romans 5:8, 9).

Christ, as He said to Paul, He says to you, "9 My grace is sufficient for you" (2 Corinthians 12:9). If you have not paid attention to what I have being saying thus far, please remember at least this one point as you go on in life; Christ said that His "grace is sufficient for you." It does not matter how vile, how debase, how abhorrent, how repulsive, how sickening, how horrifying your sins are, Christ said that His "grace is sufficient for you." Christ can make you clean from all of your sins. He will forgive you, if you go to Him with a contrite heart and ask Him to forgive you. He has promised it. Christ said,

"18 though your sins be as scarlet, they shall be as white as snow; though they be red like crimson, they shall be as wool" (Isaiah 1:18).

By Philip Mitanidis

Christ does not lie; accept His promise and become clean from all of your sins. Salvation is free. You do not have to pay for it. Christ the LORD has paid the price for you on Calvary's cross. Therefore come as you are and be clean. In doing so, you can become His daughter or His son and be bound for His Kingdom.

On the other hand, if the ceremonial law and its offerings were to be reinstated today, in the Sanctuary in Jerusalem, it will mean that Christ (Messiah) did not come in the "flesh" and die for the sins of the world. And those individuals who know that Christ died on Calvary's cross and insist on taking part in the ceremonial law and its animal sin offerings and its services, it will mean that they do not accept Christ's sacrifice on Calvary's cross. And, if Christ's death is willfully rejected by the people of this world;

The Creator of Genesis 1:1—Who is He?   By: *Philip Mitanidis*

A Question

it will mean that all of those men, woman, and children of age will die and will be dying in their sins without the hope of salvation and eternal life. Eventually, they will all die in their sins without the hope of being resurrected into eternal youthful life.

Needless to say, since Christ's death has fulfilled the sacrificial sin offering on Calvary's cross, the sacrificial offering and the ceremonial services have been discontinued in the Sanctuary. Daniel the prophet stated about 600 years before Christ came in the "flesh" that

> "27 He [Messiah of v.26] shall confirm the covenant with many for one week [seven years]: and in the midst of the week He [Messiah] shall cause the sacrifice and the oblation to cease" (Daniel 9:27).

Did you hear that dear reader?

Daniel the prophet states that the "Messiah" was going to "cause the sacrifice and the oblation to cease" in the midst of the week (3.5 years of His ministry). And because the sacrificial system ceased on Calvary's cross, so did the need for the Sanctuary, the Levitical priesthood, and its services, which took place in Jerusalem. That is why all of these years, Christ has not reclaimed the Sanctuary. He has abandoned the Sanctuary. It has outlived its usefulness. The fact that the Sanctuary, today, is under padlocks is a strong testimony that Christ the Creator has deserted it.

Remember dear reader, the reasons why the Sanctuary in Jerusalem, the priesthood, and the ceremonial law have been abandoned, it is due to the fact that the inspired Scriptures, now, teach us that "justification" and "salvation" are obtained freely only through grace by Jesus Christ, and not through the sacrifices of animals in the eastern courtyard of the Sanctuary in Jerusalem, or by works that any man should boast. Salvation from your sins is free in Jesus Christ the LORD—if you want it?

Therefore, the prophet of the LORD says, "19 Wherefore then serveth the law [ceremonial law]? It was added [to the Ten Commandments Exodus 20:3-17] because of transgressions, till the seed [Christ: Galatians 3:16] should come to whom [Abraham v.8] the promise was made" (Galatians 3:19). But, those individuals who will willfully reject Christ's sacrifice on Calvary's cross, and reject Him as their LORD, God, and Savior, and are bent on implementing the ceremonial law and its services, according to Scripture, they will perish forever.

The solemn warning is given; Christ the LORD of hosts said to the house of Judah as He says to you and to me, "24 I said therefore unto you, that ye shall die in your sins: for if ye believe not that I am He, ye shall die in your sins. 25 Then said they unto Him, Who art Thou [You]? And Jesus saith unto them, Even the same that I said unto you from the beginning"(John 8:24, 25).

To reiterate, salvation is free only through Jesus Christ the LORD of hosts (Acts 4:12; Isaiah 43:11; 47:4; Hosea 13:4), if you want it, and not by the sacrificial offering of animals in the eastern courtyard of the Sanctuary in Jerusalem.

Therefore, the above presentation begs the question, by deliberately rejecting Jesus Christ, as their LORD, God, and Savior, and His supreme sacrifice on Calvary's cross, how are Jews, Muslims, and Christians saved?

If you need more detailed information on Salvation please read my book called "According to a Promise" by: *Philip Mitanidis*. BEEHIVE PUBLISHING HOUSE INC.

The Rejection of God the Creator

Although today, the rejection of Christ, by the children of Israel, is prevalent; historically, the rejection started with their forefathers who walked with Christ their God from the start of their journey, from the fields of Raamses. They chose to reject Him many times before they reached Mt. Sinai, and after in the Promised Land. In fact, they built idols of gold and silver in His presence and worshipped them!

What were they thinking?

According to Moses and Apostle Paul, after the children of Israel rebelled a number of times on the way to Mount Sinai, they stopped and settled at the foot of Mount Sinai. There, with repentant hearts, the children of Israel agreed and said to Moses,

The Rejection of God the Creator

"All that the LORD hath said will we do."

And when they did, they built a Sanctuary for Christ the LORD of hosts to abide with them in their camp. And when the Sanctuary and its furniture were complete, the children of Israel erected the Sanctuary in the middle of their camp. After that, they dedicated the Sanctuary to Christ the God of Israel. And during the dedication, Christ the LORD of hosts accepted His dwelling place in the "most holy place" of the Sanctuary. And in the beginning of the second year of their stay at the foot of Mount Sinai, Christ the LORD of hosts lifted Himself up in the form of a cloud and led the children of Israel to a place called Kadish-barnia, which is at the south end of the Negeb. And there, Christ the LORD said to the children of Israel to go and possess the Promised Land called Cannan. Instead, the children of Israel rebelled, rejected Christ the LORD God of Israel, and chose to make captains to take them back to Egypt. And when they finally realized that there was no food or water in the desert, they scrapped the idea. Instead, they decided to go and possess the Promised Land by disobeying Christ's command that they should not go to war with the Canaanites. And when the army of Israel got slaughtered by the Canaanites, they came running to Moses seeking refuge.

Since the children of Israel had a mind of their own and did not want to obey Christ's leadership, Christ in His mercy did not take them back to Egypt to be killed; instead, He let them live their lives under His protection, in the wilderness, until their children grew up, and chose to possess the Promise Land.

And when their children inherited the Promised Land, they lived in contentment most of the time, under the rule of Joshua. But, after, during the time of the Judges, the children of Israel rejected Christ the God of Israel many times. In fact, if you were to read the book of the Judges and the book of wars, you will notice the rebellious periods where the children of Israel rejected Christ their God and went to worship the gods of their pagan neighbors.

Near the end of the Judges, Samuel came onto the scene in the 11th century BC to lead and judge Israel. But, when Samuel became old in the 10th century BC, the children of Israel, at one point, stared

The Rejection of God the Creator

at Nahash the pagan King of Ammon in admiration. Influenced by the pomp and splendor of the king's presence, the elders of the children of Israel went to Samuel in Ramah and said to him, "5 Behold, thou [you] art old, and thy [your] sons walk not in thy [your] ways: now make us a king to judge us like all the nations" (1 Samuel 8:5).

Stunned by their request, Samuel replied to the elders of Israel; "But you have a King who has sustained you, protected you, and looked after your well-being. Why do you need an earthly king?"

They replied and said, "12 Nay; but a king shall reign over us." 1 Samuel 12:12. "6 But the thing displeased Samuel, when they said, Give us a king to judge us. And Samuel prayed unto the LORD. 7 And the LORD said unto Samuel, Hearken unto the voice of the people in all that they say unto thee [you]: for they have not rejected thee, but they have rejected Me, that I should not reign over them." 1 Samuel 8:6, 7

Contrary to Samuel's will, the children of Israel (Jacob) rejected Christ the LORD God of Israel; instead, the people chose Saul, a Benjamite, to be a king over them (1 Samuel 12:12).

Unfortunately, pride had swept over King Saul during his forty years of reign. He was more willing to please his subjects than Christ the LORD of hosts. At the end, he sought support from the witch of Endor, and the following day, lost his life during the battle with the Philistines.

King David, chosen by God the Christ, brought the people back to worship Christ the LORD of hosts. And with his son Solomon, he started the plans to build a Sanctuary for Christ in Jerusalem because the Sanctuary in "Shiloh" was destroyed, due to the apostate condition of the children of Israel, which was influenced by their leaders. Christ (Shiloh) allowed the Philistines to destroy the Sanctuary that was built for Him by Moses.

After King David died (971 BC) on his fortieth year of his reign, Solomon settled on his throne, and started to build the Sanctuary in Jerusalem on his fourth year. Seven years later he completed the building of the Sanctuary and then concentrated on the furniture. When the furniture was complete, he had the

The Rejection of God the Creator

Sanctuary dedicated to Christ the God of Israel.

Christ accepted the Sanctuary for His dwelling place and promised Solomon that if his successors on the throne would reign over the people as his father David did, there would be someone on the throne perpetually; but, if those who occupy the throne, would do evil and,

> "6 go and serve other gods, and worship them: 7 Then will I cut off Israel out of the land which I have given them; and this house, which I have hallowed for My name, will I cast out of My sight; and Israel shall be a proverb and a byword among all people: 8 And at this house, which is high, every one that passeth by it shall be astonished, and shall hiss; and they shall say, Why has the LORD done thus unto this land, and to this house? 9 And they shall answer, Because they forsook the LORD their God, who brought forth their fathers out of the land of Egypt, and have taken hold upon other gods, and have worshipped them, and serve them; therefore hath the LORD brought upon them all this evil." 1 Kings 9:6-9

Although the admonition and warning were given to Solomon, right after the dedication of the Sanctuary, during his twilight years, unfortunately, Solomon fell into apostasy. He tried to please his many wives who worshipped their diverse pagan idols. By placing these pagan gods in the groves and in around the palace, the children of Israel were influenced to do the same. And when Christ the LORD saw what Solomon was doing, He said to him that his kingdom would be divided. But for the sake of his father David, He would allow the tribes of Benjamin and Judah to remain in Jerusalem.

And so it was, after forty years on his throne, Solomon lost his throne (931 BC), and his kingdom was divided into two as follows: The "house of Israel" consisted of ten tribes and the "house of Judah" consisted of two tribes— Benjamin and Judah.

These two houses, for most of their existence served the pagan

The Rejection of God the Creator

gods of their neighbors; and if that was not bad enough, most of the time fought with each other for supremacy. The king of the "house of Israel" eventually was removed by the Syrian forces in 722 BC; and the people were scattered all over the land. Likewise the king of the "house of Judah" was removed in 586 BC from his throne. Jerusalem and the Sanctuary were demolished to the ground by the Chaldeans; and the remnant of the "house of Judah" were taken into the seventy years of captivity by King Nebuchadnezzar.

And when the seventy years of captivity were expired in 536 BC, the Persian king made a decree, which stated that the Jews and the children of Israel wherever they were in the Persian kingdom, they could return to Jerusalem. Unfortunately, only a small number returned to Jerusalem; the rest preferred to stay where they were.

Those individuals who returned to Jerusalem, they put their energy into self-serving enterprises instead of rebuilding the Sanctuary of Christ the LORD of hosts. After they were reprimanded, they began to spend the time rebuilding Jerusalem and the Sanctuary. And when the Sanctuary was rebuilt, the Sanctuary paled in comparison to the previous Temple (Solomon's Temple).

In addition, there was another problem; the throne and the king of Israel were missing. And they are still missing today, just as Christ the LORD of hosts had warned. (See 1 Kings 9:3-9) And the other obvious thing that was missing was Israel's territory. Israel's territory spanned from Dan (north of the Sea of Galilee) to the Negib (south of the Dead Sea to the borders of Egypt) and eastward from the Mediterranean Sea beyond the Jordan River. Now it is down to the vicinity of Jerusalem.

The other thing that was missing from the "house of Judah" was the zeal and excitement and the preparation for the coming of "Shiloh" (Messiah), which was revealed to them by Jacob and by Daniel the prophet. For over four hundred years, well more like six hundred years, if we start the calculation from Daniel's captivity (606 BC). But even before Daniel's time, the prophets of Christ the LORD kept revealing the coming of the Messiah in the "flesh" and His death. Jacob, if you remember, about 3,400 years ago, said to his son Judah to expect "Shiloh" (Messiah) to come from his tribe.

The Rejection of God the Creator

Isaiah, about seven hundred BC (745-685 BC), also foretold Christ's rejection, sacrifice, and death by the following overall statements; said, "3 He is despised and rejected of men; a man of sorrows, and acquainted with grief: and we hid as it were our faces from Him; He was despised, and we esteemed Him not.

"4 Surely He hath borne our griefs, and carried our sorrows: yet we did esteem Him stricken, smitten of God [His Associate], and afflicted.

"5 But He was wounded for our transgressions, He was bruised for our iniquities: the chastisement of our peace was upon Him; and with His stripes we are healed.

"6 All we like sheep have gone astray; we have turned every one to his own way; and the LORD [His Associate] hath laid on Him the iniquity of us all.

"7 He was oppressed, and He was afflicted, yet He opened not His mouth: He is brought as a lamb to the slaughter, and as a sheep before her shearers is dumb, so He openeth not His mouth.

"8 He was taken from prison and from judgment: and who shall declare His generation? for He was cut off out of the land of the living: for the transgression of my people was He stricken.

"9 And He made His grave with the wicked, and with the rich in His death; because He had done no violence, neither was any deceit in His mouth" (Isaiah 53:3-9).

As you have read, in reference to Christ the LORD God of Israel, Isaiah said,

"He is despised and rejected of men;"
"He hath borne our griefs, and carried our sorrows:"
"He was wounded for our transgressions,"
"All we like sheep have gone astray;"
"He was oppressed, and He was afflicted, yet He opened not His mouth:"
"He was taken from prison and from judgment:"
"And He made His grave with the wicked, and with the rich in His death."

Yes! The above forecast of Christ's ill treatment and rejection by His own people who are "called by His name," and others, was

The Rejection of God the Creator

eloquently put, when Isaiah the prophet of the LORD of hosts said, "He is despised and rejected of men."

Likewise about five hundred BC (627-580 BC), during the span of five rapid successive kings of Judah, Jeremiah the prophet also advised and warned the people not to serve other gods; but the children of Israel chose to have one foot in righteousness and the other foot in sin.

> Jeremiah said, "1 HEAR ye the word which the LORD speaketh unto you, O house of Israel: 2 Thus saith the LORD, Learn not the way of the heathen, and be not dismayed at the signs of heaven; for the heathen are dismayed at them. 3 For the customs of the people are vein: for one cutteth a tree out of the forest, the work of the hands of the workman, with the axe. 4 They deck it with silver and with gold; they fasten it with nails and with hammers, that it move not. 5 They are upright as the palm tree, but speak not: they must needs be borne, because they cannot go. Be not afraid of them; for they cannot do evil, neither also is it in them to do good."
>
> "11 Thus shall ye say unto them, The gods that have not made the heavens and the earth, even they shall perish from the earth, and from under these heavens. "12 He hath made the earth by His power, He hath established the world by His wisdom, and hath stretched out the heavens by His discretion." "10 But the LORD is the true God, He is the living God, and an everlasting King: at His wrath the earth shall tremble, and the nations shall not be able to abide His indignation."
>
> "6 Forasmuch as there is none like unto Thee, O LORD; Thou art great, and Thy name is great in might. 7 Who would not fear Thee, O King of nations? for to Thee doth it appertain: forasmuch as among all the wise men of the nations, and in all their kingdoms, there is none like unto Thee" (Jeremiah 10:1-5, 11, 12, 10, 6, 7).

The Creator of Genesis 1:1—Who is He? *By: Philip Mitanidis*

The Rejection of God the Creator

The prophets of old directed the people to worship Christ the Creator (Jeremiah 10:10, 11, 12), and not the created, especially the obsession with things, which man's imagination conjures up. The children of Israel were to worship Christ their "King" (v.10) and not their idols. Jeremiah advised, "Learn not the way of the heathen" (v.2).

The warning was echoed by Christ the Creator and by His prophets throughout the centuries to the children of Israel. They were warned not to worship other gods, such as men, women, devils, icons, images, idols, money, etc., etc. He told them what would happen if they chose to serve other gods; but, again, they did not listen. And because they did not listen, they were blinded by satanic influences to a point where their pride became their down fall. And to their detriment, many chose to serve heathen gods.

And, if idol worship was not bad enough, on numerous occasions, during the 70 years of captivity, Ezekiel, about five hundred and eighty BC (593-570 BC), during Zedekiah's time, like the other contemporary prophets of Christ the LORD, warned and revealed how the priests rejected God the Christ, polluted Christ's Sanctuary with drunkenness, vomit, stink, flies, maggots, having sex with the worshipers in the Sanctuary, and by facing eastward to worship the sun from within the Sanctuary.

Can you imagine that?

These priests polluted the Creator's Sanctuary, and by their examples, the children of Israel fell into the same sinful acts. They put their idols on top of their flat rooftops, groves, and on either side of the many roads to exalt and worship them—whenever they passed by them. The children of Israel settled into sinful living; they abandoned Christ the LORD God of their fathers, and taught their children to do the same, as they do today. And when Jeremiah and Ezekiel exposed their sinful acts and gave the warning, the kings of Judah would not listen to the counsel of the LORD. Therefore, they brought the retribution upon themselves by the mighty hand of King Nebuchadnezzar. In fact, King Zedekiah made Nebuchadnezzar so mad that in his fury, he demolished Jerusalem, the House of God, killed Zedekiah's family, put his eyes out, and

The Rejection of God the Creator

took him to Babylon. There, he died a miserable death. It did not have to be that way. If only he, his advisors, and the false prophets listened to Jeremiah, they could have avoided the siege of Jerusalem, saved the Temple, and Judah from a gruesome ordeal of seventy years of bondage by the Babylonian king.

The Jews and the Levite priests spoke proudly that they were the Covenant keeping people. Although they claimed that they kept the Covenant, in essence, they had departed from the ways of Christ the Creator who is the LORD God of Israel.

> The prophet wrote: "7 For the priest's lips should keep knowledge, and they should seek the law at his mouth: for he is the messenger of the LORD of host." And Christ the LORD of hosts adds, "8 But ye are departed out of the way; ye have caused many to stumble at the law; ye have corrupted the covenant of Levi, saith the LORD of hosts. 9 Therefore have I also made you contemptible and base before all the people, according as ye have not kept My ways, but have been partial in the law" (Malachi 2:7-9).

And because they were disreputable, we are told, when Christ the Creator came to His own people, in the "flesh," they did not want to hear the truth and the error of their ways (Job 21:14), which He was speaking to them about. They did not want to repent for their sins, and therefore they did not want Christ to reveal their sinful living. So, they chose not to go to Christ the LORD of their forefathers and be saved (John 5:40). The prophet John observed, "11 He [Christ] came unto His own [the children of Israel], and His own received Him not" (John 1:11).

Because the leaders and the priests of the high counsel of Israel chose not to "keep" the ways of Christ the LORD of hosts, who is the LORD God of their fathers, He rejected them, and made them "contemptible" and "base" before all the people to observe.

For over seven hundred years, before Christ came in the flesh, the prophets came and gone with their messages, in order to prepare the children of Israel for the coming "Shiloh" (Messiah). But the

The Rejection of God the Creator

priests and leaders of the house of Judah did not prepare themselves to receive their Messiah. Even worse, the house of Judah did not prepare its citizens for the coming of "Shiloh" (Messiah). The LORD used strangers to wake the house of Judah to the fact that the Messiah, their King had arrived. This event took place when a caravan from the east came to Jerusalem. The strangers from the caravan revealed to Herod the pagan king and to the house of Judah that the "Messiah" (Christ) had arrived.

Don't you think that it should have been the other way around?

And it was not until the common people, and the shepherds who saw the star (holy angels) shining over the manger that took upon themselves to spread the news that the Messiah (Christ) had come. It was not the priests or the scribes of Judah looking for the Messiah; it was strangers, who came from a far country, and said,

"Where is He that is born King of the Jews?" Matthew 2:2

Once the wise men revealed to Herod the pagan king and to the priests and to the scribes of Judah that the Messiah, the King of Israel had arrived, a person would think that the high priest would have ordered an investigation and join in the revelation that the King of Israel had arrived in the "flesh" (Isaiah 9:6, 7; Luke 1:35; Isaiah 49:15, 16). Instead they rejected Him; and went about ignoring His arrival for over 30 years. They also ignored to prepare the people for His acceptance and for His Ministry.

Likewise, before Christ's ministry began thirty years later, Christ's cousin, John the Baptist, was sent to the house of Judah to prepare the people of Judah for the Messiah's (Christ's) appearance. John was to personally acknowledge and identify Christ (Messiah) to the people.

And when Christ started His ministry from the town of Nazareth, He did many miracles and stated to the children of Israel that He was the Messiah and the God of their fathers. And to authenticate His claims, He quoted the Old Testament references. But regardless of those Scripture references, His claims, and His miracles did not convince all of the children of Israel that He was

The Rejection of God the Creator

the LORD God of their fathers; instead it enraged them, and called Him a "blasphemer." They would not believe Him. They would not go to Him and be saved Christ said to them, "40 ye [all of you] will not come unto Me, that ye might have life" (John 5:40).

The majority of the Jews chose not to accept Christ as the Messiah, and as their LORD God and Savior. But, what more could Christ do to convince the children of Israel that He was the Messiah? In fact, some even wondered and said, "31 When Christ cometh, will He do more miracles than these which this man [Christ] hath done?" (John 7:31)

In return, Christ the Messiah said something very penetrating and disturbing to the Jewish leaders, and to the house of Israel 2,000 years ago. They did not like the following remarks, which Christ made to them. In fact, they were so adamant; they even conspired as to how they could kill Him on many occasions.

This is what Christ (Messiah) said unto them,

> "24 I said therefore unto you, that ye [all of you] shall die in your sins: for if ye believe not that I am He [the LORD God of their forefathers and Messiah], ye shall die in your sins. 25 Then said they unto Him, Who art Thou [You]? And Jesus saith unto them, Even the same that I said unto you from the beginning" (John 8:24, 25).

Although the warning was given personally to the Jews by Christ, they chose not to believe Christ's claims, the prophetic fulfillment of His coming in the "flesh," and His miracles. They accused Him of being possessed by the devil, and the miracles He was performing, they said that they were done by the devil. But, if Christ was doing all of the miracles by the hand of the devil, why was the devil so anxious to prove to the world that Christ was the "Messiah"? And more importantly why would the devil work through Christ to bring the people into repentance from their evil ways in order to be saved? There is something wrong with the Jewish accusation don't you think? Satan hates Christ the LORD, and he also hates those who repent from their sins. In fact, Satan

The Rejection of God the Creator

persecutes (Isaiah 59:15) people who are penitent for their sins and become the children of Christ. Therefore, Satan could not have been working through Christ the LORD to bring about salvation for the people.

Anyway, the Jews chose to reject Christ their LORD, God, King, and Savior. Just like many of their forefathers did; they would not take heed to the prophets of old. Neither would they hear the words of Christ the LORD God of their fathers when He said to them that He was the One the prophets of old wrote and spoke about. Christ's warning to their forefathers was:

"6 But if ye shall at all turn from following Me, ye or your children, and will not keep My commandments and My statutes which I have set before you, but go and serve other gods, and worship them: 7 Then will I cut off Israel out of the land which I have given them; and this house [the Sanctuary in Jerusalem], which I have hallowed for My name, will I cast out of My sight; and Israel shall be a proverb and a byword among all people:

"8 And at this house [the Sanctuary], which is high, every one that passeth by it shall be astonished, and shall hiss; and they shall say, Why hath the LORD done thus unto this land, and to this house? 9 And they shall answer, Because they forsook the LORD their God, who brought forth their fathers out of the land of Egypt, and have taken hold upon other gods, and have worshipped them, and served them: therefore hath the LORD brought upon them all this evil" (1 Kings 9:6-9). (See Deuteronomy chapter 28 also.)

Even the prophets of old warned and testified before His people that the children of Israel left Christ the Creator for other gods a number of times, and engrossed themselves by offered their children as sacrifices to them.

Nonetheless because they chose to reject Christ, at one point, near the end of Christ's ministry, overlooking Jerusalem, Christ the LORD God of Israel became emotional and cried over His

The Rejection of God the Creator

perishing people—saying:

> "37 O Jerusalem, Jerusalem, thou [you] that killest the prophets, and stonest them which are sent unto thee, how often would I have gathered thy [your] children together, even as a hen gathereth her chickens under her wings, and ye [all] would not!" (Matthew 23:37)

Time and time again, Christ would call the children of Israel (Jacob) unto Himself, but they would not come to Him and "have life." Even when Jesus Christ came in the "flesh," He outwardly claimed for three and a half years to all of the people who were outside and inside the city of Jerusalem that He was their LORD, God, King, and Savior; but they still rejected Him.

And to testify publicly that Christ was their King, LORD, God, and Savior; He rode a donkey to Jerusalem, as a King who showed his kingship. When the leaders of the Sanhedrin saw Christ riding on a donkey with a colt following and coming to Jerusalem with a multitude of people, they were afraid that finally Christ was going to set up His Kingdom. When the destitute and common people, especially those that were healed by Christ, and those that were resurrected from their dusty deathbeds, saw Christ riding on a donkey, they started to shout "Hosanna," "Hosanna" to the Highest. When others saw Christ coming to Jerusalem as a King, they to joined in the shouts of Hosanna's. As Christ the Creator rode on the donkey with a colt following Him, the people shouted for joy. They placed their garments and palm branches before His path to Jerusalem. They acknowledged Him as their King. And when Christ entered in Jerusalem, to their disapproval, the Jewish rulers very quickly said to Christ, "Stop these people from shouting." But Christ the Creator said to them, "Even if they stopped shouting in joy, the rocks will shout in their stead. The rocks will proclaim Me." Christ revealed to the Jewish priests and rulers, again that He was the King of Israel. He claimed before them that He was their "Saviour" (Hosea 13:4; John 5:40). And to put them at ease, He also told them that His Kingdom was not of

The Rejection of God the Creator

this world, but that did not sit too well with them. They were still afraid of the large following He had throughout the land.

Here is the confirmation: "6 And the disciples went, and did as Jesus commanded them, 7 And brought the ass, and the colt, and put on them their clothes, and they set Him thereon. 8 And a very great multitude spread their garments in the way; others cut down branches from the trees, and strawed them in the way. 9 And the multitudes that went before, and that followed, cried, saying, Hosanna to the son of David: Blessed is he that cometh in the name of the LORD; Hosanna in the highest. 10 And when He was come into Jerusalem, all the city was moved, saying, Who is this? 11 And the multitude said, This is Jesus the prophet of Nazareth of Galilee. 12 And Jesus went into the temple of God, and cast out all them that sold and bought in the temple, and overthrew the tables of the moneychangers, and the seats of them that sold doves" (Matthew 21:6-12).

This was the second time Jesus removed the merchants from the temple. The fact that the moneychangers were back at the temple to do business, they did not regard Christ as an authority. The Jews were more interested in doing business than to keep the Sabbath (Saturday) holy, and to keep the Sanctuary and its courtyard free from trade.

After Christ overthrew the tables of the moneychangers, He "13 said unto them, It is written, My house shall be called the house of prayer; but Ye [all of you] have made it a den of thieves. 14 And the blind and the lame came to Him in the temple; and He healed them. 15 And when the chief priests and scribes saw the wonderful things that He did, and the children crying in the temple, and saying, Hosanna to the son of David; they were sore displeased" (Matthew 21:13-15).

Instead of accepting Christ as their King and Savior, the leaders of Judah were "displeased," and contrived ways to set an entrapment to kill Him via one of Christ's disciples named Judas Iscariot.

This event of Christ's betrayal took place at night during the celebration of the "Passover."

The Rejection of God the Creator

After the Passover celebration, in the upper room, Jesus took His disciples to Mount Olives in a place called Gethsemane. And when they arrived there, Christ "32 saith to His disciples, Sit ye [all of you] here, while I shall pray. 33 And He taketh with Him Peter and James and John, and began to be sore amazed, and to be very heavy; 34 And saith unto them, My soul is exceeding sorrowful unto death: tarry ye here, and watch" (Mark 14:32-34).

And when He withdrew from them about a stone throw away, He kneeled down and prayed. "42 Saying, Father, if thou [you] be willing, remove this cup from Me: nevertheless not My will, but thine, be done. 43 And there appeared an angel unto Him from heaven, strengthening Him. 44 And being in an agony He prayed more earnestly: and His sweat was as it were great drops of blood falling down to the ground. 45 And when He rose up from prayer, and was come to His disciples, He found them sleeping for sorrow, 46 And said unto them, Why sleep ye? rise and pray, lest ye enter into temptation" (Luke 22:42-45).

"43 And immediately, while He yet spake, cometh Judas, one of the twelve, and with him a great multitude with swords and staves, from the chief priests and the scribes and the elders. 44 And he that betrayed Him had given them a token, saying, Whosoever I shall kiss, that same is He; take Him, and lead Him away safely. 45 And as soon as he was come, he goeth straightway to Him, and saith, Master, master: and kissed Him" (Mark 14:43-45).

"48 But Jesus said unto him, Judas, betrayest thou [you] the Son of man with a kiss?" Luke 22:48

And when they succeeded capturing Him, His own people, who are called by His "name" (2 Chronicles 7:14), tried Him in the halls of the Sanhedrin that night. The high counsel, and the priests of Israel, found Christ the Creator guilty because He claimed before them that He was the Messiah (Christ), their King, and the LORD God of Israel. (See Mark 14:61, 62; John 1:49.)

Caiaphas the high priest said, "What more proof do we need that this man is a blasphemer?" (See Matthew 26:63-65) With that

The Creator of Genesis 1:1—Who is He?   By: *Philip Mitanidis*
The Rejection of God the Creator

kind of encouragement from the high priest, in the morning they sent Him to Pilate, the Roman governor, to be tried in his court. After Pilate tried Jesus Christ, he did not want to get involved with the Jewish religious affairs, so he sent Him to Antipas Herod the third, the king of Galilee (Luke 3:1), who was in Jerusalem for the festivities. Herod, who believed that Christ was John the Baptist that was resurrected from the dead, tried Christ, but because Christ would not perform a miracle before him, and because he did not want to take the responsibility for His outcome, he sent Christ back to Pilate.

As Christ was escorted back and forth, the crowd kept getting bigger and bigger. By now, it had swelled with not only the locals but with individuals who came from other towns. The crowd waited in anticipation to see the outcome of Christ's trial.

They brought Christ the Creator of the universe before mortal man (Pilate) to be judged again.

But Pilate not willing to condemn Christ, he said to the crowd, "Here is your King!"

Why? They chanted before Pilate; "We cannot have this man to be a King over us?"

Most of the Jewish leaders and their followers rejected Christ their King, during Pilate's rule, just as their forefathers rejected Christ their King during the time of Samuel. They chose Saul instead. Christ the Creator said to Samuel, "7 they have not rejected thee [you], but they have rejected Me, that I should not reign over them" (1 Samuel 8:7).

Raising his voice, Pilate said; "But He is your King!"

They shouted and condemned themselves by saying, "We have no king but Caesar!"

And then, Pilate said to them; "What will ye then that I shall do unto Him whom ye [all of you] call the King of the Jews?"

They chanted; "Crucify Him!" "Crucify Him!"

Pilate said; "But! He is innocent!"

And in unison, the crowd shouted even louder; "Crucify Him! Crucify Him! Crucify him!"

Pilate said to the crowd; "My hands are innocent of this man's

The Rejection of God the Creator

blood."

In return, their vicious cry, prompted by satanic evil angels, resonated throughout the halls of the court; "Let His blood be upon us and upon our children!"

And when the children of Israel pronounced the curse upon themselves and upon their children, Pilate released Barabbas the criminal to them; and permitted the soldiers to take Christ (Messiah) the LORD God of the universe "into the common hall" to be scourged with the death penalty.

Pilate had Christ whipped with a whip, which had iron hooks tied to the ends of the horse's hairs; and every time the whip struck Christ's back, the iron hooks clawed and tore His flesh, and the blood came gushing out, leaving Him feeble and tired.

If Christ was whipped less than thirty-nine times, according to the Roman law, He would have been spared. If He was whipped more than thirty-nine times, it meant that He was receiving the death penalty. A person is more likely to endure a severe whipping; but, in Christ's case, those deadly whippings, which went beyond thirty-nine strikes, tore the muscles on His back, brutally, rendering Him incapable of lifting His own cross on His shoulders.

After they finished whipping Him, He was handed to a group of Roman soldiers. Then, they stripped Him from His clothes and took a scarlet robe and placed it over His naked shoulders, which stuck onto His bleeding torn back. They also made a crown of thorns, and stuck it on top of His head. And, as the thorns tore the flesh around His head, the blood ran down His face and neck. And when they blindfolded Christ, they placed a reed in His right hand; and they bowed the knee before Him, and mocked Him, saying, "Hail, King of the Jews." After that, they spit on Him, pulled His beard, and hit His face. And while they spit on Him, pulled His beard, and slapped His face, they asked Him mockingly, "Prophecy, and tell us who slapped you?" "Who spit on you?" "Who pulled your beard?" "Who struck you?" "Tells us if you can?"

Christ kept His silence. But you know what? He was not really silent. I say that because His prophetic words have been echoing down the corridors of time, in all ages, as a witness that this event

The Rejection of God the Creator

would take place before His chosen people.

In compassion for His people, and as a witness of His claims, Christ the Creator, the LORD God of Israel uttered the following words to His people nearly seven hundred and sixty years before He suffered this awesome, painful, humiliating, and inhumane ordeal.

Christ the Creator of verse one said,

> "6 I gave My back to the smiters, and My cheeks to them that plucked off the hair: I hid not My face from shame and spitting" (Isaiah 50:6).

Christ the Creator the LORD God of Israel did not retaliate at His abusers. He could have called from heaven upon thousands of His holy angels to deliver Him. Or, He could have called any one of the angels who were hovering anxiously above Him. Or He could have called the holy angels who were guarding the people from satanic influence. Or, He could have called even upon the angels who were watching intently upon the horrible scene, from a distance. They too could have delivered Him in a split second from His agonizing ordeal; but all they could do is watch and wait for His command. But, do you know that command never came from His lips because He had promised Adam and Eve that He was going to come and save them and their offspring from their eternal death.

And that promise was repeated again nearly seven hundred and forty years before Christ came in the "flesh." Christ the Creator of Genesis 1:1 spoke the following words to His people, and to those who sincerely wanted to be saved from their sins. He said,

> "15 Can a woman forget her sucking child, that she should not have compassion on the son of her womb? yea, they may forget, yet will I not forget thee" (Isaiah 49:15).

Christ did not forget His people. He had promised it. He does not lie. He was going to offer Himself a sacrifice for their sins and for the sins of the world. And anyone who wants to be saved would be saved through His precious blood. (See Revelation 1:5.)

The Rejection of God the Creator

Christ the Creator, the LORD God of Israel from Isaiah 49:14 added:

> "16 Behold, I have graven thee upon the palms of my hands; thy walls are continually before Me" (Isaiah 49:16).

Decision was made. Christ the Creator of His universe would not call for His deliverance. He focused upon His mission, which led Him to Calvary's cross, and nothing could deter Him from accomplishing His mission, which was to save man from his sins, and fulfill the "promise" that He made to Adam, Noah, Abraham, Isaac, Israel, David, etc. He desired to save the penitent sinner from his death, and that is what He was going to do. Christ was going to pay for your sins and my sins on Calvary's cross so that you and I can have a choice of eternal life or eternal death?

After mortal man finished beating, spitting, and mocking Christ the God of His universe, they took Him and led Him, as a sheep to slaughter, to a hill called "the skull." There they placed the Creator of the universe on the wooden cross and nailed His hands and feet to it. And when they finished doing that, they lifted the cross with its victim, with ropes, up above the hole, which they had dug, and allowed the wooden cross to fall abruptly into the hole. The weight and the thrust of the cross, which fell into the hole, further tore the flesh of the Redeemer's hands and feet. They continued to pull the cross with its victim by the ropes into an upright position, leaving a trail of blood flying from His body through the air. And when the cross, with its victim remained upright, they filled the hole with rocks and soil to secure the cross in its place and left Christ hanging there in the scorching sun.

There, in a place called Golgotha, they crucified Christ the Creator of the universe who is "the God of Israel" (Matthew 15:31), who is the God of Abraham, the God of Isaac, the God of Jacob, the God of Moses, the God of David, the God of Isaiah, the God of John, the God of Paul, the God of Daniel, the God of Mark, the God of Jennifer, the God of Erick, the God of Susan, the God of Philip...

The Creator of Genesis 1:1—Who is He?   By: *Philip Mitanidis*

The Rejection of God the Creator

It was prophesied many times before that the Creator (Christ the Messiah), when He came in the "flesh," He was going to be rejected by His own people who are called by His name (John 1:11). And because they chose to reject Him, as their LORD, God, King, and Savior, He was going to choose the Gentiles to carry on with His Gospel message (Acts 13:45, 46). In fact, nearly seven hundred and fifty years before the event of the coming of Christ the Creator in the "flesh" took place and His rejection, prophetically, Christ uttered the following words to the children of Israel;

> "23 I will say to them which were not My people, Thou art My people; and they shall say, Thou art my God" (Hosea 2:23).

Likewise, Apostle John testified and said, "11 He [Christ] came unto His own, and His own received Him not" (John 1:11).

Luke also witnessed that the children of Israel rejected Christ the LORD of hosts by saying,

> "44 the next Sabbath day [Saturday] came almost the whole city together to hear the word of God. 45 But when the Jews saw the multitudes, they were filled with envy, and spake against those things which were spoken by Paul, contradicting and blaspheming.

> "46 Then Paul and Barnabas waxed bold, and said, It was necessary that the word of God should first have been spoken to you: but seeing ye put it from you, and judge yourselves unworthy of everlasting life, lo, we turn to the Gentiles" (Acts 13:44-46).

Although the apostles turned to the Gentiles because the Jews in that generation refused to accept Christ, it does not mean they are excluded from the plan of salvation, which is in Jesus Christ the

The Rejection of God the Creator

LORD. Salvation is for every human being on planet earth; Christ died for all of us. Christ the Creator hung on the cross on top of Calvary's hill for you and for me, while His precious blood, which cleans the penitent sinner from his sins, dripped, and dripped, and dripped to the ground from His torn back, from His torn forehead, from His torn palms, and from his torn feet. And in His pain and agony of stress, He died of a broken heart because His own people, who are called by His name, rejected Him; and because the weight of the sins of the penitent sinners pressed upon Him violently, intensely, and mercilessly.

Christ the Creator died on that cruel cross for you and for me. Later, He was buried, but the grave could not hold Him captive because He was sinless. Three days later, when He had risen, He spoke to Mary Magdalene (John 20:17, 18), and shortly after, He went to heaven temporarily before He saw His disciples again. Now He is getting ready to come back to planet earth to take His people home. And, as He prepares for His second coming, He still remembers how He was nailed upon the wooden cross, upon the hill called the "Skull."

Christ the Creator while He was looking down upon us through the corridors of time, said,

"16 Behold, I have graven thee [you] upon the palms of
My hands; thy [your] walls are continually before Me"
(Isaiah 49:16).

Christ the Creator of His universe still longs for His people. He still longs for you and for me. He remembers you every time He looks at His wounds.

But, how about you dear reader, when you remember Christ the Creator of Genesis 1:1; John 1:1, 3, and 10, do you remember Him stripping Himself from all of His powers, so that He could come in the form of helpless baby, in order to save you? Do you remember that He has put on the garb of humanity? He has identified Himself with the human race. He is one of us, and that we are His "brethren." And do you remember His awesome love for you,

The Rejection of God the Creator

which caused Him to come and save you? Do you think of these things when you think of Christ? Do you?

Looking at Christ the Creator of Genesis 1:1 hanging on Calvary's cross, can you comprehend what it cost Him to save you and the other penitent sinners? Can you really comprehend what it cost Him to save His universe? This awesome Spirit Being, whose creation cannot contain Him, gave up His immeasurable powers and His creation, to His Associates, so that He could come to planet earth in the "flesh" to save you.

Can you comprehend that?

And even more awe-inspiring, and overwhelming is the fact that Christ the Creator of Genesis 1:1 came in the "flesh," as a helpless baby at the risk of losing His life. Can you comprehend that? All it would have taken for Him to lose His life was to sin once. That's it! He would have been condemned to death by His own law (the Ten Commandments, Exodus 20:3-17), which says, "the wages of sin is death" (Romans 6:23). And, if He did sin once, while He was on earth, or anywhere else for that matter, He would have died; and you and I would not be here discussing the Creator and His awesome sacrifice for us because once Christ the Creator died permanently, His whole creation, and everything that is in it would have vanished. In fact, even space would vanish. If Christ sinned, the only Individuals that would exist would be Christ's two Associates. And Christ's two Associates would exist in a setting almost to what it was before Christ the Creator created the universe and everything that is in it. And that would not be very "good" because Christ would not be there.

Can you comprehend the love of Christ for you, and what it cost Him to save you? If you can, then you are more perceptive and wiser person than the prophets of old. And, if you can understand at least, in part, His amazing love for you and for the human race, don't be like our forefathers by rejecting Him and His salvation for you.

Your salvation, dear reader is free—if you want it? Your salvation has been redeemed by the Creator's love and blood on Calvary's cross. Christ the LORD of hosts loves us, that is why He

The Rejection of God the Creator

is calling from heaven and says to you and to me,

> "4 Come out of her [Babylon], My people, that ye be not partakers of her sins, and that ye receive not of her plagues" (Revelation 18:4).

Christ died for you. It is your choice to make what you want to do with your life. Personally, I say, don't reject Christ and Christ's salvation for you; as others have done; choose eternal life. Don't be influenced by those that are "damned who believe not the truth, but had pleasure in unrighteousness" (2 Thessalonians 2:12).

My prayer for you is that you will be amongst the saved, and Christ's protection will be over you, when the horrifying deadly plagues fall upon the unsaved and upon the ecosystem of the earth, after "the Sign" of Christ's second coming appears in heaven (Matthew 24:30; Rev. 6:14). ***

Christ the Creator loves you, and cares what happens to you; He has proven that fact on Calvary's cross for you.

Isn't that enough?

Don't let pride be your demise by rejecting Christ the LORD of hosts as your Savior, as others have done; "they say unto God, Depart from us; for we desire not the knowledge of Thy [Your] ways" (Job 21:14). They have made their choice. Now, it is your choice to make. I hope and pray that you make the right choice by encouraging you to:

> "1 COME, let us sing unto the LORD: let us make a joyful noise to the Rock [Christ] of our salvation."

> "3 For the LORD is a great God, and a great King above all gods."

> "5 The sea is His, and He made it: and His hands formed the dry land. 6 O come, let us worship and bow down: let us kneel before the LORD our maker." Psalm 95:1, 3, 5, 6.

The Rejection of God the Creator

And, when Christ the Creator of Genesis 1:1 comes the second time to take His people to the third heaven, we shall see Him face to face in His Kingdom. There in order to understand His supreme sacrifice, we can ask Him of His great love for us, and of His great sacrifice for us. And while we are gathered around Him, many times, we will hear the little children asking Him,

"6 What are these wounds in Thine [Your] hands?"
Christ the Redeemer will answer,

"Those with which I was wounded in the house of My friends" (Zechariah 13:6).

LLLLLLLLI

***   If you are not familiar with the "sign" in Matt. 24:30 and Rev. 6:14, please read the unexpected timely message, to a perishing world, in my book called, "The Sign in Matthew 24" By: *Philip Mitanidis*, BEEHIVE PUBLISHING HOUSE INC.

"8 Our help is in the name of the LORD, who made heaven and earth." Psalms 124:8

SUPPLEMENTS

Although the previous chapters overwhelmingly reveal Jesus Christ, the God of Israel, as the sole Creator of "all things," and the reasons why people and religious institutions reject Christ the LORD of host, as the Creator of Genesis 1:1, John 1:1, 3, 10, here are few more reasons why many people and religious institutions reject the application of Moses' writings to Jesus Christ the LORD of hosts.

A Prophet and a Man_____ You will find many individuals, defiantly or ignorantly, will tell you, Jesus Christ is only a "prophet" and a "good man." In fact, two thousand years ago, many Jews believed that Christ was only a man; they even went as far as to ask Him, "25 Who art [are] Thou [You]?" And "53 whom makest Thou Thyself?" Christ "25 said unto them, Even the same that said unto you from the beginning" (John 8:25, 53). Jesus Christ the LORD of hosts told them that He was their "King." He told them that He was the LORD God of their fathers. And He also told them that He was the "Christ" (Messiah) of whom the prophets of old looked forward to see His day, and some of them saw it.

But you know what? Just because Christ the Creator of Genesis 1:1 stooped down from His awesome Spirit form, into the form of a man (John 1:1, 14, 41), in order to save man from his eternal death, many Jews, Muslims, Buddhists, Christians, and other individuals still rejected Him today. Today, many individuals and many religious institutions refuse to accept Christ the LORD of hosts, as the God of Israel, as the sole Creator of His universe, as the "Messiah" and as their personal Savior. But then again that is their choice and we should respect it.

By reading John 1:1, 14, 41, 3, and 10, in the New Testament, and the verses, which we already have read from the Old Testament, one would think that it would suffice for a person to conclude that the Messiah (Christ) is God the Creator of Genesis 1:1; unfortunately that is not the case. Many individuals, contrary to the inspired Hebrew and Greek Scriptures, still choose not to believe and accept Jesus Christ the LORD that He is the sole Creator, Savior, and the LORD God of Israel. They still view Him today as a prophet, as a philosopher, and as a good man.

Re Bible Translations_____ Another method that is commonly used, by some people, to reject Jesus Christ the LORD of hosts, as the God of Abraham, as the LORD God of Israel, and as God the Creator of Genesis 1:1, John 1:1, 3, 10 is to use their favorite Bible translation. By using certain Bible translations, many people have the tendency to reject the Hebrew and the Greek inspired Scriptures, which state unequivocally that Christ is God the Creator of His universe. By using the mistranslated verses from these Bible translations, Christ the LORD God of Israel is placed beneath someone. And that cannot be true because Christ the LORD is not subjected to anyone as a lesser God. You cannot find a single verse in the entire Hebrew and Greek inspired Scriptures to conjure up the idea somehow that Christ is a lesser God than God the Father, or God the Holy Spirit in order to support the idea that Christ cannot be the God of Abraham or the all powerful Creator of His universe.

What most theologians and men of the cloth do, most of the time, is to refer to Jesus Christ as a lesser God while He was in the flesh to save sinners from their sins. But, by Christ coming in the flesh, does that make Him a lesser God than God the Father or God the Holy Spirit?

As per Scripture, of course not!

But contrary to people's demeaning remarks that Christ is not that all-powerful Creator, listen to Jeremiah's statements where he says that He (Christ) created "by His power." And "by His discretion." Jeremiah says,

> "12 He hath made the earth by His power, He hath established the world by His wisdom, and hath stretched out the heavens by His discretion" (Jeremiah 10:12).

Did you notice? Christ created the earth by His "power," by His "wisdom," and by His "discretion." The earth was not created by someone else's "power," "wisdom," or "discretion." And to confirm that fact, Apostle John adds, "10 the world was made by

Him [Christ]" (John 1:10). "3 All things were made by Him [Christ]; and without Him [Christ] was not any thing made that was made" (John 1:3).

As you can see, there is no confusion as to who is the sole Creator of "all things."

Although we have the undisputed clear-cut statements in the above verses that the sole Creator is Christ the LORD of hosts, there are those who will still object and oppose the above statements and try to disprove them with their favorite mistranslated Bibles.

For example, individuals who are taught to believe that "God" the "Word" (Christ) of John 1:1 "was a god," they will use their mistranslated Bible (NWTCGS), to prove their point.

On the other hand, if an individual believes that the "Word" (Christ) of John 1:1 is "God" that individual would refrain from using the (NWTCGS) Bible and use the (Amp.) Bible or the (CEV) Bible to prove his or her point because it states, the "Word" "was truly God" (John 1:1). (CEV).

What happens, in cases as the above, when an objector objects to someone who reveals what the Greek text states in John 1:1, is an argument or an objection by the objector that is based upon outside opinions rather than "thus saith the LORD." But in most cases, the objections by the objector are based upon thus saith the translators or thus saith man or thus saith the church.

If the objector had a sincere interest in the inspired Scriptures of God the Holy Spirit, and wanted to know what was true, don't you think that the first thing the objector should have done, when he or she was confronted with the revelation of the Greek Scriptures, was to compare his or her own Bible translation with the Greek text for herself or himself to see if it was right or wrong?

The answer of course is yes; the objector should have done that!

If the objector did that, he or she would have known that the "Word" (Christ), is "God." Therefore, if the objector was sincere, he or she would stop referring to his or her mistranslated Bible verse, in order to support his or her argument because the quotation "was a god" is nowhere to be found in John 1:1 of the Greek inspired Scriptures.

But, if a person is not sincere and accepts the mistranslated Bible verses that person begins to quote the mistranslated verses to others as if they were inspired. And, if you were to ask that individual who said that Christ "was a god," more than likely, you will hear something like this; "God said so," or "It is written in John 1:1." In doing so, the emphasis is put upon God and upon the Bible prophet. Therefore that individual, to his or her detriment, believes that the quotation "was a god" is God sent!

Furthermore, if you were to read the incorrect translation, in John 1:1, you will observe that it places Christ (the Word) in the past tense. It says, Christ "was a god."

So, if Christ "was a god," once upon a time, what is He now?

Do you know?

Obviously, as per the (NWTCGS) Bible, Christ "was a god." That means that He is not "a god" now; and that statement brings to mind more questions than answers and further contradictions.

Therefore those individuals who believe in their mistranslated Bible verses, it is obvious, when they are mirrored against the Greek text, they cannot sustain their church doctrines. As hard as they try, they cannot sustain their church doctrines because the Hebrew and the Greek Scriptures unmasks these man-made doctrinal theories. The Greek Scriptures do not support doctrinal theories and opinions, which claim that Jesus Christ the LORD of hosts is not the Creator of His universe and the LORD God of Israel.

I mention the doctrinal theories because people and religious institutions use their man-made theories to alter the inspired Scriptures of God the Holy Spirit.

So, I have to ask, who are these men and women who alter the word of God the Holy Spirit in John 1:1? Are they God sent? Are they prophets of God? If so, was Apostle John not a prophet of God, is that why his word, in John 1:1, now has been changed by these people to read, "was a god"? And, if Apostle John is not a prophet of God, do we make void all of his writings (five books in the New Testament)?

What do you think?

But, according to the inspired Greek Scriptures, there is no confusion in John's statement. We are told that Christ is "God."

John testifies to that fact; he says in the Greek text, "and God is the Word." (Translation is mine.) Can anyone dispute John's statement? Obviously, as per the inspired Greek Scriptures, the answer is no! Therefore, Christ should be addressed by His name "God" as the prophet John and as the prophets of the Old and New Testaments have done over 3,000 times.

Needless to say, the conversation should stop right now because the added words "was a god" cannot be found in the Greek inspired text of John 1:1. Please note: I said "In the inspired Scriptures." I did not say in people's favorite mistranslated Bibles and man-made doctrinal theories.

And since the uninspired added words "was a god" do not exist in the Greek inspired Scriptures, we cannot or should not discuss them any further, as being inspired words of God the Holy Spirit.

Therefore, God the Christ is not "a god" as some would like us to believe by the use of their favorite Bible translations, verbiage, and theories. Christ is not "a god" because the added words "was a god" do not exist in the Greek inspired Scriptures.

To confirm that the words "was a god" do not exist in the inspired Greek Scriptures, here are John's words in the Greek text; "ΚΑΙ ΘΕΟΣ ΗΝ Ο ΛΟΓΟΣ" (and God is the Word). As you can see, the words "was a god" or "is a god" in the predicate of John 1:1 do not exist. Therefore, because of these very facts, there are no amounts of Bible translations, manmade theories, or words of gymnastics that are capable of changing the Scriptural fact that Christ is "God."

So, don't let your pride hinder your relationship with Christ the Savior; and don't reject the Bible doctrinal truth, as it is written in the Greek inspired Scriptures, by clinging to your mistranslated favorite Bible verse, which reads other than "and God is the Word." But, if you insist on using the mistranslation from the (NWTCGS) Bible, or any other mistranslated Bible verse or verses, remember, according to the inspired Scriptures:

> *Whatever name you give Jesus Christ, with your misquoted Bible verse or verses, you will also make Christ's Associates (God the Father) the same.*

For anyone to say that Jesus Christ the LORD of hosts "is a god," or "was a god," or "a prophet," or "a good man," by using their favorite mistranslated Bible and theories, remember, Scripturally, you will also make God the Father "a god," "a prophet," or "a good man."

Does anyone want to go down that road and make those demeaning claims? If one does, then, I have to ask, who is their God?

So, avoid man-made theories, additions, and deletions of Scripture. God the Holy Spirit condemns these kinds of actions and impositions that are brought upon his holy words because they lead people into doubt and into perdition.

> Paul warns: "8 though we, or an angel from heaven, preach any other gospel unto you than that which we have preached unto you, let him be accursed" (Galatians 1:8)

So! Under such severe condemnation, do laymen, clergy, and Bible translators still want to claim and say that Christ the LORD God of Israel "was a god," "a prophet," or "a good man"?

Sadly, many still answer yes! They prefer to believe what they want; and that is OK because they, as free moral agents, have that right in the sight of God their Creator. Christ the Creator is not going to hit them over their head and say, "Do as I say or else." Because retribution does not come right away, as it did with the children of Israel, people believe what they want, say what they want, and do evil whenever they want. That is why there are thousands upon thousands of religious denominations out there. They pick and choose, which translation or translations of the Bible they can use to sustain their doctrines with. They in essence say,

> "14 unto God, Depart from us; for we desire not the knowledge of thy [Your] ways" (Job 21:14).

Therefore, please be mindful what you read from the various diversified Bible translations. I say that because I am putting the emphases on the translators of the New Testament for the various discrepancies, which exist in their Bible translations. The discrepancies are quite obvious; it can be readily seen that the translators vary the translation of the Greek Scriptures into English in their respective Bibles. It should be noted; many New Testament Bible translations not only contradict the Old Testament writers, but these translations also contradict each other. By reading these New Testament translations, you will find in many of these translations, a number of verses that are translated from the Greek language into English are full of inconsistencies. Therefore they are misleading. In order to avoid all of these discrepancies, one has to go directly into the Greek inspired Scriptures and verify what they are saying; otherwise a person can be easily mislead from the true contents of the verse or verses and conclude, as many already have that Jesus Christ the LORD of hosts is not the Creator of "all things," and that He is not the LORD God of Israel. That is why you will find many people base their religious doctrines and beliefs upon their favorite Bible translation or translations. In doing so, they stand firm in their beliefs in contradiction to the Greek inspired Scriptures.

Nonetheless, if you are not able to find a Bible that is translated correctly from the Hebrew and the Greek languages, make the corrections of the various verses, which are not translated correctly at the back of your Bible, if you have room there? If you do not have room there, then write them in one of your notebooks, so that you will be able to refer to these corrected verses at will, whenever you are confronted by someone's mistranslated Bible.

So, be careful, which Bible translation you use to base your Bible doctrine on and teach it as a Bible truth because if your doctrine is wrong, you will not only deceive yourself, but you will also deceive others to believe a lie. In doing so, Scripture in the Old and New Testaments warn, their blood will be upon your hands, if they perish? But, if you

> "16 Take heed unto thyself [yourself], and unto the doctrine; continue in them: for in doing this thou [you] shalt both save thyself, and them that hear thee [you]" (1 Timothy 4:16).

Commentators_____ Another severe problem that exists in the religious world is the fact that many religious institutions teach their followers to place their trust, or faith, if you like, in the church fathers, leaders (Imams), rabbis, priests, and the multitude of Bible commentators who set their church's doctrines.

If you are a Christian fundamentalist, by reading the above comment, you probably thought of a number of religious institutions, which do teach their followers that only certain individuals in their church are able to give the right answers from the Bible. And in many cases, the church says to their followers that only certain individuals are able to understand what the Bible says. Or the church claims only certain individuals, within the church, are holy enough for God to work with or reveal His will. Or the church only recognizes certain few holy men as the prophets of God, and so on, and on, go the beliefs of men and women.

Now without me writing page after page about church leaders, popes, holy men, rabbis, Imams, commentators, etc., etc., what I would like to do at this point is to collect all of these individuals with their fancy titles and lump them all into the category of commentators because that is all they are. I say that's all they are because, if these individuals were holy men of God, they will be holy. They would not dethrone Christ the LORD God of Israel by the use of their man-made religious doctrines, theories, comments, and take His glory away from Him, which is given to Him by His two Associates (God the Father and God the Holy Spirit). If they were men and women of God, they would not do that. They would elevate Christ the LORD of hosts as the prophets of old do.

So! Why don't they?

If you said that they do; then ask yourself, why do the doctrines of these churches teach their followers to believe differently from each other? If these men and women are God inspired, in all of these churches, why don't they all believe in the same doctrine or in the same God? Why do they all say something different and do not believe in Christ the LORD God of Abraham? Why don't they believe that Christ is God and the sole Creator of Genesis 1:1? Stop and think for one moment, well preferably more than one moment, but stop and think of the implications these so-called holy men and women fester amongst each other with their so-called holy messages? These individuals not only have created resentment with each other, but they even have gone to war with each other killing millions of people throughout the history of planet earth. In fact, they are still at it today, as you read this book! How can these men and women, claim that they are holy, and at the same time, go against Christ the LORD God of Israel, when He specifically has commanded, "Thou shalt not kill"? Obviously, a person has to conclude that they are not holy. If they were holy, they would live their lives within the Ten Commandments (Exodus 20:3-17), which Christ the LORD of hosts gave to the children of Israel "to give unto us" (Acts 7:38) the Gentiles. But, if these commentators and churches do not live within the holy precepts of the Ten Commandments, a person can further say with Isaiah "there is no light in them" (Isaiah 8:20).

Scripture reveals in individuals, who choose to live in sin that "there in no light" or truth "in them." But, how will you know if they are not lying to you? How will you know if they are speaking the truth?

Consider the first obvious fact, which stands out in the religious world. Consider the tens of thousands of churches with their prophets and commentators. All of these churches claim that they speak the truth. They claim that they do not lie. Obviously they all cannot be speaking the Gospel truth because every one of these religious institutions believes differently in the Gospel doctrine (2 John 9). So how can they all claim that they are speaking the truth? True, they all might have some doctrinal truth, or they might speak the truth to a degree, but they do not speak the whole truth. Therefore there are thousands upon thousands of religious institutions that do not speak the Gospel truth.

Having said that, how are you to know which one of these institutions is not lying to you?

The test is simple. Scripture tells us,

> "20 to the law and to the testimony: if they speak not according to this word, it is because there in no light in them" (Isaiah 8:20).

As I said, the test is simple. It is not complicated. They must speak, teach, and live by the moral law, as it is given in Exodus 20:1-17. And they must speak, teach, and live according to the testimony that is given by Jesus Christ and by His prophets of old. Therefore, let me reiterate, the churches and their prophets and their commentators must abide by the Ten Commandments as they are given to us in Exodus 20:3-17. They must keep the Ten Commandments not to be saved but because they are saved and because that is "the whole duty of man" (Ecclesiastes 12:13). And they will abide by the inspired Scriptures (the Gospel doctrinal testimony: 2 John 9) and teach the people to do the same.

In other words, if a religious person claims to be speaking the truth, but he or she is not abiding or living within the Ten Commandments, as they are given in Exodus 20:2-17 that individual is lying. And if that individual does alter the inspired Scriptures (the testimony and the doctrine, 2 John 9) that individual is further lying to you.

On the other hand, if an individual allows the Gospel message of Jesus Christ the LORD (Mark 1:1) to come through by allowing Scripture to interpret Scripture that individual is not lying to you. And when that individual does not understand some of the inspired Scriptures, like Daniel the prophet that individual will admit that he or she does not understand it; and therefore that individual will refrain from making a comment about that portion of the Scripture. That individual will not willfully lie and re-crucify Christ; he or she will not willfully or knowingly lie. In addition, Christ the LORD said, "by their fruits ye shall know them." (See Matthew 7:15-20.) And we are also told, "If any man speak, let him speak as the oracles of God"

> "11 If any man speak, let him speak as the oracles of God; if any man minister, let him do it as of the ability which God giveth: that God in all things may be glorified through Jesus Christ, to whom be praise and dominion for ever and ever. Amen" (1 Peter 4:11).

A person will not add, delete, or alter the word of God in order to support his or her opinions or religious doctrinal beliefs.

Scripture tells us: "Whosoever transgresseth, and abideth not in the doctrine of Christ, hath not God. He that abideth in the doctrine of Christ, he hath both the Father and the Son" (2 John 9).

According to Isaiah 8:20, those are few ways you will know if an individual is speaking the truth or not?

So, the big question is, why do people place their trust or faith upon the thousands of commentators who do not agree amongst themselves, and upon the Bible doctrinal Gospel truth? Should not the people of planet earth go to God in prayer for their answers, instead to commentators who advocate their followers to live in sin, and false information? Obviously the answer is yes! People should definitely go to God for their needs, whatever they might be?

Remember this fact, God the Holy Spirit is the Author of the Bible; therefore God the Holy Spirit is able to provide you with the Gospel truth, if you seek it; just as he did with the prophets of old.

So, dear reader, why would you put your trust in the Bible commentators, when you and I have been advised to go to God first? And if we want to know what His holy word is saying to us, we are to study His word and allow Scripture to interpret Scripture for us. In other words, we are to allow the prophets of God who have written God's word to interpret His word for us.

We are to place our trust in the word of God for His doctrinal truth, and not in the opinions of the various Bible commentators who are not God sent, or are not recognized by Him, as His spokes' persons. So, be careful whose comments you accept as the Gospel truth. Ask yourself, who are these people? Put them to the test, and see if they are God sent? And that includes me.

People should put their trust and "$_8$ help...in the name of the LORD, who made heaven and earth." Psalms 124:8

Does a day equal 24 hours? _____ Having stated earlier, in chapters one and two, the scientific and Biblical facts for you, let me add one more point and say that there is a lot of speculation about the time period of a day; some religious institutions claim that one creation day, in Genesis chapter one, means one million years. And some religious institutions claim that one creation day equals to one thousand years.

It is stated in some doctrinal beliefs that the "evening" of Genesis 1:5 equals to 500 years. Likewise, they say that the

Does a day equal 24 hours?

"morning" also equals to 500 years. Therefore the statement, in Genesis 1:5, "5 and the evening and the morning were the first day," according to their belief, a day equals to one thousand years. The assumption is made that all of the creation days in Genesis chapter one (verses 5, 8, 13, 19, 23, 31) equal to six thousand years, plus one rest day (Sabbath), the total equals to seven thousand years.

How they came to the conclusion that a day equals to 1,000 years is by misquoting Scripture, and by rejecting the empirical statement that a day equals to twenty-four hours. Although you cannot find a single verse in the entire Bible, which states that a creation day equals 1,000 years, you will notice that the theorists use a verse that refers to God the Creator and what a time period means to Him and not to you or to me.

The misquoted verse, which is used to make the claim that a day equals 1,000 years is derived from 2 Peter 3:8. The verse reads; "8 that one day is with the LORD as a thousand years" (2 Peter 3:8).

So, to God, a day equals one thousand years; but, does a day equal to 1,000 years for you and for me? Or, does a day equal to twenty-four hours?

If you insist that a day equals to 1,000 years, explain it to your landlord and to your mortgage holder and tell them that they will not receive their payments on the first day of every month because your day equals to 1,000 years—they have to wait.

Nonetheless, I did say that the verse in 2 Peter 3:8 is misquoted. The verse is not quoted in its entirety, in order to explain what the apostle is saying. In fact, the verse is self-explanatory; it says "8 that one day is with the LORD as a thousand years, and a thousand years as one day."

So, which is it? Do 1,000 years equal to a day? Or does a day equal to one thousand years for you—that is, if you are able to live that long?

Obviously, neither because for you and for me a day equals to twenty-four hours; but to God, a day is "as" "one thousand years" and one thousand years is "as" one day. To God, time is irrelevant because He is from "everlasting to everlasting." He is eternal. Therefore time is only applicable to His creation and to the created beings therein.

So, what does this verse (2 Peter 3:8) have to do with the creation verses of Genesis chapter one?

As you can see, absolutely nothing! It's only an analogy.

As I stated before, the creation verses in Genesis chapter one are self-explanatory; they state that "the evening" (night) and "the morning" (day-light) equal to one day. And one day equals to twenty-four hours. Job acknowledges that a day consists of night and daylight. He said, "3 Let the day perish wherein I was born" (Job 3:3).

Furthermore, in confirmation that the creation of the heaven, ecosystem, man, and beast were completed in six twenty-four hour days comes by the mouth of God the Creator of Genesis 1:1. Standing on top of Mount Sinai, He said to the children of Israel, "8 Remember the Sabbath day [Saturday], to keep it holy. 9 Six days shalt thou [you] labour, and do all thy [your] work: 10 But the seventh day is the sabbath of the LORD thy God: in it thou shalt not do any work, thou, nor thy son, nor thy daughter, thy manservant, nor thy maidservant, nor thy cattle, nor thy stranger that is within thy gates: 11 For in six days the LORD made heaven and earth, the sea, and all that in them is, and rested the seventh day; [Saturday] wherefore the LORD blessed the sabbath day, and hallowed it" (Exodus 20:8-11).

Christ the LORD God of Israel (v.2), in the above verses, claims that He created the "11 heaven and earth, the sea, and all that in them is," in "six days," and on the seventh day, the children of Israel were to rest and keep the Sabbath day holy. In fact, the children of Israel were told to celebrate the Sabbath day from sunset to sunset.

Here is Moses' statement: "32 from even unto even, shall ye [all of you] celebrate your sabbath" (Leviticus 23:32).

So, what day is the Sabbath day?

According to the fourth Commandment (Exodus 20:8-11), the Sabbath is the seventh day of the week, which is Saturday; and the first day of the week is Sunday—check your calendar.

As God requested it, the seventh day Sabbath was kept every week by the children of Israel (Jacob), during their thirty-eight years of wandering in the desert. It was kept in the Promised Land; and

Does a day equal 24 hours?

they are still keeping the seventh day Sabbath today. That is quite a testimony, in confirmation that a day equals to twenty-four hours!

On the other hand, if the creation days and the Sabbath were one million years each, as some believe, or one thousand years each, then the children of Israel should not be working today at all because they would be living in the seventh day Sabbath. Therefore God the Christ should not have told them to keep one twenty-four hour day holy out of seven—but He did! Does that mean Christ the Creator does not know the duration of a day? Or, the theorists, who claim that a day equals 1,000 years, are the ones who do not know the duration of a day?

What do you think?

Furthermore, given that Moses claims that a day equals to twenty-four hours, should not that suffice?

Moses wrote, "14 And God said, Let there be lights in the firmament of the heaven to divide the day from the night; and let them be for signs, and for seasons, and for days, and years: 15 And let them be for lights in the firmament of the heaven to give light upon the earth: and it was so. 16 And God made two great lights; the greater light to rule the day, and the lesser light to rule the night: He made the stars also. 17 And God set them in the firmament of the heaven to give light upon the earth, 18 And to rule over the day and over the night, and to divide the light from the darkness: and God saw that it was good. 19 And the evening and the morning were the fourth day" (Genesis 1:14-19).

You know, I am tempted to continue with the above scenario of 1,000 years, but I know better not to because when we consider objections that are based upon man-made theories, and argue outside of the empirical statements of the Bible, the dialogue could continue almost for ever.

Therefore, if you claim that your day equals to one million years or one thousand years, I would be compelled to say to you that you are not from this planet.

By the way, how can Christ the Creator of Genesis 1:1, who spoke the universe into existence, take 6,000 years to create the ecosystem of the earth, when the scientific community tells us that the universe came into existence in approximately 53 μseconds?

The Experiment

Let us finish a little bit of unfinished business before you go for a break; or better still, go for a break and then come back.

Earlier, if you recall, we were involved in a little experiment. During our little experiment, I said that I was sorry for leaving you hang on that point of our experiment. The point of our experiment was based upon what Christ the Creator had said to His tempters. If you remember, Christ the Creator of Genesis 1:1, when He came in the "flesh" 2,000 years ago, said to the Pharisees, Sadducees, priests, and to the crowd,

> "46 had ye believed Moses, ye would have believed Me: for he wrote of Me. 47 But if ye believe not his writings, how shall ye believe My words?" (John 5:46, 47)

The question, which I asked earlier, was "What did Moses write about Jesus Christ?"

I do not know if you continued with the experiment or not, but this much I do know, my experience has been that people have a tendency to get stuck when they are asked the question, what did Moses write about Jesus Christ the LORD? You should not be surprised when I say that over ninety percent of the people get stuck. They cannot answer the question what did Moses write about Jesus Christ the LORD of hosts, as per the inspired Scriptures of the Bible. So, don't feel bad if you fall in that category because many of these people, to whom I have posed the question, are prominent theologians, Bible students, and men of the cloth.

On the other hand, you will find a small percentage of people, who manage to quote few prophetic verses from the Torah, in order to show what Moses wrote about Christ the Creator.

The two most common verses that are quoted are as follows:

> "15 And I will put enmity between thee and the woman, and between thy seed and her seed; it shall bruise thy head, and thou shalt bruise his heel" (Genesis 3:15).

> "15 The LORD thy God will raise up unto thee a Prophet from

The Experiment

the midst of thee, of thy brethren, like unto me; unto him ye shall hearken" (Deuteronomy 18:15).

And not to frequently, I have found the following verse quoted:

"10 The sceptre shall not depart from Judah, nor a lawgiver from between his feet, until Shiloh [the LORD of hosts] come; and unto Him shall the gathering of the people be" (Genesis 49:10).

If you are wondering why I wrote [the LORD of hosts] in the above verse, it is simple; I stated that fact because, it was Christ the LORD of hosts who dwelt in His Sanctuary, in between the two cherubims, in Shiloh. Therefore He is identified by the name of "Shiloh"—remember? If you do not remember, read 1 Samuel chapters 1 - 4, and notice in particular 1 Samuel 1:3; 2:2; 4:4. If you recall, as we have studied, Christ the LORD of hosts moved from Shiloh, into His new Sanctuary in Jerusalem, which was made in part out of cedar wood. Thus, according to Moses, the LORD of hosts, who dwelt in His Sanctuary in "Shiloh," was to come to His people. Moses wrote, "10 The sceptre shall not depart from Judah, nor a lawgiver from between his feet, until Shiloh come; and unto Him shall the gathering of the people be" (Genesis 49:10). Moses identifies "the LORD of hosts," who dwelt in Shiloh, by the name of "Shiloh." And "Shiloh" is personified as the Messiah of whom the prophets looked forward to His coming, in the "flesh," to His own people. Moses adds, "unto Him [Shiloh] shall the gathering of the people be." "Shiloh" (Christ the LORD God of Israel) tried to gather His people unto Himself, 2,000 years ago, but the majority did not come to Him to be saved. The prophet of old says, "11 He [Christ] came unto His own, and His own received Him not" (John 1:11).

Moreover, once in a while, I have heard the following verse quoted, which is taken from the time period when Balaam the prophet was asked to curse the children of Israel when they were camped in the land of Moab in their fortieth year. Balaam, who

The Experiment

came all the way from the land of Mesopotamia to curse the children of Israel, said to King Balak, "17 I [Balaam] shall see Him, but not now: I shall behold Him, but not nigh: there shall come a Star out of Jacob, and a Sceptre shall arise out of Israel, and shall smite the corners of Moab, and destroy all the children of Sheth" (Numbers 24:17).

If you have time, read Numbers 24, and observe the beauty of the camp of Israel, before they subdued the rest of Canaan.

But, going back to the above four verses; I have to ask, is that all Moses wrote about Christ the Creator?

Obviously the answer is an emphatic no!

Having said that, since you have read the previous chapters in this book, you should have the answer or you should have scored a very high percentage by your answer. If you did not, then the following pages are especially for you; they give the answer again to the question "What did Moses write about Christ the LORD?"

See! I did not leave you hanging after all!

Thus far we have found out that the Creator of Genesis 1:1; John 1:1, 3, and 10 is Christ the Messiah (John 1:1, 14, 41).

And this same Creator acknowledges that He is the LORD and God of Israel. Christ said, "7 I will take you to Me for a people, and I will be to you a God: and ye shall known that I am the LORD your God, which bringeth you out from under the burdens of the Egyptians" (Exodus 6:7). And when the children of Israel accepted Christ the God of their fathers as their LORD and God, He brought the children of Israel out of the hand of Pharaoh, and led them from the fields of Raamses to the foot of Mount Sinai. And there at the foot of Mount Sinai, the children of Israel listened to Christ the LORD God of Israel when He spoke to them from the top of the mountain saying,

> "2 I am the LORD thy God, which have brought thee [you] out of the land of Egypt, out of the house of bondage" (Ex. 20:2).

There at the foot of Mount Sinai, after the children of Israel made a Covenant with Christ and accepted Christ the LORD of

The Experiment

hosts as their LORD, God, and Savior, Christ dwelt in a tent with the children of Israel and walked with the children of Israel all the way into the Promised Land. In fact, Christ the God of Israel acknowledged that He walked with the children of Israel from Egypt and all the way into the Promised Land.

When Christ the LORD of hosts was brought to live in a tent, in Jerusalem, at one point, Christ confirmed the fact that He walked with the children of Israel by saying to Nathan the prophet, "5 Go and tell My servant David, Thus saith the LORD, Shalt thou build Me an house for Me to dwell in? 6 Whereas I have not dwelt in any house since the time that I brought up the children of Israel out of Egypt, even to this day, but have walked in a tent and in a tabernacle. 7 In all the places wherein I have walked with all the children of Israel spake I a word with any of the tribes of Israel, whom I commanded to feed My people Israel, saying, Why build ye not Me an house of cedar?" (2 Samuel 7:5-7)

If you recall, David's son did build the Sanctuary in Jerusalem. And during the dedication of the Sanctuary to Christ the God of Israel, Christ accepted His new Sanctuary, as His new dwelling place. Historically, Christ the LORD God of Israel dwelt in His Sanctuary in Jerusalem until King Nebuchadnezzar utterly destroyed Jerusalem and the Sanctuary to the ground in 586 BC.

But, until then, the psalmist acknowledged the fact that it was Christ the LORD God of Israel who dwelt in the "most holy place" of the Sanctuary, above the "mercy seat," by saying, "1 THE LORD reigneth; let the people tremble: He sitteth between the cherubims;" "9 Exalt the LORD our God, and worship at His holy hill; for the LORD our God is holy" (Psalms 99:1, 9).

So, historically, as per the Torah and as per the prophets of old, they all reveal to us that Christ the LORD God of Israel dwelt with the children of Israel in His Sanctuary, and was worshiped by the children of Israel on and off throughout their history.

Apostle Paul confirms the fact that it was Christ who interacted and dwelt with the children of Israel. He explains in his overview of what Moses wrote in the Torah about Christ the LORD God of Israel by saying,

The Experiment

"1 MOREOVER, brethren, I would not that ye should be ignorant, how that all our fathers were under the cloud [Exodus 13:21], and all passed through the sea [Ex. 14:21, 22; Isaiah 51:50]; 2 And were all baptized unto Moses in the cloud and in the sea; 3 And did all eat the same spiritual meat [Ex. 16:15]; 4 And did all drink the same spiritual drink [Ex. 17:6, 7]; for they drank of that spiritual Rock that followed them: and that Rock was Christ [Χριστος].

"5 But with many of them God [Christ] was not well pleased: for they were overthrown in the wilderness. 6 Now these things were our examples, to the intent we should not lust after evil things, as they also lusted. 7 Neither be ye idolaters, as were some of them; as it is written, The people sat down to eat and drink, and rose up to play"

"8 Neither let us commit fornication, as some of them committed, and fell in one day three and twenty thousand [23,000]," in the camp of Israel that day. And then, the apostle identifies whom they tempted. Paul says that the children of Israel tempted "Christ" (Χριστον) the God of Israel.

Here is the confirmation: "9 Neither let us tempt Christ [τον Χριστον], as some of them also tempted, and were destroyed of serpents [Numbers 21:4, 5]" (1 Corinthians 10:1-10).

Please note, for your convenience, I have placed in brackets in the above overview the cross-references of the events mentioned by Apostle Paul and Moses.

Having reiterated the above information for you, as you have read, Apostle Paul's overview does reveal what Moses wrote about Christ the LORD of hosts in the Torah (the five books of Moses). Unfortunately, the reason most people cannot find Christ the LORD God of Israel in all of Moses' writings is due to the fact that people do not know that Christ is the sole Creator (Genesis Chapter one, John 1:1, 3, 10); the "King of Israel" (Isaiah 44:6, Matthew

The Experiment

21:4, 5: John 1:49), the "first and the last" (Isaiah 48:12, 13; Revelation 1:17, 18), the "LORD of hosts" (Isaiah 37:16), "Jehovah" (Psalm 83:18), etc., etc. And because people do not know that Christ is the only Creator of the universe, they cannot relate to Christ the Creator in the Old Testament by His name "LORD God," or identify Him as the LORD God of Israel as the three overviews have done (Nehemiah 9, Psalms 78, and 1 Corinthians 10:1-10). When most people think of Christ, they think of a "Messiah," they do not think of Christ as Christ the Creator and as the LORD God of Israel. In fact most people, when they look for Christ in the Old Testament, they look for the word "Christ." What many individuals fail to grasp is the fact that the character name "Christ" was used to identify God the Creator of Genesis 1:1 when He came in the "flesh" to save man from his sins. But, even though Christ the Creator is acknowledged by the character name of "Christ," He is still addressed in the New Testament by His name "LORD" and "God," just as He is addressed by that very same name in the Old Testament. As we have seen, all of the prophets of old address Christ by the name "LORD God" because that is His name.

Therefore, if you are looking for Christ the God of Israel in the Old Testament, you will find Him by the name of "LORD," "God," "LORD God," and by few character names, such as "the Creator," "the Most High," "the LORD of hosts," "the King of Israel," "the God of Israel," "the first and the last," "Rock," "Saviour," "Jehovah," etc., etc. And when you do that, you will find Christ the Creator of Genesis 1:1 in almost every chapter of the Torah. (For more detailed information on Christ's character names read my book "Moses Wrote About Me" *By Philip Mitanidis*, BEEHIVE PUBLISHING HOUSE INC.)

So, did you have the right answer to the question, "What did Moses write about Jesus Christ the Creator?"

Here is the answer by Apostle Paul who confirms, in a nutshell, the facts of what Moses wrote in the Torah about Christ the LORD God of Israel. (Answer: 1 Corinthians 10:1-10. See page 362.)

As we conclude, just remember about ninety-six percent of Moses' writings are all about Christ the Creator of Genesis chapter

The Experiment

one. Christ the Creator has testified to that fact. Christ said, "Moses Wrote About Me," Christ did not say, Moses prophesied about me, neither did Christ say, Moses wrote about My Associates (God the Father). Christ said, "Moses wrote about Me," period. And then, Christ added, "But if ye [all of you] believe not his writings, how shall ye believe My words?" (John 5:46, 47)

In fact, in His previous remarks, Jesus included all of the Old Testament Scriptures. He said,

> "39 Search the scriptures...they are they which testify of Me" (John 5:39).

So, dear reader, did you get the right answer?

Congratulations!

At this point, do you believe Christ's words when He said, "Moses wrote about Me"? Do you believe Moses' writings are about Christ the LORD God of Israel; do you believe Christ when He says that the Scriptures, Old Testament, "testify of Me," or, are you going to make some kind of an excuse, and disagree with Christ the LORD of hosts, as many religious institutions and people still do? Remember, if you disagree with Christ's statement, you in essence are calling Christ the Creator the LORD God of Israel a liar?

Do you really want to do that?

I hope you had a thought-provoking study.

Declaration

This is what Christ (Messiah), "28 the everlasting God, the LORD, the Creator of the ends of the earth" says, "11 Ask Me...concerning the work of My hands...12 I have made the earth, and created man upon it...My hands, have stretched out the heavens, and all their host have I commanded." "24 I am the LORD that maketh all things; that stretcheth forth the heavens alone; that spreadeth abroad the earth by Myself." "4 Thus saith the LORD of hosts, the God of Israel; Thus shall ye [all of you] say unto your masters; 5 I have made the earth, the man, and the beast that are upon the ground, by My great power and by My outstretched arm."

And God the Holy Spirit agrees with Christ the Creator when He spake by the mouth of John, saying, "10 the world was made by Him [Christ]." Moses agrees; he said, "2 Thou [You] hadst [has] formed the earth and the world, even from everlasting to everlasting, Thou art God." Isaiah also said, "16 Thou [You] hast made heaven and earth." And Apostle Paul adds, "16 all things were created by Him [Christ] and for Him [Christ]," "17 and by Him [Christ] all things consist" (Isaiah 40:28; 45:11, 12; 44:24; Jeremiah 27:4, 5; John 1:10; Psalms 90:2; Isaiah 37:16: Colossians 1:16, 17).

QUESTIONS

1). a). Who created the heavens and the earth?
   b). What is His full name? c). What are His character names?
2). When did the Creator create the heavens and the earth?
3). How did the Creator create the universe and everything that is in it?
4). On which day of the creation week did the Creator create the sun?
5). On which day did God the Creator create man?
6). In whose image did the Creator create man?
7). How many people did the Creator create, and what were their names?
8). Did these created beings have any children before they sinned (broke the Ten Commandments)?
9). How many years has it been since man first sinned on planet earth?
10). Because of their sin, from where were these first created beings banished?
11). Before these created beings were expelled from their home, what promise was made to them, by whom, and was the promise conditional?
12). After the promise was made, did the people in general, accept the Creator as their God?
13). What did the antediluvians do in defiance to the Creator's will?
14). Because the antediluvians abandoned the Creator and polluted the earth with sin, what did God the Creator say to Noah He was going to do?
15). Before the flood came, how many people desired to be saved?
16). How many years did Noah preach the Gospel to the antediluvians?
17). Who and what was saved in the big ark (ship), which Noah built?
18). Where did the big ship land after the flood?
19). a). What were the names of Noah's three children?
    b). Who was the oldest, the youngest, and the second-born?
20). Which child did Noah curse?
21). Where eventually the children of Noah's three sons go to live?
22). After Noah, to whom was the message of salvation given to pass on to the people of planet earth?
23). From which tribe was Moses?
24). a). Who was the oldest; Moses, Aaron, or Miriam? b) Who was the youngest?
25). a). Why did Moses flee from Egypt? b). Where did he go?
26). a). Where was Aaron when Christ the LORD asked him to go and meet with his brother Moses? b). Why was he asked to meet with

Questions

Moses?

27). Where did the two brothers (Moses and Aaron) meet?

28). a). Whose children did the Creator ask Moses and Aaron to bring out of Egypt? b). Why, and in what field did they meet before they left Egypt?

29). Where did God the Creator take the children of Israel, who were in bondage in Egypt, to stay for a year?

30). What was audibly revealed to Moses and to the children of Israel from the top of Mount Sinai?

31). How did the children of Israel respond to God's audible revelation?

32). Why did the children of Israel fear the Creator's audible revelation?

33). What was Moses' advice to the children of Israel?

34). What was the response by the children of Israel to Moses before the children of Israel heard the words of the Covenant?

35). What other law or laws were given to the children of Israel by the pen of Moses?

36). How was the Covenant (agreement) ratified between God the Creator and the Children of Israel?

37). When were these laws given?

38). When and why was the ceremonial law implemented?

39). a). After the children of Israel entered into agreement with God the Creator, what did God the Creator ask the children of Israel to build for Him? b). And why did He make that request?

40). After the dedication of the Sanctuary, what did God the Creator do?

41). After the children of Israel were counted and organized into groups around the House of God the Creator, how did the children of Israel know when to move and when to camp?

42). When did God the Creator and the camp of Israel move from Sinai?

43). Where did Christ the Creator take the children of Israel from Sinai?

44). After their journey, to Kadesh, what did the Creator ask the children of Israel to do?

45). Before the children of Israel decided to fulfill the Creator's command, what did the children of Israel decide to do first?

46). How many spies were sent to Canaan by the children of Israel?

47). How many spies, when they came back, gave good report?

48). What were the names of the spies who gave good report?

49). Why do you think not all of the spies gave good reports on the land of Canaan?

50). What was the response of the children of Israel to the Creator's command to go and possess the land of Canaan?

Questions

51). After the children of Israel refused to go and possess the Promised Land, what did they want to do?
52). What desire did the Creator grant the children of Israel, after they refused to possess the Promised Land?
53). How many years did the children of Israel wander in the wilderness?
54). a). How many people died in one day from snakebites in the camp of Israel while they were in the desert of Arabah? b). Did any children die from the snakebites?
55). How many people from the original group, who came out of Egypt, crossed the Brook of Zered, and went into the land of Moab?
56). a). What happened to Moses after he saw the Promised Land? b). Where is he now?
57). Who took over the leadership after Moses' death?
58). Where was the camp of Israel located before they crossed the River Jordan?
59). What happened when the soles of the Levi priest touched the water of the River Jordan?
60). What did the leaders of Israel do when they were crossing the River Jordan?
61). What event was celebrated when the children of Israel camped at Gilgal, and what was done to all of the males?
62). a). What city was overthrown first by the children of Israel? a) Was anyone saved from that city? b). What were their names?
63). a). After the children of Israel secured the majority of the land of Canaan, what did they do with the land? b). What tribe did not receive a portion of the land?
64). Where was the House of God (Sanctuary) pitched after the children of Israel crossed the River Jordan?
65). Why was the Ark of the Covenant removed from the House of God during Samuel's priesthood?
66). What happened to the Ark of the Covenant after its removal from the Sanctuary in Shiloh?
67). What happened to Dagon (the Philistines fish god) in his temple?
68). Why did the Philistines return the Ark of the Covenant to the Hebrews?
69). How did the Philistines return the Ark of the Covenant?
70). a). Where was the Ark of the Covenant taken by the Hebrews? b). How long did it remain there? c). Who removed it from there?
71). a). Who built the House of God in Jerusalem? b). What was the parcel of land called where the House of God was built?

The Creator of Genesis 1:1—Who is He?   By: *Philip Mitanidis*   369
Questions_____

72). Why was the second King of Israel not allowed to build the House of God?
73). What did King Nebuchadnezzar do to the House of God, which was in Jerusalem?
74). What happened to the residence of Jerusalem at the third siege of Jerusalem when King Nebuchadnezzar demolished the place?
75). How long did Nebuchadnezzar keep the children of Israel in bondage?
76). Who released the children of Israel from their bondage and let them go back to Jerusalem?
77). a). When the Sanctuary was rebuilt by the children of Israel, after they returned to Jerusalem from their 70 years of bondage, what happened to the Ark of the Covenant? b). After the dedication of the Sanctuary, to God the Creator, was the Shekinah glory present in the Sanctuary?
78). Where can the Ark of the Covenant be found today?
79). a). How do we know that Christ the Creator dwelt in His Sanctuary in between the two cherubims, up until 586 BC. b). Who saw Him?
80). Can the Shekinah glory of Christ the Creator be seen in the Sanctuary, which is in Jerusalem today?
81). By what name is God the Creator addressed in Psalms 83:18?
By what character name is God the Creator commonly addressed these days?
82). What does the name Christ mean?
83). Who are the Creator's Associates, and what are the Creator's Associates names
84). Did the Creator fulfill the "promise" He made to Adam and Eve regarding their salvation?
85). a). When did God the Creator fulfill His "promise" to Adam and Eve? a) Do we have proof of this fulfillment?
86). Why did God the Creator allow Himself to be stripped from all of His powers and come to planet earth in the "flesh"?
87). Why did God the Creator allow His own people (the children of Israel) to crucify Him?
88). a). Did the Creator die? Is He still dead? b). If not where is He now?
89). a). While Christ the Creator was in the "flesh," on earth, who reigned on Christ's throne and over Christ's universe? b). How long is this Individual going reign on the Christ's throne and over the Christ's universe?
90). Did Christ the Creator create the universe and everything that is in it

The Creator of Genesis 1:1—Who is He? By: *Philip Mitanidis*
Questions

all by Himself?
91). What promise did Christ the Creator make to His disciples and to the penitent sinner before He departed for heaven?
92). How close do you think is the Creator's second coming?
93). How many prophetic events are left before Christ the Creator comes the second time to take His penitent people to heaven?
94). a). Are you ready for the journey to heaven? b). Who do you want to come with you?

Bibliography

Mitanidis Philip *"Moses Wrote about Me"* BEEHIVE PUBLISHING HOUSE INC. 2011. pp. 163-168

www.ingramcontent.com/pod-product-compliance
Lightning Source LLC
Chambersburg PA
CBHW071235160426
43196CB00009B/1071